Violence and the Struggle for Existence

Violence

and the

Struggle

Work of the Committee on Violence of th

EDITED BY

LITTLE, BROWN AND COMPAN

for # EXISTENCE

Department of Psychiatry, Stanford University School of Medicine

David N. Daniels, M.D.
Assistant Professor of Psychiatry, Department of Psychiatry, Stanford University School of Medicine;
Consultant in Psychiatry, Palo Alto Veterans Administration Hospital

Marshall F. Gilula, M.D.
Postdoctoral Fellow, Department of Psychiatry, Stanford University School of Medicine;
Research Associate, Institute for the Study of Human Problems, Stanford University

Frank M. Ochberg, M.D.
Former Resident, Department of Psychiatry, Stanford University School of Medicine;
Special Assistant to the Deputy Director, National Institute of Mental Health

FOREWORD BY *Coretta Scott King*

oston

To

The Reverend Dr. Martin Luther King, Jr.
1929–1968

AND

Senator Robert F. Kennedy
1925–1968

WHO BELIEVED IN THE AMERICAN DREAM OF PEACE,
EQUALITY OF OPPORTUNITY, AND FREEDOM FOR ALL OUR PEOPLE

WHO OPPOSED VIOLENCE IN HUMAN AFFAIRS

WHO, TO THE MOMENT OF THEIR DEATH, SOUGHT RECONCILIATION
AND UNITY AMONG US

Members of the Committee on Violence

Department of Psychiatry, Stanford University
School of Medicine

David N. Daniels, M.D., and Frank M. Ochberg, M.D.
COCHAIRMEN

Thomas E. Bittker, M.D.

R. Charles Boelkins, M.Sc.

Peter G. Bourne, M.D.

J. Christian Gillin, M.D.

Marshall F. Gilula, M.D.

George D. Gulevich, M.D.

Beatrix A. Hamburg, M.D.

Jon F. Heiser, M.D.

Frederic W. Ilfeld, M.D.

Jay M. Jackman, M.D.

P. Herbert Leiderman, M.D.

Frederick T. Melges, M.D.

Richard J. Metzner, M.D.

Alan J. Rosenthal, M.D.

Walton T. Roth, M.D.

Alberta E. Siegel, Ph.D.

George F. Solomon, M.D.

Richard C. Stillman, M.D.

Robert L. Taylor, M.D.

Jared R. Tinklenberg, M.D.

Edison J. Trickett, Ph.D.

Alfred E. Weisz, M.D.

Contributing Authors

Thomas E. Bittker, M.D.
Resident, Department of Psychiatry, Stanford University School of Medicine, Stanford

R. Charles Boelkins, M.Sc.
Research Associate in Psychiatry, Stanford University School of Medicine, Stanford

Peter G. Bourne, M.D.
Former Resident, Department of Psychiatry, Stanford University School of Medicine, Stanford; Assistant Professor of Psychiatry, Department of Psychiatry, Emory University Medical School, Atlanta

David N. Daniels, M.D.
Assistant Professor of Psychiatry, Department of Psychiatry, Stanford University School of Medicine, Stanford; Consultant in Psychiatry, Veterans Administration Hospital, Palo Alto

J. Christian Gillin, M.D.
Former Resident, Department of Psychiatry, Stanford University School of Medicine, Stanford; Clinical Associate, Laboratory of Clinical Psychobiology, National Institute of Mental Health, Chevy Chase, Md.

Marshall F. Gilula, M.D.
Postdoctoral Fellow, Department of Psychiatry, Stanford University School of Medicine; Research Associate, Institute for the Study of Human Problems, Stanford University, Stanford

George D. Gulevich, M.D.
Assistant Professor of Psychiatry, Department of Psychiatry, Stanford University School of Medicine; Director, Inpatient Psychiatric Service, Stanford University Hospital, Stanford

Robert F. Harris, B.S.
Research Assistant and Student, Stanford University School of Medicine, Stanford

Jon F. Heiser, M.D.
Former Resident, Department of Psychiatry, Stanford University School of Medicine, Stanford; Staff Psychiatrist, Oakland Naval Hospital, Oakland

Frederic W. Ilfeld, Jr., M.D.

Resident, Department of Psychiatry, Stanford University School of Medicine; Graduate Student in Sociology, Stanford University, Stanford

Jay M. Jackman, M.D.

Former Resident, Department of Psychiatry, Stanford University School of Medicine; Graduate Student in Anthropology, Stanford University, Stanford; Assistant Director of Community Psychiatry, Mt. Zion Hospital, San Francisco

Frederick T. Melges, M.D.

Assistant Professor of Psychiatry, Department of Psychiatry, Stanford University School of Medicine, Stanford

Richard J. Metzner, M.D.

Resident, Department of Psychiatry, Stanford University School of Medicine, Stanford

Frank M. Ochberg, M.D.

Former Resident, Department of Psychiatry, Stanford University School of Medicine, Stanford; Special Assistant to the Deputy Director, National Institute of Mental Health, Chevy Chase, Md.

Alan J. Rosenthal, M.D.

Assistant Professor of Psychiatry, Department of Psychiatry, Stanford University School of Medicine, Stanford

Mary M. Shapiro, B.A.

Senior Research Assistant, Department of Psychiatry, Stanford University School of Medicine, Stanford; Research Assistant in Psychiatry, Veterans Administration Hospital, Palo Alto

Alberta E. Siegel, Ph.D.

Professor of Psychology, Department of Psychiatry, Stanford University School of Medicine, Stanford

George F. Solomon, M.D.

Associate Professor of Clinical Psychiatry, Stanford University School of Medicine, Stanford; Chief, Psychiatry Training and Research Section, Veterans Administration Hospital, Palo Alto

Richard C. Stillman, M.D.

Former Fellow, Department of Psychiatry, Stanford University School of Medicine, Stanford; Clinical Associate, Experimental Group and Family Studies Section, National Institute of Mental Health, Chevy Chase, Md.

Robert L. Taylor, M.D.

Resident, Department of Psychiatry, Stanford University School of Medicine, Stanford

Jared R. Tinklenberg, M.D.
Instructor, Department of Psychiatry, Stanford University School of Medicine, Stanford

Edison J. Trickett, Ph.D.
Former Postdoctoral Fellow, Department of Psychiatry, Stanford University School of Medicine, Stanford; Assistant Professor of Psychology, Department of Psychology, Yale University, New Haven

Alfred E. Weisz, M.D.
Assistant Professor of Psychiatry, Department of Psychiatry, Stanford University School of Medicine, Stanford

I t is gratifying that a scientific study of violence and methods for its reduction is being undertaken by scholars, particularly in the United States. Violence in our country has unique features, especially for black people, and its scope generally is vastly greater than in other industrial nations. We need to know why.

Only a short time before his death, when he addressed the convention of the American Psychological Association in September, 1967, my husband expressed the hope that social science would apply itself to urgent issues.

I am deeply appreciative of the dedication of this work to him along with Senator Robert Kennedy. It is ironic that men who sought to eliminate violence in human affairs should have died by violence, and this reason alone should stimulate serious study to lead to its ultimate elimination in civilized society.

Mrs. Martin Luther King, Jr.

Atlanta

Acknowledgments

A volunteer group effort, such as the one culminating in this book, comes to fruition through the contributions of many people. We, the editors, on behalf of the Committee on Violence, express deep appreciation of all those in the Stanford community who helped us and gave encouragement during the course of our work.

This work could be carried out only in a setting that fosters the development of all its members. Thus we are indebted to David Hamburg, Professor and Chairman of the Department of Psychiatry, who has brought to this department a profound appreciation for the scientific method; a deep concern for the critical, current social issues; and a spirit of egalitarian professional cooperation.

We appreciate the helpful critiques of Rudolf Moos, Peggy Golde, and Irvin Yalom; the encouragement of Thomas Gonda, Erich Lindemann, and Melvin Sabshin; the interest and cooperation of Robert Baker, Lloyd Cutler, Walter Menninger, and Frank Zimring of the National Commission on the Causes and Prevention of Violence; and the participation in our symposium of Albert Bandura, John Kaplan, and Sherwood Washburn.

We are indebted to Mary Shapiro for the technical editing of the entire book, for her many valuable contributions to content and style, and for her assistance throughout the project.

We are grateful to the group of Stanford faculty wives who volunteered their time and energy after the assassination of Robert Kennedy. These women—especially Barbara Baxter, Ruth Franklin, Jewelle Gibbs, Rachelle Marshall, Judy Nadel, and Mary Noyes— reviewed manuscripts, assisted in research, and helped with typing.

Many members of the Stanford Hospital staff helped our committee during various stages of the work. Special thanks are due

Spyros Andreopoulos, Kathryn Borg, Jane Duff, and Joan Foley and the administrative assistants and secretaries who helped, often under great time pressures—Elizabeth Armstrong, Barbara Cleave, Hazel Eickworth, Liz Hoskinson, Ruby Lee, Ann Morey, Valarie Munden, Margo Percival, Cathy Rapson, Eileen Rogers, Evelyn Schmeisser, Sally Thomasson, Joan Wolfe, Virginia Yauman, and Lu Yutzy.

The firm of Keogh and Marer provided free legal consultation. Syntex Corporation underwrote a portion of our expenses, as did the publishers of *Look* magazine.

We give our personal thanks to Judy Daniels, Maryann Erickson, and Lynn Ochberg for their suggestions, patience, and support during the work of the committee and the writing and editing of the manuscript.

The function of a preface—to make brief introductory remarks—is encompassed in the Introduction: The Crisis of Violence. Here we simply wish to state that the task of reducing violence lies ahead. We ask those who read this volume to join with us in thought and action in the effort to understand and limit man's violence.

DAVID N. DANIELS
MARSHALL F. GILULA
FRANK M. OCHBERG

Stanford University
June 1969

Contents

Part II
CURRENT ISSUES *of* VIOLENCE *in the* UNITED STATES

Part III
RECOMMENDATIONS *and* CONCLUSIONS

Violence and the Struggle for Existence

Introduction

THE CRISIS OF VIOLENCE

David N. Daniels, M.D., Marshall F. Gilula, M.D.,
and Frank M. Ochberg, M.D.

A crisis of violence exists in the United States. The point is *not* that Americans are more violent than ever before, or even more violent than people from other nations [8]. The point is that today's violence threatens the existence of our species. Scientific knowledge and mass communications confront us with this truth. We build awesome instruments and institutions of destruction and bring reflections and portrayals of violence into every home. We all face the specters of nuclear weapons, a long and unpopular war, interracial riots, campus unrest, political assassinations, battered children, and unknown assailants. These reminders make the violence that surrounds us more apparent than ever before. Americans are worried and alarmed by the violence that we see everywhere. Indeed who among us can claim immunity from violence?

No longer can a single one of us remain apathetic to the crisis of violence. Both collectively and individually we must see that we are at a turning point in our nation's history. In this crisis, as in every crisis, we are offered the choice of either turning back to inadequate ways of dealing with conflict or looking ahead for more adaptive methods. We must see the danger that violence poses to all life and turn now—not tomorrow—to finding and pursuing adaptive alternatives.

Thus our group, the Committee on Violence, wrote this book in the hope of contributing to the understanding and reduction of violence in our country. We believe that Americans are sufficiently

1

alarmed to recognize that we are in a crisis of violence, concerned enough to search for alternatives, and resourceful enough to change.

The Committee on Violence

The Committee on Violence of the Department of Psychiatry at Stanford University was formed the day after Robert Kennedy died. On that day some of us felt outraged, some of us felt confused and almost apathetic, and others felt frustrated. All of us were shocked and deeply saddened. At our first meeting we groped for some way in which we as behavioral scientists, primarily psychiatrists and psychologists, could contribute to resolving the crises of violence in our country. We felt that there is no substitute for each individual's being concerned, doing his own thinking, and getting involved in the struggle to cope with violence. Undoubtedly our professional and personal values influenced our decisions that day and the work that followed. Primarily these values stem from the helper-healer tradition of medicine and psychology with its goals of reducing suffering and promoting understanding. Obviously these values and goals create a bias against behavior destructive of human life and well-being, in short, against violence.

We decided to begin by reviewing and evaluating current issues of violence and their roots. This decision in turn was based upon our conviction that seeking information about complex conflictual issues before simply acting or reacting to them is in itself an important aspect of coping with conflict. Reviews of immediate relevance and interest for our group were the effect of mass media on violence, the phenomenon of assassination, the controversy about gun legislation, the use of violence to resolve conflict, and the relationship of mental illness to violence. Soon other reviews were added to these: collective violence by minority groups, the relation of drugs to violence, and theories of violence and aggression including biological, psychodynamic, and environmental bases of violent behavior.

Members divided into task groups and established a series of seminars on violence in which professors, resident physicians training in psychiatry, psychology fellows, and students participated equally. Communications with the National Commission on the Causes and Prevention of Violence were established. Dr. Milton Eisenhower, Chairman of the Commission, invited one of us (D.N.D.) to consult with the Commission in Washington, and several Commission members visited us at Stanford to exchange ideas.

We gradually formulated three goals. First, we hoped to prepare a review of violence from a psychiatric and psychological point of view and make recommendations based on our findings. In doing so, we tried to combine both academic and action orientations to produce a scholarly review, yet one that would be useful to the general public, lawmakers, and professionals. Second, we hoped to stimulate communication and research within the academic community. Since our viewpoints on violence reflect our particular professional disciplines of psychiatry and psychology, the reader is encouraged to examine the many contributions of other fields, such as criminology, history, law, political science, and sociology, in order to attain a well-rounded view of the phenomenon of violence. Third, we hoped that our work might help lay a foundation for a multidisciplinary institute at Stanford for the study of aggression and violence.

Our preliminary findings were forwarded to the National Commission and were presented at a Symposium on Violence on November 16, 1968, at Stanford Medical Center. By this time two important themes had emerged, and they became the themes of this book.

Violence and Adaptation

First, one way to understand violence is in the context of man's struggle to adapt to his environment. Whether a desperate, impulsive effort to resolve personal conflict (as in homicide) or a planned and sanctioned group activity (as in war), violence is part of the struggle to resolve stressful and threatening events.

Second, the current issues of violence troubling Americans—assassination, homicide, civil disorder, campus disturbances, and war—all reflect our struggle to keep pace with a rapidly changing world by continuing to use violence to solve conflict at a time when violent responses are becoming increasingly maladaptive. In today's technological era we believe that adaptive alternatives to violence are needed urgently because the survival value of violent aggression, whatever its value might once have been, is diminishing rapidly.

Although these themes concerning violence and adaptation do not explain all violence, they are useful in bringing together the various theories of violence described in Part I. They also help make understandable the various current issues of violence reviewed in Part II. However, before a synopsis of the book is presented, it is essential to define terms and describe the process of adaptation in humans.

Definition of Terms

Various writers attribute different meanings to terms like aggression and violence. The resulting ambiguity makes necessary the defining of two groups of terms: (1) aggression and violence; and (2) adaptation, adjustment, and coping. In our seminars we found that these terms have quite different meanings for different disciplines and individuals. Indeed the chapter authors do not always use the terms exactly as defined below, nor do they agree unequivocally upon these definitions. For instance, in the chapter Biological Bases of Aggression, the authors restrict the use of aggression to attack behaviors, as experimental biologists frequently do. Nonetheless, *aggression* [3, 6, 11] is defined here as the entire spectrum of assertive, intrusive, and attacking behaviors. Aggression thus includes both overt and covert attacks, self-directed attacks, dominance behavior, such defamatory acts as sarcasm, and such assertive behaviors as forceful and determined attempts to master a task or accomplish an act. A broad, rather than restrictive, definition of aggression is selected because relationships between the underlying physiological mechanisms and the social correlates of dominant, assertive, and violent behavior are still poorly understood. Hence this definition encompasses, but is broader than, the definition of aggression in animals common to experimental biology [1], which says that an animal acts aggressively when he inflicts, attempts to inflict, or threatens to inflict damage upon another animal. Usually this implies another animal of the same species, since predatory activity often is not considered as aggression.

Violence [11] is destructive aggression and involves inflicting physical damage on persons or property (since humans so often symbolically equate property with the self). Violent inflicting of damage is often intense, uncontrolled, excessive, furious, sudden, or seemingly purposeless. Furthermore, violence may be collective or individual, intentional or unintentional, apparently just or unjust. Some extend the concept of violence to include inflicting psychological damage and infringing on human rights [12]. In man it is possible to broaden the meaning of violence in this way because psychosocial equivalents of physical destruction can be described.

Adaptation means the behavioral and biological fit between the species and the environment resulting from the process of natural selection [2, 10]. In man adaptation increasingly involves modification of the environment as well. A point to stress here is that behavior, especially group-living behavior in higher social species like man, is a crucial element in natural selection [4]. Adaptive behaviors are those that enhance species survival and, in most instances, individual survival. In contrast, *adjustment* is behavior of a group or individual that temporarily enhances the way we fit with the immediate situation. Its main value is in gaining time when no reasonable course of action is feasible. Adjustment does not usually result in an enduring alteration of behavior structure or patterns [7, 11]. In fact adjustment may have biologically maladaptive consequences in the long run. Since violence often has short-run adjustive value, it may be used even when its long-run adaptive consequences are adverse. In addition, rapid environmental change or extraordinary environmental circumstances may render formerly adaptive behaviors largely maladaptive [4]. In other words, behaviors appropriate to past environmental conditions can work against survival in changed or unusual environments.

Coping is goal-oriented, problem-solving behavior that occurs when a stressful stimulus interrupts important plans of action. It represents the continuing and usually successful struggle of an individual or group to meet environmental demands for change. Hence coping usually accomplishes tasks or goals with adaptive consequences. Put another way: "Behavior may be considered to serve coping functions when it increases the likelihood (from a specified vantage point with respect to a specified time unit) that a task will be accomplished according to standards that are tolerable both to the individual and to the group in which he lives" [9]. Coping behaviors involve primarily a present and a future orientation, information-seeking, and active problem-solving efforts. While each specific sequence of task-oriented behaviors may or may not have adaptive value, coping taken as a whole is an adaptive rather than adjustive human process.

A Definition of Human Adaptation

Every culture prescribes the range of coping behaviors available to its people, but within this range individual adaptive behavior often is forged and tested in times of stress, and especially during times of crisis. Stressful and new situations ironically offer us both the danger of failure and the opportunity for learning. Either the situation itself or unpleasant feelings about the situation (including massive anxiety) may block our usual resources and prevent problem-solving; aggressive reactions that are both indiscriminate and protective may occur. We may show primitive forms of behavior: passive adjustment, withdrawal, falsely blaming others, indiscriminate rage, violence, or confusion.

Alternately, stressful events provide a constructive challenge and expanded opportunity for learning. In a stressful situation that is not overwhelming, we seek information helpful in dealing with the situation and try to apply this information [5]. From information-seeking and subsequent exploratory behavior come not only greater utilization of information and eventual mastery of new situations, but also a sense of heightened self-awareness, enhanced coping skills, and personal growth.

A number of commonly occurring stressful life situations that may challenge and develop our coping skills have been recognized [5]. These are associated with the turning points or transitions in life and include adolescence, separation from parents, marriage, and parenthood. Other challenging transitions involve cultural crises, such as war and the threat of war; rapid technological change; and physical events, such as drought, earthquakes, and famine. These transition points in life provide important opportunities for learning and developing more sophisticated ways of coping with problems.

We have marvelous adaptive abilities for coping with varying, even extreme, situations. These abilities result from cultural evolution interacting with our biological evolution. Culturally we survive through complex communal living. Through our living groups we obtain satisfaction, develop identity, and find meaning in life. Basic social values are of special cultural importance, for they determine the limits of acceptable behavior, especially during times of stress. Biologically we are uniquely endowed for complex communal living. Such biological characteristics as the upright posture, prehension, speech, prolonged infancy and maturation, and profound development of the brain—all favor and allow for rich, dynamic, and varied living. Development of the cerebral hemispheres has played an especially important role in adaptation, for the cerebrum constitutes the biological basis of higher intelligence, self-awareness, language, and flexibility [2].

Thus through the interaction of biological evolution and cultural evolution, we have the equipment for adapting to and molding diverse environments. But this ability to adapt by manipulating the environment is now our cause for greatest concern, for in changing the environment, man changes the conditions necessary for his survival. We now are seeing an unprecedented acceleration of various man-made changes, which call for accompanying changes in man, changes which we are having difficulty in making. While biological change is extremely slow, cultural change theoretically occurs at least every generation, although some aspects of culture (e.g., technology) change faster than others (e.g., beliefs and customs). The term *generation gap* not only describes how we today view the "battle of the generations" but also alludes to the speed of cultural change and how people have trouble keeping pace. Living in the electronic age, we watch televised accounts of preagricultural-age violence and feel our industrial-age mentality straining to cope with the environment.

Since survival results from the long-range adaptiveness of our behavior, *knowledge of our adaptive mechanisms is essential for understanding the role of violence in human behavior and existence.* Although various aspects of violence are examined in the chapters that follow, this theme—violence and the struggle for existence—and variations upon it can be seen throughout.

Organization of the Book

The book is divided into five chapters on theory (Part I), eight chapters on current issues of violence (Part II), and two summarizing chapters (Part III). The theoretical chapters review the scientific data bearing on the roots of aggression and violence and provide a perspective for understanding the many forms of violence. Although diverse, all the theoretical chapters stress the *interaction* of environmental factors with the individual's intrinsic potential for aggressive behavior. Here, as elsewhere in the book, views are presented that are complementary rather than mutually exclusive.

Chapter 1, Biological Bases of Aggression, examines representative examples from the great wealth of animal studies and human biological data bearing directly on the problem of aggression and violence. Aggression in both animals and man is viewed as a potentially adaptive behavior pattern having its origins in genetically coded neural mechanisms that are acted upon by both hormonal and psychosocial factors. Given the internal mechanisms, aggression is viewed as a response to a variety of stimuli originating in the individual's environment. The evidence presented casts strong doubt on the position that aggression is an inherent preprogrammed drive resulting from a disturbance of internal homeostasis.

Chapter 2, Psychodynamic Aspects of Aggression, Hostility, and Violence, presents a modern view of psychoanalytic theory of aggression and violence. Aggression in the form of violence is described as primary when it occurs in association with frustration of basic needs, and as secondary when it endures and becomes associated with achieving gratification, problems arising during childhood development, and current conflicts. Violence is viewed as the need to take action to reduce tension and as a substitute for thinking things out. The chapter relates human development, fulfillment of personal needs, and the psychological (often unconscious) meanings of violent acts.

In Chapter 3, Environmental Theories of Violence, the specific environmental contributions to violence, especially group violence, are reviewed in terms of social learning, frustration, and various situational factors potentiating violence, such as a low expectancy of punishment, boredom, and group contagion. Here the view is presented that violence not only occurs as a consequence of frustration and environmental provocations, but also can be a socially learned behavior independent of any frustrations.

Chapter 4, Anger and Attack, brings together elements from a number of theories as it builds a cybernetic model for understanding anger and violence. People subjectively make varying assessments about the likelihood of reaching goals. These "subjective probabilities" are reflected in specific affects (feelings) that are part of how we appraise outcomes. Anger is seen as occurring when, during the appraisal of outcomes, there is a reversal of optimism to pessimism, which is brought on by an external interference that the individual feels he can eliminate through his own actions. The special conditions leading from anger to attack are reviewed. In man these include especially "dashed hopes" and personal distortions that occur during the appraisal process.

Chapter 5, Alternatives to Violence, deals systematically with the variety of possible effective nonviolent strategies for resolving conflict, especially intergroup conflict. These strategies range from negotiations to strikes, protest, and nonresistance. In addition, limitations of collective violence and factors leading to violence rather than nonviolence in settling conflicts are discussed.

While the chapter on alternatives provides a transition from the other theoretical chapters in Part I to the eight chapters in Part II that deal with current issues of violence in the United States, our hope is that all the theoretical analyses will offer a substantial background for understanding these complicated current issues that are of such grave concern to Americans. The choice of material covered in the current issues section is an outgrowth of our interests as psychiatrists and psychologists, the goals of our committee, and the year in which this book was written.

Chapter 6, The Choice of Collective Violence in Intergroup Conflict, naturally follows Chapter 5, since it reviews the conditions that lead to so-called civil disorder or riots. The ghetto riot, an event of great current concern, is used as an example of the process and factors conducive to group violence. The chapter discusses the grievances and characteristics of the "rioter," the psychological and social forces at work, and the situational factors involved. The author then proposes a model explaining the occurrence of riots and suggests that a similar process applies to other minority groups in conflict with established ways and authority—for instance, to current student "revolt" on college campuses.

Television daily brings portraits of such violence and many other forms of violence into all our homes, poor and affluent alike. Indeed television has been called the universal appliance of the ghetto. Drawing upon basic data of social learning in children and data concerning the exposure and effects of the mass media on the audience, Chapter 7, Violence in the Mass Media, presents the interrelations among social learning, mass media—especially television—and violence.

Next are two companion chapters dealing with the firearms controversy. Chapter 8, Firearms Control and Violence, reviews the data on gun deaths, especially homicide. The relation of gun availability to homicide is discussed in terms of lethality of weapons, comparative studies with other advanced Western countries, impulsivity, the murderer-victim relationship, and the effects of restrictive legislation. Chapter 9, The Gun Law Controversy, first analyzes public opinion about gun controls, groups favoring and opposing strong gun controls, and the arguments of both proponents and opponents of gun legislation. Then the psychological and social issues underlying the controversy are explored in detail. Finally, views from other nations of violence in America are presented. These views further support the evidence that the controversy over gun laws represents in microcosm the major issues in the crisis of violence in the United States.

Chapter 10, American Presidential Assassination, presents a narrative of the eight assassination attempts (each was by firearms) and examines the matrix formed by the assassin's mental disorder, the victim's fatalism disposing him to assassination, and factors in the social environment. In this chapter, as in other chapters in the current issues section, elements drawn from various theories presented in the theoretical section help to make understandable the particular issue under discussion. Here with the phenomenon of assassination, factors in the individual's life history combine with environmental determinants to produce the attack.

In Chapter 11, Mental Illness and Violence, the available data on the relation of mental illness to violence are examined. The authors review studies that compare rates of violent acts by discharged mental patients with the same rates in the general population. These studies reveal that mental patients on the average are no more violent than other citizens. Then factors in the individual that help to predict violent acts are presented. Special attention is given to the "pre-assaultive" state and the role of alcohol in violent acts.

Another clinically oriented review, Chapter 12, Drug Use and Violence, explores the connections between drug usage by specific subgroups and the occurrence of violent behavior. This chapter employs the cybernetic model of violence presented in Chapter 4 in explaining the interactions among social, psychological, and pharmacological factors that augment or diminish the propensity for violence. While particular attention is focused on "speed" (methamphetamine), alcohol, and marihuana and their users, other mind-altering drugs also are considered. These include narcotics, LSD (lysergic acid diethylamide), barbiturates, and the major tranquilizers (phenothiazines). Finally, characteristics of the delirious state are explored.

The last of the eight current issues chapters, Case Studies of Violence, presents three vivid psychiatric case histories of killings by mentally disordered individuals. The third and longest case study draws upon the murderer's autobiography and excerpts from the fortuitous tape recording of the actual murder. The intent of Chapter 13 is to show how the life experience of the individual, gun availability, drug abuse, and unbearable current conflict together can culminate in violent behavior.

Although these thirteen chapters bring together in one volume diverse theories and many issues of violence, there are topics we should like to have covered: a cross-cultural comparison of violence, and violence in historical perspective. Furthermore, we did not attempt a systematic review of the most poignant issue—war. Nevertheless, in the final chapter we do present some views on war and the struggle to adapt.

The final two chapters present a summary of recommendations and a synthesis of conclusions. While each of the foregoing thirteen chapters concludes with implications and recommendations for the reduction of violence relevant to the topic under discussion, Chapter

14, Summary of Recommendations, pulls together our major recommendations. Not all these require formal national programs on a collective basis; individuals can act upon some suggestions immediately. Moreover, we hope that the reader will use these recommendations and the material from which they are derived to draw his own conclusions, then act upon them. Chapter 15, Violence and the Struggle for Existence, presents a synthesis of issues and theory showing how concepts from adaptation, crisis, and coping theory are one way to "tie it all together." The chapter includes a discussion of the exceptional amount of violence in man and our unique recourse to mass genocide—war. The case is presented here for the anachronism and danger of man's violence in this complex, crowded world of ours. The authors emphasize that recognizing and understanding the threat violence poses to man's existence are only a beginning to the determined search for and pursuit of alternatives.

References

1. Carthy, J. D., and Ebling, F. J. (Eds.). *The Natural History of Aggression.* New York: Academic, 1964.
2. Dobzhansky, T. *Mankind Evolving.* New Haven: Yale University Press, 1962.
3. Gould, J., and Kolb, W. L. *A Dictionary of the Social Sciences.* New York: Free Press, 1964.
4. Hamburg, D. A. Emotions in the Perspective of Human Evolution. In Knapp, P. D. (Ed.), *Expression of the Emotions in Man.* New York: International Universities Press, 1963.
5. Hamburg, D. A., and Adams, J. E. A perspective on coping behavior. *Archives of General Psychiatry* 17:277, 1967.
6. Hinsie, L. E., and Campbell, R. J. *Psychiatric Dictionary* (3d ed.). New York: Oxford University Press, 1960.
7. Kluckhohn, C. The Limitations of Adaptation and Adjustment as Concepts for Understanding Cultural Behavior. In Romano, J. (Ed.), *Adaptation.* Ithaca: Cornell University Press, 1949.
8. Richardson, L. F. *Statistics of Deadly Quarrels.* Pittsburgh: Boxwood Press, 1960.
9. Silber, E., Hamburg, D. A., Coelho, G. V., Murphey, E. B., Rosenberg, M., and Pearlin, L. I. Adaptive behavior in competent adolescents. *Archives of General Psychiatry* 5:354, 1961.
10. Simpson, G. G. The Study of Evolution: Methods and Present States of Theory. In Roe, A., and Simpson, G. G. (Eds.), *Behavior and Evolution.* New Haven: Yale University Press, 1958.
11. *Webster's Third New International Dictionary.* Springfield, Mass.: Merriam, 1966.
12. Wheeler, H. A moral equivalent for riots. *Saturday Review* 51:19, May 11, 1968.

Part I

THEORIES *of* AGGRESSION *and* VIOLENCE

tained in studies of the genetics, the neurophysiology, and the endocrinology of aggressive interactions. The changes in aggressive behaviors that are produced by experiences occurring early in life—namely, isolation, deprivation, and learning—are outlined in the third section. The final section describes four events that can generate aggressive responses: superficial pain, threats to status, invasion of personal space, and overcrowding.

Adaptive Aggression and Evolution

A basic tenet of the theory of evolution is the concept of adaptation to the environment. Because the environment in its very broadest sense is in a continuous state of change, it demands changes of living organisms. In the earth's history environmental alterations have generally occurred slowly enough so that millions of different species have kept pace with the changes. It is this *process* of keeping pace that is called evolution, and the *method* of keeping pace is called adaptation. Each change in the environment requires that some corresponding adaptation must take place in those organisms which are directly affected by the change.*

Because of the tremendous amount of inherent variation in any population of sexually reproducing organisms (animals as opposed to plants), there always will be some individuals better prepared than others to meet new environmental requirements. For instance, if the average winter temperature were to drop severely over a period of years, those animals with more dense fur or better thermal regulatory mechanisms would be more likely to survive and reproduce than would animals unable to withstand the colder temperatures.

Survival alone, however, is meaningless if an animal does not reproduce, for it is only by reproducing that the surviving animal can contribute to the survival of the entire species. Unlike the lower animals, though, a nonreproducing man or woman *can* contribute to the survival of the human species by a variety of means: through research in medicine or psychology and by making advances in law, politics, engineering, or the fine arts. Species survival, whether human or nonhuman, is dependent on the species' gene pool, the reservoir of potential variation. Evolution is a consequence of the natural selection (differential survival and reproduction) of those

* For the interested reader, two outstanding volumes present a comprehensive treatment of the theory and data of evolution: Mayr [54] and Moody [58].

individuals who are best fitted—i.e., adapted—to the demands of the environment.

From the premise that evolution occurs as a response to a changing environment, one can infer that the rate of evolutionary change will be dependent on the rate of change of the environment. The oceans are the most stable gross environments, although there have been changes in temperature and salinity. Bodies of fresh water are less stable than the oceans, while terrestrial environments, which lack the stabilizing influence of a fluid medium, are the most widely variable of all. In general the evolutionary rates of animals inhabiting these different environments have been correspondingly slow or rapid [58].

Although humans have had great influence on nonhuman evolutionary histories, man's major and recent biological impact has been to remove himself from the strictures of biological evolution. Where early man's primate ancestors were subject to environmental change, modern man (at least from Cro-Magnon) has increasingly subjected the environment to his control. This reversal of control has taken place because of man's unique adaptation—his brain. The human brain is an acutely specialized organ which, through its evolutionary development, has been the foundation of language, cultural tradition, and breathtaking scientific achievements. But although man seems now to be free of selection by natural (as opposed to man-made) environmental pressures, he appears to face even greater dangers. These dangers—such as overpopulation, environmental pollution, and nuclear holocaust—present themselves because man is able to produce major changes in his sociocultural environment more rapidly than his genetic heritage will permit him to adapt to the changes.

Niko Tinbergen [75], a pioneering leader in the study of animal behavior, has reflected on man's propensity to kill other members of his species. In coming to the conclusion that man is an "unhinged killer," he says

There is a frightening, and ironical paradox in this conclusion: that the human brain, the finest life preserving device created by evolution, has made one species so successful in mastering the outside world that it suddenly finds itself taken off guard. One could say that our cortex and our brainstem (our "reason" and our "instincts") are at loggerheads. Together they have created a new social environment in which, rather than ensuring our survival, they are about to do the opposite. The brain finds itself seriously threatened by an enemy of its own making. It is its own enemy. We simply have to understand this enemy.

THE PROBLEM OF DEFINITION

There is abundant evidence that aggressive behaviors serve a positively adaptive function and promote the survival of a species. But what is aggression? The answers are many and depend for their inclusiveness or exclusiveness on the discipline providing the definition. In general, vertebrate zoologists limit aggression to within-species encounters. Carthy and Ebling [14] define it as follows: "An animal acts aggressively when it inflicts, attempts to inflict, or threatens to inflict damage on another member of his own species." This definition, however, is obviously too limited to apply to the human animal. It seems logical to assume that destructive violence aimed at others' physical possessions and property represents damage inflicted on the person who owns them. Thus one could argue that human aggression and violence is defined by the *intention* to hurt another individual, either physically, psychologically, or financially, whether the hurt is threatened, attempted, or actually accomplished.

Some scientists believe Carthy and Ebling's definition to be too restrictive because in eliminating between-species conflicts, it exempts all the predatory behaviors as well as defenses against predation. Washburn and Hamburg [79] have reviewed the data on aggression in Old World monkeys and apes as the data bear on the problem of human aggression. They conclude that ". . . if one is concerned with aggressive behavior in man, the degree to which human carnivorous and predatory activity is related to human aggressiveness should be kept open for investigation and not ruled out by definition." Moyer [59] has recently made an interesting attempt to define different types of aggressive behavior by defining the stimulus situations which elicit them, suggesting that each type has a distinct biological basis. The seven types of aggression that Moyer has named and identified are as follows: (1) predatory aggression, (2) intermale aggression, (3) fear-induced aggression, (4) irritable aggression, (5) territorial aggression, (6) maternal aggression, and (7) instrumental aggression. For some of these seven types Moyer has found evidence for rather specific involvement of different areas within the brain's emotional control center, the limbic system. For other types there are research data that implicate the male and female sex hormones as playing major roles in the initiation or inhibition of aggression. Finally, the class of instrumental aggression is simply his acknowledgment that aggressive behaviors can be learned and that once learned are more likely to appear in future situations resembling those in which they were learned.

An appeal to the instinctiveness of aggression has been made by

Kahn and Kirk [43], who have proposed that aggression be considered as a drive which is an ". . . inborn, biologically rooted, directionally oriented energizer of behavior that is elicited by frustration of other drives and needs necessary to the survival of the species and the individual organism." (See Chapter 2 of this book.) However the appeal to innate drive mechanisms not only presents a sticky problem for disentanglement by the behavioral scientist but also raises the outmoded dualism of nature versus nurture.

Because aggression and violence have been defined and interpreted so differently by the various scientific disciplines, and because there is presently no consensus opinion of the best definition, the present chapter will use the terms to mean *any kind of behavior that threatens to damage, attempts to damage, or in fact does damage another individual or his property.* Note that this definition is *deliberately* more restrictive than that offered in the Introduction (see page 4). The reason is a simple one: Most of the data presented in the following sections have been obtained in studies of animal *behavior* in both natural and laboratory settings. Behavior is observable, without any argument; but the attribution of a reason, motive, or purpose to an animal's behavior is a scientist's construction and may not agree with the animal's "reason," "motive," or "purpose." Psychiatrists are probably justified in arguing that in man aggression includes ". . . such assertive behaviors as forceful and determined attempts to master a task or accomplish an act" [27]. However, to extend the meaning of this definition to the behavior of animals seems quite unwarranted. It is delightful to watch a very small kitten trying its hardest to scale the heights of the family-room sofa. Is the kitten being aggressive, or is he merely exploring vigorously in a new environment? This homely example illustrates the complex problems of definition and interpretation one faces when trying to disentangle the interrelated behaviors that include approach, attack, avoidance, withdrawal, exploration, and play.

Those who study animals' behavior cannot ask their subjects why they behaved in a certain way. Rather, they must accumulate observational instances of a behavior, noting each time the consequence of the act, and then by inductive reasoning determine the probable function of that act. Thus if a particular facial expression regularly is followed by the withdrawal of another animal, the observer infers that the expression is a warning or threat that means "go away." The second step in inferential reasoning—and the one that many observers do not like to make—is that the performing animal meant, "You go away or I will attack you because you are too close to my baby and that makes me angry." Until animals can tell the observer *why* they did what they did, there is no justfication for defining as "aggression" the broad spectrum of behaviors that anthropomorphically resemble human endeavors.

ADAPTIVE FUNCTIONS OF AGGRESSION

Contemporary man exists because in his evolutionary history he responded aggressively to those situations in which his life, his family, or his society were threatened. For man, as well as for animals, aggressive behaviors have served a variety of adaptive purposes that Lorenz [50] has suggested include spacing the animals, maintaining a dominance hierarchy, and aiding natural selection through regulation of breeding. One major function of aggression between members of the same species is to increase the distance between the two individuals or the two groups. If there is sufficient suitable habitat, then it is biologically more sound if the animals are evenly distributed rather than concentrated in one locale. There is suggestive evidence, which will be discussed later, that high population density is a major factor in accentuating disruptive influences in an otherwise stable society.

A second function of aggression derives from the fact that in many mammalian species social interactions are regulated by some system of ordering individuals, variously designated a dominance hierarchy, a peck order, a hook order, or having the key to the executive washroom. For some animals the structuring system operates only during special periods such as the breeding season or the birth season. For other animals the system is always present and inescapable. Almost all the higher primates, including man, are born, mature, and die within an overriding, structuring system. The function of primate dominance hierarchies is to maintain social stability within the group. For example, each member of a baboon group (excluding infants) knows his relative status with respect to the other animals and regulates his social interactions accordingly. Thus a stable hierarchy affords a strong measure of predictability: Individuals know which behaviors are permissible with which animals [19].

While the concept of dominance implies aggressive or assertive behaviors, in fact a dominance hierarchy minimizes the occurrence of overt fighting within a group. Instead the animals employ a special set of behavior patterns that are safe substitutes for fighting. Different facial expressions, postures, tail positions, and vocalizations are used to signal the motivational states and intentions. Threats made without physical contact replace actual attack; deferential behaviors, shown in response to a threat, acknowledge subordinance and prevent physical abuse. If an established dominance hierarchy is artificially broken down either by removal or introduction of animals, severe fighting will erupt in a group of monkeys, and it will persist until the hierarchy is reestablished [72].

The third major function of within-species aggression is that of natural selection for the individuals or groups best adapted to their environment. All the hoofed animals have restricted breeding seasons during which females are in estrus and the males in rut. The rutting males combat fiercely in ritualized but severe fighting to collect and maintain a harem of breeding females [53]. The males who are stronger and better fighters will cover more females and sire more offspring than will smaller, weaker, or sickly males. Similarly, in many species of primates where there are strong dominance hierarchies, it is the most dominant males that mate at the optimal time for conception. Lower-ranking males are not excluded from reproductive activities but copulate before or after the critical 24-hour period surrounding the time of ovulation. Thus the dominant males father more infants than do the subordinate males, who are generally neither in the prime of life nor in prime physical condition.

THE CAUSATION OF AGGRESSION

Any attempt to determine the causation of behavior is fraught with difficulties. There is, however, a convenient way to examine some of the problems. Medical science has found that the most basic requirements for sustaining life are directly controlled by internal, chemical-neurological networks, which function without conscious control. Most thoroughly understood are the mechanisms that control eating, drinking, and breathing. These drives are called *homeostatic* because they energize behaviors that seek to stabilize an internal chemical system at a balance point.

The body's tissues require oxygen, which is transported from the lungs by the blood; but they also require that carbon dioxide be removed from the tissues, and this too is accomplished by the blood. Although carbon dioxide is a by-product of energy production in the tissues, it is the pressure of carbon dioxide gas dissolved in the blood that regulates the rate of inhalation and exhalation by the lungs. A cluster of cells (called a baroreceptor) located in the carotid artery is sensitive to the pressure of the dissolved carbon dioxide gas. As the CO_2 pressure increases, the baroreceptor in the carotid artery responds by signaling the diaphragm to pump faster, thereby increasing the rate at which CO_2 is removed from and O_2 added to the blood by the lungs. That this is a reflex mechanism, not subject to conscious control, can be tested simply by holding one's breath to prevent removal of the carbon dioxide gas: An explosive exhalation will be triggered reflexly when the baroreceptor tells the diaphragm to start pumping. Similar homeostatic mechanisms signal the needs for food (by lowered levels of blood sugar) and water (by dehydration of water-sensitive tissues).

The scientific picture becomes much less clear when one examines what are called nonhomeostatic drives. Sexual activity has been the most carefully studied, and it appears that organisms can function normally without ever engaging in any sexual behavior, even though there are chemical and neurological systems which organize and regulate sexual appetites. Aggressive behavior has also been labeled as a nonhomeostatic drive, but there is far from unanimity of opinion in this case (see Chapter 4). As the following sections of this chapter will demonstrate, there is an extensive neurological-hormonal system (or possibly systems, if one accepts Moyer's approach) involved in the initiation, the expression, and the inhibition of aggression. Although there is internal regulation, most of the evidence suggests that the initiation of aggressive behaviors is basically dependent on external factors. Given our present state of knowledge of aggressive behaviors, the best one can say is that unlike a simple reflex, or a homeostatic drive mechanism, aggression is dependent in a very complex way on both internal and external factors.

Tinbergen [75] has suggested that the problem of causation must be approached with the knowledge that one is dealing with three subquestions which are related to each other by a temporal dimension. In asking the question "What makes an animal fight?" one is asking the following: (1) What are the immediate, effective, internal, and external factors? (2) What were the particular social experiences in this animal's developmental history that predisposed him toward aggressive behavior? (3) What were the historical selection pressures that fostered the evolution of aggressive behavior in this species? The answer to each of these subquestions will be quite different, yet they are obviously interdependent. The immediate factors always operate on an animal, which has had a particular developmental history, and to which he has brought a species-typical genetic heritage. Although his individual complement of genes is unique, they are drawn from a species' gene pool that determines, within general limits, his inborn neurological, chemical, and behavioral characteristics.

The following section will examine the role of internal factors in aggressive behaviors. The evidence for *genetic* control of aggression is scanty beyond the well-documented finding that both natural and artificial selection can accentuate the intensity and frequency of aggressive behaviors in animals. The *brain* is unquestionably the most important internal factor in aggressive behaviors, although its role is complex and not completely understood. Finally, some important findings will be presented to demonstrate that the *sex hormones* affect the expression of aggressive behaviors by means of their action both before and after birth.

The Role of Internal Factors

The evolutionary history of any species must always remain shrouded by the mists of time. Although bones leave fossil records, past behavior is ephemeral and can only be inferred from the probable function of the fossilized bones. Similarly one can only make inferences about the probable historical selection pressures that operated on a given species. But, fortunately, natural selection operates to preserve those genes and gene combinations that determine particularly adaptive neurochemical mechanisms and behavior patterns. In general where there is no margin for error and the adaptive value is very great, basic mechanisms come under absolute genetic control. For example, the molecular structure of enzymes that regulate protein synthesis must not vary if the organism is to survive and develop normally. It is the genetically programmed internal factors that provide the essential substrate for other neurochemical events as well as behavior. Unlike some behavior patterns—many variations of which may ultimately achieve the same purpose—the biochemical and neural foundations of behavior are extremely precise and consistent from one individual to another. Abnormalities, distortions of balance, or any type of pathology occurring in these foundations of behavior can have profound consequences for the early development and later expression of specific behavior patterns.

THE GENES AND AGGRESSIVE BEHAVIOR

The normal human has twenty-three pairs of chromosomes, one pair of which determines the sex of the individual: Normal genetic males have one X and one Y sex chromosome, while normal genetic females have two X chromosomes. About one child in two hundred is born with a major chromosomal abnormality [78]. Of these about one-third are abnormalities of the sex chromosomes [63]. While some chromosomal abnormalities are surprisingly commensurate with a completely normal life, many others are not. There is a well-documented association between chromosomal abnormalities and intellectual impairment—mongolism being the best known example [49]. Some males have an extra X chromosome, called Klinefelter's syndrome (XXY), which is frequently associated with mental and emotional disturbance, while others may lack a Y chromosome and have only the X (Turner's syndrome: XO).

A less frequent anomaly is the presence of an extra Y chromosome, creating the XYY or "super-male" syndrome. It has been speculated that the extra male chromosome might make a man "more manly" than normal and, by deduction, more aggressive or more prone to violent behavior.

The possibility that the XYY syndrome may "cause" a man to be extremely violent has recently received extensive and spectacular coverage by the news media following the murder trials of two XYY men. In Australia Lawrence Hammell was acquitted of murder, while in France Daniel Hugon received a lesser penalty than usual for murder. In each case the defense rested heavily on the claim that the defendant had decreased personal responsibility for the crime because of the effects of the chromosomal abnormality. However, on March 6, 1969, in the first American court test, the Superior Court of Los Angeles ruled that there was insufficient scientific evidence of any relationship between the XYY chromosomal abnormality and abnormal human behavior.

Recently Kessler and Moos (personal communication) have reviewed the literature on the XYY abnormality. They found *no convincing evidence* for a relationship between the XYY pattern and specific morphological, physiological, or behavioral characteristics. They urge that extreme caution be exercised by those making statements about the behavior traits of XYY individuals until much more data have been collected. An important step in this direction has been taken by researchers at Yale–New Haven Hospital where the chromosome patterns of newborn infants are determined by computerized routines. Of the four thousand babies checked, eighteen have been found to have gross chromosomal abnormalities—nine of which were anomalies of the sex chromosomes [51].

As suggested previously, it is common knowledge that animals can be bred selectively to enhance specific behavioral characteristics. Several strains of dogs, pit bulls, fox terriers, and Doberman pinschers, for example, have been bred for enhancement of their special attacking and killing abilities. Similarly, fighting cocks are bred selectively and trained to fight to the death an opponent they have never seen before. The brave bulls of Spain and Mexico are also bred for fierce fighting characteristics. Although aggressive behavior is a result of the interaction of many genes, that it does have a firm genetic foundation was amply demonstrated by Scott [70]. He crossed very aggressive basenjis with very docile cocker spaniels and found that the puppies scored midway between their parents on tests of aggressiveness.

Beyond the simple statement that there are gross genetic influences on aggressive behavior in humans, at the present time there is insufficient evidence to enable valid predictions of future aggressive or violent behavior to be made on the basis of genetic information alone.

THE BRAIN AND AGGRESSIVE BEHAVIOR

Quite unlike the genetic picture, there is so much research information on the brain and its control of aggressive behavior that a review chapter such as this can do little more than summarize the major topics. (For a more technical, sophisticated discussion the reader should consult Clemente and Lindsley [16], Grossman [29], and House and Pansky [40].) And because the brain and central nervous system (especially man's) are the most complex single product of evolution, both the descriptive terminology and experimental procedures are also exceedingly complicated.

The neuropsychologist's research techniques are predicated on at least two fundamental principles underlying the action of the central nervous system. First, certain responses that are critical for survival become neuromotor reflexes and are genetically programmed. For example, foreign matter reflexly elicits tears if it is on the eye, sneezing if it is in the nose, and coughing if it is in the throat. Second, different sites within the brain work on a check-and-balance system often involving reciprocal inhibition—thus the embarrassment one is caused when the cough or sneeze reflex inhibits the swallowing reflex. But frequently learning can produce voluntary control of reflex protective mechanisms, as exemplified by the use of contact lenses, snuff, and tobacco.

Research on the anatomy and physiology of the brain involves a variety of techniques that include direct and indirect electrical stimulation, injection of drugs and hormones, and surgical removal (ablation) of small portions. Because nerve tissue operates by the conduction of minuscule electrical currents, scientists can place a microelectrode down into a particular part of the brain and give that area a brief electric jolt. If the area is one that starts a particular behavior pattern or a muscular response, the artificial stimulation through the electrode will initiate that response. If the area is one that stops or inhibits a behavior, the behavior will cease during the period of stimulation. If an area responsible for starting a response is ablated, that response will not occur (unless it can be started elsewhere). Similarly if an inhibitory or "stop" area is removed, the behavior that it controls will continue. For example, an area of the hypothalamus inhibits eating. If it is destroyed, an animal will persistently overeat and become obese.

The principal regions controlling aggression are believed to lie deep in the temporal lobes and in the subcortical structures, known collectively as the limbic system, which extend almost continuously from the forebrain to the brainstem. These regions include the ventral septum, the preoptic area, the amygdala, the stria terminalis, the hypothalamus, portions of the thalamus, and other less well-defined areas [18]. Figures 1, 2, and 3 provide a crude neuroanatomical road map of the human brain.

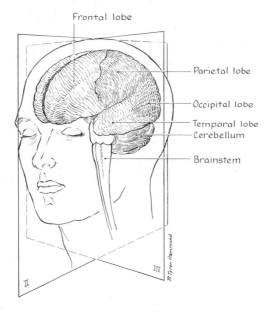

FIG. 1.   Three-quarter frontal view showing location of the brain within the head and the four major lobes of the cerebrum. A cut made along Plane II, called a midline section, reveals the anatomical relationships shown in Fig. 2. Similarly, a cut along Plane III, called a coronal section, reveals the structures shown in Fig. 3.

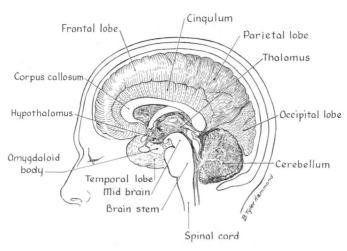

FIG. 2. Midline section (Plane II of Fig. 1) through brain illustrating gross physical relationships between structures implicated in the origin and control of aggressive behaviors. The location of the amygdaloid body, which lies deep within the temporal lobe, is shown by a dotted outline.

Among the earliest studies of brain function that found changes in aggressiveness were those by Bard [4], Bard and Mountcastle [5], and Klüver and Bucy [45]. Using techniques far less precise than those available today, these investigators removed massive portions of the

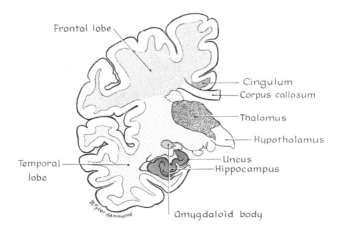

FIG. 3. Coronal section (Plane III of Fig. 1), showing only the right half of the brain. Limbic system structures visible include the amygdaloid body, hippocampus, hypothalamus, thalamus, and cingulum.

cerebral cortex in both cats and monkeys. The behavioral changes they observed included a range of effects from extreme docility to extreme ferocity. In the thirty years since these pioneering studies, major advances have been made in the knowledge of brain function and its regulation of behavior.

The results obtained by Flynn and his co-workers [24] illustrate the complexity of the brain mechanisms that are gradually being unraveled in his and many other laboratories. In studying the reactions of cats to rats, Flynn has noted two types of attack by the cat: a rage attack and a quiet biting attack. He has shown that the rage attack, following stimulation of the hypothalamus, is a directed, well-performed chase and attack. The rage attack, however, does not change to eating after the death of the rat; in fact, a cat will stop eating to attack when stimulated through the implanted electrode. Flynn reports that a variation of only a few millimeters in the site of stimulation within the lateral nucleus of the amygdala will either enhance or delay the attack.

A long series of experiments with cats has been reported by Brown and Hunsperger [10]. Their results demonstrate the neural complexity underlying not only aggressive behavior but also its corollaries, threat and withdrawal. In the cats they studied, using brain stimulation by implanted electrodes, Brown and Hunsperger found that there was no simple one-to-one relationship between their experimental procedures and the behavior displayed by the cats. Four general behavior patterns could be elicited—threat, threat followed by attack, threat followed by escape, and escape—but the pattern elicited was dependent upon the location of the electrode, the intensity of the stimulating current, and the sociophysical environment. Attack and escape behaviors were not found in different areas but rather were neurologically inseparable. Nor was the neuroanatomy of the threat system a simple unit: Threats could be elicited by stimulation of areas in the midbrain, the hypothalamus, and the amygdala.

It seems that all too often laboratory investigators are prone to forget that the spectrum of threat, attack, and withdrawal behaviors (known collectively as agonistic behaviors) are adaptive *social* behaviors and that their evolution has occurred in the context of a species' general social interactions. Several fascinating studies of brain control of aggression have been conducted in which the animals were observed postoperatively in a social situation. Rosvold, Mirsky, and Pribram [65] let eight rhesus monkeys live together until they had established a dominance hierarchy. Then the number three ranked monkey had her amygdala removed and, after recovering to normal health, was returned to her social group. The investigators found that she became more dominant, unpredictably aggressive, and vicious. She became the most dominant member of the group, while the males formerly ranked first and second fell to seventh and eighth.

Delgado and his associates at Yale University have conducted many similar studies of aggression in rhesus monkeys living in a social situation by using the technique of radio telemetry [18]. The monkeys have stimulating electrodes placed in various parts of the brain that modulate agonistic behaviors. The electrodes are connected by fine wires to a battery and control mechanism, which the animal wears as a small pack on his back. An FM radio signal sent to the pack will deliver, through complicated electronic circuitry, a small electrical stimulation to the brain through the electrode. After the initial finding that they could strongly inhibit threat and attack reactions by stimulating the caudate nucleus, Delgado placed the control lever inside the testing cage. The other group members learned very rapidly that after they pressed the lever, the dominant animal, of whom *they* were afraid, would behave in a fearful, submissive manner.

Conversely, Delgado has reported that telemetric stimulation of different brain areas can elicit attack and that the elicited aggression appeared not to be a stereotyped response but rather was indistinguishable from spontaneous activity. Elicited attacks were modulated by sensory inputs and were appropriate to changes in the location and attitude of the attacked animals. A very significant point about Delgado's research is that the experimental monkeys do not behave in a vacuum. Rather they are continuously sensitive to the presence and behavior of other members of their social group. He points out that existing social relationships still are effective, that friendships and coalitions still operate, and that dislikes and antagonisms remain effective even when an animal's behavior is being artificially "controlled" by the experimenter.

Robinson and his group working at Tulane University have also presented evidence that aggressive behaviors have their origin in brain mechanisms [64]. By telemetric stimulation of a nucleus in the hypothalamus of rhesus monkeys, Robinson has been able to elicit threats and attacks by a subordinate to a more dominant monkey. He found that the threat-attack behaviors were reliably elicited by the stimulation and that over a period of several days of testing, the dominance relationship between the two animals could be reversed.

The surprising finding was that, although the status relationship had been artificially altered by brain stimulation, the newly formed status relationship persisted unchanged, and without additional brain stimulation of the formerly subordinate monkey, for the duration of the study, a period of several months.

The research studies summarized here barely scratch the surface of the available data. However, they do provide a strong indication of the evidence implicating brain mechanisms in the initiation, modulation, and inhibition of agonistic behavior. Turning now to human subjects, there are numerous clinical conditions that involve disruptions of the neurological control of aggressive behavior. One group of these conditions is caused by a disturbance of the cerebral cortex that releases the subcortical centers from higher control. Usually sufficient cortex is involved to produce other symptoms, such as dementia or disorders of sensation, speech, and movement. This type of syndrome may occur in acute drug intoxications, after head injuries, in the elderly, in chronic alcoholics, and in drug addicts. All degrees of emotional responsivity, irritability, fighting, and violent temper outbursts are commonly seen; furthermore, many crimes of violence have been committed by people with cortical pathology—particularly when intoxicated (see Chapter 12). Prior to the availability of the modern tranquilizers, prefrontal lobotomies often were performed to reduce the occurrence of extremely destructive behaviors, directed both to the self and to others, by some chronic mental patients. However, this procedure was not found to be helpful in patients who repeatedly committed violent acts for personal gain [25].

A second group of clinical conditions derives from disease or pathology of the subcortical structures in the limbic system (see Fig. 3). A tragic example of this type of disturbance occurred with encephalitis lethargica. Also known as "sleeping sickness," the disease was widespread from 1915 to 1926. A few months after recovery children often developed marked impulsiveness and destructiveness —including violent attacks on others, sexual offenses, self-mutilation, and destruction of property. The brain areas mainly affected by the disease were the basal ganglia, the hypothalamus, and the periaqueductal gray of the brain stem [38].

A great deal of attention has been given to the relationship between temporal lobe pathology and aggression. Irritability, impulsiveness, and a low threshold for aggressive behavior have been found in about 50 percent of those patients with "temporal lobe epilepsy," a condition in which small brain lesions are found in regions deep within the temporal lobe—the amygdala, the uncus, and the hippocampal areas. However, rage as an accompaniment to an epileptic seizure is rare. Seizure discharge within the brain, or electrical stimuli involving the temporal lobes, usually produces fear, not rage. Environmental stimuli, on the other hand, seldom cause fear but frequently trigger rage. Gloor [28] has speculated that electrical stimulation or seizure discharge may be akin to the physiological reaction to unknown threats, leading to fear or flight, while the more mundane stimuli of everyday life may provoke rage because they are known and less feared.

Mark and Ervin [52] have defined a clinical entity, the "dyscontrol syndrome," with four categories of prominent symptoms: (1) senseless brutality, (2) pathological intoxication (a well-known clinical phenomenon where a relatively small amount of alcohol seems to release inordinately wild behavior), (3) sexual assault, and (4) multiple serious automobile accidents. In persons having a history of episodic dyscontrol, Mark and Ervin have occasionally found focal brain disease of the limbic system or temporal lobe. Anticonvulsant therapy or small surgical lesions in the involved area, or both, are said to improve many of these patients. Diseases of the hypothalamus have confirmed its role in the control of aggression in man. Acute destruction of, or tumors located in, the anterior hypothalamus have resulted in increased aggressiveness, while patients with small tumors in the posterior hypothalamus are often apathetic, somnolent, and inactive [68].

In summary, while it is clear that destruction or stimulation of many brain areas (either experimentally or in disease) may cause a deviation from "normal" in the expression of aggressive behavior, the neurological control of aggression is extremely complex and incompletely understood. Clinical applications, including diagnosis and treatment of obvious brain disorders, therapy for persons with disordered control of their behavior, as well as prediction, prevention, and control of inappropriate aggression, have so far been minimal and await further progress in basic research.

THE SEX HORMONES AND AGGRESSIVE BEHAVIOR

That males are generally more aggressive than females is one of the oldest and best known facts of both animal and human behavior. It is only recently, however, that a sound, scientific reason for this has been found. Interdisciplinary research by physiologists, endocrinologists, psychologists, and psychiatrists has been converging on the discovery that the way in which the mammalian brain functions later in life is to a very large extent determined by the hormonal, physical, and social stimuli to which it is exposed *before* birth as well as immediately after birth. This discussion is deliberately limited to the sex hormones because there is good evidence for their direct involvement in aggressive behavior. Though there is substantial literature on the relation of other hormones to aggression—particularly the adrenal hormones—only indirect relationships have been demonstrated. (Additional information can be found in Newton and Levine [60] and Clemente and Lindsley [16].)

For about twenty-five years scientists have known that permanent changes could be induced in the sexual behavior of rats and guinea pigs if the animals were treated with sex hormones before and after birth [35]. It now has been clearly established that the brain of the young mammal is affected by the presence or absence of the sex hormones during certain critical stages in its development. These hormones are normally produced in very small but measurable amounts by the adrenal glands long before the sex glands become functional. There are several types of both the male and the female hormones, called androgens and estrogens, respectively; most important for the present discussion is the role played by the male hormone testosterone.

During embryological development of the fetus there is a stage at which the animal's future reproductive system is undifferentiated; that is, it is neither malelike nor femalelike. The unformed genital tract will develop as a male's under the influence of microscopic amounts of androgens, which are secreted appropriately either by the adrenals of the fetus or those of the mother, while the absence of androgens will cause the genital tract to develop as a female's [36]. However, not only the reproductive organs themselves but also the neural mechanisms mediating sexual behavior undergo differentiation by the action of testosterone. Harris and Levine [36] have found that if testosterone is administered to female rats during the critical period of differentiation (which occurs about two to four days after birth in the rat) it "leads to disorganization of the nervous elements underlying the expression of female behavior." These androgen-treated females do not engage in normal female sexual behavior, and they develop more rapidly and achieve a greater body weight than do normal females.

The significance of these results derives from the finding that the brain and central nervous system, which ultimately control all behavior, are channeled toward a particular way of functioning by chemical events that may occur before birth. Most important is the fact that the behavioral changes are *not* limited to sexual behavior.

Young, Goy, and Phoenix [81] treated pregnant rhesus monkeys with testosterone during the second quarter of fetal development and found that profound and long-lasting changes were produced in the female infants. Their overall pattern of social behavior was incredibly similar to that shown by males and hardly at all like normal females. Their play patterns involved rough-and-tumble play, mauling, biting, threatening, chasing, and mounting. Although too young for adult sexual behavior, Goy's masculinized females displayed the male mounting behavior frequently and the female sexual invitation posture very infrequently.

Since male hormones can produce apparently permanent changes in behavior through their action on the brain during sensitive developmental periods, one immediately faces the question: Can abnormal hormone conditions during fetal or neonatal life so alter the organization of the human brain that very aggressive or violent behavior patterns become more probable? There is one suggestive line of evidence that this may be true. Ehrhardt and Money [22] have studied ten girls, aged about 4 to 14 years, whose mothers received therapeutic treatments during pregnancy with synthetic hormones related to androgens. Using interviews and sex-role preference tests, they classified nine of the ten girls as "tomboys" on the basis of their preference for boys' toys, their athletic energy, their outdoor pursuits, and their minimal interest in feminine frills, doll play, baby care, and household chores. Ehrhardt, Epstein, and Money [21] observed fifteen girls whose adrenal glands, because of a defect in enzyme metabolism, produced excessive amounts of androgens prior to birth. Their condition became known because their external genitals were masculinized at birth. Immediate treatment with cortisone reversed the biochemical abnormality and surgery corrected the masculinized genitals. However, like the ten masculinized girls described above, they remained tomboys in their play activities and showed little interest in typical feminine pastimes. The long-term consequences of fetal masculinization are not yet clear because the girls did retain typical conceptions of romance, marriage, and motherhood. Obviously strong weight must be given to the counterbalancing forces of early social learning experiences in the home.

The Role of Early Social Experiences

In seeking answers to the causation of aggression, one finds abundant experimental evidence indicating that the social experiences of infancy play a crucial role in shaping later behavior patterns. All mammals require some degree of maternal attention and contact, in the form of nursing and grooming, if they are to survive. In many mammalian species infants are born in litters, a pattern which ensures that the littermates provide each other with extensive and intensive social experience during infancy and adolescence [61]. The babies of higher primates are extremely dependent on maternal care for nourishment, transportation, and protection. Usually only one infant at a time is born to each female, but the births tend to be clustered within a limited period of time, so that as a result the young monkeys grow up in the company of age-mates [47]. Starting at about 6 months of age the young monkey plays tirelessly with other infants, explores his environment, and learns the "language" of his species. Behavior patterns develop, are modified and perfected, until the animal takes his place as a full adult member of his group.

The many studies by Harlow and his coinvestigators [31–34] have demonstrated the critical necessity for social experience with mother and peers if infant rhesus monkeys are to become normal adults. Rhesus monkeys that have had no social experience before adulthood show a variety of aberrant behaviors. One characteristic of these animals is that they may be markedly and inappropriately aggressive to other rhesus. Females, even though in the full bloom of physiologically normal estrus, will attack male partners who attempt to copulate [33]. Such an attack is an *extremely* unlikely event in the repertoire of normal feral (wild) animals.

By dint of great patience and persistence on the part of a few breeding males, several of Harlow's socially deprived rhesus females were inseminated and subsequently gave birth; others were artificially inseminated. Maternal responsiveness by the twenty "motherless mothers" took one of two forms—both abnormal. Seven of the mothers were passively indifferent to their babies: unresponsive to cries, screams, and attempts to suckle; and unprotective in the presence of humans. Another eight of the females were brutally intolerant of their infants. Several babies were nearly killed, some had fingers or toes bitten off, and all needed humane intervention to save them. The severity of the mothers' aggressiveness waned as the infants grew up, while the babies became very adept at avoiding and escaping from maternal attacks. Interestingly, the infants who experienced brutality were themselves significantly more aggressive during the eight months they were studied than were the infants raised by normal mothers. They no doubt learned the value of being aggressive—how else to get at mother's breast?—and the aggressive elements were accentuated at the expense of more typical infant behaviors. In addition the infants of motherless mothers showed significantly less social play and fewer sexual postures than the control infants. The remaining five motherless mothers were classified as showing "borderline adequate" maternal behavior. However, three of these five did have some minimal social experience with peers during the first year of life [2].

Adult male rhesus without infantile and juvenile social experience also display behavioral abnormalities [33]. Sexual behavior is the most bizarrely altered: Mounts may be oriented to the head or the side of the female; masturbation is very common, even in the presence of a normal, receptive female; and the female's sexual invitation is likely to elicit an attack rather than a mount. Socially deprived male monkeys also respond inappropriately when threatened by a human. Rather than threatening back or attempting to attack, the deprived male goes into an orgy of self-biting. Unless their long, razor-sharp canine teeth are removed, these males will severely mangle their own arms, hands, legs, and feet by their repeated, self-directed aggression.

The most severe behavioral pathology occurs following total social and perceptual isolation for periods longer than three months during the first year of life [34, 66]. Rowland [66] imposed two isolation conditions on infant rhesus monkeys separated from their mothers. The *early isolates* were isolated from birth to 6 months of age, and the *late isolates* from 6 months to 12 months of age. Fourteen days after leaving their isolation booths, pairs of infants were placed in a monkey "playroom" with pairs of control infants. Rowland found massive deficits in all the isolation-reared infants' social behavior. The *early isolates* displayed signs of intense fear of the control infants and tried to avoid all social interactions. The *late isolates*, on the other hand, were violently aggressive toward the other yearlings. In fact it was necessary to discontinue the daily playroom social testing because the control infants were in danger of being severely wounded.

The early and late isolate monkeys were studied again when they were almost 3 years old. In the course of testing one isolate with either one adult, one same-aged peer, or one infant, Mitchell [57] found that the isolates still behaved in a very abnormal fashion. Compared with the control subjects, the isolates engaged in significantly fewer play and sex behaviors and displayed significantly higher frequencies of hostile and fearful behaviors. Continued testing of the isolates, when they were 4½ years old, revealed that the males would violently—and totally inappropriately—attack infants, adolescents, or adults of either sex [56].

In summary, these experiments show that rhesus monkeys, after experiencing total social isolation for more than three months during their first year of life, suffer severe and increasingly pathological consequences, especially in the realm of threat-attack-avoidance behaviors. How does one interpret these findings? It is most unlikely that during solitary confinement the infants *learned* to be aggressive, for how would they have learned? It is also unlikely, though not impossible, that aggressive patterns were learned during the initial social encounters after isolation. Another explanation might be that the high frequency of attack behaviors was the result of a *failure to have learned* the positive, affiliative, friendly behavior patterns during isolation. But this too is inadequate because one still faces the question, why then were attack behaviors (in the late isolates) and escape behaviors (in the early isolates) so frequent?

Is there any evidence to suggest that the elements of agonistic behavior, which include the continuum of escape-threaten-attack, are unlearned responses? Yes, but not particularly for attack behaviors. Recall the discussion (p. 28) of Brown and Hunsperger's findings that electrical stimulation of portions of the midbrain, hypothalamus, and amygdala will variously elicit avoidance, threat, or attack patterns. The anatomical loci from which threats can be elicited are contiguous with and may overlap the loci of avoidance and escape patterns. There is also suggestive evidence that escape and attack are very primitive mammalian social behaviors [9] and that with the evolution of increasingly complex forms of social organization and social interaction, these primitive patterns have been overlaid and suppressed. For example, the courtship patterns of many species involve behaviors whose function is to reduce the conflicting motives of attack and flight, which are aroused by the close proximity of the mate [73].

It might thus be argued that escape or attack (or both) occur so frequently in isolated monkeys because these patterns are unlearned responses to a fear-evoking, novel stimulus—another monkey. They are prepotent because isolation from normal mother and normal peer experience prevented normal social learning, not only of alternative response patterns but also of the stimulus characteristics of a social partner. Therefore, without normal early socialization and the acquisition of learned inhibitions, certain configurations of stimuli may automatically induce escape or attack responses.

There is very intriguing evidence that a specific communication pattern can elicit an unlearned, apparently innate response in young rhesus monkeys. Sackett [67] raised eight infant rhesus from birth to 9 months of age in individual isolation cages, one wall of which was a rear-projection screen. Pictures of monkeys engaged in various social behaviors were projected on the screens, and the behavior of the infants was scored during each picture. During one part of the experiment the picture duration (2 minutes) was fixed and controlled by the experimenter, while in a second phase the infant monkey controlled the total duration of his exposure to a given picture. A touch on a lever would project a picture for 15 seconds, after which it would go off; reexposure required another lever touch. Sackett reported that at about 3 months of age the infants began showing signs of extreme disturbance and fear when pictures of monkeys giving social threats were shown on the screen. Soon afterward they stopped lever-touching when the threat pictures were projected but not for pictures showing other social behaviors. He concluded that the data gave strong evidence for the existence of innate recognition mechanisms which led to complex behavioral responses. Extrapolating from these data, one might predict that there also exist stimulus configurations which will elicit attack behavior from a socially naïve monkey. Further research on the ontogeny of agonistic behavior may shed light on the causation of aggression.

The accentuation of aggressive behaviors by rearing in isolation is not limited to primates. Kahn [42] has reported that isolation-reared mice were more aggressive than those having normal social experiences with a mother and littermates. Similarly, Banks [3] and King and Gurney [44] have found more fighting in mice isolated during infancy. Birds also may display higher levels of aggression when reared alone instead of in a group [46].

However, there is also contradictory evidence—as so often occurs in every stage of scientific investigation. The contradictions also emphasize the extreme caution required of any investigator seeking to generalize experimental results to species or genera different from the experimental subjects. Fox terriers, a strain of dogs that has been artificially selected for fighting ability, will begin fighting their own littermates at about 7 weeks of age if they are left with their mothers. In some instances it has been necessary to separate the litter to keep the puppies from killing each other. However, if fox terrier puppies are brought up alone without mother or littermates until the age of 4 months, they do *not* fight with normally raised terriers, even when attacked [26].

Melzack and Thompson [55] reared twenty-one Scottish terrier puppies under different conditions of social deprivation between 1 and 10 months of age. When tested with a normally reared dog in a competitive food-getting situation, the isolates "lost" 57 of 64 competitions. Furthermore, they did not respond—except with quiet passivity—to the growling and snapping of normally reared dogs. Their nonaggressive withdrawal patterns seem to resemble the behavior of the early isolate monkeys described above.

Summarizing the consequences of early social isolation, there seem to be two quite consistent patterns emerging: After isolation from normal mother and peer experiences, an animal is very likely to display either markedly *increased* aggression or markedly *decreased* aggression. There seems to be no middle ground. Although diametrically opposed, the consistency of results is remarkable considering the enormous variability among the isolation techniques, the duration of isolation, the behavioral measures employed, and phyletic differences of the animals. It certainly appears that there is some common, underlying mechanism whose action is profoundly altered *away from the normal state* by imposition of social isolation. Further theoretical development must await the results of carefully controlled studies that consider brain function, hormone activity, and genetic constitution within the context of behavioral modification by means of social isolation.

When searching out the causation of aggression, thoughtful consideration must be given to the effects of learning. Although the immediately preceding discussion presented major evidence that aggressive behaviors may be unlearned, it also is true that specific learning experiences may strongly accentuate the probability of occurrence of aggressive interaction. Washburn and Hamburg [79] have suggested that interspecies differences in aggressivity may be related to the ease with which some species learn aggressive responses. They argue that "the result of evolution is that behaviors that have been adaptive in the past history of the species . . . are easy to learn and hard to extinguish." Note carefully that this proposition does not imply that aggression is either innate or learned but only that different species may show differences in their *readiness* to learn under certain conditions.

The incidence of swimming in different primate species illustrates Washburn and Hamburg's thesis. Unlike marine mammals, the monkeys and apes possess no particular structural adaptation for swimming. Man is a rather capable swimmer, and if an individual has received training, he can in fact swim rapidly and for long distances. It is no doubt true that early man swam across rivers or to islands to achieve a safe retreat long before he used logs or vine ropes for the same purpose. Since the ability to cross natural water barriers in search of food, mates, or safety would have been of adaptive value, swimming patterns became easily learned behaviors. (One might also argue that swimming first occurred as a corollary to water-gathering, bathing, or perhaps just the sensual pleasure of taking a cooling dip on a hot afternoon.) In any case, chimpanzees and gorillas not only do *not* swim but actively attempt to avoid contact with any amount of water larger than they can drink [69, 76]. Zoos and research stations frequently use a water-filled moat to contain these powerful apes within a restricted space. The rhesus monkey on the other hand is an excellent swimmer and does not hesitate to enter water. It seems quite likely that in some extreme situation a chimp or gorilla could swim—or learn to swim—but because the behavior has never had great adaptive significance, the animals are prone neither to enter water nor to learn to swim. Obviously if swimming became essential to survival, those animals that did not drown would reproduce and presumably contribute to the next generation whatever propitious combination of genes enabled them to learn to swim. Many generations of such selection for individuals easily able to learn to swim would no doubt result in a population that learned to swim much more readily than their swimming-but-just-barely ancestors. Such is the course of evolutionary change under the pressure of natural selection for a peculiar trait.

Laboratory workers at the Roscoe B. Jackson Memorial Laboratory in Bar Harbor, Maine, have explored the conditions under which it is possible to train a mouse to be very aggressive or very submissive. If a house mouse without social experience after weaning is placed in the home territory (e.g., living cage) of another naïve mouse, the interloper will be attacked. By techniques of pairing a mouse with another mouse for very brief periods, one can train the animal to become either very aggressive and dominant (because he always wins) or very fearful and submissive (because he is always attacked and loses). Different "training" programs can produce winners or losers, fighters or cowards—behaviors and attributes that the animal carries into new situations with strange animals. Rats have been trained to fight by putting a pair into a box with an electric grid floor. After conditioning, the animals will rear on their hind legs and spar with forefeet and mouth when a signal associated with shock is turned on. By "fighting," the animals postpone the onset of foot shock.

Thus isolation, deprivation, and early training experiments all provide strong evidence that aggressive behaviors in many mammalian species have their origin in neural pathways that have become genetically coded during the evolutionary history of the species. But while the genetic code enables the expression of attack and flight behaviors without the normal social learning opportunities, aggression is frequently displayed in inappropriate circumstances with generally maladaptive consequences. This finding accentuates the importance of the early developmental period for acquiring learned inhibition and control over the occurrence of aggression. When animals behave hyperaggressively without evident control or inhibition —as often occurs as a consequence of prolonged early social deprivation—it is tempting to see that behavior as analogous to human violence.

Role of Immediate-Present Events

Unlike man, the nonhuman animals live almost exclusively in the present. Excluding instinctual thought-for-the-'morrow behaviors (e.g., nut-gathering and -burying by the squirrel), the temporal sequence of individual elements and larger behavior patterns occurs as a response to the temporal sequence of immediate stimulus inputs. The response to the immediate present is of course modulated by both past experience and momentary internal physiology, but these factors simply provide the framework within which responses are made to perceived stimuli. However, even this latter statement must now be qualified by Van Lawick-Goodall's [76] discovery that chimpanzees fabricate tools, carry them until they can be appropriately used, and then apply them in a way that indicates that they were made specifically for use in an unspecified future situation.

Not only perceived stimuli—those occurring at time "now"—but also short-term external conditions can be described as immediate instigations to aggressive behavior in mammals, and it would be a lifetime's task to describe accurately just a portion of them. As a consequence, the details must be abstracted to generalizations and to classifications that always seem to be forced compromises possessing loopholes, exceptions, and loose ends. The classification offered here is only one of many that are possible and undoubtedly reflects the authors' particular attitudes and orientations. A variety of studies suggest that aggression may occur (1) as a response to pain, (2) as a response to a threat to status, (3) as a response to the invasion of personal space, and (4) as a consequence of overcrowding. The four instigations to aggression suggested here reveal successively more complex stimulus situations. Accompanying the increase in complexity is a decrease in the accuracy with which one can single out a specific event as "the cause" of aggression. However, these are the events or conditions reported to elicit aggressive behavior in animals that seem to be most directly relevant to an investigation of the biology of aggression and violence in the human animal.

AGGRESSION INDUCED BY PAIN

Of all the sensory modalities, pain is the most universal and probably the least understood. In addition to specialized nerve endings, pain is perceived when the stimulus input to any modality exceeds some threshold: Extremely loud sounds, bright light, high or low temperatures all cause pain just as surely as a physical blow or a tear in the skin. Superficial pain (as distinguished from a deep somatic pain like a backache) and especially that arising in the extremities is probably the most consistently reliable single cause of aggression [70]. Feeling pain, the animal displays aggression to whatever has been perceived as causing the pain. The aggressive response both removes the source of the painful stimulation and prevents a repetition. Such a response is usually a highly adaptive one, for it functions to preserve the integrity of the organism. Behaviors that terminate or avoid pain are learned very rapidly and, once learned, are extremely difficult to extinguish.

Animals with a "brain" as primitive as the nervous system of the planaria (a flatworm) can learn that certain events are reliably followed by pain [41]. Such pain-signaling events can induce a change in behavior. Animals with complex brains readily learn that an event is a *threat* of pain, and they will respond as aggressively to the perceived threat as to the perceived pain. It is interesting to speculate that in man psychological pain and the psychological threat of pain represent analogues to physical pain. The "superficial pain" of a verbal insult frequently instigates the same response as a sharp slap in the face, while the deep "somatic pain" caused by a severe psychological loss, such as the death of a loved one, is as incapacitating as a blow to the solar plexus.

AGGRESSION INDUCED BY THREATS TO STATUS

In many mammalian species there is a typical social organization that is structured by interindividual status relationships. The structural effects of status differences may be seasonal—as in the breeding harems of elephant seals [48]—or they may be year round, as in rhesus monkey groups [20]. Despite their often despotic appearance, it is inarguable that firmly established and mutually recognized status differences actually minimize the frequency and severity of aggression in complex social organizations. Bernstein and Mason [7] have reported a significant decrease in aggressive interactions as a status hierarchy is worked out in a group of rhesus monkeys. Once established, the hierarchy is maintained primarily by threats (of pain) and gestures of submission. If, however, an individual wishes to elevate his own status, it can be done only by displacing another of higher status. In the animal world such a confrontation is rarely settled without physical aggression.

Experiments with rats [6] have shown that a new rat placed in an existing group of rats will be severely attacked by members of the group. He is recognized immediately as not belonging to the group —probably because he lacks the characteristic "group odor." Should he survive the stress and injury of the initial attacks, the stranger may become an integrated member of the group.

Southwick [72] has reported on an illuminating experiment that he conducted with a group of rhesus monkeys (*Macaca mulatta*) at the Calcutta Zoological Gardens. Extensive observations determined the baseline frequency for each of twenty behaviors occurring in a social group of seventeen monkeys composed of adults, juveniles, and yearlings of both sexes. At intervals after the group had stabilized, new animals were placed in the 25- by 40-foot enclosure. Southwick found that new juveniles were attacked by the resident juveniles but ignored by the adults; new adult females were viciously attacked by the resident females; and new adult males were similarly attacked by the adult males (but not the boss male) and to some extent by the females. For each class (juvenile, adult female, adult male) of introduced animal, it was found that the class whose status was threatened was most active in agonistic responses toward the stranger.

A well-established finding is that in macaque monkeys aggressive behaviors in a seminatural situation occur most frequently during the period immediately following group formation. Although the animals are chosen so that the age-sex class distribution mirrors the composition of a natural group, the animals are usually strangers to each other. During the first hour after eleven rhesus monkeys were placed in a 24- by 48-foot compound, Bernstein and Mason [8] recorded 195 behavioral interactions, of which more than 50 percent were attacks and threats. The frequency of aggression during the first hour was more than 20 times greater than that observed during any 1-hour period for the balance of the study. Aggression and responses to aggression comprised 82 percent of all behaviors. The most dominant male directed more than 90 percent of his aggressive behaviors to other adults and less than 10 percent to the juveniles. Similarly the adult females directed their aggression primarily to each other, while the juveniles were aggressive only toward each other and a subadult female. The status hierarchy observed at the end of the first hour after group formation did not change significantly during the remaining 75 days the group was observed.

The status-structured social organization common to many macaque and baboon (*Papio*) species bears some resemblance to the hierarchical relationships typical of many human organizations. Obvious examples are the military services, large business and industrial corporations, and educational institutions. Each has its characteristic organizational structure, but all share the common element of assigning differential status and rank within the hierarchy. As do the nonhuman primates, humans know their own rank as well as that of most others in the hierarchy and regulate their interactions accordingly.

The sharp observer of everyday, commonplace interactions will be able to detect rank differences between individuals if he is aware of the occurrence of many subtle, nonverbal behaviors. Between two men with different rank in the same organization, the lower-ranking man usually will defer to his superior by opening doors; by following rather than leading through narrow passageways; by conceding first chance at the water cooler, or the bar, or the hors d'oeuvres; by offering to get the coffee; by speaking less and listening more; and in many other ways too numerous to mention. Accustomed to receiving these acknowledgments of his rank position, a superior will first detect the elements of a challenge when a closely ranked inferior ceases acting deferentially and assumes behavior patterns consistent with those occurring between rank-equals. Recognizing a threat to his status, the threatened individual may initiate a variety of repressive measures designed to "put the upstart in his place."

One can argue, with more than superficial meaning, that the violence generated by black-white or by student-administration confrontation is the inevitable consequence of a subordinate's vigorous challenge to a superior's rank (see Chapter 6). In our nation both college students and black citizens represent large minority groups that have long been relegated to very low-status positions in the American power structure. Virtually devoid of the power to influence decisions that directly affect their lives, representatives of these two groups have posed an often violent challenge to the supervening levels of power. Those individuals and institutions whose status has been and is now being directly threatened are responding, in most cases, with powerful and often violent countermeasures.

AGGRESSION AS A RESPONSE TO THE INVASION OF PERSONAL SPACE

The concept of territoriality has a long and checkered history in zoology and ethology [1, 11, 74]. Although having a range of interpretations, territorial behavior in essence is the defense of a fixed, geographically demarcated area against intrusion by certain other members of one's own species. Territorial defense consists more in warning others that "this land (tree, hole, pond) is mine" than in physical combat over possession. It is a common phenomenon among fish, birds, and many mammals [39]. In most species territoriality occurs seasonally, particularly during breeding, nesting, and rearing of the young. While the arguments about the origin, structure, and function of territoriality are many [17, 80], the import for this discussion is that defense of territory serves an adaptive function by enhancing differential survival and reproduction.

There is a heated debate over whether or not true territorial behavior occurs in the more advanced primates—monkeys, apes, and man. At present the available evidence suggests that the gibbon is probably the only territorial primate [13, 23]. However, an extremely biased but popular best seller, *The Territorial Imperative* [1], attributes most of man's ills to his drive to conquer and maintain a geographical territory. Resolution of this debate will come only when there are substantially more hard scientific data than are now available. A number of monkey species, especially those which travel and forage for food on the ground rather than in the trees, are organized into closed social groups that range widely over a given area. These are called "closed groups" because they are strongly resistant to having outsiders join the group [71]. The monkeys living in closed groups are generally quite aggressive, and a dominance or status hierarchy is a prominent feature of their social organization. Such groups will typically "defend" against invasion the particular location where they happen to find themselves.

A Swiss zoologist, Hediger, is generally credited with being the first to recognize the importance of spatial relationships between *individual* animals and between animals and man [37]. Hediger has suggested that an animal lives and moves at the center of two concentric spheres whose size depend on the status of a potential interactor. The inner or smaller sphere is the defense or attack space, while the larger or outer sphere is the flight or withdraw space. If a predator enters the flight space, the animal will run away until the predator is again outside the withdrawal space. If, however, the predator chases his prey and in fact crosses into the defense space, the animal will attack and fight. Most social interactions require that members of one's *own* species must approach very closely. That the status of the potential interactor determines the dimensions of individual space can be easily determined by noting the different distances to which a mother monkey will permit another infant or an adult female to approach her. Relative status seems to be the major factor in determining the size of the spheres of personal space.

It seems a logical argument that in those nonterritorial species, perhaps including man, the function of personal space is like that of territoriality. Personal space is by analogy a sort of portable territory, moving with the individual rather than being fixed by physical markers. Hall, in his book *The Hidden Dimension*, presents fascinating cross-cultural evidence for the sanctity of personal space in humans and its ramifications for nonverbal communication [30]. Hall details the very important cultural differences in the closeness to which another individual is tolerated. An American may well feel uncomfortable, if not actually threatened, by the Frenchman who insists on conversing at a distance of 18 inches. Feeling threatened by another's closeness, an individual may very well become aggressive —certainly verbally if not physically.

Faced with growing populations and increasing densities, man finds his personal psychological space as well as his personal physical space undergoing a forced shrinkage. When others become intolerably close, and there are no means of escape, aggression becomes increasingly probable. Thelma Veness, writing of hostility in small groups of people, has suggested that aggression may be prompted by the feeling that one is becoming lost in the crowd, that one is no longer distinctive. To be too closely crowded by others may arouse concern for one's identity, and she argues that "there is a special sense in which an 'overpopulated' situation applies to human existence—that there just never seems to be room enough for all the 'selves' seeking establishment and recognition" [77]. Provocative as these suggestions may be, their validation depends on research that has not yet been conducted. There is a wealth of evidence from animal studies which shows that invasion of territory—fixed or portable—elicits an attack upon the intruder. Both intuition and common sense suggest that the too-crowded human will also react aggressively toward those who are crowding him, if he has no way to escape.

AGGRESSION AS A CONSEQUENCE OF OVERCROWDING

The factor of high population density is a general condition that greatly increases the probability of aggression and violence. High density per se is not causally related directly to aggression but rather has its effect by profoundly altering behavioral and physiological regulatory systems. Overcrowding produces internal changes that ramify to directly affect the situations which are immediate instigations to aggression [15].

Scientists have found that all animal populations, whether the individuals are solitary or gregarious, have a density limit (the number of individuals per unit of area) that is typical for that given species. In many cases the habitat—including food and water, nesting spots, and predators—is such that the local population never reaches the maximum possible density. But in optimal habitats where there are few or no external factors to limit population growth, the density will stabilize at or near the maximum for the species [15]. Many experimental studies have shown that growth-limiting factors develop *within* the population through physiological changes that decrease the birth and survival rate while increasing the death rate.

The general mechanism that limits population growth is the activity of the adrenal glands. These secrete hormones that have widespread effects on the body's internal mechanisms. The adrenals are one of the body's emergency defense organs and normally secrete their hormones when either physical or psychological stress demands defensive responses. The adrenals are designed to handle relatively short-term stress, shutting off after the emergency has been met. If, however, stress is prolonged, the glands must continue to secrete the necessary hormones after the available supply has been expended. When this occurs, the adrenals grow larger (hypertrophy) in the attempt to meet the body's demands.

Under conditions causing long-term adrenal activation, there are profound physiological changes within the organism: Body growth is suppressed; the formation of disease-fighting antibodies is suppressed; the resistance to infection decreases; the viscera and gut undergo degenerative changes; the composition of the blood changes; and the reproductive organs either cease functioning or function incompletely [15]. Out of all the stress-producing events or conditions that have been studied, high population density has probably the most severe long-term effects.

Where animal populations (and perhaps human populations) approach the critical density level, significant changes occur in the normal pattern of social interaction. The frequency of social contacts between individuals is enormously increased, and the "pace" of life accelerates. The increased population size means that individuals are less likely to recognize other individuals and more likely to respond to them as outsiders, as nonmembers of the group. Similarly the social hierarchy that would normally regulate interactions begins to malfunction because the animals do not know their own or others' relative status. When these conditions occur, there is frequently an increase in the number of aggressive interactions. Social signals indicative of status rank, which normally inhibit fighting, are either not given or not attended to.

Calhoun [12] has described what he calls a "behavioral sink" that may develop when albino rats are experimentally overcrowded. Certain males engage in repeated, vicious, dominance fights and occasionally go berserk and even attack females and infants. Other males become completely passive and withdraw from all social interaction by crouching in corners or hiding in nest boxes. "Probers" are those males which, according to Calhoun, become hypersexual but homosexual, extremely active, and often cannibalistic.

Although there is an unfortunate lack of data for other than rodent populations, one can infer that high population densities would affect several of the aggression-causing relationships previously described in this chapter. The breakdown of structures that maintain social stability would result in increased fighting, more superficial pain, and therefore still further increased fighting. Personal space would be violated more frequently, inducing aggressive responses.

One can only speculate about the response of *Homo sapiens* to extremely high population densities, inasmuch as there have been no research studies. Certainly there are a number of cities that appear to be natural laboratories for research—Hong Kong, Tokyo, Calcutta, New York, and the *barrios* of several South American cities. Do the inhabitants of these cities—or their most densely populated sectors —behave more aggressively than one would expect? Do individuals show altered physiological profiles that would indicate a stressful social situation? Is there any evidence for a reduction in the reproductive rate? At a time when many scientists—from anthropologists to zoologists—believe that world overpopulation is the single most important threat to man's survival as a species, there is a frightening dearth of evidence about man's response to high population densities.

Conclusions

In this chapter we have examined in some detail selected examples of a wealth of research data that bear directly on the problem of violence and aggression. Aggressive behavior by both animals and man serves an adaptive function and has its origins in genetically coded neural mechanisms that are acted upon by hormonal and psychosocial factors. Unlike previous, popular accounts of aggression, the present chapter argues that aggression is a basic behavioral response that has multiple determinants whose precise effects vary with the sex, the age, and the species of the organism. The aggressive response can be elicited in situations that are threatening to the integrity (either physical or psychological) of the individual and as such is an adaptive mechanism promoting the survival of the individual as well as the species. However, violence—aggression gone awry —is only a short-term coping mechanism that enables adjustment but which in the long run will prove maladaptive to both the individual and the species. Viewed in this way, it is clear that appropriate aggression is not harmful and that attempts to extinguish all forms of aggressive behavior will prove as maladaptive as continued acceptance of violence.

In conclusion, it is urged that there be an immediate intensification of research effort devoted to understanding the origins, the expression, and the elicitation of aggression. Basic medical research in neurophysiology, the biochemistry of the endocrine systems, and the implication of genetic abnormalities must be increased one hundredfold. Nonetheless, available studies of situational factors evoking aggression in animals indicate clearly that careful attention must be given to culturally and institutionally determined child-rearing practices that subtly bias the child toward using aggressive behaviors as coping mechanisms. Furthermore, both human and animal studies indicate that specific neural and hormonal mechanisms underlying aggression can be understood and controlled—and hence offer one important avenue for controlling violence.

References

1. Ardrey, R. *The Territorial Imperative*. New York: Atheneum, 1967.
2. Arling, G. L. Effects of Social Deprivation on Maternal Behavior of Rhesus Monkeys. M.Sc. thesis, University of Wisconsin, 1966.

3. Banks, E. M.   A time and motion study of pre-fighting behavior in mice. *Journal of Genetic Psychology* 101:165, 1962.
4. Bard, P.   Central nervous mechanisms for emotional behavior patterns in animals. *Research Publications of the Association for Research in Nervous and Mental Disease* 19:190, 1939.
5. Bard, P., and Mountcastle, V. B.   Some forebrain mechanisms involved in expression of rage with special reference to suppression of angry behavior. *Research Publications of the Association for Research in Nervous and Mental Disease* 27:362, 1947.
6. Barnett, S. A.   *The Rat: A Study in Behavior*. Chicago: Aldine, 1963.
7. Bernstein, I. S., and Mason, W. A.   Activity patterns of rhesus monkeys in a social group. *Animal Behaviour* 11:455, 1963.
8. Bernstein, I. S., and Mason, W. A.   Group formation by rhesus monkeys. *Animal Behaviour* 11:28, 1963.
9. Bourliere, F.   *The Natural History of Mammals*, tr. by H. M. Parshley. London: Harrap, 1955.
10. Brown, J. L., and Hunsperger, R. W.   Neuroethology and the motivation of agonistic behavior. *Animal Behaviour* 11:439, 1963.
11. Burt, W. H.   Territoriality and home range concepts as applied to mammals. *Journal of Mammalogy* 24:346, 1943.
12. Calhoun, J. B.   Population density and social pathology. *Scientific American* 206:139, 1962.
13. Carpenter, C. R.   A field study in Siam of the behavior and social relations of the gibbon *Hylobates lar*. *Comparative Psychology Monographs* 16:1, 1940.
14. Carthy, J. D., and Ebling, F. J.   Prologue and Epilogue. In Carthy, J. D., and Ebling, F. J. (Eds.), *The Natural History of Aggression*. New York: Academic, 1964.
15. Christian, J. J.   Endocrine Adaptive Mechanisms and the Physiological Regulation of Population. In Mayer, W. G., and Van Galder, R. G. (Eds.), *Physiological Mammalogy*, Vol. I. New York: Academic, 1963.
16. Clemente, C. D., and Lindsley, D. B. (Eds.).   *Aggression and Defense: Neural Mechanisms and Social Patterns*. Los Angeles: University of California Press, 1967.
17. Crook, J. H.   The adaptive significance of avian social organization. *Symposia of the Zoological Society of London* 14:181, 1965.
18. Delgado, J. M. R.   Aggression and Defense Under Cerebral Radio Control. In Clemente, C. D., and Lindsley, D. B. (Eds.), *Aggression and Defense: Neural Mechanisms and Social Patterns*. Los Angeles: University of California Press, 1967.
19. DeVore, I. (Ed.).   *Primate Behavior: Field Studies of Monkeys and Apes*. New York: Holt, Rinehart & Winston, 1965.
20. DeVore, I., and Eimerl, S.   *The Primates*. New York: Time, Inc., 1965.
21. Ehrhardt, A. A., Epstein, R., and Money, J.   Fetal androgens and female gender identity in the early-treated adrenogenital syndrome. *Johns Hopkins Medical Journal* 122:160, 1968.
22. Ehrhardt, A. A., and Money, J.   Progestin-induced hermaphroditism:

IQ and psychosexual identity in a study of ten girls. *Journal of Sex Research* 3:83, 1967.

23. Ellefson, J. O. A Natural History of Gibbons in the Malay Peninsula. Ph.D. thesis, University of California, 1967.

24. Flynn, J. P. The Neural Basis of Aggression in Cats. In Glass, D. C. (Ed.), *Neurophysiology and Emotion*. New York: Rockefeller University Press, 1967.

25. Freeman, W. Psychosurgery. In Arieti, S. (Ed.), *American Handbook of Psychiatry*, vol. 2. New York: Basic Books, 1959.

26. Fuller, J. L. Cross-sectional and longitudinal studies of adjustive behavior in dogs. *Annals of the New York Academy of Sciences* 56:214, 1953.

27. Gilula, M. F., and Daniels, D. N. Violence and man's struggle to adapt. *Science* 164:396, 1969.

28. Gloor, P. Discussion Following Brain Mechanisms Related to Aggressive Behavior (Kaada, B.). In Clemente, C. D., and Lindsley, D. B. (Eds.), *Aggression and Defense: Neural Mechanisms and Social Patterns*. Los Angeles: University of California Press, 1967.

29. Grossman, S. P. *A Textbook of Physiological Psychology*. New York: Wiley, 1967.

30. Hall, E. T. *The Hidden Dimension*. Garden City, N.Y.: Doubleday, 1966.

31. Harlow, H. F., Dodsworth, R. O., and Harlow, M. K. Total social isolation in monkeys. *Proceedings of the National Academy of Sciences of the United States of America* 54:90, 1965.

32. Harlow, H. F., and Griffin, G. A. Induced Mental and Social Deficits in Rhesus Monkeys. In Osler, S. F., and Cooke, R. E. (Eds.), *The Biosocial Basis of Mental Retardation*. Baltimore: Johns Hopkins Press, 1965.

33. Harlow, H. F., Joslyn, W. D., Senko, M. G., and Dopp, A. Behavioral aspects of reproduction in primates. *Journal of Animal Science* 25:49, 1966.

34. Harlow, H. F., Rowland, G. L., and Griffin, G. A. The effect of total social deprivation on the development of monkey social behavior. *Psychiatric Research Reports of the American Psychiatric Association* 19:116, 1964.

35. Harris, G. W. *Neural Control of the Pituitary*. Baltimore: Williams & Wilkins, 1955.

36. Harris, G. W., and Levine, S. Sexual differentiation of the brain and its experimental control. *Journal of Physiology* 181:379, 1965.

37. Hediger, H. *Wild Animals in Captivity*, tr. by G. Sircom. London: Butterworth, 1950. (*Wildtiere in Gefangenschaft*. Basel: Benno Schwabe, 1938.)

38. Hill, D. Aggression and Mental Illness. In Carthy, J. D., and Ebling, F. J. (Eds.), *The Natural History of Aggression*. New York: Academic, 1964.

39. Hinde, R. A. *Animal Behaviour: A Synthesis of Ethology and Comparative Psychology*. New York: McGraw-Hill, 1966.

40. House, E. L., and Pansky, B. *A Functional Approach to Neuroanatomy*. New York: McGraw-Hill, 1960.

41. Jacobsen, A. L. Learning in flatworms and annelids. *Psychological Bulletin* 60:74, 1963.
42. Kahn, M. W. Infantile experiences and mature aggressive behavior of mice: Some maternal influences. *Journal of Genetic Psychology* 84:65, 1954.
43. Kahn, M. W., and Kirk, W. E. The concept of aggression: A review and reformulation. *Psychological Record* 18:559, 1968.
44. King, J. A., and Gurney, N. L. Effect of early social experience on adult aggressive behavior in C57Bl/10 mice. *Journal of Comparative and Physiological Psychology* 47:326, 1954.
45. Klüver, H., and Bucy, P. C. Preliminary analysis of functions of the temporal lobes in monkeys. *Archives of Neurology and Psychiatry* 42:979, 1939.
46. Kruijt. J. P. Ontogeny of social behavior in Burmese Red Junglefowl (*Gallus gallus spadiceus*) Bonnaterre. *Behaviour* [Suppl. 12], 1964.
47. Lancaster, J. B., and Lee, R. B. The Annual Reproductive Cycle in Monkeys and Apes. In DeVore, I. (Ed.), *Primate Behavior: Field Studies of Monkeys and Apes.* New York: Holt, Rinehart & Winston, 1965.
48. LeBoeuf, B. J., and Peterson, R. S. Social Status and Mating Activity in Elephant Seals. Paper presented at the American Association for the Advancement of Science, Dallas, Dec. 1968.
49. Lejenne, J., and Turpin, R. Somatic Chromosomes in Mongolism. In Kolb, L. C., Masland, R. L., and Cooke, R. E. (Eds.), *Mental Retardation.* Baltimore: Williams & Wilkins, 1962.
50. Lorenz, K. Ritualized Fighting. In Carthy, J. D., and Ebling, F. J. (Eds.), *The Natural History of Aggression.* New York: Academic, 1964.
51. Lubs, H. A., and Ruddle, F. H. Chromosomal abnormalities in 4,000 consecutive newborns. *Genetics*, 1969. In press.
52. Mark, V., and Ervin, F. R. *Violence and the Brain.* New York: Harper & Row. In press.
53. Matthews, L. H. Overt Fighting in Mammals. In Carthy, J. D., and Ebling, F. J. (Eds.), *The Natural History of Aggression.* New York: Academic, 1964.
54. Mayr, E. *Animal Species and Evolution.* Cambridge, Mass.: Belknap, 1963.
55. Melzack, R., and Thompson, W. R. Effects of early experience on social behaviour. *Canadian Journal of Psychology* 10:82, 1956.
56. Mitchell, G. D. Persistent behavior pathology in rhesus monkeys following early social isolation. *Folia Primatologica* 8:132, 1968.
57. Mitchell, G. D., Raymond, E. J., Ruppenthal, G. C., and Harlow, H. F. Long-term effects of total social isolation upon behavior of rhesus monkeys. *Psychological Reports* 18:657, 1966.
58. Moody, P. A. *Introduction to Evolution* (3d ed.). New York: Harper & Row, 1963.
59. Moyer, K. E. Kinds of aggression and their physiological basis. *Communications in Behavioral Biology* 2:65, 1968.

60. Newton, G., and Levine, S. (Eds.). *Early Experience and Behavior*. Springfield, Ill.: Thomas, 1968.
61. Rheingold, H. L. (Ed.). *Maternal Behavior in Mammals*. New York: Wiley, 1963.
62. Richardson, L. F. *Statistics of Deadly Quarrels*. Pittsburgh: Boxwood, 1960.
63. Robinson, A., and Puck, T. T. Studies on chromosomal nondisjunction in man. II. *American Journal of Human Genetics* 19:112, 1967.
64. Robinson, B. W. Summary of symposium, The Physiology of Fighting and Defeat. Presented at the American Association for the Advancement of Science, Dallas, Dec. 1968.
65. Rosvold, H. E., Mirsky, A. F., and Pribram, K. H. Influence of amygdalectomy on social behavior in monkeys. *Journal of Comparative and Physiological Psychology* 47:173, 1954.
66. Rowland, G. L. The Effects of Total Social Isolation upon Learning and Social Behavior in Rhesus Monkeys. Ph.D. thesis, University of Wisconsin, 1964.
67. Sackett, G. P. Monkeys reared in isolation with pictures as visual input: Evidence for innate releasing mechanism. *Science* 154:1468, 1966.
68. Sano, K. Sedative neurosurgery; with special reference to posteromedial hypothalamotomy. *Neurologia Medico-Chirurgica* 4:112, 1962.
69. Schaller, G. *The Mountain Gorilla: Ecology and Behavior*. Chicago: University of Chicago Press, 1963.
70. Scott, J. P. *Aggression*. Chicago: University of Chicago Press, 1958.
71. Southwick, C. H. Patterns of intergroup social behavior in primates with special reference to rhesus and howling monkeys. *Annals of the New York Academy of Sciences* 102:436, 1962.
72. Southwick, C. H. An experimental study of intragroup agonistic behavior in rhesus monkeys (*Macaca mulatta*). *Behaviour* 28:182, 1967.
73. Tinbergen, N. *Social Behaviour in Animals*. London: Methuen, 1953.
74. Tinbergen, N. The functions of territory. *Bird Study* 4:14, 1957.
75. Tinbergen, N. On war and peace in animals and man. *Science* 160:1411, no. 3835, 1968. Copyright 1968 by the American Association for the Advancement of Science.
76. Van Lawick-Goodall, Baroness J. *My Friends the Wild Chimpanzees*. Washington, D.C.: National Geographic Society, 1967.
77. Veness, Thelma. Introduction to Hostility in Small Groups. In Carthy, J. D., and Ebling, F. J. (Eds.), *The Natural History of Aggression*. New York: Academic, 1964.
78. Walzer, S., Breau, G., and Gerald, P. S. A chromosome survey of 2400 normal newborn infants. *Journal of Pediatrics* 74:438, 1969.
79. Washburn, S. L., and Hamburg, D. A. Aggressive Behavior in Old World Monkeys and Apes. In Jay, P. C. (Ed.), *Primates: Studies in Adaptation and Variability*. New York: Holt, Rinehart & Winston, 1968.
80. Wynne-Edwards, V. C. *Animal Dispersion in Relation to Social Behaviour*. Edinburgh: Oliver & Boyd, 1962.
81. Young, W. C., Goy, R., and Phoenix, C. Hormones and sexual behavior. *Science* 143:212, 1964.

2. Psychodynamic Aspects of Aggression, Hostility, and Violence

George F. Solomon, M.D.

This chapter presents a psychodynamic view of aggression and violence from a psychoanalytic frame of reference. The theories presented here are not necessarily exclusive of others, but, rather, relate closely to the biological and social factors discussed in Chapters 1, 3, and 4. Psychodynamics refers to the relationship among forces, conscious and unconscious, internal and external, present and past, which influence or determine behavior. Violence, the exertion of physical force to injure or destroy, is accompanied by the emotion of anger or hostility (terms that connote somewhat different degrees of feeling of resentful displeasure, antagonism, or enmity), which may or may not be consciously perceived by the perpetrator. Anger or rage may be expressed, suppressed (not communicated), or repressed (kept from consciousness). Though the concern of this book is mainly with expressed and acted-upon emotion, I shall consider here more general concepts concerning hostile feelings and aggressive drives. As will be discussed, the term *aggression* can be used to include assertive as well as hostile behaviors. I shall touch upon the complex issues of the relationship of aggression and violence to instinct, to frustration, to learning, and especially to defense mechanisms, coping, and adaptation.

Anger must reach a certain intensity before resulting in violence, though of course some deliberate or accidental violence may not be the consequence of hostile feelings. The threshold for the emergence of violent action may vary from individual to individual, in part on the basis of biological differences. Lesser degrees or partial expressions of hostility or antagonism may present themselves as irritability, annoyance, unfriendliness, pouting, grudges, peeves, jealousy, and temper. It is important to consider what forces allow hostile feelings, resulting from current conflict or persisting as the residual of old hurts, to become actions. Of course hostility and violence can be directed against the self in depression and in suicide, which are not subjects of this chapter.

The unconscious of the adult primarily represents a collection of thoughts, feelings, experiences, and fantasies of his or her childhood. Forces that operate to produce violence may have been conscious and even normal at certain phases of infancy and childhood. It is only when destructive motivations have not been mastered in the early years of life that they reappear at later points in one's life or under conditions leading to reactivation of old conflicts. Cultural and social factors, which are elaborated upon elsewhere, can encourage, fortify, or discourage both the expression of innate capacities for aggression as well as earlier, infantile types of aggressive behavior. Child-rearing practices in terms of specific types of family interactions and gratification and frustration of instinctual needs are both expressions of and determinants of cultural character and behavior patterns and traits; these arise as adaptations to specific circumstances [8].

Instinctual Basis of Aggression

FREUD'S CONCEPTS

Though the terms *instinct* and *drive* tend to be utilized interchangeably in the psychoanalytic literature, Freud's German term *trieb* was poorly translated as "instinct." The term *drive* implies a state of readiness for a certain type of behavior. *Instinct* implies a set, inborn pattern of behavior that is complete and automatic in response to a given stimulus. Thus drive is, of course, the better concept for the human being.

Freud relatively neglected aggression in his early theories and had difficulty in accounting for sadism, masochism, and the mass destruction of war on the basis of his existing concepts of (1) the pleasure principle—the individual seeks pleasure and avoids pain, (2) instincts as falling into either sexual-libidinal or self-preservative classes, and (3) motivation as based on seeking to reduce tension [12]. Since he saw instinctual aims as regressive (tending toward earlier, more primitive goals), in 1922 Freud [10] postulated a drive toward nonbeing analogous to the catabolic (tissue destructive) component of metabolism in contrast to the anabolic (tissue building) component.

Aggressive drives were then defined as based on a death instinct (Thanatos), and libidinal (affectionate and sexual) drives on a life instinct (Eros). In *Civilization and Its Discontents* Freud [11] took the pessimistic view that civilized man's increasing need to repress his destructive instincts leads to outbreaks of ever more violent wars. This last of Freud's two-sided instinctual theories is his least accepted.

Some psychoanalysts do not accept aggression as a primary drive but rather see aggression as only one other way that instinctual aims are striven for in response to frustration of pleasure-seeking motivations [19]. Of those psychoanalysts who do regard aggression as an independent drive, most do not base this drive on a death instinct [9]. Aggressive drives have also been described as part-instincts related to libidinal forces rather than as independent drives (libido refers to energy or drive in the service of relationships and sexuality, in a general sense). The psychoanalytic concept of fused libidinal and aggressive drives is reflected in so-called oral-sadism and anal-sadism [34]. Oral-sadism results both from the destructive imageries accompanying ingestion and devouring and from the reaction to frustration of oral aims like biting and its psychological derivatives (e.g., sarcasm). Anal-sadism arises from ambivalent infantile attitudes intrinsic to bowel control and elimination of feces that may involve pleasure and pride as well as revulsion. Hostile impulses related to anal conflict and imageries may be reflected in smearing and its derivatives (e.g., slander) or in defiant holding-back attitudes.

ETHOLOGICAL EVIDENCE

The questions of the instinctual status of aggression and of the relation of aggression to hostility remain. Evidence from comparative biology, more thoroughly reviewed in the preceding chapter, is relevant to human instinct theory. Lorenz [22], the ethologist, studied animal behavior and was impressed by the universality of fighting among fish, birds, and lower mammals. He presents a strong case for aggression as an instinct evolved in the service of survival of the species, which is relatively easy to understand in terms of predator and prey. However, he also sees intraspecies aggression as serving adaptive evolutionary functions. Aggression promotes survival of the fittest with consequent genetic benefits. Aggression in animals also contributes to population regulation and is utilized for defense of territory. Territorialism favors reproduction and rearing of young and contributes to the stability of the family, tribe, pack, and more complex forms of social organization. Rituals, submissive behavior, and social bonds have strong aggression-inhibiting functions among animals.

Though the *capacity* for destructive behavior clearly has biological routes, it is not entirely clear whether the tendency to *manifest* such behavior is intrinsic or needs to be evoked. Aggression is also subject to significant modification by environmental factors. Animals tend to attack especially when frustrated or frightened. Clark [6] found aggression in mice to be elicited only under specific circumstances. He noted that fighting patterns could be modified by experience, that an animal could learn solutions other than attack, and that aggression diminished as social order increased. What is impressive here is the high degree of modifiability of animal behavior (formerly considered innate), whether it be reproductive, nurturant, or aggressive. Even rats need to have had the experience of being mothered to be able to nurse their young.

AGGRESSIVE DRIVES AS
ASSERTIVE VS. DESTRUCTIVE

Accepting at least a capacity for expressing aggression as innate, it seems important to differentiate destructive aggression from a drive toward mastery or competence [36]. The word *aggression* derives from Latin roots meaning "to move toward." If one views aggression in terms of assertion and growth, destructiveness assumes a reactive character. Destructiveness is a response to circumstances and is derived from a biological drive but is not instinctual in and of itself. The child appears to be delighted to be able to accomplish a new feat independent of receiving praise or interpersonal gratification. This kind of gratification is evidence of a basic tendency toward achievement and growth [33]. There appear to be important universal motivations toward seeking stimulation and novelty as well as toward stimulus-reduction and clinging to the familiar.

There is experimental evidence that avoidance of novelty and familiarity-seeking are increased by impoverishment of experience during early development and by states of heightened arousal that include anxiety [23]. Mice reared in a barren environment avoid exploration of a new environment and are timid and frightened, whereas those which had repeated experiences with new "toys" and objects are bold and adventuresome later in life. Either a schizophrenic patient or a subject given the stimulant drug amphetamine will choose to reduce arousal by viewing emotionally neutral slides he has already seen rather than going on to view scenes he has not yet seen, naturally preferred by a normal subject to avoid boredom.

As will be discussed further, the familiar that is sought by man may include the tumultuous and violent, a repetition of unsatisfactory but well-known childhood experiences [32].

Some individuals fail to distinguish between assertion and destructive aggression, just as some people perceive all tender, affectionate feelings as sexual. In the case of aggression such confusion may lead to timidity and unassertiveness or to violent expressions of assertive strivings.

Infantile Modes of Expressing Aggression

Whether the baby's first cry is a primary instinct or a reaction to the frustration of separation from the all-providing womb, the ability to display discomfort vocally and bodily is present at birth. Such undifferentiated discomfort may be a precursor to anger as well as other noxious emotions. As development progresses, other physiological functions and anatomical parts become agents for the expression of anger—biting, clawing ("tooth and nail"), spitting, striking, kicking, throwing objects [30]. Such actions aim to destroy or hurt the frustrating object (or its symbolic equivalent).

As maturity ensues, cognitive abilities, judgment, and the variety of interpersonal and social skills that characterize a well-functioning human being serve to express, control, and direct a person's aggressive energies.

Links Between Aggressive and Sexual Drives

Sadism refers to the libidinization (making sexual) or pleasurization of aggression or violence. The merging of pleasurable or sensuous perceptions with the act of inflicting harm disguises the anger or rage inherent in the original impulse [3]. This disguise serves the purpose of repression, i.e., keeping the painful feelings from awareness. Such repression of the underlying hostility results from guilt or from fear of retaliation. Fortification of aggression by libidinal drives also aids the movement from fantasy to action because of the increased impetus of dual motivation and the tendency for pleasure-seeking to manifest itself in behavior. Sexual sadism also may function to limit and isolate the expression of hostile impulses to interactions with willing partners. For instance, one sadist stated that sadists are generally kind people and gave an example of his group's paying the hospital bill of a favorite masochist injured in a motorcycle accident! Sadism can also be related to identification with the aggressor and to avoiding frightening passive experiences by being the initiator of an act.

Rape is clearly an act combining aggressive and sexual drives. The ethologists have pointed out the intimate connection between aggressive and sexual drives in the animal. They describe the many similarities and often precarious separation between the behavioral patterns of fighting and mating. Since slang and folk expressions provide clues to unconscious associations, it is noteworthy that the terms *screw* and *fuck* refer both to sexual intercourse and interpersonal hostility. A child observing parental sexual relations often interprets intercourse as assault, a relatively common basis for later sexual inhibitions. Motives of power, control, and even destruction readily link up with sexual motives. Unconsciously an act of rape can represent forceful violation of the mother, not only as pleasure-seeking, a taking of what is not offered, but as an act of revenge against the mother for her rejection or against the father in response to envy or in reaction to his hostility.

Murder, which sometimes accompanies rape, may be a culmination of the destructive impulse or the wish to destroy the mother before she tells the father. "I punish to avoid being punished." Using force also can be a means to extract love that is perceived as unlikely to be freely given. "I'll never get what I want unless I take it." The object of assault can represent mother or nonmother. An uneducated, culturally deprived but bright young man raped a prim librarian, the pure, intelligent, "upper-class" ideal he felt he could never achieve, the antithesis of the devalued, promiscuous, illiterate, unloving mother, represented by the three prostitutes he had married. We see thus that there are many ways in which sexual and aggressive energies and motives can and do fuse.

Hostility and Violent Aggression

PRIMARY (REACTIVE) AGGRESSION

I should like to distinguish between "primary" aggression and "secondary" aggression. Neither term refers to the basic aggressive drive as such, the biological underpinning of both these forms of aggression, or to the assertive, nonhostile forms of aggression. Primary aggression refers to hostility and attack that is reactive and proportional to a frustrating situation. Its release serves to reduce tension and, if complete, permanently discharges the emotion. "Getting it out of one's system" or "off one's chest" prevents repression and subsequent buildup of hostile impulses. Repression costs psychological effort to maintain and may lead to the emergence of neurotic symptoms that serve both to aid the repression and to express the hostility in disguised forms. Of course the repressed once-primary aggression may break through and appear later aimed at original or substitute objects.

Primary aggression is a product of the formula:

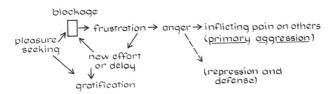

The sequence occurs in temporal relation to inciting events. Elicitors of primary aggression are to be found in the immediate environment of the individual. Primary aggression is common in the infant and young child because the propensity for frustration is great. The infant cannot meet his own needs. Only as the trait of basic trust evolves from experience with a predictable, need-satisfying parent can frustration be handled through learning to expect and wait for future gratification. Primary aggression can occur at any age. Usually the adult, as a result of acquiring language and learning other forms of socialization, is capable of channeling and controlling aggressive impulses into acceptable behaviors, even when circumstances might justify hostile attacking behavior. Of course even killing is socially acceptable and usually without guilt in the killer in the face of ultimate provocation, i.e., self-defense, and in war, which is impersonalized and rationalized, serving—however maladaptively—more to resolve social than personal conflict.

Control of reactive anger occurs by channeling emotion through higher brain centers involved in cognition, symbolization, and inhibition. Explosive rage, a dangerous form of primary aggression, may be the result of "short circuiting" from lower brain centers mediating emotion to those portions of the brain controlling motor action. For instance, a cat with its entire cerebral cortex (the portion of the brain mediating the "highest" level of function) surgically removed can show "sham rage"—behavior appropriate to anger and attack. A "blown fuse" can occur under conditions of intense stimulation or overwhelming anxiety, because of impaired brain function (from disease or drugs), or consequent to relatively deficient control and coping devices. Such control techniques must be learned during development, largely through observing parental examples and by identifying with adult behavior. To be able to apply under stress the ways one has learned to handle anger, one must have strong adaptive capability (ego strength). This strength is a product of the stored memories of previously mastered stresses and tasks [33].

Individuals prone to reactive rage may go to great lengths to avoid provocation. They fear their own anger and may suffer from so-called instinctual anxiety because of the tendency for their aggressive impulses to overwhelm reason and all ego functions. For these people anger becomes a real threat to the integrity of the personality. On the other hand, overcontrol and inhibition of primary aggression may predispose to later explosive breakthroughs and to secondary aggression. A total dampening of primary aggression also may lead to seriously inhibited character development or a chronic, life-long apathy.

SECONDARY (DEFENSIVE) AGGRESSION

Secondary aggression refers to hostile or violent behavior that is entirely disproportional or even unrelated to current provocation. Secondary aggression is most often manifested by aggressive personalities who have a "chip on the shoulder" or a "short fuse" and may be ready to do battle on impulse. Their aggression taps a warehouse of previously stored hostility that seeks expression at any opportunity. "Senseless" killing can be a manifestation of secondary aggression in its most extreme form. There is often only flimsy or no apparent motivation or provocation. (The first two cases in Chapter 13 are illustrative.) Secondary aggression occurs in conjunction with emotional conflict and maladaptive, unrealistic behavior but is not specific to one form of psychiatric disorder and may be manifest in the immature, neurotic, psychotic, or psychopathic (antisocial) individual. Were the "warehouse of hostility" analogy totally true, the release of anger should eventually deplete the store of hostility that had accumulated from old hurts. But this does not seem to happen. The aggressiveness in these individuals continues to express itself over and over again in a compulsive, repetitive fashion, a phenomenon to be discussed further. Even when disastrous consequences ensue from the expression of aggression, these individuals continue to repeat the old pattern of behavior for seemingly trivial or groundless reasons and may come to be regarded as "never learning by experience."

It is the secondary form of aggression that causes the greatest concern from both psychological and sociological points of view. Relatively little of man's destructiveness is clearly reactive or "justified." Understanding the causes of secondary aggression may help its prevention and treatment. There are particular phases of human development when personality traits crystallize into permanent or lasting forms of thought or action. These have been termed *critical learning periods*. Traits arising through an original mastery of the developmental task of a given period are termed *primary autonomous ego traits* [33]. Traits that arise out of attempts to master or repair conflict arising from traumatic influences at a particular phase of development are termed *secondary autonomous ego traits*. The latter may represent the best adjustment the individual was able to make at that time.

Secondary traits, like scars, retain evidence of old wounds and succeed in varying degrees at healing old injuries. The specific way of behaving that once served a useful coping function may assume a life of its own relatively uninfluenced by logical reasoning or later environmental demands. Becoming a bully may have been highly adaptive in the slum, but belligerence may not be useful after the scholarship to college has been obtained. A middle-class group may ostracize or avoid the belligerent individual, may consider him bad or crazy, and does not understand his behavior, even though it often represents a once-normal and useful pattern. It is very hard to abandon a behavioral pattern that previously had "survival" value.

LIFE CRISES AND SECONDARY AGGRESSION

Since secondary aggression is one outcome of relative failure to master successfully the tasks of critical periods of life, further consideration of developmental crises is in order.

The original life crisis may be birth itself. Other childhood crises include weaning, toilet training, going to school, joining the gang, and puberty. As an individual attains maturity, he encounters adult crises that include educational, marital, occupational, or parental crises. Other crises arise from circumstances of living, e.g., sickness, birth of siblings, loss of loved ones, and catastrophe. Each takes its toll or makes its contribution. Mastery of small doses of threat adds to the strength of the personality and helps the individual meet future threats. Such strength can be regarded as the sum of the stored memories of masteries minus the stored memories of defeats. Thus to be strong, there must be challenge, not provided in the overprotected or "spoiled" child, but challenges must not have been so great as to overwhelm the coping capacity. Specific developmental stages and their relation to aggression now will be discussed.

Infant ("Oral") Phase

Secondary aggression can represent a coping mechanism by which an individual attempts to attain some type of internal equilibrium or homeostasis, to reduce anxiety, and to fulfill needs. Aggressive traits such as greed, insatiability, constant demands for attention, or toughness may compensate for feelings of deprivation, worthlessness, and vulnerablity related to the earliest, nurturant (oral) phase of development.

Histories of maternal deprivation and neglect and of parental loss have been documented as relatively common in the violence-prone and antisocial person [7]. When earliest biological and emotional needs are associated with lack of gratification and repeated frustration, the demands themselves come to serve as alarm threats to the organism and disturb psychological homeostasis. For example, the wish itself for love and tenderness, perhaps evoked through contact with a desirable other person, may produce anxiety and set in motion avoidances and defenses. Hostility is one way of driving others away when one is afraid of his own affectionate wishes. Aggression can reflect not only the reaction to frustration but also a desperate seeking of gratification to reestablish some sort of equilibrium. Bowlby [5] has pointed out that the initial phase of mourning in reaction to loss is protest, an angry cry for mother (or, later, other love-objects). Blocked mourning can result in a protesting, angry life attitude.

Only when gratification is predictably forthcoming does the primary trait of basic trust emerge [8]. The unloved person feels worthless and unlovable. He displays perpetual cravings for reassurance and gratification that never seem to be satisfied, leading to new frustrations that may be reacted to with anger and violence. The intensity of need for external love for one's very existence explains the intensity of the fight for these needs. There is often a precarious balance and conflict between this tendency toward violence and the tendency to repress all aggressiveness through fear of losing love or fear of receiving still less in the future.

Toddler ("Anal") Phase

Defiant behaviors (or their converse, compliant ones) tend to arise from issues around maturational demands and acculturation processes of the toddler period, which include not only control of the sphincters but also locomotion, speech, and the appreciation of time [33]. The first great struggle between biological drives and social demands tends to occur over the issues of bladder and, especially, bowel control. Extreme and opposite outcomes tend to result from unresolved tensions around particular developmental issues. In this case defiant behavior is more heroic, requiring greater strength than compliance, which may occur in the child whose "spirit was broken" through coercion. Lack of self-control also can reflect difficulty at this stage; for instance, histories of childhood enuresis are common in impulsive adults.

An individual fixated (psychological maturation relatively arrested) or regressed (emotionally taken back, at least in part) to the toddler phase under the influence of current stress or conflict is still or again at a point in life when he did not fully appreciate the meaning of time. Action is closely related to the sense of time [4]. The antisocial "psychopathic" person lives in the "here and now," often oblivious to the future consequences of his acts; he "wants what he wants when he wants it." A firm sense of reality is tied to an appreciation of the meaning of time. Mastery of the sense of time is manifested by the trait of patience. For those with a one-dimensional sense of time, the past is merged with the present. Old hurts are still there, and old coping devices, once useful, are still operating.

Action patterns involving motility—fight or flight reactions, for example—generally have their roots in the toddler phase, but some motor patterns may have an even earlier basis. Doing or going can represent attempts to actively recapture the joy of the passive motion of infancy, the soothing of being carried or rocked, a highly pleasurable and security-providing sensation to the baby [31]. Action can also serve as reassurance against nonbeing or as a defense against passivity and dependency: "I am alive"; "I can get what I need on my own." When action modes of coping become merged with hostile emotions, violence may ensue.

"Oedipal" Phase

The beginnings of sexual impulses, which careful childhood observation and depth psychotherapy have shown to become first manifest during the nursery school period, set the stage for an emotional crisis, the Oedipal phase of development, that may involve conflicts predisposing a person to later aggression. This phase comprises selecting the parent of the opposite sex as the first conjugal candidate and the parent of the same sex as the first potential rival. Although such fantasies are not realizable, the Oedipal phase need not be seriously conflictual. It often becomes so as a result of seductive or punitive behavior on the part of parents who themselves have unresolved sexual conflicts. Also the child may have difficulty at this phase resulting from a lack of mastery of previous developmental tasks. The child with a history of earlier deprivation, for example, may not be able to relinquish his sexual strivings for his mother. Successful resolution of the Oedipal situation implies "I'll get a girl (or boy) of my own someday" or "To heck with you, I'll go out and play with the kids" attitudes and a readiness for identifying with the parent of the same sex.

One maladaptive outcome of Oedipal conflict is secondary aggression. The individual is angry and dissatisfied. He figuratively is pounding on the bedroom door to gain admittance. Exaggerated fearfulness may be a consequence of "castration anxiety" related to apprehension concerning the consequences of forbidden wishes and rivalrous feelings. Since the unconscious operates on the "talion principle" of "an eye for an eye, a tooth for a tooth," imageries of sexual mutilation may result from forbidden sexual impulses. Hostility projected onto one's father may make him seem more fearful. A defense against such fears is a counterphobic daredevil, flying-in-the-face-of-danger attitude.

Peer Group ("Latency") Phase

Establishing peer group relationships is an important phase of development, which occurs at a time of relative absence of sexual pressure in the preadolescent years (latency). The gang can strongly influence behavior and is an important source of the we-they idea. Many of the effects of maternal deprivation can be overcome by wholesome peer group relationships, a phenomenon demonstrable in experiments with monkeys [16]. However, the aggressive child may be ostracized from his peer group, which may lead to further aggression, obnoxious and antisocial behavior. Another possibility is the alliance of hostile youngsters in an antisocial group, in which aggression is mutually reinforced [29]. For some people the "cops," "fuzz," or "pigs," represent the hated, feared parent. Such a group provides protection and support, meaningful but not threateningly intimate relationships, and a collective myth that expresses and rationalizes aggressive fantasies. Of course gang aggression is based on many interacting factors, only one aspect of which is psychodynamic. Similarly, antiauthority attitudes, when developed to meet specific cultural needs, may not be pathological and often are essential to social evolution and progress.

Identification and Aggression

FAILURE OF IDENTIFICATION

The antisocial person has failed to identify successfully with an appropriate older person of the same sex. Society's values are taken in and assimilated largely in the context of meaningful, affectionate relationships with individuals who hold those values. (The "asocial personality," whose manifest behavior may be similarly deviant and socially unacceptable, is the "normal" result of an abnormal environment and successful identification with an unsuitable figure, e.g., the thief who learned his trade from his loving father.) There is documentation of absence, death, brutality, or passive uninvolvement of the father in the past histories of male criminals and psychopaths [1]. The ability to utilize the father as a model may be made more difficult by his being unloved and disparaged by the mother. She may have chosen a weak man to whom she could feel superior or a "bad" husband by whom she could feel abused.

Identification with a strong, admired father figure is often made difficult or impossible by social forces. In the culture of poverty the role of the male is devalued, and any family stability and economic security often must be provided by the mother. A father who cannot find work and who may not even be able to be acknowledged as head of the household lest welfare payments be denied is not likely to be seen as someone worthy of emulation. This type of father figure makes a secure sense of masculinity very difficult for a boy to obtain. In reaction he may utilize aggression as a way to "prove" his masculinity, for which no suitable model exists and about which he feels so unsure. Hostile behavior as "manly" also may represent a denial or reaction against passive, dependent, infantile wishes, the wishes themselves serving as a source of rage, since the individual has so often experienced frustration of these demands.

When the conscience or superego is adequate, anxiety ensues as a signal when guilt-provoking impulses occur. The anxiety of guilt-anticipation motivates avoidances of or defenses against the forbidden impulses. A generous, compassionate Jesuit brother, chaplain of a juvenile detention center, who had been a tough slum kid himself, had a rich repertoire of devices ranging from humor to flight to avoid provocation. "I'd hurt someone if I got mad, and I'd really hate myself for it; so I know I have to do something when I tense up."

IDENTIFICATION WITH THE AGGRESSOR

Aggression or violence may result from identifying with the aggressor. If a child has a hostile, cruel parent or parent-substitute, he can become a subdued, submissive, frightened, or even masochistic individual, or he can become equally as aggressive, angry, and mean as his tormentor. Those who act violently very often have been the victims of violence. They actively do what they passively fear—"If you can't beat them, join them." The parent in the so-called battered child syndrome (severe injuries inflicted upon young children) is not so much sadistic as extremely rigid, judgmental, and unrealistic in perceiving undesirable behavior even in infants as willful, defiant, and voluntary [20]. His or her victimized children may become cruel.

Aggression or sadistic coping has its counterpart in the masochistic attitude, in which the individual makes the best of a bad situation. The masochist derives pleasure from self-punishment, which seems to reduce guilt, and symbolically seeks parental love by suffering and self-effacement [2]. Masochism has been termed "the act of loving a sadist." The collection of abuse, injustice, and suffering not only serves purposes of atonement but can be a way to bribe love or gain pity as a substitute. Sexual motivation may merge with aggression in masochism as in sadism. The balance between sadism and masochism is often precarious, and frequently shifts occur between the two positions. The tormented may become the tormentor.

IDENTIFICATION WITH PARENTS' CONFLICTS

Aggressiveness may result not only from identification with an overtly aggressive parent but from identifying with a hostile component of the parent's personality, which is unconscious and indirectly expressed. Adelaide Johnson [18] pointed out that the child may develop "holes" or "lacunae" in the conscience corresponding to similar less obvious defects in the parent. The resulting "Swiss cheese conscience" lacks controls in specific areas reflecting unresolved parental conflicts. A father, for example, may show inordinate interest and fascination in his son's fights. Even punishment, especially when inconsistently applied, may convey a parent's pleasure at an ostensibly unacceptable activity. A parent may ignore the child except when he is aggressive. Being noticed is an extremely important motivation, since the infant cannot survive without coming to the attention of the parent. Much behavior that seems and may even be perceived by the perpetrator as defiant is actually a compliance with a parent's unconscious wishes. The parent gets the child to do for him and vicariously enjoys what he or she would have liked to be able to do. The father of an 8-year-old arsonist, one of the youngest children ever committed to the California Youth Authority, broke into a smile and chuckled with delight as he told of an earlier incident in which the boy had attempted to assault his younger brother with a meat cleaver, implying, "That's my boy!" Similarly mothers can encourage aggression quite unconsciously because they want to bring out traits in the boy corresponding to their fantasies of the masculine image.

A child's actions tend to be identifications with parental actions in preference to parental precepts or ideas. The son of a military officer aggressively and violently pursued "peace," not realizing that his style of action, though not the content of his thought, was like his father's. Parents may be concerned with appearances and communicate that what *seems* to be is more important than what is. A dichotomy between behavior and nominally held principles can arise, thereby making "morals" meaningless in terms of behavior [14]. Such individuals' ideals are often unrealistic and operationally functionless. A thug reported "great admiration" for Albert Schweitzer.

Aggression and Self-Concept

A self-concept as a bad or mean person often underlies violent behavior. A parent may project the hostile portion of his own self on a child or may identify one child with an unwholesome figure of his own past. A young criminal, whose prominent parents were "pillars of the community," was actually, and unbeknown to him until adulthood, the son of his father's brother, a murderer. Clearly he always had been identified by his "parents" with the biological father. A label can become an inner command or, in computer terminology, a program. Sartre [27] describes the child Genet's being told, "You are a thief," an event "which stopped all other forms of living." Genet did not merely want to steal, nor did it matter that he actually stole; what was most significant was that he was a thief, "a truth, an eternal essence . . ." ". . . If he is a thief, he must always be one, everywhere, not only when he steals, but when he eats, when he sleeps, when he kisses his foster mother." Sartre tells how Genet at the age of ten already felt his destiny. ". . . He knows to the last detail the life that he will have to sip drop by drop."

The rejected child's image of being bad also can serve to preserve his hope that mother would love him were he only good. He must continue to behave destructively lest the reality of her unconditional disinterest be demonstrated, a fact that would be too painful to face.

The concept of self-image may provide an important link between organic and psychological factors in the causation of violence. The child who is impulsive, hyperactive, and destructive as the result of brain damage or dysfunction is often labeled as naughty and bad. Though the original behavior was involuntary, perpetuation of destructiveness and aggressiveness can result from the individual's perception of himself as evil. A postencephalitic youngster had to learn in psychotherapy that it was "Mr. Cephalitis," not he, who was bad even after the rages associated with temporal lobe seizures were controlled by anticonvulsants [28].

Aggression as Self-Punishment

Acting out aggressively without regard to the moral implications of one's behavior may not reflect a failure of development of the conscience but can result from the repression of a cruel, even sadistic, conscience, which is an inner representation of the cruel, punitive parent. Usually there is a concomitant deficiency in the positive, benevolent aspects of the superego (the residue of approbations and prohibitions, roughly equivalent to the conscience), namely, deficiencies in stored memories of praise and in the ego ideal (the desired self-image). Thus too much as well as too little conscience may lead to violence. One explosive, apparently "immoral" young man said, "I guess I think nothing I do is wrong because I really think everything I do is wrong." He made no differentiation between acceptable and antisocial behaviors. His miserable childhood had seemed little more than an endless series of beatings at the hands of incredibly cruel grandparents whom he could never please. To allow himself to perceive his utterly unreasonable superego would be to hate himself viciously.

A punitive conscience also can express iself unconsciously through punishment-seeking behavior [25]. Assault, like other forms of criminal behavior, can be a way to evoke punishment and retaliation, to assuage and appease a cruel conscience, and to attenuate painful feelings of guilt. In view of the aforementioned talion principle characteristic of the thinking of the unconscious, violence particularly may be the means to provoke punishment, which would be fantasied itself as violent. Violence is used to get violence. As already mentioned, even punishment may be sought out in preference to being ignored, and some individuals feel that the only attention they can evoke is in the form of punishment. As suicide may be an attempt to murder an inner representation of a hated other person, murder may be a way to be killed. This psychodynamic mechanism is a potent argument against the death penalty, which thus may induce more murders than it deters [24]. For example, a San Quentin inmate recently has made several publicized attempts to go to the gas chamber because it is his "constitutional right" to be executed.

Fixed, Repetitive Patterns of Aggressive Behavior

Aggressive, even violent, behavior may take the form of fixed or repetitive actions entirely out of keeping with the demands or limitations of the real situation. Each form of action tells a story of its own, e.g., the strong-arm robber's standing up with his gun (that has both sexual and aggressive symbolism) to a feared, envied father, but why must the story be told over and over again? To understand action patterns, one must be aware that somewhere in the constellation of behavior and action there is an element of pleasure. It is often worthwhile to emphasize the *process* versus the *content* of a specific behavior.

Child psychiatrists have noted that children manifesting a repetitive play pattern generally are responding to current anxiety. The therapist then seeks out sources of conflict or stress in the child's present environment. It is as though doing something definite counteracts the feelings of indefiniteness in one's life and serves as a means of gaining active control over a situation that is otherwise out of control. Freud [13] stated that compulsion represents a search for certainty when the individual is beset by uncertainties. He pointed out that the act may no longer be related to the person whom the individual loves or hates but is self-preservative and self-stabilizing. The compulsive behavior pattern may become a source of gratification in and of itself. Intrigued by analogies to principles of physics, Freud likened repetition compulsion to inertia; once something gets going, it tends to keep going.

Insecurity implies that the individual is unsure of what is going to happen in the reality of the immediate or foreseeable future. Such insecurity may represent an overprinting on the present and future of a past that was unpredictable in many important ways—because of inconsistent parental behavior, early losses of significant loved ones, parental discord, or frequent changes of residence. These are the kinds of life events so often found in the histories of violent persons. On a more subtle level such uncertainty may be based on parental ambivalence or bipolarity of attitude communicated to the child in the form of contradictory messages and signals, both verbal and nonverbal. In their most malignant form such conflicting messages are manifested as the "double bind" that Bateson and Jackson consider a causal factor in schizophrenia [35]. The double bind is characterized by the individual's inability to comment on the communications being expressed in order to make a correct discrimination as to which level of communication he will respond. To illustrate, a "double-binding" parent may accuse the child of being unfriendly yet recoil physically when the child makes an affectionate approach. If the child says, "You don't love me," the parent's denial, "Of course I do," is expressed in a cold, unloving manner. The aggressive deviant often comments on the "hypocrisy" of his parents, who said one thing and acted in another way. To him verbal communication is often meaningless, irrelevant, or unbelievable.

The perpetuation of the feelings of uncertainty, and how these feelings lead to chaotic anticipations of the future, need further clarification. It is as though the road ahead is seen through a rear-view mirror or "past-colored" glasses. Then aggressive reactions and defenses associated with the original anxiety-provoking situations may continue to operate. Such reactions actually can become enhanced because the dangers are elaborated in fantasy and become exaggerations of the original perceptions. Acts associated with successful coping with original stresses can, in and of themselves, become pleasurized and serve as sources of gratification. Unfortunately, new situations or stresses may render formerly effective coping devices now inappropriate and maladaptive and create new turmoil in life, which may in turn be handled by the formerly effective but now out-of-date methods.

Action patterns also often have an addictive quality. Action may be a "shot in the arm" to allay basic anxiety or depression. Though there may be other pleasurable qualities that satisfy defiant (anal), exhibitionistic, or competitive urges, the most tenacious and repetitive are the "pacifier" (oral) types of gratification. An act (as a *transitional object*), like the child's security blanket, may be clung to for dear life as a substitute for and representative of the mother [32, 37]. When there was violence in the relationship with a parent, violent action may be a security-providing parent-symbol, needed to allay anxiety, no matter how ineffective and unsatisfactory the act really is or the parent really was. The person who provokes fights may be symbolically seeking the mother who gave him spankings. Once again, bad parents or their symbolic representatives, which may be an aggressive action pattern, are better than nothing at all. Thus seemingly irrational and unrewarding behavior is a mechanism to provide certainty and security, ingredients essential to human existence.

Sensation-Seeking

Violence can be a form of sensation-seeking or thrill-seeking behavior. Violent actions stir strong emotional reactions not only in others but in the perpetrator himself. Emotionally impoverished individuals, deprived of affection in childhood and not deriving gratification from current interpersonal relations, may seek strong feelings for the sake of the sensations themselves [21]. Rather than seeking interpersonal closeness, which is perceived as threatening or unrewarding, the individual regressively seeks a state of excitement or pleasure as may have existed in the earliest relationship with his mother. The sensation-seeker wants a shortcut to the bliss of the child in his mother's arms.

It has even been suggested that the need for excitement in some individuals is the result of low physiological responsivity to stimulation or to more rapid adaptation to stimulation [26]. Hebb [17] was one of the first to emphasize that stimulation may be sought under conditions of low arousal. Thus the organism can be motivated to increase as well as to reduce tension. Boredom motivates action, sometimes in the form of violent action. Strong sensation may be needed to feel alive, real. Drug-taking, itself related to lessened control and sometimes to paranoid states predisposing to violence, is often a form of sensation-seeking. It may not matter greatly to the user whether he is sedated, stimulated, or has other forms of alteration of consciousness from drugs, as long as he feels *different*, feels something. Sensation-seekers often report having received little parental expression of tenderness.

Cruelty and Paranoia

Man has a unique propensity for cruelty as a result of his capacity for fantasy and psychological defense. His violence toward other men may not be assuaged by submissive behavior on the part of the victim, as is the common case in animals. Cruelty, sometimes the result of sadism as already discussed, can also be a result of paranoid ideas and attitudes. These are states of feeling victimized, persecuted, or threatened. In paranoia there is often also a sense of being important and powerful. Paranoid ideas are accompanied by irrational hostility and fear of others. Cruelty and violence can also result from displaced aggression in which the victim, a scapegoat, is a substitute for the person who engendered the hostility. Even among lower animals some displacement of aggression is seen. A dominant male monkey teased by a human may attack subordinate members of his group. Paranoid mechanisms involve the defense of projecting one's feelings onto another person and perceiving these feelings as directed against oneself. Paranoid attitudes often underlie individual and mass aggression.

The core of paranoid states seems to lie in feelings of helplessness and powerlessness and in lack of basic trust in the predictable, reliable meeting of basic needs. An infant or child whose signals of need go unattended and whose care is based primarily on parental desires or routines, e.g., the mother who feeds the baby when *she* feels hungry, or by the clock, develops not only reactive rage, which may be projected, but a sense of impotence. In turn, grandiosity and power-seeking can be defenses against feelings of helplessness. Those who give up trying to get love may substitute power. Hitler was concerned with control and authority, not with popularity. A clinical vignette poignantly illustrates these concepts. A patient believing himself to be Jesus Christ suffered a severe paranoid schizophrenic illness for several years despite a variety of somatic treatments and attempts at intensive psychotherapy, during which he never "opened up." Finally, his therapist gave up and arranged transfer to a back ward. At their last interview the therapist began to weep in despair, disappointment, and frustration. The patient asked incredulously, "Do you mean I've created a *feeling* in you? My mother never felt anything; she dusted me off like the furniture." He went on with an outpouring of emotion to relate his guilt over incestuous feelings toward his mother who, though unaffectionate and unemotional, had been sexually provocative. All his delusions immediately melted away, and recovery has been maintained for six years. This patient felt totally unable to elicit an emotional response in another person, a feeling that had been reinforced by an unhappy marriage to a frigid woman. He compensated by fantasies of omnipotence.

Halleck [15] states that the subjective feeling of helplessness is crucial in the genesis of criminal and violent behavior. Violence is used to combat this painful emotion or indirectly to keep it from consciousness. Helplessness not only may represent a residual of childhood powerlessness but results from oppression by society, by significant others, or by the inner representation of unreasonable parents, a cruel conscience. If one acts, he seemingly is not helpless, has a sense of freedom, and believes that he can influence his environment. The doer feels master of his own fate. Violent coercion is one ultimate way to have impact upon a world perceived as unresponsive and oppressive.

In the third case in Chapter 13, murder ensued in the context of perceived loss of all freedom of choice and the consequent sense of entrapment. When the killer-to-be was given no choice, he felt he had no other options. His interpretation of the situation was "paranoid." Both the ghetto dweller, who sees the possibility of change yet feels impotent in effecting social betterment, and the student, who has no role in policy-making in his huge, impersonal, bureaucratic, research-oriented, establishment-dominated university, may riot in frustrated, angry response to their sense of futility and powerlessness. Acquiring a feeling of effectiveness and importance is a potent antidote to hostility and suspiciousness.

From Fantasy to Action

The translation of fantasy into action in some instances may relate to a basic fantasy once having been confirmed in reality. The brutal father is a *real* threat, lending credence to the castration anxieties of the Oedipal phase. The first killer described in Chapter 13 had a history of repeated overt mother-son incest, a very rare phenomenon. Conversion of a basic fantasy into action sets the stage for the acting out of other fantasies. The border between thought and action may become blurred so that what is conceived and what is done seem tantamount to the same thing. The psychopath may regard thought as if it were behavior [14]. Thus we have the possibility of the intention to do something substituting for the action itself. If he *thought* of it, it is as if he *had* done it. "But I meant to return the car" is supposed to excuse the fact that the car was not returned.

The impulse-ridden character acts in conjunction with thought. He does not look before he leaps. Thought that is anticipating and inhibiting in the light of reality considerations does not occur. Impulsivity is related also to the need for immediate tension reduction, tension being experienced as an overwhelming threat. Any tension, then, is like the hunger of the infant. Action is then less toward the positive aim of achieving a goal (pleasure) but of eliminating tension (pain).

Confusion of thought or fantasy and action relating to developmental defects in acquiring conceptual thinking, impulsivity in terms of tension release, and impoverishment of learned coping strategies and ability to plan may be mutually reinforcing phenomena in the production of violent behavior.

The Mob

Some "stored" hostility, which represents the heritage of inevitable frustrations, lies latent in all of us. Aggression and violent behavior may be elicited in otherwise peaceful and law-abiding citizens under group pressure or "mob psychology." Guilt is relieved through being aware that others dare act on hostile feelings, and shame is inoperative since all are doing the same. The individual conscience is superseded. Once released, instinctually derived forces may overwhelm individual ego controls. The Balinese have been known as an extremely peaceful people for centuries. Not only did they participate in the recent genocide of the Chinese in Indonesia, but many old feuds among themselves were settled by killing once the social prohibitions against violence had broken down.

The leader of a group may subtly induce the group to act out his impulses, just as the parent may the child. To speculate, Mayor Daley's communications at the time of the 1968 Democratic Convention, which can be interpreted as implying permission and expectation of the police to use violence, may have represented his own hostility to those attempting to disrupt the Convention. This implication stands in sharp contrast to the communications of the London Chief of Police prior to the massive demonstrations at the American Embassy. The British authority made it unequivocally clear that restraint was expected of the unarmed bobbies and that such restraint would be a source of credit.

Recommendations: Coping with and Controlling Hostility

Various socially acceptable mechanisms are available to cope with hostility. These have to be learned to be accessible for use in later life in handling new increments of primary aggression, lest such reactive aggression be expressed violently or added to the store of unconscious hostility through repression. Verbal expressions of anger may prevent discharge of angry feelings by action. Name calling and epithets have a use, but being so close to emotions themselves, not only do they discharge anger, they may provoke emotional counterreaction. Expressing resentment as thoughts may be more acceptable and less psychologically injurious to others. In addition, the conversion of emotion from a percept (subjective sensation or feeling) to a concept (an idea expressed by language symbols) itself is a step toward control and mastery. Conceptual thinking is a product of a later, more mature phase of development than perceptual thinking. Conceptual thinking can be used to handle aggression via relatively sophisticated defenses such as intellectualization and rationalization. The mechanism of sublimation, which discharges emotion acceptably through changes in aim or object, can take place in the case of aggression through sports, competition, rivalry, debate, and nonviolent protest. Sublimation is a particularly effective mechanism since it aids *constructive discharge* rather than repression of one's aggressive energies.

While society should encourage expressing aggression in nonviolent ways lest it be repressed to emerge later in malignant secondary forms, it must reinforce inner controls against violence by labeling violence as bad and unacceptable. All people, especially children, can be taught that the emotion of anger should be listened to as a signal that can be useful to set in motion an attempt to identify a thwarted goal and to bring into play appropriate coping responses. One should not be able to feel removed in distance from the consequences of one's acts, and the concept of personal responsibility should be reinforced. For instance, it is doubtful whether a bombardier would pour napalm on civilians if he had to do it directly and not from the remote-control, push-button cockpit. The public should be aware of signs of secondary aggression, paranoia, and displacement of aggression in order to avoid electing those who advocate violence, see Communists and conspiracies around every corner, and look for scapegoats.

Not only is the human capable of projection, he is capable of identification and of empathy. He can perceive what another is feeling and be troubled by another's pain. He can extend the loyalty and love he feels for his family to larger groups, hopefully to humanity. The hope of mankind lies not only in successful defenses against and sublimations of hostile impulses but in the promotion of affection and identification with one's fellow man.

Acknowledgment

I am very grateful to my father, Joseph C. Solomon, M.D., Associate Clinical Professor of Psychiatry, University of California School of Medicine, San Francisco, for his direct help and for the use of several of his original concepts.

References

1. Anderson, R. E. Where's Dad? Paternal deprivation and delinquency. *Archives of General Psychiatry* 18:641, 1968.
2. Berliner, B. Libido and reality in masochism. *Psychoanalytic Quarterly* 9:322, 1940.
3. Bieber, I. Sadism and Masochism. In Arieti, S. (Ed.), *American Handbook of Psychiatry*, vol. 3. New York: Basic Books, 1966.
4. Bonaparte, M. Time and the unconscious. *International Journal of Psycho-analysis* 21:427, 1940.
5. Bowlby, J. Grief and Mourning in Infancy and Early Childhood. In Eissler, R., et al. (Eds.), *Psychoanalytic Study of the Child*, vol. 15. New York: International Universities Press, 1960. P. 9.
6. Clark, L. D. A comparative view of aggressive behavior. *American Journal of Psychiatry* 119:336, 1962.
7. Craft, M. *Ten Studies into Psychopathic Personalities*. Bristol (Eng.): Wright, 1965.
8. Erikson, E. *Childhood and Society* (2d ed.). New York: Norton, 1969.
9. Fenichel, O. *Psychoanalytic Theory of Neurosis*. New York: Norton, 1945.
10. Freud, S. Beyond the Pleasure Principle (1922). In *The Standard Edition of the Complete Psychological Works of Sigmund Freud*, tr. and ed. by J. Strachey with others. London: Hogarth, 1955. Vol. 18, p. 7.
11. Freud, S. Civilization and Its Discontents (1930). *Standard Edition*, 1961. Vol. 21, p. 64.

12. Freud, S. The Ego and the Id (1927). *Standard Edition*, 1961. Vol. 19, p. 19.
13. Freud, S. Notes upon a Case of Obsessional Neurosis (1909). *Standard Edition*, 1957. Vol. 10, p. 155.
14. Greenacre, P. Conscience in the psychopath. *American Journal of Orthopsychiatry* 15:495, 1945.
15. Halleck, S. L. *Psychiatry and the Dilemmas of Crime. A Study of Causes, Punishment and Treatment.* New York: Hoeber Med. Div., Harper & Row, 1967.
16. Harlow, H. F. Social deprivation in monkeys. *Scientific American*, Nov., 1962. P. 1.
17. Hebb, D. O. *The Organization of Behavior.* New York: Wiley, 1949.
18. Johnson, A. M., and Szurek, S. The genesis of antisocial acting out in children and adults. *Psychoanalytic Quarterly* 21:323, 1952.
19. Kardiner, A., Kurush, A., and Ovesey, L. A methodological study of Freudian theory. *International Journal of Psychiatry* 2 (1):489, 1966.
20. Kemp, C. H. The battered child syndrome. *Journal of the American Medical Association* 181:17, 1962.
21. Levy, D. M. Primary affect hunger. *American Journal of Psychiatry* 94:643, 1937.
22. Lorenz, K. *On Aggression.* New York: Harcourt, Brace & World, 1966.
23. McReynolds, P. Exploratory behavior: A theoretical interpretation. *Psychological Reports* 11:311, 1962.
24. Menninger, K. *The Crime of Punishment.* New York: Viking Press, 1968.
25. Nunberg, H. The sense of guilt and the need for punishment. *International Journal of Psycho-analysis* 7:420, 1926.
26. Quay, H. C. Psychopathic personality as pathological stimulation-seeking. *American Journal of Psychiatry* 122 (2):180, 1965.
27. Sartre, J. P. *Saint Genet: Actor and Martyr.* Translated by B. Frechtman. New York: Braziller, 1963.
28. Sarvis, M. Psychiatric implications of temporal lobe damage. *Psychoanalytic Study of the Child* 15:454, 1960.
29. Scharr, J. H. Violence in juvenile gangs. *American Journal of Orthopsychiatry* 33:29, 1963.
30. Silverberg, W. *Childhood Experience and Personal Destiny.* New York: Springer, 1952.
31. Solomon, J. C. Passive Motion and Infancy. *American Journal of Orthopsychiatry* 29:650, 1959.
32. Solomon, J. C. The fixed idea as an internalized transitional object. *American Journal of Psychotherapy* 16 (4):632, 1962.
33. Solomon, J. C. *Synthesis of Human Behavior.* New York: Grune & Stratton, 1964.
34. Szasz, T. On the psychoanalytic theory of instincts. *Psychoanalytic Quarterly* 21:25, 1952.
35. Weakland, J. H. The Double-Bind Theory of Schizophrenia and Three Party Interaction. In Jackson, D. D. (Ed.), *The Etiology of Schizophrenia.* New York: Basic Books, 1960.

36. White, R. W. *The Abnormal Personality*. New York: Ronald, 1964.
37. Winnicott, D. W. Transitional objects and transitional phenomena. *International Journal of Psycho-analysis* 34:89, 1953.

Selected Readings

Aichorn, A. *Wayward Youth*. New York: Viking, 1935.

Cleckley, H. *The Mask of Sanity*. Philadelphia: Mosley, 1941.

Donnelly, J. Aspects of the psychodynamics of the psychopath. *American Journal of Psychiatry* 121:1149, 1964.

Frank, J. D. *Sanity and Survival. Psychological Aspects of War and Peace*. New York: Random House, 1967.

Friedlander, K. Formation of the antisocial character. *Psychoanalytic Study of the Child* 1:189, 1945.

Greenacre, P. *Trauma, Growth, and Personality*. New York: Norton, 1952.

Harlow, H. F. Love in infant monkeys. *Scientific American* 200:68, 1959.

Hartmann, H., Kris, E., and Loewenstein, R. M. Notes on the Theory of Aggression. In *Psychoanalytic Study of the Child*, vols. 3, 4. New York: International Universities Press, 1949.

Lampl-DeGroot, J. Neurotics, Delinquents and Ideal Formation. In Eissler, K. (Ed.), *Searchlights on Delinquency*. New York: International Universities Press, 1949.

McNeil, E. B. Psychology and aggression. *Journal of Conflict Resolution* 3:195, 1959.

Masserman, J. (Ed.) *Violence and War with Clinical Studies*. Science and Psychoanalysis, vol. 6. New York: Grune & Stratton, 1963.

Montague, M. F. A. *Man and Aggression*. New York: Oxford University Press, 1968.

Redl, F., and Wineman, D. *Children Who Hate*. Glencoe, Ill.: Free Press, 1951.

Storr, A. *Human Aggression*. New York: Atheneum, 1968.

Winnicott, D. W. The Anti-Social Tendency and Others. In *Collected Papers*. London: Tavistock, 1958.

Zilboorg, G. *The Psychology of the Criminal Act and Punishment*. London: Tavistock, 1954.

3. Environmental Theories of Violence

Frederic W. Ilfeld, Jr., M.D.

The two previous chapters presented the biological and psychodynamic theories of aggression and violence. Although these chapters considered some environmental bases for aggression, they dealt in large part with inherent factors. It is clear that there is no constant aggressive reaction to specific stimuli in the human being. Stimuli that lead to violence are varied and complex, and tendencies toward violence may last beyond the anger state. Even more striking are the differences in the amount of observable violence among individuals and among different cultures. To account for such phenomena, one must explore the major environmental roots of violence. These are prior social learning, frustration, and various instigating stimuli. I shall discuss each of these theoretical formulations and indicate what each implies concerning the prevention of violence.

The reader will recall that violence is defined in the Introduction to this book as destructive aggression, involving the inflicting of physical damage upon person or property. Elsewhere violence is considered as an act of "intense, willful physical harm committed by an individual or a group against himself or another individual or group" [14]. It is categorized in various ways, such as individual or collective, overt or covert, legitimate or illegitimate. Violence is also recognized as only one of many forms of aggression. Examples of other types of aggression with destructive consequences are open verbal disputes—for instance, ridicule; covert verbal aggression, such as sarcasm, gossip, or rumor; a breach of expectation or other obstructionism; avoidance and withdrawal of support. In addition, aggression has been defined as including the entire spectrum of assertive, achieving, intrusive, and attacking behaviors and thus need not be always destructive. These distinctions between violence and other

79

types of aggression are highlighted because this chapter focuses on environmental theories only as they pertain to violence alone. However, these theories frequently, but not invariably, apply to the other manifold forms of aggressive behavior.

Violence as a Consequence of Social Learning

Authors who have explored the relationship between violence and social learning hold that prior learning is a critical factor in determining the amount of violence later displayed. Attention is paid particularly to child-rearing practices and to membership in certain groups or subcultures advocating or highly valuing violence.

Bandura and Walters [3, 4] have reviewed exhaustively those facets of prior experience that are associated with violence. From their and others' field and laboratory observations, several conclusions have been drawn. Destructive aggression can be learned in accordance with the tenets of learning theory just like any other response. Habits of violence are acquired largely through imitation, as discussed later, or through the direct rewarding of destructive aggressive behavior. Preceding frustration is not necessarily required.

Like other learned responses violence can be inhibited either by the use of aversive stimulation or through strengthening incompatible positive responses. *Aversive stimulation* refers to those factors that are painful to the individual so inflicted and which commonly suppress the behavior occurring at the moment. Punishment, shame, and guilt are all known to act in this capacity. The term *incompatible positive responses* refers to actions that are contradictory to the act of violence; it is not possible, or at least it is very difficult and improbable, that both would occur at the same time. Examples of such incompatible responses include eating, lovemaking, state of muscle relaxation, anxiety, nonviolent protest, or idiosyncratic cultural antagonists to aggression such as smiling. The former mechanism, inhibition through aversive stimulation, has received much more study and investigation than the latter. This is unfortunate, because the strengthening of incompatible positive responses may have a greater potential for the control of violence.

Bandura and Walters point to considerable evidence which shows that physically aggressive-punitive parents tend to have physically aggressive children. In general it has been found that punishment by an authority figure seems to inhibit direct violence toward the punitive person and is associated with high destructive aggression toward other possible targets. Is this heightened violence derived from the pain and frustration of the parental punishment? Perhaps so; but Bandura and Walters claim that there is another factor operating which is all-important in the learning of violence—that of imitation or modeling.

Experimental laboratory studies have demonstrated repeatedly that children exposed to adult models of physical aggression will in later play display more physical aggression than children not so exposed. For example, in a series of experiments by Bandura and his associates [4], the general experimental design consisted of three groups of nursery school children: one group exposed to adult models of violence, a second exposed to adults who displayed inhibited and nonaggressive behavior, and a third control group not exposed to any particular adult models. The children observing violence watched the adult models exhibit physical and verbal aggression toward a large inflated plastic doll. In contrast, the children observing the adult models who were not violent saw adults sitting very quietly, totally ignoring the doll and the instruments for violence that had been placed in the room. Immediately after this exposure the children were placed in the same play setting. Those who had observed the violent adult models displayed a great number of precisely imitative violent behaviors, whereas such behaviors rarely occurred in either the children observing the other adults or the control group. Furthermore, in other experiments the success of the model's violence in achieving desired goals has been shown as a crucial factor in determining the degree to which a violent pattern of behavior will be reproduced by the child observer.

Violence in the mass media recently has become a hotly debated topic. The importance of the mass media for social learning is highlighted by the estimate that school-age children spend more of their time in front of the television set than in the classroom. Since mass media are such a crucial ingredient in the learning of violence, a complete chapter (Chapter 7) has been devoted to its discussion; hence it will not be considered further here.

In sum, physical punishment by parents does not inhibit violence and most likely encourages it. It both frustrates the child and gives him a model to imitate and learn from. The learning of violence through modeling applies to more than just parental behavior. It is also relevant to examples set by the mass media, one's peer or other reference groups, and local and national leaders.

Another investigational approach to violence and its child-rearing antecedents is that of comparing different socialization practices over several cultures [2, 23]. While this method has some obvious limitations, such as variable reliability of data and poor control of variables other than those under immediate study, still its benefits are great. The cross-cultural method provides an independent testing ground for hypotheses derived from field or laboratory studies. For instance, if modeling is thought to be an important factor in learning violence, then one might expect individual violence such as personal crime to have high incidence in societies where military glory is highly emphasized. Indeed a comparison of a sample of 30 cultures showed such an association between incidence of personal crime and emphasis on military glory to be highly statistically significant [23]. In cultures where military glory is emphasized, there is a high incidence of personal crime; the converse holds for cultures with low emphasis on military glory.

Similar cross-cultural comparisons have been made between several indicators of violence (incidence of personal crime; emphasis on military glory; bellicosity of a society; and killing, torturing, or mutilating one's enemies) and various aspects of child-rearing [2, 23]. Of these four indicators of violence at least three occur significantly more frequently in cultures with the following practices:

1. High positive pressure is exerted by adults toward making children behave (1) in a self-reliant manner and (2) in a high-achieving manner.
2. High amounts of anxiety are aroused in the child by his failing to behave (1) in a self-reliant manner and (2) in a high-achieving manner.
3. Exclusive mother-son sleeping arrangements (i.e., absence of father from the room) last for prolonged periods of greater than one year.

What are the meanings of these cross-cultural findings? First, it must be realized that associations, even if highly significant, do not of themselves show causation. Further research must be done to ascertain whether the above child-rearing factors are necessary, sufficient, or simply contributing antecedents to violence. While one might devise a number of interpretations to explain the data, two points are clear. First, there are consistent heightened levels of violence for certain cultures. Second, these cultures with high amounts of violence are characterized by certain child-rearing patterns. Learning achievement behavior, socialization for self-reliance, and frequent absence of the father from the living quarters appear to be of importance.

The bulk of social learning for most people, from school age through adulthood, occurs among one's peer or reference groups. These are groups that command one's allegiance and are deemed by the individual to be meaningful or valuable to him. The group norms (expected standards of behavior) and values (shared beliefs) are critical for shaping the individual group member's perceptions, cognitions, and actions. For example, a shared belief among many United States citizens is that communism is inherently evil: Communist leaders aim to dominate the world, exploit other people, and distort the truth. This country's mission is to contain communism. Conversely, the view of many Soviet citizens toward the United States is nearly a mirror image of our view of them—our leaders are bad, we are imperialistic and dominating, we exploit our own and other people, and we distort the truth. Reality is not the same for observers belonging to different groups. To the Russian, the United States is a threat, but his country is peace-loving; to the United States citizen, these relations are reversed.

The importance of one's group membership in determining his beliefs and actions with particular reference to violence is emphasized by Wolfgang and Ferracuti [24]. They propose that violent behavior results primarily from cultural factors—the norms and values of one's reference groups. Their thesis is that violence is an expected and accepted mode of problem-solving in certain subcultures. Violence as a means of coping with one's life stresses and as a demonstration of masculinity and toughness is a highly valued behavior for some groups. For example, in this country there is evidence that modes of expression of destructive aggression in children vary among the social classes. Lower-class boys appear more likely to be oriented toward direct expression of violence than are middle-class boys. This can be seen in the greater acceptance and prevalence of fighting among lower-class boys. On the other hand, the middle-class youngster is more likely to turn any violent impulses inward upon himself, and as an adult he is more likely to commit suicide. Put another way, the prevalence of violence depends largely upon how much it is incorporated into the customs of one's reference groups.

IMPLICATIONS

Some general corrective measures implied by the social learning theory of violence are the reduction of punitive parental socialization practices, the refinement and implementation of behavioral responses incompatible with violence, the provision of competent and nonviolent masculine models, and modification of the values or else "dispersal" [24] of the members of subcultures of violence.

It is generally accepted that the strongest internal controls are developed by children whose parents have shaped their behavior by affection, praise, and reason rather than by physical punishment or deprivation of privileges. This is not to say that punishment does not have its place in child-rearing, only that it should take a secondary role in socialization and be used selectively. Punitive parental behavior might be reduced through public opinion against violence and through more effective parental education about child-rearing practices.

Deficient male identification as an antecedent of violence is suggested by studies of delinquency and by one of the cross-cultural findings presented earlier. A recent study of delinquency [1] compared a group of juvenile offenders with a matched sample of nondelinquent youth who were similar in age, race, socioeconomic status, and community delinquency rate. Compared to the nondelinquents, delinquent youth were less likely to have a father in the home during childhood. Also the reader will recall the previously mentioned finding of the statistically significant association of exclusive mother-child sleeping arrangements for at least one year, with three of the four cross-cultural measures of violence. This finding might be associated with later deficiencies in identification with the father. In any case, providing the young who are lacking desirable male models with a competent and caring "big brother," foster father, or constructive peer group experience appears both operationally feasible and effective in enhancing new learning. Care must be taken, though, for such models must not only be able to relate meaningfully to the youngster but must demonstrate behavior that can be rewarded in the disadvantaged youth's environment.

Childhood training for achievement and self-reliant behavior correlates significantly with measures of violence in cross-cultural comparisons. The feasibility and particularly the desirability of changing such child-training goals are questionable at best, since achievement and self-reliance are necessary for much of man's productivity and adaptation. Still our child training might emphasize more the importance of cooperation and regard for others, equally essential ingredients for productivity and adaptation.

Peer groups often serve as breeding grounds for violence. The actions necessary for violence, the use of toy weapons, and the practice of mock killing are mastered at a youthful age with imitation being a primary mode of learning. Then with the onset of puberty, violence as a symbol of masculinity may become part of the group culture. How to divert these youthful gangs from destructive to constructive activity remains an unresolved issue. Certainly a central task is changing the belief of many youth gangs that violence and manliness are inherently linked. Such a change might be accomplished by providing successful nonviolent models of masculinity.

Wolfgang and Ferracuti [24] comment on modifying subcultures and reference groups where violence is highly valued. They suggest that a community-worker approach to handling juvenile and delinquent gangs, development of indigenous leadership, community action programs, and community service centers all fail to modify the existing norms and values of the delinquent gang. They claim that these programs of community development do not modify people's attitudes and beliefs about violence. Such programs of community development are seen as a holding action or a containment policy —"stop-gap measures of temporary containment of conflict." According to Wolfgang and Ferracuti, before the subculture of violence can be replaced by nonviolence, the former must be disrupted, dispersed, disorganized. They advocate territorially dispersing the members who share intense commitment to the violence value and relocating them within the majority culture setting of nonviolence. In making this proposal, these authors avoid consideration of the serious consequences of uprooting people. Typically there follow widespread confusion, anxiety, and depression [18], making emigration a rather unacceptable mode of modifying subcultures of violence. The issue of dispersion raises several further questions: First, do people not have any rights (whether they are "violent" people or not) to choose where they live? Second, is it correct to assume that the "majority culture" will accept or tolerate "violent" people placed in their midst? Willingness to go and willingness to incorporate are two important factors determining the feasibility and desirability of dispersion.

Another caution must be taken with Wolfgang and Ferracuti's proposal for group dispersal. They are concerned with disrupting a group's value preference for violence, and this solution should not be generalized to a current major social problem—inner-city ghettos. Dispersion of a community does not rectify any of the abject physical and social conditions of our ghettos. Relocation and resocialization will not correct disease, poverty, unemployment, poor education, low self-dignity, or lack of community self-determination. As discussed in Chapter 6, American ghettos at this moment are not primarily subcultures of violence; there is not as yet a deep value commitment to the practice of violence. More basically they are subcultures of frustration—from social discrimination and from political and economic impotency. Thus the violence of the ghetto is better understood as a consequence of frustration and not simply a result of social learning. Guidelines for rectifying such conditions of frustration are amply provided by the Kerner Commission Report [19]. However, unless alternatives to violence are employed for coping with ghetto frustrations, there remains the threat of the adoption and institutionalization of the values and practices of violence.

Violence as a Consequence of Frustration

Of all the proposed causes of violence, frustration and other situational factors are the most hotly debated, not because they play a questionable role in violence but because they are more apparent and modifiable. In contrast to man's inherent nature or his social learning, frustration and situational variables are most visible as contributors to violence and are more easily changed.

In its broadest sense frustration results from an interference with ongoing, goal-directed activity [5, 6, 8, 16]. There is a violation of the individual's expectations. Frustration may take highly varied and complicated forms. It may stem from a threat to one's life or to the thwarting of a basic or important individual need, such as hunger, thirst, sex, or self-dignity; it may arise from competition. Conflict within or among an individual's different roles in society breeds frustration. Too little or too much social control engenders frustration. Frequently frustration is built into the organizational matrix or value systems of a society such as our "institutionalized white racism," in which prejudice is incorporated into society's structure [19].

It is not the aim of this chapter to elucidate the many different possible frustrations inherent in this or other human societies. Rather the primary interest lies in the mechanisms by which frustration may become translated into violence. Originally the frustration-aggression hypothesis stated that (1) aggression is the naturally dominant response to frustration, and (2) frustration is regarded as an inevitable antecedent of aggression [8]. This construct has had to be modified because in some individuals and cultures physical aggression is not the typical response to frustration. In many instances other behavior patterns, such as apathy, resignation, or evasion, follow frustration. Also, as discussed previously, modeling or imitation by itself is sufficient for the display of aggressive responses, frustration not being a necessary antecedent.

Later work [4–6] characterized the relation of frustration and violence as follows. Frustration as its primary effect increases the motivational or energy level of the individual. This in turn leads to more vigorous use of that behavior in the individual's habit repertoire which is elicited by the stimulus situation. Thus the response to the heightened motivational state engendered by frustration depends both on the stimulus situation at the moment and on the personality characteristics of the individual (i.e., his dominant habit patterns). An example of a stimulus situation that in the presence of frustration may discourage violence is the presence of a large visible police force in a potential riot area. Examples of personalities for whom the dominant response to frustration is not violence are those past and current practitioners of nonviolent political action. Although they may have been aggressive people, it is difficult to picture Martin Luther King, Jr., or Mahatma Ghandi becoming violent under even the most provocative circumstances. To summarize, the critical factors seem to be (1) awareness of prevailing expectations, (2) elucidation of those situations that produce intense and frequent frustration, (3) identification of those stimuli in addition to frustrations that elicit violence (discussed in the following section), and (4) knowledge of which personalities are more likely to react to frustration with a violent response.

One particular factor included under situations that produce intense and frequent frustration should be emphasized, because it is currently causing an especially high frustration among large numbers of our society. This is the violation of human dignity and pride. Institutionalized racism, the prejudice built into the structure of our society, with its myth of Negro inferiority in particular, breeds rage and potential violence [8]. In a similar vein, Spiegel [22] views this country's chief social strain as a historical incompatibility between our democratic ideals and our substantial authoritarian practices, which keep many from full participation in our democracy. Hopefully there remain potent political, economic, and legal modes for dealing with this frustration and a willingness of our society to abolish racism [19]. If not, violence may be the last resort in minority peoples' bid for self-respect and self-determination. (See Chapter 6 for an extensive discussion of this issue.)

Another phenomenon that is strongly associated with violence and might be categorized under frustration is the restriction of sexual relations. Comparative cross-cultural studies demonstrate a statistically significant association between punishment of extramarital intercourse and incidence of personal crime; military glory; bellicosity; and killing, torturing, or mutilating one's enemies [23]. This relationship between high restriction of extramarital intercourse and prevalence of violence is very striking. One might argue that the frustration of sexual restrictions leads to violence. However, this correlation may represent a general association between restrictive sexual practices and violence. Perhaps this association is due to "violent cultures" punishing any transgression, not just extramarital intercourse. Or violence may be due in part to the damming up of sexual energies. Another possible explanation might be that violence and affectionate lovemaking are incompatible responses; one cannot occur in the presence of the other.

Another group of frustration-type antecedents to violence are those encountered on the community and national level. These are so numerous and variable in nature that only a listing and not an extensive discussion will be undertaken. Experimentally, intergroup conflict has been shown to originate from two groups competing for goals that only one group can obtain, to the dismay and frustration of the other group; conflict and increased likelihood of violence develop from mutually unobtainable goals [20]. Also rapidly developing and innovating societies and emerging nations, with their jockeying for power and wealth and their shifting values and dominance hierarchies, are more susceptible to violence than stable societies. Social stress, whether caused by poverty, overcrowding, low level of employment, skills, or education, can predispose toward violence [15]. Fast rates of improving economic conditions are generally associated with rising expectations and internal political instability [11]. Further factors engendering the institutionalized violence of warfare include the quest for increased resources (natural resources, people, or economic or political power), the distortions of ethnocentrism and national images and ideologies, the expectation of solution of internal problems, the presence of a warmaking institution, the desire for self-determination, and inadequate or distorted communication with other nations [9, 10].

IMPLICATIONS

Examination of the relationship between frustration and violence carries several implications for the prevention of violence. There can be regular and periodic assessment and reduction of those frustrations that are widespread and involve significant and important goals. Next, at least in principle, prevailing expectations that cannot be fulfilled can be lowered. Finally, it must be recognized that unnecessary or indiscriminate use of force may heighten frustration and increase the likelihood of escalated violence or even serve as a triggering or precipitating incident for violence.

Among the multitude of frustrations in America today, several seem to stand above the rest in current importance: those of the failure of many minority group individuals to achieve dignity and self-pride, and of poor communities to effectively communicate their grievances and attain control of their own destinies. Expectations have been increased but not fulfilled. For many of our people the conditions of poverty, discrimination, unemployment, and lack of skills, when combined with unfulfilled expectations for improvement, foster disillusionment and disappointment and tear away at self-esteem and dignity. In correcting these social conditions which produce intolerable frustration, one should recognize that "give-aways" and paternalism do little to enhance the recipient's dignity and self-esteem [12]. In large part the organization and effort must come from the disadvantaged community itself, with the more prosperous society assisting with necessary training and resources when requested and appropriate.

While one may attempt to reduce frustration in human life, its elimination is impossible and even undesirable. Frustration and conflict play a basic role in human existence; where they cannot be reduced, our task is to keep them at a tolerable level and guide the responses to them into constructive rather than destructive actions. Hence nonviolent ways of resolving conflicts born out of frustrations must be developed and employed. Briefly these include improved modes of conciliation and communication of grievances; the institutionalization of programs of evaluation and change (ombudsman system); and such forms of pressure without bodily violence as propaganda, subversion, boycotts, strikes, sabotage, and nonviolent action (see Chapter 5 and Jerome Frank [9]). All of these methods have great promise for situations of frustration where other solutions have seemingly been exhausted.

Violence as a Consequence of Instigating Stimuli

Besides frustration there are other important situational contributors to violence [7]. They act as stimuli conducive to violence. The more important ones may be listed as follows: a precipitating event, a low expectancy of punishment, the ready availability of means (weapons, policy, army), alcohol intoxication, boredom, group contagion, and strong obedience to authority. Impending violence often may be prevented or elicited by manipulating any of these factors.

Precipitating events stem from a variety of phenomena ranging from personal threats and arrests to shootings and news media coverage of violent events. These may sometimes be modified or eliminated by practicing less threatening modes of communicating, by using less violent means of social control, and by reducing widespread transmission and sensationalizing by mass media of any such potentially instigating stimuli.

The show of strong yet constrained physical force can be a powerful deterrent to threatened violence, in that expectancies for punishment are raised. However, excessive and unrestrained force can act as an instigating stimulus to the outbreak of collective violence, since the display of abusive force increases the frustration and the anger of the victim population. This suggests the use of adequate but judicious physical force as a possible alternative in the prevention or control of violence. When this is done, the consequences and limitations of violence as a strategy for conflict resolution should be kept in mind (see Chapter 5).

The likelihoood of violence can be enhanced by the ready availability of highly lethal means of destruction, such as firearms (see Chapter 8), or, on a larger scale, the presence of armed forces. Experiments suggest that even the casual sight of a gun can catalyze violence [7]. It should be noted that people are not killed just by other people; man-made weapons such as knives, guns, bombs, and so forth are often necessary for violence to occur and in all cases increase the amount of destruction done. The widespread distribution of such weapons can be monitored and controlled through legislative means.

Individuals with a past history of violence or those under the influence of alcohol consistently are shown to have a higher probability for violence (see Chapters 11 and 12). Persons who have a history of alcoholism or violence should be recognized as being a high risk, and their access to weapons of destruction should be limited.

Boredom, the presence of other individuals all with the same emotion, and obedience to an inspiring leader may all serve as catalysts to violence. Group contagion may be a potent contributor to violence, since numbers, as in a gang, can provide a releasing effect for aggression. Boredom may be a possible force toward violence, since man has a natural desire for stimulation and excitement. Strong obedience to a legitimate authority and a desire to win the leader's approval can act as a major motivating force either for or against violence, depending upon the leader's desires and orders. The relationship of obedience to authority and the practice of violence has recently been highlighted in a series of carefully controlled laboratory experiments [17]. The laboratory procedure consisted of the experimenter's ordering a naïve subject to administer increasingly more severe punishment (electric shock) to a "victim" in the context of a learning experiment. (The victim was a confederate of the experimenter.) In general, it was found that the proportion of obedient subjects willingly inflicting high levels of electric shock upon the "victim" [62 percent] greatly exceeded the expectations of the experimenter and his colleagues. The general conclusion was that obedience to authority plays a greater role in our behavior than we "individualistic," "free-will" oriented Americans believe.

In the prevention of violence all three factors of boredom, group contagion, and obedience to leaders may be faced. Meaningful tasks and recreation can be found. Dangerous groups can be encouraged to take constructive action. If all else fails, they can be dispersed, and leaders advocating violence can be apprehended.

Crowd violence—panics and riots—is an example bringing a number of aforementioned factors together, particularly frustration and various instigating stimuli. Social scientists have discussed this topic under the rubric of "collective behavior." They agree that collective or mob violence is not dependent upon established group norms and values. Rather the norms in crowd violence are emergent or spontaneous and not formalized, and thus crowd violence is greatly dependent upon situational conditions. The conditions predisposing to mob violence have been discussed by Smelser [21] as comprising the following:

1. Structural conduciveness—social conditions, such as overcrowding, that are conducive to crowd violence
2. Structural strain—conflict among a group's values or norms; frustration of expectations
3. The growth and spread of a generalized belief that identifies the source of the strain, attributes certain characteristics (evil motives) to this source, and recommends that violent actions be taken to relieve the strain
4. A precipitating incident
5. The mobilization of participants for action—a matter of leadership and communication

6. The relative absence of social control and a low expectation of punishment

Smelser views each of these six conditions as necessary for the production of crowd violence, and all six together are thought to be sufficient. One should note that situational determinants, such as a widespread frustration or prevalent existing social conditions (e.g., boredom, precipitating event, group contagion, expectation of punishment), appear more relevant for collective violence than are social learning factors (child-rearing practices, reference group's norms and values).

Comment

In this chapter major environmental determinants of violence are reviewed, and their implications for the prevention of violence are discussed. Environmental causes are separated into several theoretical categories. Violence may be seen as a consequence of certain kinds of social learning. Having punitive parents, learning through imitation of violent peers of leaders, having inadequate or insecure male identification, acquiring excessively high-achievement and self-reliant behavior, and belonging to subcultures highly valuing violence are all social factors predisposing to violence. Violence may also be viewed as a consequence of various kinds of frustration endured by individuals and groups. Elevated and unfulfilled expectations and the intensity and frequency of frustration are important factors here. A third group of antecedents are a number of stimulus situations conducive to violence: a precipitating event, a low expectancy of punishment, the ready availability of destructive means, alcohol intoxication, boredom, group contagion, and strong obedience to authority.

In their discussion of violence, authors often tend to emphasize only one approach or frame of reference to the exclusion of others. Yet no one explanation by itself is sufficient to account for all the phenomena of violence. For example, it is generally recognized that humans, males in particular, have an inherent capacity for violence. But violence is highly variable among individuals and different societies, often because of differences in child-rearing practices and cultural value systems. Furthermore, certain situational factors such as intense or widespread frustration and an instigating event frequently are necessary to trigger a violent action. Thus in planning the prevention and reduction of violence, one must ascertain which of these various theories of causation are most salient to the situation at hand. The important issue to be faced is not why man is violent but *when* and *under what conditions* he becomes so. Different modes of intervention may then be utilized in accordance with the different causal factors involved.

Thus the analysis of violence proposed here is primarily multidimensional. For a given instance of violence, whether it be assassination, warfare, riots, or personal crime, the antecedents must be carefully determined. Such antecedents may be easily recognized, or they may be ambiguous or complex. Solutions to violence will vary in accordance with the nature of its causes.

Besides a multidimensional approach, a second perspective taken in this chapter and throughout the book is the view of violence as one means in man's struggle to adapt. Violence is one possible mode of coping with individual and group life stresses. It is a mechanism by which man can deal with his social environment. While man's response to frustration and to social learning cues has changed only slowly (if at all), our technology and environment have changed rapidly. We propose that violence is rapidly becoming less functional for man because of our increasing technological efficiency in killing and the lessened feedback and inhibition of our acts because of man-made weapons. As an adaptive technique, violence is becoming an anachronism. There are other, usually more effective, modes of handling current-day problems. We need alternatives to violence for man's success, and indeed survival, in the future. Several such alternatives are considered in Chapter 5.

Overall it should be apparent that there are no quick or easy solutions to our violent behavior. Certain measures such as counterforce may be effective in the short run, but institutionalizing socially constructive activities, modifying socialization practices that foster violence, and rectifying current situational contributors to violence all are relevant and important and require immediate attention and further study. While the problem at times seems overwhelming, at least we know that violence need not be inevitable and that prevention is possible. Hope is provided by knowing that not all peoples are equally violent; violent behaviors which are learned can be unlearned; frustrations can be alleviated; weapons can be limited; and men can find peaceful alternatives for resolving conflicts.

References

1. Anderson, R. E.   Where's Dad? Paternal deprivation and delinquency. *Archives of General Psychiatry* 18:641, 1968.
2. Bacon, M. K., Barry, H., and Child, I. L.   A cross-cultural study of correlates of crime. *Journal of Abnormal and Social Psychology* 66(4):291, 1963.
3. Bandura, A., and Walters, R. H.   *Adolescent Aggression.* New York: Ronald, 1959.
4. Bandura, A., and Walters, R. H.   *Social Learning and Personality Development.* New York: Holt, Rinehart, & Winston, 1963.
5. Berkowitz, L.   *Aggression: A Social Psychological Analysis.* New York: McGraw-Hill, 1962.
6. Berkowitz, L. (Ed.).   *Roots of Aggression: A Re-Examination of the Frustration-Aggression Hypothesis.* New York: Atherton, 1969.
7. Berkowitz, L.   Experiments on Automation and Intent in Human Aggression. In Clemente, C. D., and Lindsley, D. B. (Eds.), *Aggression and Defense: Neural Mechanisms and Social Patterns.* Los Angeles: University of California Press, 1967.
8. Dollard, J. D. L., Doob, L. W., Miller, N. E., Mowrer, O. H., and Sears, R. R.   *Frustration and Aggression.* New Haven: Yale University Press, 1939.
9. Frank, J. D.   *Sanity and Survival: Psychological Aspects of War and Peace.* New York: Random House, 1967.
10. Fried, M., Harris, M., and Murphy, R. (Eds.).   *War: The Anthropology of Armed Conflict and Aggression.* Garden City, N. Y.: Natural History Press, 1968.
11. Frieraband, I., and Frieraband, R.   Conflict, crisis, and collision: a study of international stability. *Psychology Today*, May, 1968.
12. Goodenough, W. H.   *Cooperation in Change: An Anthropological Approach to Community Development.* New York: Russell Sage Foundation, 1963.
13. Grier, W. H., and Cobbs, P.   *Black Rage.* New York: Basic Books, 1968.
14. Ilfeld, F. W.   Overview of the causes and prevention of violence. *Archives of General Psychiatry* 20:675, 1969.
15. Maccoby, E. E., Johnson, J. P., and Church, R. M.   Community integration and the social control of juvenile delinqency. *Journal of Social Issues* 14:38, 1958.
16. McNeil, E. B.   Psychology and aggression. *Journal of Conflict Resolution* 3:195, 1959.
17. Milgram, S.   Conditions of obedience and disobedience to authority. *International Journal of Psychiatry* 6:259, 1968.
18. Murphy, H. M. B.   *Flight and Resettlement.* New York: UNESCO, 1955.
19. *Report of the National Advisory Commission on Civil Disorders.* New York: Bantam, 1968.
20. Sherif, M.   *In Common Predicament: Social Psychology of Intergroup Conflict and Cooperation.* Boston: Houghton Mifflin, 1966.

21. Smelser, N.J. *Theory of Collective Behavior*. New York: Free Press, 1963.
22. Spiegel, J. P. Psychosocial factors in riots—old and new. *American Journal of Psychiatry* 125:281, 1968.
23. Textor, R. B. *A Cross-Cultural Summary*. New Haven: Human Resources Area Files Press, 1967.
24. Wolfgang, M. E., and Ferracuti, F. *The Subculture of Violence*. London: Tavistock, 1967.

4. Anger and Attack

A CYBERNETIC MODEL OF VIOLENCE

Frederick T. Melges, M.D.,
and Robert F. Harris, B.S.

Anger triggers violence when man becomes blinded by his rage. Reason, foresight, empathy, and morality—all of man's unique endowments become eclipsed by unchecked fury. Discovering how and why he becomes so blinded is the purpose of this inquiry.

This chapter will attempt to answer the following questions: First, what are the nature and function of anger as an emotion, affect, and motive? Second, what are some of the common circumstances engendering anger in humans? Third, when does anger lead to attack? Our intent is not to be exhaustive but rather to propose a frame of reference that may provide simple yet workable approaches to the above questions. Since our focus is on some of the special features of human anger and aggression, we shall not deal with those aspects that are common to both humans and animals.

Our frame of reference centers around the subjective probability of reaching goals—that is, how likely the person feels that his goals will be reached. A great deal of human consciousness consists of structuring goal priorities and planning to meet goals [25]. Holloway [16] has pointed up the need for a theoretical model that specifically applies to human anger and aggression. Such a model would have to take into account man's goal-striving activities and his unique capacities for long-term expectations about his and others' goals. Although these expectations usually facilitate man's adjustment to changing environments, they also make him vulnerable to

This project has been supported in part by a Research Scientist Development Award (NIMH Grant No. MH 29163–02) made to Dr. Melges.

unfulfilled and distorted expectations that may in turn lead to anger and attack.

Our thesis is that anger occurs when a plan of action toward a valued goal is interrupted by an interference specific enough to warrant attack. Attacking takes place when alternate plans of action seem blocked or when the expected rewards for attack appear to override other outcomes.

Before we explore theoretical ramifications and empirical data, let us point out that the basic ideas are simple: If you don't get what you expect and think you deserve, you get mad. You attack if that seems the only way you can get what you want or protect what you have. Although these experiences are common to everyone, the issues are not quite that simple. Why do you get mad rather than anxious or depressed? Why do you attack rather than give up or seek another goal? In the hope that our model provides answers to questions like these, we urge the reader to introspect and see how various aspects of our model fit his own experiences.

We shall explore various aspects of our thesis at some length. First, we shall describe a cybernetic model of emotion and motivation. This model centers around plans of action and subjective probabilities of reaching goals. Second, we shall deal with anger as a subjective feeling state—that is, as an affective signal predicting outcomes and prompting motives toward action. Third, we shall point out how anger in humans usually reflects different forms of unfulfilled expectations. Fourth, we shall show how the experience of anger occurring as a result of certain distortions of perceptions and personal needs may lead to attack and violence. By attempting to look at man from within as he looks out at his involvement with others and relates this involvement to his past, present, and future, we hope to capture a view that will give us not only greater understanding of anger but also guidelines for dealing constructively with anger.

This chapter aims at integrating some of the other theories described in this book into a composite model. A number of our concepts are derived from ongoing research projects yet to be published. We use the general model for emotion and motivation described in detail by Pribram and Melges [36], of which the model of anger and attack presented here is an extension. Some important revisions and clarifications, however, have been added. We believe that this proposal in its present form integrates other theories while at the same time making them more precise and operational.

Three theories frequently are utilized to explain violence—psychoanalytic, frustration, and social learning theory. Our cybernetic model explaining violence incorporates aspects of each of these theories while rejecting other features. Although limitations of space do not permit a detailed comparison, we shall point out briefly some of the fundamental similarities and differences. The arguments are more fully presented in the work of Pribram and Melges [36], and many of the following points will become clearer as the reader becomes familiar with the model presented here.

The importance of relationships between people, emphasized by psychoanalytic theory, is basic to our model. Also stressed is the psychoanalytic concept of "signal" affects [12] that alert the individual to changes in himself and his environment, but we believe that the psychoanalytic concept of "drive discharge" of affects is misleading and nonoperational. We hold that drives are not inherited programs of action tendencies with innate drivenness and directionality, but rather drives are best conceived as stimuli arising from imbalances of physiological regulation that through experience become associated with specific response patterns. For example, hunger does not lead to eating because of an inherited program of responses, but rather eating is the response that the infant learns will deal with the stimulus of hunger. This argument has special relevance to the explanation of attack behavior on the basis of a supposed aggressive drive. Since at the present time no physiological imbalance is known that would lead to an inner stimulus necessitating attack behavior, this raises doubts about an aggressive drive or drive stimulus leading to attack. Thus we propose that there is no innate aggressive drive or drive stimulus that arises from periodic physiological needs as with hunger, thirst, sex, and so forth. Although certain individuals may have inherited high activity levels, making them more predisposed to action, the action does not have to take the form of attack. In essence, the stimuli that prompt attack originate from environmental and social factors, not from within the body [38]. Thus attack upon objects and persons is a learned response usually associated with the affect of anger. And as we shall see, anger usually stems from the appraisal of certain kinds of frustrating and social situations. Furthermore, when one "expresses aggression," he is not "discharging" pent-up energy derived from an aggressive drive, but rather he is putting to action a state of physiological and muscular preparedness associated with anger.* Although the act of attacking may feel like a release of "drive tension," it is far more operational to conceive this as a muscular action that breaks up a positive feedback loop between

* Although classic psychoanalysis still holds to the "drive discharge" notion, there are some neo-Freudians [18] who take a similar position to ours.

the affect of anger and the physiological arousal associated with the motive to attack. Thus attacking "relieves" the person from the physiological arousal that, once initiated by anger, may aggravate the unpleasant aspects of anger.

Emphasizing anger as a signal about reaching goals, including the important goals of interpersonal relations, thus makes our position much closer to frustration and social learning theories. In line with frustration theory we highlight the role of unfulfilled expectations, but, in addition, we outline the ways in which expectations often become distorted and unrealistic. Since many frustration theories are rooted in drive concepts, however, we differ from frustration theorists by minimizing the role of drives as an explanatory principle. Evoking behavior through rewards and punishments, stressed by social learning theories, is placed within the general framework of emotions as appraisals of reinforcement, including those reinforcements coming from imitation and identification. The latter processes are fundamental to the development of specific goal orientations and the value placed on reaching certain goals.

Our focus on inner feeling states emphasizes the subjective dimensions of anger and attack. It is in this realm of subjective experience that action—whether kindness or attack—has its roots. What springs forth as action can be best understood in terms of what is felt.

A Cybernetic Model of Emotion and Motivation

The term *cybernetic* is derived from a Greek word meaning "steersman" [42]. A steersman navigates his ship on the basis of anticipated and present outcomes. Information or "feedback" about these outcomes enables him to keep the ship on course, that is, headed for its designated goal. Some of this information may be derived from special equipment, such as maps, sextants, and radar. These tools allow him to anticipate the possible outcomes and to adjust his ship accordingly. Other information about outcomes comes from memories of situations similar to the present. In these past situations some courses of action turned out favorably, others unfavorably. These memories, now triggered by present stimuli such as wind and rain, give rise to expectations that in turn help guide the steersman toward the most favorable course in the pursuit of his ultimate destination. But the steersman, as a man rather than a computer, does not have a one-track mind. While reaching his destination is a goal of high priority, he has many other goals that he thinks about at the same time. Certain of these goals, such as staving off hunger or saving the lives of his crew, may temporarily become more important than his goal to keep on course. These other goals may become priorities when events interrupt the usual procedures on his ship. It is here that emotion plays its part.

Emotions occur when there is an interruption of an ongoing plan of action. This interruption of a plan is not necessarily a blockade or interference. Termination of a plan of action, when a goal is either reached or not reached, is an interruption that gives rise to feelings of satisfaction or disappointment, respectively. A third type of interruption occurs when a plan of action (which includes a train of thought) is intruded upon by a stimulus such as a sunny day, a beautiful picture, a melody, and so forth. These intruding stimuli evoke either conscious or unconscious associations about the probability of reaching other goals in terms of past experience with similar stimuli.

Emotions are processes involved with the appraisal of outcomes in light of the interruption. The appraisal focuses on the chances of reaching the goals that concern the person at the moment. This process of appraisal is manifested in awareness by different feeling states, termed affects, that serve as signals of the underlying emotional process. Thus according to this model emotions are defined as the *processes* involved in appraising the likelihood of reaching goals, whereas affects are feeling *states* that signal the specific nature of the appraisal. What the person feels—the affects—are thus only part of the emotional process. For example, the affect of fear is a state of mind that reflects the appraisal of a threat of possible injury to one's body. This distinction between the signal and the process is important for the understanding of emotion.

A great deal of confusion among students of human behavior occurs because subjective feeling states (affects) have been equated with the cognitive and physiological processes (emotions) that give rise to the signals. Furthermore, affects and emotions often are not differentiated from motives. Motives are action tendencies prompted by the emotional appraisal process. The confusion is analogous to equating a traffic signal with the processes of evaluating and responding to the traffic signal. The expectation signaled by a red light is that there might be cross traffic at the intersection, so I had better stop. Green and yellow traffic lights signal the expectations that the intersection will be clear, so I may continue, or that there might be cross traffic, so I had better slow down. The traffic lights thus function to tell what outcomes to expect at a given time and location. The signals prompt motives (that is, go, caution, or stop) in terms of the expectations about what is likely to occur at that moment and at that intersection. But there is nothing about a red light per se that suggests cars will be crossing the intersection; this expectation is learned. Once learned, the red light itself can spur the motive to stop without the awareness of the expectations it signifies. Analogously, affective signals are similar to the traffic lights, but of course they come from within the body and are not external perceptions. They reflect the underlying emotional appraisals, and when a given affect is felt, it signifies that certain outcomes are to be expected at that moment. This leads to certain motives. When a person is asked why he did something, however, he may not be aware of how he appraised the outcomes in the situation. He may merely say: "I did it because I *felt* like it." Therefore, in order to understand an affective signal like anger, it is necessary to relate the affect to the specific kind of appraisal of outcomes that it reflects.

Thus in this model we make distinctions between emotion, affect, and motive. Emotion is the process of appraisal of outcomes. Affect is a conscious feeling state that reflects the appraisal. Motive is the action tendency prompted by the appraisal to which the affect draws attention.

The process of emotional appraisal involves evaluating not only the chances of reaching the goal in mind at the moment of interruption but also all other goals relevant to the situation. For example, if an enemy ship is detected ahead, the steersman appraises not only the risk the new distraction poses in terms of reaching his destination but also its threat to the lives of the crew, his own life, his family ties, and so forth. His appraisal incorporates information from his special navigational instruments, from his crew, and from his past experience. It also takes into account which goals are most valued. In circumstances of undeclared war, saving the lives of his crew may rank highest; whereas destroying the enemy ship may be the most important goal in times of declared war. As all these outcomes are weighed in light of new and remembered information, the appraisal process is reflected in rapidly changing feeling states (affects). These different feeling states serve as a composite signal of the appraisal of all the outcomes with which one is concerned. They reflect the person's overall estimate of his chances of reaching the goals that concern him at the moment. As a composite inner signal, a given affect summarizes the feedback about anticipated outcomes. Thus if the outcomes are uncertain or ambiguous, one experiences anxiety. If it appears that one's central goals cannot be reached, depression and hopelessness set in. If plans of action seem adequate to meet the task, one feels confident.

Thus according to this model different affects reflect different subjective probabilities of reaching intended goals. They are signals of "How well am I doing?" and "What is likely to happen?" [12]. Affects alert the person to changes in his present and anticipated environment, and they keep his attention on these changes until appropriate adjustments have been made. While serving as overall predictors of outcome, affects also prompt motives; that is, certain kinds of appraisals lead to specific action tendencies. These motives, before being put to action, are again subjectively appraised in terms of "What would happen if such and such were done?" For example, the steersman, fearing the risk of death to his crew and himself, appraises the consequences of his motive to retreat. He considers the possibilities that lives might be saved, there might be loss of face, he might be court-martialed, and so forth. These anticipations, coupled with the prospects of possible victory and the expected rewards of righteously fulfilling his duty, may keep him from retreating and lead him to attack. Thus through the emotional appraisal of outcomes, different motives or action tendencies are evaluated; the motives finally selected for action are those which minimize risks and optimize valued outcomes.

In summary, the process of emotion arises when a plan of action is interrupted. The function of emotion is to change or reinstate goals in light of (1) the subjective probabilities of reaching the goals and (2) the value of specific goals. The affects that reflect these processes alert the person to the possible need for changing goals and plans. A given appraisal of outcomes, signaled by an affect, helps one change his motives or intentions so that subsequent action will produce the most favorable outcome in the situation. These relationships are depicted in Figure 4. Since these relationships provide the background for understanding our thesis about anger and attack, some further definitions are in order as we explain the diagram.

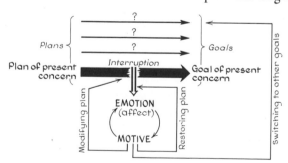

FIG 4. Function of emotions and motives in monitoring plans and goals

Plans of action refer to hierarchically organized sequences of intended action [34]. They are similar to the programs of a computer. Programs are made up of subroutines to meet various contingencies in the pursuit of ultimate goals, such as solving a mathematical problem. Unlike most computers, however, man usually knows his goals and is continually estimating his chances of reaching them in terms of envisioning and evaluating predictions about his plans. Also, as with the example of the steersman, he appraises the chances of reaching the many goals he holds in mind at the same time. Yet with rare exceptions man can carry out only one plan toward a given goal at any one time. In Figure 4 this focus on one plan linked with one goal is portrayed by the heavy line marked "Plan of Present Concern" and "Goal of Present Concern." The other plan-goals, held in mind but not being carried out, are shown by the lighter lines. The "Plan of Present Concern" is the one being carried out because past experience indicates that this plan most likely will reach the "Goal of Present Concern." Plans of action are hierarchically organized according to which plan is most relevant to the goal most valued at the moment.

Goals are the desired outcomes of action. They can be short-term, long-term, or continuous as well as strictly personal or shared with other people. At any given moment the motive for a goal can be evoked when events occur that (1) must be dealt with for survival and the maintenance of other goals or (2) arouse possibilities of developing further plans and goals for the individual's self-enhancement. An example of the former is the steersman's perceiving the enemy ship. The original goal of keeping on course was replaced for the moment with the goal of dealing with the intruder. An example of the latter would be discovering stray cargo. In this instance taking valuable merchandise on board would further the central task of transporting goods as well as opening up further possibilities. Whereas events in the environment can evoke specific goals at a particular time, the selection of which goals are being pursued usually depends on factors other than just the immediate environmental demands.

One of these factors is the value of a goal. A goal takes on value when it is basic to survival, when there has been considerable investment of time and energy in pursuing it, when it is shared with other people important to the person, and when it meshes with a host of other goals being maintained or pursued by the person. The goal's value relates to the intensity of an affect aroused by interrupting a plan. For example, if the steersman, standing on a windy deck, cannot light his pipe, he is apt to be only mildly annoyed. Appearance of the enemy ship, however, threatens the investment he has made in the journey thus far. The enemy ship endangers the lives of his men and raises uncertainties about reaching many other goals. Intense affect is thus felt, for many other goals hinge on the immediate goal of dealing with the enemy ship.

In Figure 4 we show how an interference (the vertical bar) to the "Plan of Present Concern" not only poses a threat to the "Goal of Present Concern" but also may threaten other plans and goals (as indicated by the question marks). Interrupting the "Plan of Present Concern" initiates the emotional process, which is comprised of the appraisals of outcomes, including the appraisal of motives before they are put to action. All this occurs very rapidly and is *reflected* in different affects. As soon as the emotional appraisal finds a motive that, in light of situational demands, minimizes overall risks and optimizes reaching the most valued goals, this motive is put to action. Later the actual outcomes of this action, along with further anticipated outcomes, are again emotionally appraised in terms of the subjective probabilities of reaching the valued goals.

As indicated in Figure 4, motives or action tendencies can take three general forms: (1) modifying the plan of present concern, (2) restoring the plan of present concern, and (3) switching to another goal or set of goals. Different affective or feeling states are associated with appraisals of various outcomes and give rise to different motives. Modifying the plan of action means that sequences or subroutines of the larger plan are altered in the attempt to reach the original goal. The steersman, for example, might deviate off course for a few hours in order to avoid the enemy ship but later return to the original tack. To do this, he would have to have considerable confidence in his predictions and the efficacy of his subplans, that is, the speed of his ship, the efficiency of the crew, and so forth. Restoring the plan of present concern involves eliminating or screening out the interference. Defensively the steersman might minimize the threat posed by the enemy and forge ahead, seemingly unaffected by the threat. This type of defensive maneuver could arise from extreme states of anxiety that often lead to ignoring the unwelcome inputs. Or he could restore the original plan by attacking the enemy and thereby eliminating the blockade. As we shall show in the next section, anger spurs attack. Finally, switching to another goal arises when this switch helps avoid unfavorable outcomes or when the approach of other goals is expected to yield greater rewards than pursuit of the original goal. If an unfavorable outcome, such as death or mutilation, seems likely to occur, the steersman may switch to a plan of retreat, which avoids the danger. As an example of switching to more rewarding goals, the discovery that the ship was not alien but rather a friendly pleasure vessel filled with voluptuous Tahitian women would spark exhilaration and (forgive the terminology) approach to other goals.

This model highlights the role of emotion and motivation in adapting to changing environments and fulfilling internal needs. It also helps clarify the difference between defense and coping mechanisms [15], as discussed in the Introduction to this book and in Chapter 15. Coping strategies are conceived here as those motives that attempt to accommodate to novel events through either modifying the plan of current concern or switching to a different goal and plan. Defense mechanisms, on the other hand, consist of motives that attempt to restore the interrupted plan by distorting or screening out the interference. Defenses attempt to restore the original plan without adequate appraisal of outcomes, whereas coping strategies are more future-directed: They aim at getting around the blockade, avoiding it if it poses a real threat, or using it as a stimulus to open up other plans and goals. Of course if an adequate appraisal of outcomes indicates that eliminating the interference is the only way to deal with the situation, then attack represents coping. On the other hand, if attack is spurred by the attempt to take revenge and "right" past wrongs, then attacking is defensive. The key difference between defense and coping thus is that coping takes into consideration future outcomes, whereas defense aims at maintaining the present or restoring past plans.

In summary, the role of emotions in guiding action by changing plans and goals is the basis for this cybernetic model. The term *cybernetic* might be stretched a little for our purposes to include not only *feedback* about what has happened or is happening but also *feedforward* to that which might happen. The appraisal of *anticipated* outcomes, based on past experience, is fundamental to all emotions [36]. A key feature of this feedback-feedforward system is that the affect felt is an outcome itself. Once experienced, the feeling state can also become an anticipated outcome that may be either desired or shunned. If it is a pleasant feeling, measures may be taken to maintain it or arouse it once again. If unpleasant, the aim may be to relieve the feeling or prevent its being experienced again. In this way we have a truly cybernetic loop: A given affect, such as joy, initially reflecting the high subjective probability of reaching valued goals, is sought after at a later time as a desired outcome in itself. Furthermore, subsequent appraisals of overall outcomes may include the chances of becoming joyous. Thus emotions and the accompanying affects mediate action by reflecting present and anticipated outcomes and also by becoming anticipated outcomes in themselves.

Anger as a Subjective Signal

We are now prepared to specify the unique features of anger that differentiate it from other affects. In terms of our cybernetic model the kind of affect experienced depends on the appraisal of outcomes. This appraisal essentially involves interrelating three expectations: (1) the subjective probability of reaching valued goals, reflected in varying degrees of optimism or pessimism; (2) the degree of control the person believes he has over the outcomes, that is, what he himself can do about them; and (3) how much he can trust and rely on other people in the situation.

The appraisal of outcomes reflected in the emotion of anger thus is as follows: (1) At a time when the individual is quite optimistic about completing the plan of present concern, he meets an unexpected interruption that suddenly reverses his optimism to pessimism. In other words, the interruption comes at a time when the person feels he deserves to reach his goal. (2) The interruption is a specifiable, usually external interference that the person feels he can eliminate through his own action. He thus feels that he has control over the eventual outcome—something can be done about it [37]. (3) Certain individuals or groups cannot be trusted and relied upon to change the outcomes and may even be antagonistic to one's own plan.

These emotional appraisals, experienced as anger, prompt motives to restore the interrupted plan by attacking the interference. Despite interruption the initial optimism carries over so that there is still hope that the plan will reach its goal. The specificity of the interference makes its removal seem possible. Since the plan is of major concern to the individual, not to others, he must rely on his own actions to effect the change. Restoring the status quo ante, rather than modifying the plan or switching to other goals, is the selected motive because of these appraisals of outcome.

For example, suppose that you have been promised a raise in salary and have every reason to believe that you will get it. You feel that you deserve it and that it has been long overdue. You are so sure of it that you have made many plans and commitments as to how the extra money will be used. But then at the last moment your boss informs you that you will not get the raise. The reason, he explains, is because a colleague claimed you rarely get to work on time. Angered, perhaps furious, you feel that this sudden turnabout was unnecessary and undeserved. You aim to do something about it. Your first act is to prove your colleague wrong; you are certain that you can do this. Thus in this example of anger-arousal the lack of expected rewards changed initial optimism to pessimism, and the interference was specific enough to do something about it. Quite possibly the interference can be eliminated and the original plan restored.

Similar situations to the above example, but with differences in the appraisal of outcomes, give rise to other affects. If you were uncertain about the possibility of a raise, unsure about what you could do about it, and doubtful as to how much to rely on others, you would feel anxious. Or, if you felt that no matter how hard you tried, your efforts would never accomplish this goal, you would feel hopeless and depressed [27].

Whereas the type of affect experienced reflects specific appraisals of outcomes, the intensity of a given affect stems largely from the value of the goals being pursued. The more valued the goals are, the greater the intensity of the affect. In this way the intensity of anger ranges from mild irritation to rage. In the above example if fury results, it is because there was considerable investment in getting the raise, and further plans and goals, perhaps shared with other persons, hinged on obtaining the extra money.

The subjective sensations and attitudes, which have been experimentally shown to accompany anger, portray a mixture of optimism and pessimism, show the tendency to take action, and reveal the feeling of alienation from other people. A host of studies [2, 6, 23, 26, 35] indicate that, compared to other affects such as anxiety and depression, anger is experienced as an active, potent sensation, largely localized in the skeletal muscles, and having both pleasant and unpleasant feeling tones. In a pilot study that we performed [29], the experience of anger, compared to that of depression and anxiety, was associated with greater optimism and a sense of control over outcomes. Unlike the pleasant affects studied (that is, love, joy, and calmness), however, anger was associated with greater pessimism, a marked feeling of unrelieved tension, and alienation from other people.

Having detailed the nature of the appraisal of outcomes reflected in anger, let us repeat the basic thesis: Anger occurs when a plan of action toward a valued goal is interrupted by an interference specific enough to be attacked. But as we shall point out later, anger does not lead on, willy-nilly, to attack. Still, the possibility of restoring the plan through attacking is part of the appraisal of outcomes signaled by anger.

Dashed Hopes and Anger in Humans

In humans the experience of anger often stems from dashed hopes. The lack of expected rewards in the example of "losing" an anticipated raise portrays this. Or take the example of an adolescent boy whose girl friend led him to believe that she would soon agree to having sex. He had courted her for several weeks and had spent all his earnings on her. But when he made his move, she refused. Furious, he retaliated, striking her across the face with an iron poker.

These examples of dashed hopes show that when a reward is expected but then is not received, anger is apt to occur. This lack of expected rewards is different from a physical obstacle or an antagonist that blocks the pursuit of a goal. In the example of the appearance of the enemy ship, while there is a blockade of the original plan, it is not just because expected rewards did not materialize. Such a blockade as the enemy ship opposes the carrying out of the plan. The lack of an expected reward, by contrast, does not necessarily come from someone or something's obstructing a plan. Rather the interruption comes from the failure to achieve an outcome that is required for completing or furthering one's plans. Dashed hopes thus stem from the lack of an expected positive outcome rather than the occurrence of a negative event. Since humans have extensive expectations for rewards relating to a host of different plans, they are especially vulnerable to dashed hopes and resultant anger.

Both dashed hopes and blockades give rise to frustration—that is, the initial feeling of distress when the pursuit of a goal is interrupted. The specific feeling that arises after the initial frustration depends on the appraisal of outcomes. Hence, as Lazarus [23] and Berkowitz [1] point out, not all frustration leads to anger and aggressive tendencies. If the block is a powerful antagonist or predator, fear is the probable reaction. If the block takes place at a time when the individual is not very sure about reaching the goal, disappointment rather than anger is apt to be felt. An interference usually gives rise to anger when the individual is highly committed to a plan of action and not only expects but also feels he deserves to reach the goal. The closer he is to the goal, the more likely it is that frustration will be followed by anger [24].

The expectation that one deserves to reach a goal stems from more than just being close to the goal. It also involves believing that the goal (1) has been earned—that considerable time has been invested in it, (2) has been promised by other individuals with whom there is an explicit or implicit contract, or (3) is long overdue in terms of having equal rights with other people. To *deserve* something thus touches on many of man's special attributes—his extended time sense, his interpersonal relations, and the social-moral codes of action through which he organizes his community living. In these areas other animals have only limited capacities. Yet man is capable of far-reaching temporal, interpersonal, and moral expectations. Because of them he is also especially vulnerable to dashed hopes within each of these arenas. Common examples, dealt with in the next sections, are these: (1) feeling rushed, delayed, or constricted; (2) feeling misunderstood; and (3) feeling righteous and wronged. Dashed hopes from these circumstances frequently give rise to anger because there is a reversal of optimism to pessimism, the belief that one can regain control over the outcome, and the expectation that one must set things right himself rather than rely on others.

It should be stressed that these circumstances for dashed hopes have been selected for discussion because they involve common expectations peculiar to humans. But they do not include all the types of dashed hopes experienced by man. Certainly, the hope for adequate food, water, and other physical necessities is common to both men and animals. People deprived of these elements will feel that fundamental strivings and needs have been thwarted. Anger and attack are likely to result, particularly if the people involved did not expect to be deprived. Since hunger arouses a desperate need upon which all other plans hinge, it perhaps has been the most frequent precipitant of anger and aggression in severely disadvantaged peoples. In this chapter, however, we shall restrict the discussion to some of the more subtle expectations that have become common in Western civilization.

FEELING RUSHED, DELAYED, OR CONSTRICTED

In the complex social organization of Western civilization, time has become an organizing principle par excellence. A host of plans have to be processed simultaneously. Therefore, a timetable of how and when these different goals will be reached governs a great deal of current and anticipated behaviors. Deadlines and appointment times, as well as new opportunities, have to be responded to at specified times. These timetables place demands on performance that often cannot be realized.

The frustration of being rushed—of having too much to accomplish within a short period of time—is a common precipitant of anger. Though man holds in mind many simultaneous plans and goals, he can act upon only one at a time or at most a very few. He usually has to focus his consciousness on one plan at one time. If he has enough time to act on one plan at a time, he may well have confidence that each of his goals will be realized. But if he has to accomplish many of these goals within a given period of time, his optimism for reaching the separate goals is often reversed to an overall pessimism, for he cannot do all things at once. Since a time limit often seems arbitrary and unnecessary, he is apt to get mad at those people who place time demands on him.

On the other hand, if he does not meet the required deadlines, others may get mad at him if the completion of their plans depends in turn on his accomplishments. Being held up or delayed makes the probability of reaching goals appear far off. The more distant an event is in the future, the less it is endowed with a sense of reality [19]—that is, the less likely it seems that the event will actually take place.

If possible future courses of action seem blocked and the person feels that he has few choices available, he is apt to feel constricted. Not only may he feel oppressed by those who limit him to only a few opportunities [9], but also any interference with the plans he is carrying out is apt to lead to anger, for to give them up would be to give up everything. Having few plans available makes one value those he has more highly. Under such circumstances he must restore the plans or lose all.

More than any other animal, man lives in an extended temporal domain. His "life-space" includes his foreseeable future—the choices open to him and the traditions that define what he can rightfully expect. He is likely to defend these temporal boundaries just as much as the land on which he lives. It is tempting to speculate that in the temporal domain feeling rushed and feeling constricted are respectively analogous to "crowding" and "transgression of territoriality" within the spatial realm. The latter spatial factors are well-known precipitants of aggression (see Chapter 1) and relate more to meeting basic survival needs than the examples of dashed hopes described here.

FEELING MISUNDERSTOOD

Bronowski [5] emphasizes that the capacity for extensive empathy is a trait which distinguishes man from other animals and also from any kind of conceivable robot or automaton. In terms of our model, empathy may be defined as the capacity to experience what another person is feeling with regard to *his* plans and goals, that is, *his* strivings and hopes. Most people feel that they deserve to be understood by at least someone in this way. But this expectation of empathy from another person is charged frequently with hopes that are rarely realizable in the adult. Getting a complete picture of another's view is impossible unless one has lived that person's life.

Yet since the expectation of empathy from those close to a person is often quite high, many individuals are vulnerable to having their hopes of being understood thwarted. Perhaps this expectation stems from transferring the illusion of complete understanding during earlier mother-infant interactions to later adult-adult relationships. Mere proximity to another person often carries with it the expectation that the other understands what most concerns the individual. Furthermore, he may expect this empathy without communicating his feelings. Paradoxically, attempts at communicating may lead to the discovery that the partner does not understand him. Consequently, the person then feels misunderstood by those he had hoped and expected to understand him the most. He becomes angry, for he is not getting what he felt he deserved. Perhaps this process accounts in part for the fact that the vast majority of homicides and acts of violence take place among couples, relatives, and close friends rather than between criminals (see Chapter 8). The disillusionment of not being understood is more apt to lead to dashed hopes and resultant anger in such close relationships.

Jealousy is a common instance of expecting empathy without clearly communicating one's feelings, needs, and strivings. For example, a husband may expect absolute fidelity from his wife and also may expect her to understand his need for such faithfulness without communicating the nature of this need. He expects her to understand what he does not want her to know, that is, his insecurity about being a man, something he may not be able to admit even to himself [41]. Since he may feel that she should understand his psyche even better than he does, her behavior becomes the mirror in which he expects to find a false, yet expanded image of himself. Thus the chances for feeling misunderstood are high. First, because of his hypermasculine facade she may not know of his need to be reassured that he is manly. Second, if she acknowledges this need, he may feel chagrined that she knows his feelings of inadequacy as a man. Third, if she dutifully plays the games of supporting his need for reassurance, he may be vaguely aware of the superficiality and lack of real understanding in the relationship. In each of these instances the husband may feel that he is not being understood in the way he deserves, partly because he is unaware or unsure of how completely he wants to be understood. The likelihood for dashed hopes, in terms of feeling misunderstood, are thus high.

The illusion of empathy is set up not only through personal contracts, such as marriage, but also on the basis of perceived similarities. Here the part is mistaken for or identified as the whole. For example, I am black, and you are black; therefore, you and I have similar, if not identical, hopes, strivings, and frustrations. In this instance there is little attempt to see the individual as an individual, apart from expectations I have for him by virtue of our identical race and similar backgrounds. The converse of this is also common: I am black, and you are white; therefore, I expect that you cannot understand, or even begin to understand, my feelings and goals. Moreover, though I do not expect you to be able to empathize, I believe that you should; and since I cannot expect you to do what you should do, you are thus against me. By not understanding me, you are not giving me what I deserve.

FEELING RIGHTEOUS AND WRONGED

Expecting fairness and equal rights with others is an ingrained aspect of moral development and is common to diverse cultures [21]. Morality involves the expectation that one's property, values, and sense of worth will not be trespassed or violated. What seems fair and just involves judgments of what the person feels he deserves in terms of rewards for meeting his own standards, and those of his fellows, relative to the benefits that others appear to be getting. These comparisons are difficult and lack firm criteria. The vagueness of the criteria makes the chances for dashed hopes quite high. Since certain individuals or groups often seem favored, the criteria seem to shift, making others feel that they are being maligned or wronged. A moral code, a shared plan of action, then seems interrupted and must be restored in order to make the pursuit of goals just and fair for all people.

The chances for feeling wronged are even greater during periods of rising expectations when promises, often laced with moral righteousness, are being made to disadvantaged peoples. Such groups have already felt wronged; they feel doubly wronged if promises are not fulfilled. To put off or take away their burgeoning hopes leaves them righteously indignant and, often understandably, ready to attack (see Chapter 6).

It is especially difficult in the vague area of human values to determine what is fair or unfair or whether hopes are being realized. Yet guiding religious, political, or ethical myths may be the individual's most prized possessions. When these values are challenged, it is similar to having one's territory threatened, for fundamental aspects of the self are being violated. William James [17] put it well: "In its widest possible sense, . . . a man's Self is the sum total of all that he CAN call his. . . ." And what is his includes, perhaps most importantly, what he believes in, for beliefs serve to sustain the pursuit of meaning and commitment into the future. To challenge them, or even not recognize them, threatens the self. Feeling wronged, the individual prepares to defend what he deems inalienable.

In summary, in addition to reflecting reactions to actual blockades in the pursuit of goals, anger often signals unfulfilled hopes and expectations. It is ironic that man's special capacities for foresight, empathy, and morality, all of which help him adapt to anticipated environments, nevertheless make him vulnerable to many forms of dashed hopes with resulting frustration and anger. Sustaining hope is necessary to sustain ongoing commitments, yet hopes are often misconstrued. When hopes fall through, others may be to blame, but more frequently it is because the hopes had little basis in reality.

Transformation of Anger into Attack

By *attack* we mean physical assault upon another person or upon the symbols that represent him. To review our basic thesis: Attacking takes place when alternate plans of action appear closed or when the expected rewards for attack override other outcomes. The function of attack is often defensive. As outlined in Figure 4, the aim of attack is to restore the interrupted plan by eliminating the interference. Attack can be functional, especially when other solutions such as modifying the plan or switching to another goal are indeed closed or highly infeasible. Also the threat of attack as a form of retaliation can protect territorial boundaries and keep in check the acquisition tendencies of other persons or groups. Thus attack or the threat of attack is functional, for example, in times of war or in certain subcultures, such as delinquent gangs [44]. Attack may be necessary for self-assertion in the interest of self-preservation. In this sense the capacity for attack likely has had an important adaptive function in the evolution of human behavior.

But in modern societies behaviors of physical attack are becoming increasingly maladaptive if long-range consequences are considered. How well we know that defensive threats lead to senseless military buildups which ultimately point nowhere except to mutual annihilation. Moreover, attack or the threat of attack disrupts collective, cooperative plans that have been and are now the keynote of man's adaptation. We can no longer pair off against one another in groups while at the same time justifying our defensive stance as a measure necessary for survival. In today's world the survival of one group ensures the survival of another, since the destruction of one group risks the destruction of another.

Although preservation of the self and reproduction of the species have been the organizing principles of organic evolution, there is no reason to assume that our collective consciousness must now serve only these same ends. For man adaptation no longer involves merely reacting to environmental changes. *Adaptation today requires producing changes through envisioning ultimate consequences.* One of these changes may be the necessity to counter excessive competitiveness resulting from biological evolution by replacing it with moral concern for the welfare of our fellows.

The reason for our writing this chapter was not just to gain a "scientific" understanding of the problem of violence but also to conceptualize the issues so that we might achieve some understanding and control over attacking behavior. Our ultimate concern is therefore moral: Violence is bad. And violence is bad not just because it runs the risk of mutual annihilation and is therefore maladaptive in the long run. Violence is bad also because it does not embrace man's highest potentialities.

But as history has shown, there is danger in morality. What is bad should be punished; those who attack should be attacked: These are far too common sentiments. Science tells us that punishment for acts done in the past is a poor deterrent for repeat performances unless we can foster the firm expectation that the consequences of such acts will indeed entail unfortunate outcomes in the future [33]. Yet our penal policies for the most part continue to punish deviants while neglecting the rehabilitation that would help them to appraise future consequences of their acts [14]. Our moral and penal codes thus could become enriched by scientific approaches. What we need are ways to understand how men become predisposed to attack and what makes them overlook such risks as retaliation. Knowing factors like these may enable us to take appropriate preventive and rehabilitative measures.

It is well known that anger frequently precedes attack. The physiological arousal accompanying anger prepares the organism for fighting. This is part of our evolutionary and biological heritage. Once this preparation for fighting takes place, the probability for attack is increased. Thus as outlined later, diminishing the circumstances that give rise to anger will decrease the frequency of attack. Sustaining realistic hope is fundamental to this.

But not all anger leads to attack. McKellar [26] has shown that in the vast majority of instances anger remains unexpressed. When it is expressed, it usually takes the form of verbal abuse and only infrequently that of physical attack. Moreover, even in these instances the object of attack is usually nonhuman. This is interesting in light of the fact that in 98 percent of the 250 angry instances analyzed by McKellar, a human adult was stated to be the cause of anger. These findings, along with a similar review by Lazarus [23], indicate that even when anger is being experienced, there are usually coexisting potent inhibitors of attack. Consideration of other outcomes, such as the risk of retaliation, social disapproval, or transgression of ethical standards, serves to keep assaultive motives in check.

It is when these other outcomes are not appraised sufficiently or when they are seen as less important than the restoration of the present ongoing plan that anger may lead to violence. Since the latter conditions often are met in circumstances of extreme hardship, war, or self-defense, attacking is understandable. In circumstances like these the rewards for attacking clearly are evident. Moreover, attack may not be preceded by anger in times of war or self-defense, for in these instances the violent act is often a trained response, that is, an automatic response to stimuli which are part of an ongoing plan. Here the stimuli do not interrupt the plan but rather are necessary for its continuance. Hence since there is no interruption, emotion and its accompanying affective signals may not occur. For example, if a soldier has been trained to shoot the enemy, the appearance of the enemy is necessary for carrying out that plan. He may then shoot the enemy without experiencing anger. By contrast he might get frustrated and angry if the enemy did *not* appear, for then his plan would be interrupted. But in many violent acts such as occur between close friends or during mob rule, the rewards are not explicit. These violent acts are thus difficult to understand. Various kinds of breakdown in the appraisal of outcomes, as discussed next, may help give us some insight into these acts of anger.

We shall deal with types of breakdown in the appraisal of outcome process most relevant and important to humans. Again as in the section on dashed hopes, breakdowns in the appraisal process can be classified as temporal, interpersonal, and social-moral. Within these categories the respective types of breakdowns in the appraisal of outcomes are as follows: (1) taking only the present view, (2) taking only the personal view, and (3) taking action exclusively as a goal itself. In these instances since the full impact of outcomes relevant to the situation is not considered, the expectation of what will happen is thus distorted. Moreover, since entire areas of outcomes are not considered during these distortions, alternate plans of action may seem nonexistent; restoring the plan of concern, rather than modifying it or switching to other goals, becomes the focus. Thus attacking the interference is seen as the act with the greatest payoff.

TAKING ONLY THE PRESENT VIEW

If there is an almost total focus on the present, the consideration of outcomes not immediately connected with the plan of present concern may not take place. Attention is then directed only to the short-range outcomes of the present plan, and the outcomes relevant to other plans and goals may be overlooked. With only the present view an interference to the present plan is magnified greatly. Eliminating the blockade becomes the all-consuming focus. Getting around it by modifying the present plan or adopting alternate plans are options that may not come to mind when attention is restricted only to the present. The tendency to attack the blockade thus is greatly enhanced.

Among the circumstances that give rise to an exclusive focus on the present are the use of intoxicating drugs, certain forms of acute mental illness, and hopelessness about having any control over the future. Chapter 12 points to the high incidence of violent acts during drug intoxication. This may be related in part to an exclusive focus on the present. For example, after ingestion of high doses of tetrahydrocannabinol, which is the active ingredient in marijuana and hashish, one study [32] demonstrated an almost total focus on the present. Also the ability to conceptualize future consequences was markedly impaired. Under the influence of this drug even minor stresses seemed total and never-ending to the subjects. Helpless and seemingly oppressed, their blissful, euphoric state transformed quickly into tendencies to attack or into terrifying fright, for they could not see beyond the immediacy of the present stress. As self-preservation in the present became the total focus, other plans, goals, and outcomes disappeared.

Similar to the effects of mind-altering drugs, greater concentration on the present is a feature of certain forms of acute mental illness, particularly paranoid delusional states and acute confusional psychoses [28]. Here the past and future may telescope into the present, so that memories and expectations become at least partially indistinguishable from present perceptions. Deprived of time perspective, the individual may react violently to internal stimuli, that is, memories and expectations, as though they were actually taking place in the here-and-now. This makes the evaluation of long-range consequences difficult and distorts the meaning and interpretation of immediate stimuli from the environment. Temporal distortions may account in part for the violent behavior that occurs during certain phases of mental illness, particularly acute paranoid psychosis and organic brain disease (see Chapter 1). Thus without the perspective of time and consequence, immediate stimuli can become extremely threatening and can lead to violence.

Hopelessness about reaching long-term goals is another factor that favors taking only the present view. Melges and Bowlby [27] have described the kinds of expectancies that underlie different types of hopelessness. For example, the hopelessness of the sociopath—a person disposed toward criminal acts—is characterized by a belief that his own actions will have little influence on what will happen to him in the long run (see Chapter 13). He therefore tends to seize what he can get in the present without regard for ultimate consequences and goals. Moreover, many delinquents become frightened when they begin to feel hope, for this feeling has been followed frequently by disappointment and abandonment in the past. Clinard [9] and others [44] point out that deviant acts occur more frequently in subcultures deprived of opportunities. This is a major factor in certain theories of delinquency [10]. Stated simply, the predisposition to attack an interference may stem from the attitude "It is useless to wait for other things to happen or to strive for far-off goals; I must get what I can get *now*."

Since the unpleasant aspects of anger provide an immediate internal stimulus that demands attention in the here-and-now, anger itself may lead to taking the present view. Taking action in order to relieve this pent-up tension may become the major concern. In correlating changes during acute mental illness, Melges and Fougerousse [28] found that as anger increased, an intensified focus on the present occurred. Similarly using normal subjects, Melges and Ochberg [30] found that the experience of anger was associated with a sensation of "present" being more stretched out; and there was little relation between the present and the past. Thus as the distress of anger increases, the individual may progressively restrict his attention to present concerns and to motives that would relieve the tension. Focus on current frustrations is increased even further when the person has lost his mental grasp of future consequences and extended goals as a result of using intoxicating drugs, from certain forms of acute mental illness, or from despair about long-term rewards. The deprivation of physiological needs (hunger, thirst, and so forth) is also a potent factor for taking only the present view, since restoring physiological equilibrium is a plan basic to survival.

TAKING ONLY THE PERSONAL VIEW

When the appraisal of outcomes is restricted to only those outcomes that concern the individual alone, the tendency to attack an interference is enhanced because (1) other people may seem to be unimportant except as obstacles or antagonists who are in the way of the completion of the person's own plan; (2) alternate solutions, necessitating cooperation from others, appear to be unavailable; and (3) there is little empathy for the plans and goals of other people— that is, other people's plans have little value compared to one's personal plan.

The circumstances that favor taking only the personal view are complex. We shall not deal with how ingrained attitudes of distrust and suspicion arise from early family interactions. Rather we shall give some examples of current situations that often accentuate the personal view. These factors center around heightened self-concern and the inability to compare one's own views with the views that others hold.

Heightened self-concern takes place when a basic biological need or basic value is threatened or violated. In Western civilization severe threat to biological needs (food, drink, sex, and so forth) is relatively rare compared to the challenge of difference in values. A value may be defined as a continuous goal that the individual tries to gain or keep [4]. Two of these values merit special mention—the maintenance of self-esteem and the sense of control over one's destiny.

When a person feels depreciated or misunderstood by others, his self-esteem is threatened. If he is made to feel like a second-class citizen, he may become concerned solely with his own advancement while neglecting the concerns of others. Similarly if he feels misunderstood, he may make no attempt to understand the views of those who fail to understand him. In these situations since he feels wronged by others, their views are something to contend with rather than to understand. Restoring his own sense of importance becomes the focus. This may lead to attacking those who have deprived him of his self-respect.

If a person feels that he no longer has any control over what will happen to him—if he feels his own actions will have little effect—he may then feel at the mercy of others. This feeling of not being able to help oneself, as with taking only the present view, can occur during certain forms of mental illness such as organic disorders of brain function. It also can occur when social oppression exists (see Chapter 6). Since the person essentially feels unable to direct himself toward his own goals, he feels unduly influenced by the demands of the immediate environment, particularly the demands of other people. This feeling of being influenced may culminate in a persecutory delusion [31]. But even with lesser degrees of distortion the feeling that one has little control over his own destiny may lead to attempts to restore oneself as an active agent. This may involve attacking those who appear to be influencing and controlling the individual.

Aside from heightened self-concern, restricting appraisal of outcomes to those outcomes that involve only oneself may stem from an inability to compare one's own views with the views of others. This inability to juxtapose the intentions and views of others with those of oneself may be at the root of what is commonly termed projection, that is, attributing one's own motives to others. Melges, Tinklenberg, and Fougerousse [31] describe how deficits in short-term memory impair a person's ability to simultaneously keep in mind his view of himself, his view of others, and his interpretation of their view of him. Deficits in short-term memory have been demonstrated in organic brain disease [13], during psychotomimetic intoxication [32], and in schizophrenia [8]. These deficits may lead to projection in the following manner: If an individual's short-term memory is so evanescent that he loses his view of himself whenever he attempts to think about how others see him, one of two things may result: (1) He will see himself almost exclusively in terms of how he expects others to view him, or (2) he will cling to his own view of himself in order to preserve his sense of identity. In either case because he is unable to compare these various views, that is, because he is unable to hold them simultaneously in mind long enough to make comparisons, he is left with a highly personalized picture of himself and the world, relatively unmodified by the views of others. Moreover, if he clings to his self-view, he is apt to see others only in terms of this personal view. Hence he frequently projects: He sees others as carbon copies of himself. Through such a process the appraisal of outcomes in relation to other people is reduced to include only personal concerns. In short, there is a failure to empathize.

This state may make a person feel that others are out for themselves only, just as he is. This may lead him to distrust others. In fact, his own suspicious behavior may provoke suspicion in others [7]. A spiral of increasing distrust and mutual hostility may emerge with each defensive stance progressively reinforcing the suspicions about the other's malevolence [22, 43]. In effect, distrust breeds distrust, so that attacking the other may seem necessary to defend the self.

TAKING ACTION AS A GOAL IN ITSELF

While taking only the present view and personal view limits attention to the interferences with the present plan and makes alternate plans appear closed, the motive to eliminate the interference must be expected to lead to desired outcomes if attack is to take place. When the act of attacking is associated with anticipated rewards, then the performance of this act may become a goal in itself. But note that the anticipated rewards may not be derived solely from restoring the original plan and reaching the original goal. These rewards may be associated with attacking itself, so that *to attack* becomes the goal. It is then that the original goal of the plan initially interrupted may no longer be considered. The uncanny thrill of attacking, known to combatants, soldiers, and athletes, may be rooted in these associated rewards. Of course one must keep in mind that acts *in* anger may become pleasantly toned as the interference is eliminated [40], since the subjective probability of reaching the original goal is increased. But the appraisal of this outcome relates to the original interrupted plan and goal. Distortion in the appraisal process, however, arises when the act of attack becomes an exclusive end in itself rather than a means to an end.

Attacking itself may thus become a goal when attack is immediately associated with either the relief of negative feelings or the arousal of positive feelings or both. The relief of negative feelings revolves around the riddance of the unpleasant tension of anger and the change from passivity and aimlessness to activity and pursuit. We have already pointed out how the experience of anger prompts the motive to attack and also physiologically prepares the organism for fighting. Since the muscles are ready to fight, inhibiting this action leads to conflict and mounting tension. The act of physically attacking relieves some of this tension. Through past experience this relief may become associated with attacking and thereby become a desired outcome in itself. Similarly if a person feels oppressed and passive (that is, not being in control of his own destiny), to attack may give the illusion of control and self-direction. Since many oppressed people and, in the abnormal form, deviant individuals, have few if any positive goals to pursue, that is, have little to be *for*, they discover a sense of identity and purpose through finding something to be *against*. To oppose, and often to attack, restores the sense of self-direction.

This reorientation toward a goal makes the person feel less stultified. The act of attacking may do more than just relieve negative feelings; it may arouse a sense of power, righteousness, or belonging. When a violent act produces a tangible, visible effect, the violator may experience a sense of efficacy and power. He can do something; he sees that he can have an effect. And the effect need only be just that—something happening right now, usually something visibly powerful, such as fear induced in others, a stunned body, a falling building, or a street burning. He then feels "on the make" rather than passive and weak. In such a state the presence of instruments of attack—guns, knives, and so forth—may stimulate their use as a means toward greater power (see Chapter 8).

Another immediate reward for attacking is the sense of setting things right. If a person feels wronged, he may feel compelled to take revenge, even though such an act has little relevance to his other ultimate goals. During revenge, attacking becomes a goal itself. In line with the law of the talion—an eye for an eye, a tooth for a tooth—the attacker feels that he is acting righteously. However illusory, this moral self-image is immediately rewarding. Violence in the name of justice and morality can lead to tragic acts, such as severe child-beating by a parent. As Steele and Pollock [39] point out, parents who attack their children in this way feel that they have acted righteously—the child's will must be broken, he must be whipped into respecting his parents, and so forth. Even when the child has suffered fractures of the skull or limbs, many of these parents still feel that they "did right."

During riots and mob rule there is often an interaction among the feelings of righteous indignation, power, and belonging. As more and more individuals join in, each member begins to feel that he is right for acting on his angry impulses. Before long the taste of power arising from sheer numbers replaces striving for the original goal. In addition, group support helps minimize the risks to the individual by diffusing responsibility among others [20]. At the same time, group pressure makes it more difficult for the individual to back out for fear of losing face. The immediate rewards of attack, through the expanded self-images of righteousness, power, and belonging, usurp personal wisdom and foresight.

Summary

Anger occurs when a plan of action is interrupted by an interference specific enough to be potentially identified and attacked. Like all affects, anger reflects a subjective probability in reaching goals. The nature of the subjective probability, which differentiates anger from other affects, lies in the way in which outcomes of reaching goals are being appraised. Anger occurs when this appraisal consists of a reversal of optimism to pessimism brought on by an external interference that in turn the individual feels he can eliminate through his own actions.

Instead of a modification of the plan or a switch to another goal, the emotional appraisal of outcomes reflected in the affect of anger prompts a motive to restore the interrupted plan by eliminating the interference (see Fig. 4). Attacking the interference takes place when alternate plans of action appear closed or when expected rewards for attack override other outcomes.

The understanding of both anger and attack is enhanced by categorizing some of the common outcomes with which man is concerned. Aside from meeting his physical needs of hunger, thirst, and so forth, man is concerned with extensive temporal, interpersonal, and social-moral expectations and outcomes. In these realms he may become angry if actual outcomes do not meet his expectations. Hence anger often stems from dashed hopes when men (1) feel rushed, delayed, or constricted in the temporal realm, (2) feel misunderstood by other people, and (3) feel righteous and wronged in terms of prevailing social-moral expectations. Although anger also arises when a person is actively obstructed or opposed, the lack of expected rewards (dashed hopes) is perhaps just as frequent in precipitating anger in humans.

Once anger is experienced, whether arising from various kinds of dashed hopes or actual blockades, it prompts the motive to attack and prepares the organism for fighting. When anger is experienced by humans, however, only infrequently does it lead to attack. Although attacking may be functional when it is indeed the only way out of a situation, the motive to attack may be enhanced by distortions in the appraisal of temporal, interpersonal, and social-moral outcomes.

These distortions are (1) taking only the present view, (2) taking only the personal view, and (3) taking action as an exclusive goal itself. Many violent acts, except for those that are trained or socially expected responses, most often stem from an *interaction* of these distorted appraisals.

Conclusion: What to Do

Before making some general recommendations in terms of the model presented here, we must caution that expecting simple solutions for complex problems is an unrealistic hope which in itself is apt to lead to disappointment and anger. Similarly expecting immediate changes, without taking sufficient time to understand the issues and to work for long-term effects, may give rise to even greater frustration and anger.

If the model for anger and attack presented here is valid, reducing the incidence of violence may be accomplished by greater conscious awareness of those factors herein specified as leading to anger and attack. This understanding might allow for greater mastery and control over the unwitting aspects of these phenomena. More specifically, if we decrease the frequency of anger, we decrease the tendency to attack; and if we decrease distortions in the appraisal of outcomes of reaching goals, we may help prevent acting on angry impulses. To do this, the key thing is to sustain hope within the temporal, interpersonal, and social-moral arenas of human concern. Sustaining hope in these areas centers around three general factors: (1) enhancing the long-range view by making the subjective probability of reaching personal goals, such as maintaining self-respect and staving off hunger, quite high; (2) teaching and rewarding the capacity for empathy and making understanding resource people available to distressed individuals; (3) stripping attack of its immediate rewards while at the same time reinforcing behaviors that attempt to get around an interference rather than destroy it. Individuals should be taught that in the face of an interference with personal goals, the emotional appraisal should essentially include the long-range interpersonal outcomes and that the motive to attack should be replaced by seeking alternate solutions. These techniques and attitudes can be learned.

Thus preventing violence may ultimately depend on the emotional training we give our children. Educating the young, along with their parents, in our school systems about such matters might be accomplished by emphasizing role taking, rehearsing appropriate responses to anger and other emotions, and encouraging sportsmanlike conduct in athletic pursuits. Emotional training should have an equal status to intellectual development in our schools. The post-Sputnik boom in scholastic excellence unfortunately has been motivated by a defense against attack. It is time to learn to cope with the defense itself.

Using an evolutionary framework, Bowlby [3] argues that bonds between members of a socially organized species originally served the function of protection from predators. The group protects its members. Yet for modern man the functions of social bonding stretch far beyond mere defensive operations; it is through social bonds that transmission of cumulative knowledge has been possible. As Dobzhansky [11] points out, it is along these lines of a "superorganic evolution" that mankind is making its greatest strides. It is now important that our social bonding become enriched by the knowledge of how and what others are feeling and striving for, lest mankind's greatest strides tumble him into catastrophic obscurity. In short, our bonds must become less defensive and more extensive, encompassing the foreseeable futures of all peoples.

References

1. Berkowitz, L. (Ed.). *Roots of Aggression: A Re-examination of the Frustration-Aggression Hypothesis.* New York: Atherton, 1968.
2. Block, J. Studies in the phenomenology of emotions. *Journal of Abnormal and Social Psychology* 54:354, 1957.
3. Bowlby, J. *Attachment and Loss.* Vol. 1: *Attachment.* London: Hogarth, 1969.
4. Branden, N. Emotions and values. *The Objectivist* 5:1, 1966.
5. Bronowski, J. *The Identity of Man.* New York: American Museum of Science, 1966.
6. Bull, N., and Gidro-Frank, L. Emotions induced and studied in hypnotic subjects. II. *Journal of Nervous and Mental Disease* 112:97, 1950.
7. Cameron, N. The development of paranoic thinking. *Psychological Review* 50:219, 1943.
8. Chapman, J., and McGhie, A. A comparative study of disordered attention in schizophrenia. *Journal of Mental Science* 108:487, 1962.
9. Clinard, M. B. (Ed.). *Anomie and Deviant Behavior.* New York: Free Press, 1964.
10. Cloward, R. A., and Ohlin, L. E. *Delinquency and Opportunity: A Theory of Delinquent Gangs.* New York: Fress Press, 1960.
11. Dobzhansky, T. *Mankind Evolving.* New Haven: Yale University Press, 1962.

12. Engel, G. L. Anxiety and depression-withdrawal: The primary affects of unpleasure. *International Journal of Psychoanalysis* 43:89, 1962.

13. Engel, G. L., and Romano, J. Delirium, a syndrome of cerebral insufficiency. *Journal of Chronic Disease* 9:260, 1959.

14. Halleck, S. L. *Psychiatry and the Dilemmas of Crime.* New York: Hoeber Med. Div., Harper & Row, 1967.

15. Hamburg, D. A., and Adams, J. E. A perspective in coping behavior. *Archives of General Psychiatry* 17:277, 1967.

16. Holloway, R. L., Jr. Human Aggression: The Need for a Species-Specific Framework. In Fried, M., Harris, M., and Murphy, R. (Eds.), *War: The Anthropology of Armed Conflict and Aggression.* New York: Natural History Press, 1968.

17. James, W. *The Principles of Psychology,* vol. 1. New York: Dover, 1950.

18. Kardiner, A., Kurush, A., and Ovesey, L. A methodological study of Freudian theory. *International Journal of Psychiatry* 2(1):489, 1966.

19. Klineberg, S. L. Future time perspective and a preference for delayed reward. *Journal of Personality and Social Psychology* 8:253, 1968.

20. Kogan, N., and Wallach, M. A. Risk-taking as a Function of the Situation, the Person, and the Group. In *New Directions in Psychology III.* New York: Holt, Rinehart & Winston, 1967.

21. Kohlberg, L. Development of Moral Character and Ideology. In Hoffman, M. L. (Ed.), *Review of Child Development Research.* New York: Russell Sage Foundation, 1964.

22. Laing, R. D., Phillipson, H., and Lee, A. R. *Interpersonal Perception.* London: Tavistock, 1966.

23. Lazarus, R. S. *Psychological Stress and the Coping Process.* New York: McGraw-Hill, 1966.

24. Lewin, K. Time Perspective and Morale. In Watson, G. (Ed.), *Civilian Morale.* Boston: Houghton Mifflin, 1942.

25. McKay, D. M. Cerebral Organization and the Conscious Control of Action. In Eccles, J. C. (Ed.), *Brain and Conscious Experience.* New York: Springer, 1966.

26. McKellar, P. The emotion of anger in the expression of human aggressiveness. *British Journal of Psychology* 39:148, 1949.

27. Melges, F. T., and Bowlby, J. Types of hopelessness in psychopathological process. *Archives of General Psychiatry* 20:690, 1969.

28. Melges, F. T., and Fougerousse, C. E. Time sense, emotions, and acute mental illness. *Journal of Psychiatric Research* 4:127, 1966.

29. Melges, F. T., and Harris, R. F. Subjective dimensions of emotion. In preparation.

30. Melges, F. T., and Ochberg, F. M. Affective arousal and time sense in normal subjects. In preparation.

31. Melges, F. T., Tinklenberg, J., and Fougerousse, C. E. Paranoid delusions—possible mechanisms. In preparation.

32. Melges, F. T., Tinklenberg, J., Hollister, L., and Gillespie, H. Tetrahydrocannabinol (marihuana extract) and time sense. In preparation.

33. Menninger, K. *The Crime of Punishment*. New York: Basic Books, 1968.
34. Miller, G. A., Galanter, E., and Pribram, K. H. *Plans and the Structure of Behavior*. New York: Henry Holt, 1960.
35. Plutchik, R. *The Emotions: Facts, Theories, and a New Model*. New York: Random House, 1962.
36. Pribram, K. H., and Melges, F. T. Psychophysiological Basis of Emotion. In Vinken, P. J., and Bruyn, G. W. (Eds.), *Handbook of Clinical Neurology*. Disorders of Higher Nervous Activity, vol. 3. Amsterdam: North Holland, 1969.
37. Rotter, J. B. Generalized expectancies for internal versus external control of reinforcement. *Psychological Monographs* 80:1, 1966.
38. Scott, J. P. *Aggression*. Chicago: University of Chicago Press, 1958.
39. Steele, B. F., and Pollock, C. G. A Psychiatric Study of Parents Who Abuse Infants and Small Children. In Helfer, P. E., and Kempe, C. H. (Eds.), *The Battered Child*. Chicago: University of Chicago Press, 1968.
40. Titchener, E. B. *An Outline of Psychology*. New York: Macmillan, 1896.
41. Vauhkonen, K. On the pathogenesis of morbid jealousy. *Acta Psychiatrica Scandinavica*, Supplement No. 202, 1968.
42. Wiener, N. *Cybernetics*. Cambridge, Mass.: M.I.T. Press, 1948.
43. White, R. K. Misperception and the Vietnam war. *Journal of Social Issues* 22:1, 1966.
44. Wolfgang, M. E., and Ferracuti, F. *The Subculture of Violence*. London: Social Science, 1967.

5. Alternatives to Violence

STRATEGIES FOR COPING WITH SOCIAL CONFLICT

Frederic W. Ilfeld, Jr., M.D.,
and Richard J. Metzner, M.D.

Collective violence is considered by many to be a viable strategy for resolving social conflicts on both the national and international scenes. The purposes of this chapter are first to highlight some limitations of this view and next to offer several alternative strategies with high potential for success. In doing this, several differing concepts of "social conflict" are reviewed. Then the functions and limitations of collective violence are considered. The major portion of this chapter is devoted to exploring alternate strategies for handling social conflict. In particular, mechanisms for enhancing group solidarity and for promoting effective social protest and change are discussed. Many examples will be taken from the American racial crisis. This is done because American racism provides a good illustration of the phenomenon of social conflict and is a critical issue currently facing our society.

Dimensions of Social Conflict

Conflict is related to our parent topic of violence in that violence is one method of expression of social conflict and is one possible means of its resolution. As used in this chapter, the term *social conflict* refers to incompatibility or antagonism between groups of persons rather than that within an individual or between individuals.

129

(Individual conflict is treated in Chapter 2, Chapter 4, Chapter 11, and Chapter 13.) Our focus here is upon intergroup competition or incompatibility rather than intrapsychic or interpersonal conflict. Such intergroup conflict may occur among groups in a community, between communities, or between different nations and societies. Behaviorally it is manifest in several culturally patterned ways: physical aggression including violence, verbal dispute, covert verbal attack (ridicule, blame, gossip), breach of expectations, avoidance, and separation. Attitudes accompanying such behavior include hostility and negative images or stereotypes. (For a broader and more extended discussion of human conflict than this chapter can encompass, see two studies on the nature of conflict [25, 31].)

The sources of social conflict are many, with a representative list being Le Vine's [28]. Competition for scarce resources (goods or status), physical proximity, ambiguity over one's role or status in a group, absence of authoritative and legitimate rules for resolving conflicts, certain child-training practices, and adult stresses and frustrations are some potential antecedents to conflict. What should be noted here is the similarity of many of these antecedents to those of violence. A most prominent and important source of intergroup conflict is that described by Sherif's group [42] in their studies with teams of young boys in a summer camp setting. In their field experiment described later in this chapter, neither cultural, physical, nor economic differences were found to be necessary for the rise of intergroup conflict; nor were maladjusted, neurotic, or unstable tendencies necessary conditions for the appearance of intergroup prejudice and stereotypes. The sufficient condition for the rise of hostile and aggressive deeds was merely the existence of two groups competing for goals that only one group could obtain, to the dismay and frustration of the other group. Social conflict developed from these mutually exclusive goals.

The sort of conflict manifest in Sherif's boys groups can be considered realistic or rational in contrast to unrealistic or irrational conflict [13]. The term *rational conflict* refers to situations in which one's goals are made more difficult or impossible to attain through the efforts of some real opposing agent. Here conflict arises from frustration of specific, conscious expectations, and efforts are directed at countering the opposing agent. In rational conflict there exist functional alternative strategies for resolving the conflict; there are different avenues for solving the problem or reaching the goal. Contrasting with this are *irrational conflicts*, which are related not to the mutual goals of the antagonists but to the need for psychological tension release on the part of either or both of them. Irrational conflict has its primary source outside of the ongoing interaction of the opponents. Psychological tension is channeled onto the other party through such defense mechanisms as displacement and projection. Displacement involves tension release against a substitute rather than the provoking object. Projection entails attributing one's own tensions and feelings to others. The significance of irrational conflict is that here the opponent serves primarily as a target for tension release, and alternative strategies of resolving the conflict are limited in number and are not usually conscious. Thus in this chapter when alternate *strategies* to social conflict are discussed, they apply to *rational* conflict alone.

Another distinction to be made is that between tolerance of social conflict and its resolution. The difference involves more than semantics. In one view, that of *conflict resolution*, social conflict is viewed as a maladaptive outcome and as disruptive. It is thought to be produced by an interaction of strains and stresses within the social system and is something of which one wishes to be rid. On the other hand, the *conflict tolerance* view considers conflict as inevitable and as necessary for the maintenance and integration of social systems [12, 22]. For example, conflict helps to create and modify cultural standards of behavior; it produces new and energetic leadership; it provides a means of assessing relative strength; it gives increased cohesion to each of the rival groups; conflicting multiple group memberships provide social stability and prevent polarization (see next section).

Actually, it should be noted that neither the conflict resolution nor the conflict tolerance view is by itself wholly descriptive. In some contexts conflict is disrupting, while in others it is facilitating. As the reader will see, at times conflict needs to be resolved, and at times it requires tolerance. In our view the deciding criterion is whether or not the integrity of the system is threatened. In general, conflicts in which the contending parties do not share the basic values on which the legitimacy of the larger social system rests tend to threaten the disruption of the structure. Where the basic goals, values, and interests of the larger social system are agreed upon by its component groups, then social conflict may make possible the readjustment of rules and power within the social system in accordance with the needs and feelings of its individual members or subgroups.

Uses and Limitations
of Collective Violence

Inasmuch as violence is one mode of conflict resolution, we turn now from a discussion of social conflict to a consideration of the positive and the negative aspects of collective violence. Before assessing its limitations, we should first acknowledge the so-called useful or functional aspects of violence. As catalogued by Coser [13] and expanded upon in Chapter 6, these functions are severalfold. First, violence may be a means of achievement to those persons whose legitimate channels to opportunity are barred. Violence in this sense provides an opportunity for the oppressed and downtrodden individuals or groups for affirming their identity and for claiming full manhood. A second function of violence is that of a danger signal. Here the incidence of violence serves as a barometer of the degree of frustration prevalent in a society. The assumption is made, of course, that man resorts to violent action only under extremely frustrating, self-threatening, and anxiety-producing conditions. This assumption is not wholly correct; cultures may have a tradition of violence that bears no relation to frustration [48]. A final function of violence is that of a catalyst toward increased group solidarity; an external enemy engenders high cohesiveness among members of the threatened group.

For all these uses of violence one general point deserves mention—that alternative paths besides violence may achieve the same goals. Violence is not intrinsic to the achievement of masculinity or the self-realization of man. It need not be the only type of feedback that alerts society to its shortcomings. There are other effective methods of promoting group solidarity besides use of violence. Violence is not the only means to these ends, and the central aim of this chapter is to point out some of the alternate paths. But first the limitations of violence should be underscored.

Violence furthers group polarization. It increases the distance between groups in emotional understanding and in communication. If one group employs violence, the opponent is likely to retaliate in kind. Violence, whether legal or not, begets more violence. Besides counterviolence, anger, and repression, the use of violence produces fear. Such fear stifles the adversary's moral conscience and creates mistrust. It also serves to undermine in the opponent's view the legitimacy of the very goals for which one is fighting. In such an atmosphere of collective violence with its attending misunderstanding, anger, counterviolence, fear, lack of trust, and lessened legitimacy of the opponent's aims, it is clear that successful collaboration or negotiation is immeasurably more difficult.

A second limitation of violence is that if it is employed successfully by either an individual or a group—such as the use of war in the birth of our nation—then it may be increasingly relied upon for handling other conflicts. With continued success in the use of violence, whether it be in robbing banks or coercing other nations, one will come to rely increasingly upon it as an effective strategy. Violence, even when used for a "noble" cause, is ultimately self-corrupting. Although we have been taught that "fighting for one's freedom" is a virtue, we should still recognize that the very process itself makes a society more willing to embark upon the institutionalized violence of warfare as the solution in future endeavors.

A third limitation is a pragmatic one. In certain circumstances collective violence simply does not succeed in achieving desired goals. One must have substantial physical force, adequate resources, and sufficient determination. Such a limitation pertains less in the case of assassination and guerrilla tactics than in the case of open warfare.

A fourth limitation is the obvious one of significant waste and disruption for both contending parties. The loss of manpower and materials in the First World War was far too enormous to justify the end result. Vietnam has eroded the human and natural resources of all the concerned parties, yet the conflict remains unresolved. Also on the international front the specter of escalation to mutual destruction from nuclear weapons is a major barrier to the use of nuclear warfare in resolving conflict.

Finally, one must discern the destructive *long-term* effects of violence—repression, fear, mistrust. Distinction should be drawn between the short-term results of violence, which are often favorable, and its long-term consequences, which are in most cases unfavorable. Violence is shortsighted; it is not sufficiently future-oriented. Particularly in this country, with our desire for immediacy and the prominence of the "now" generation, short-term effects appear more salient than long-term consequences.

All five limitations are pertinent to dissident groups advocating violence in the United States. The use of violence undermines the legitimacy of goals; one's rival is less likely to sympathize or try to appreciate one's view. Violence is met with counterviolence, repression, misunderstanding, and divisiveness. Such increased group polarization may be desirable if one is in the American Colonies fighting against the British or if one is fighting for Algerian independence against France. It is not functional, for instance, when fighting for black independence in this country unless one is working toward eventual black separatism. Violence cannot achieve effective long-term change within a nation without risking mistrust, fear, and repression. Successful alternatives for resolving social conflict and securing meaningful social change must be found and taught.

Incomplete Strategies for Intergroup Conflict Resolution

Many traditional modes of resolving conflict have notable shortcomings. Such incomplete strategies include blaming the opponent, disseminating information or encouraging personal contact, holding conferences of leaders, escaping from the conflict situation, and practicing the policy of deterrence.

The casting of blame onto the opposing group leads mainly to a vicious cycle of recriminations. Collaboration is rarely aided by blaming the other side. When we have publicly dubbed a group as an "enemy," their persistent pursuit of their own ends is "evidence" that they are cold and calculating, which justifies our conclusion that there is no point in trying to cooperate.

It is often maintained that social conflict can be ameliorated by the dissemination of "accurate" (i.e., favorable) information to each of the contending groups to correct misperceptions about each other. While this seems logical enough, it does not always occur in practice. Psychological research [18] about perception and attitude change shows that favorable information about one's acknowledged adversary is either ignored or is reinterpreted to fit one's own designs.

Similarly, more intense exposure, such as face-to-face relations and other personal contact situations, is not invariably productive of increased tolerance. Prior prejudices and stereotypes are not automatically dissolved by personal contact alone. Contact may breed contempt as well as friendship, particularly when there are mutually exclusive goals for the participants. On the other hand, contact can reduce intergroup hostility when rivals meet in pursuit of a vital purpose that grips all participants. The conditions of the contact situation are crucial [35]. For instance, attitude change may occur at lesser levels of intimacy but meet with resistance at high levels of intimacy [47]. Gordon Allport [1] in his intensive review of intergroup contact research concluded that four characteristics of the contact situation are of the utmost importance. Prejudice is lessened when the two groups (1) possess equal status in the situation, (2) seek common goals, (3) are cooperatively dependent upon each other, and (4) interact with the positive support of authorities, laws, or custom. To this list of beneficial conditions might be added contact over a prolonged time period and contact particularly among the younger members of opposing groups.

A limitation of conferences of leaders in settling intergroup conflicts is that a leader is bound to the goals and norms of his group. It has been found that a negotiator's role in his reference group (i.e., whether a leader or a delegate) affects the way in which he represents that group in bargaining with other representatives [24]. Still, first and foremost, he must be loyal to his own group, otherwise he will be rejected as its leader or representative. Thus there are obvious restraints on leaders, inasmuch as they must embody and uphold their own group sentiments. While leaders cannot act totally as free agents in negotiating situations, still they have several very important roles in reducing social conflict. Information can be exchanged firsthand at conferences of leaders, thereby reducing the chances of misunderstanding. Also leaders can alert their peoples to whatever overriding and common goals exist among men (see later section).

Evasion—escape or separation—is effective in temporarily avoiding social conflict by the removal of one of the contending parties. Where no proximity or cooperation is necessary between the opposing parties, this strategy may be functional, but such conditions are not always met. An example of evasion as a means of avoiding social conflict is seen in our nonrecognition of Red China.

The practice of "deterrence" is in this country a widely propounded means of circumventing violent confrontations both on the national and international scenes. It assumes that one is facing an enemy whose intent is hostile and that fighting can be avoided if one or the other can amass superior capabilities to threaten the opponent. The stability of deterrence assumes that each side can quite accurately identify the adversary and assess both his capabilities to injure and the seriousness of his intent to carry out threats.

The flaws in the strategy of deterrence by armed superiority are several. Perception and accurate prediction of the enemy's resources and intent are influenced by one's feelings toward him and are hindered by poor communication with him. Studies on human judgment show that an opponent's position on a particular issue is appraised by group members as more extreme than it is. This distortion occurs through a contrast effect, in which the difference between the out-group's position and one's own is exaggerated. Similarities are obscured. The principles of human judgment and perception are such that an "enemy" who is inferior to us in power is seen as more inadequate than he really is; but when he begins to approach our power, his power is seen as equal or greater than our own. Thus where opponents have nearly equal strength, escalation of weapons is sure to follow, both because of the distorted perception caused by fear that one's enemy is stronger and because of the necessity to convincingly threaten the enemy that one will successfully retaliate if attacked.

Deterrence cannot correct for distorted perception or "accidents"; it cannot limit escalation; threats and intimidations that are required to keep the enemy at bay only serve to intensify group polarization and mistrust and may precipitate open warfare. Open conflict and "show of force" are felt by many to be necessary intermittently to display one's strength and to convince the enemy of one's determination. The practice of deterrence by armed superiority at best produces a temporary and unstable equilibrium.

A strategy avoiding many of these pitfalls is that of deterrence based on *sufficiency* of arms. Here arms are built up to the point where successful retaliation can be achieved, but weaponry for the sake of matching or surpassing the enemy's overkill potential is not attempted. This approach is theoretically possible in our age of nuclear weapons. Still the natural temptations to further "protect" oneself or symbolically defeat one's opponent by amassing more or superior weapons is difficult to resist. Also the outbreak of nuclear war by misunderstanding or accident remains a possibility.

Strategies for Social Cohesion and Control

OVERRIDING AUTHORITY

The use of political-legal structures is perhaps the most widely recognized and understood means of conflict resolution. In all societies there are formalized procedures for handling conflict that are imbedded in custom or a code of law, and these laws and customs are held by the populace to be legitimate. It is this legitimation, the acknowledgment of the reality and genuineness of law, that turns social power and control into acceptable social authority. Naturally, the use of law for social cohesion is operative only within a defined political territory. The citizens of San Francisco and of Boston are beholden to the federal laws of our country, but there are no such formal rules governing the relationships between the people of London and the people of Peking. The ultimate application of the strategy of overriding authority is seen in the frequent proposals for a world community based on law.

The basic precondition for overriding authority, whether it be in a classroom or on a national or international scale, is a moral consensus—the acceptance by all concerned parties of the legitimacy of the rules that govern their conduct and of the means for resolving conflicts that arise. Authority without moral consensus has two options: use of force or propaganda to restrain dissident elements, or change in policy and authority structure to include dissidents. Increasingly minority groups such as college students and the black population in this country are questioning old authorities and policies, at least in part because they have not had the opportunity to participate in the formation of such policy. Our national ethics dictate that legitimacy arises from active participation—this is the core of democracy. Yet we are still far from attaining full and representative participation of all groups in the decision-making process in this country.

ENHANCING GROUP IDENTITY AND PRIDE

A second means of providing social cohesion and control is by solidifying a group's identity and enhancing its members' pride [23]. Such a process unites the subfactions of the larger group into a more cohesive whole. On the other hand, it inherently neither reduces nor increases the propensity for conflict and violence with outside groups. For instance, enhanced national identity and pride, while reducing internal conflict, do not necessarily decrease the potential for conflict with other nations.

In the formation of a new positive identity, the symbols of this identity are all important, as for instance in the use of the term *black* rather than *Negro*. Black has come to stand for meaning in one's heritage and worth in one's being; Negro, conversely, is felt by many to refer to the degrading background of slavery and the impotency of second-class citizenship. Critical to the formation of new identity with its attending symbols and group pride is acceptance by outsiders. For example, blacks want and need to be seen by others as unique and important people. This does not necessarily mean that they want to secede from this country or are trying to prove themselves superior to others. Old self-images of Negro inferiority must be destroyed before a new commitment to their own pride and power emerges. Besides the changing of symbols and acceptance by others, a new identity must be consolidated with a historical elaboration of one's own uniqueness and worth. It is no wonder then that in our black population there is an upsurge in the desire for learning black history, black culture, and black languages such as Swahili. Such efforts to place one's new identity in a meaningful historical perspective are productive of increased self-esteem and should be supported. Finally, the emerging self-image must be fostered and encouraged by the surrounding social system. In the case of the black man, if he is provided no productive avenues for his increasing self-confidence and sense of worth, then violence is imminent. Hopes and expectations will have been raised without fulfillment. Ways of bettering oneself and one's community must be available to support and enhance the new identity.

OVERLAPPING GROUP MEMBERSHIPS

A major way of increasing social cohesion and controlling social disruption is one that goes unappreciated by the average observer. This is because it is largely an informal or unplanned strategy in contrast to political authority and legal planning. Such a strategy may be termed *overlapping group memberships*, in that persons belong to a variety of groups whose memberships intersect and overlap. Thus loyalties are divided; individuals place only part of their efforts into each group; basic societal cleavages along one axis with the attending threat of open conflict are avoided because one belongs to at least some of the same groups as one's adversary. There is an interlocking of group memberships with a multiplicity of loyalties and conflicts. In such a situation one conflict is less likely to cut through and polarize the group.

The importance of this phenomenon for providing social cohesion is described in several disciplines: political science [14], anthropology [22], and sociology [11, 12]. Different authors use various terms, such as structural pluralism, crisscrossing group memberships, and multiple group affiliations, but the concept of overlapping affiliations preventing intergroup polarization remains the same. Such affiliations may be based on a variety of characteristics—for example, sex, age, kinship, race, marital status, parenthood, religion, political allegiance, residence, occupation, avocations, and income.

The important questions posed to social and behavioral scientists are, first, which groups are most demanding of one's loyalties and hence most relevant for containing conflict. Next it must be determined how the membership of these groups is distributed throughout society. If one particular subgroup is not sharing a sufficient number of important group memberships with other parts of society, the chances are greater for its alienation, misunderstanding, and open conflict. It is felt by many people that this has been the case, for instance, with minority racial groups in this country. They are separated from the rest of society not only by race but also involuntarily by residence, occupation, income, and many voluntary associations such as social clubs. Another issue to which social scientists might profitably address themselves is the delineation of those factors which encourage and foster the development of overlapping group memberships. Specific techniques for promoting overlapping memberships should be investigated and applied.

SUPERORDINATE GOALS

Superordinate goals have been defined by Sherif [41] as those goals that have a compelling appeal for members of each group but which neither group can achieve without participation of the other. All parties concerned are interdependent in accomplishing a task or achieving an end state that they each desire.

Sherif asserts that such a sense of "common predicament" or common involvement is a more universal and potent factor in attaining social cohesion than common culture, common language, or common religion. Furthermore, he claims that friendship or enmity between members of groups are the results and not the causes of group interactions. These opinions are based on a series of small group studies named "the Robber's Cave experiment" [42]. This planned experiment took place at a boys' camp, where 11-year-old middle-class, American, Protestant, well-adjusted boys, all strangers to one another, were divided into two groups of twelve boys each. These two groups were isolated from each other during the first six days until each had become a cohesive organization with definite leadership structure, local customs, and a name. Then over the following week the two groups met in a series of competitive activities in which one side's victory inevitably meant the other's defeat. The result was a high level of mutual hostility. To their own groups the youngsters attributed self-glorifying qualities, but to the other they assigned those traits that labeled them as an enemy. They improvised and collected weapons, raided each other's property, and engaged in other shows of power.

Attempts were then made to restore peace, first spontaneously by a high-ranking member of one group who tried to open negotiations with the "enemy." His overtures were taken as attempts toward deception by pretended expression of reconciliation, and his departure was accompanied by a hail of green apples. His own group, far from receiving him as a hero, chastised him for making the attempt. Nor was there any response to the camp leaders' attempt to overcome the mutual stereotypes of the two groups by appeals to fair-mindedness or justice. Bringing the groups together at meals or movies was equally ineffective, for in such settings the warring factions sat apart from each other and hurled taunts and spitballs.

Finally, this mutual hostility was resolved (measured by one group's members choosing friends from the other and by a decrease in belligerent behavior) by a series of planned occurrences in which the groups had to cooperate to attain goals that neither could achieve alone. For example, a very inviting movie could be rented only if the treasuries of the two groups were combined. More compellingly, the camp water supply, secretly disrupted by the counselors, necessitated cooperative action to find the leak. Finally, when the truck carrying food and supplies for an overnight camping trip ran into a ditch and stalled, both groups had to get on the tow rope to pull it out. These series of cooperative activities toward superordinate goals had a cumulative effect in reducing intergroup hostility.

Before generalizing the results of this experiment to actual ongoing situations, its limitations must be recognized. These were only small groups of boys interacting over a relatively brief time. The boys did not regard the other group as a threat to their personal existence. There was an absence of personal enmity displaced from other situations—so-called irrational conflict. The superordinate goals were immediately apparent and clearly rewarding.

Despite the lack of exact congruence to many real life conditions, this experiment still points the way to exploring issues of conflict and cooperation in naturally occurring groups. Most critically, we must define those goals that are common to opposing groups and which require collaboration for their attainment. This can be done by group leaders or outside mediators. Oftentimes such a superordinate goal simply involves survival of the participants, as is the case of the threat of nuclear war. Frequently economic benefits or the advancement of technical knowledge results from collaboration. Once the superordinate goals are delineated, then placing them into operation can be initiated by disseminating information about the common predicament and by structuring face-to-face contact around these goals.

Strategies for Social Protest and Change

INCREASING GOVERNMENT RESPONSIVENESS

If social conflict is an inevitable accompaniment of human existence and a necessary vehicle for providing social change, then such conflict must be taken into account and constructively employed by a political system. Allowances must be made for the expression of dissent, not just so that the dissenter "lets off steam" but for meaningful feedback to those in power for adjustment and improvement of the system. For a social structure in which there is insufficient toleration and institutionalization of conflict, the presence of any conflict then threatens disruption. Such rigid systems that suppress dissent exert pressure toward the ultimate emergence of radical cleavages in society and a greater chance of violent forms of conflict [13]. We must develop ways of constructively utilizing social protest for providing meaningful social change rather than suppressing or ignoring it and risking the explosive consequences.

Does effective communication of political grievances reduce collective violence? By effective communication of grievances we mean both sharing accurate information as to what these grievances are and taking steps to resolve just grievances. There are no rigorous scientific studies answering this question, but available information seems to suggest the affirmative. The National Advisory Commission on Civil Disorders concludes that:

Virtually every major episode of urban violence in the summer of 1967 was foreshadowed by an accumulation of unresolved grievances by ghetto residents against local authorities. . . . Coinciding with this high level of dissatisfaction, confidence in the willingness and ability of local government to respond to Negro grievances was low [37].

The Commission also relates several instances of potential riot where efforts on the part of local politicians to understand and remedy the grievances of their constituents served to avert violence.

Because we pride ourselves on being a rather special bastion of democracy, the United States, in particular, needs more effective self-determination and improved feedback for a more responsive government. Our acceleration in the progress of science and technology has been matched with only minimal political reform to further realize our high hopes of a true democracy. This very circumstance—the distance between our ideals and our practices—has prompted Dr. John Spiegel, an accomplished behavioral scientist and director of the Lemberg Center for the Study of Violence, to claim:

The chief social strain in the United States has always been the incompatibility between its democratic ideals and its authoritarian practices. The rights of man, the equality among peoples, and the principle of representative government, the main items in the democratic philosophy, have from the birth of our country been pitted against an underlying and largely inarticulate authoritarianism. . . . Authoritarianism in the

United States has been maintained in two ways: (1) by the principle of exclusion of social groups from the democratic process; and (2) by the operation of pyramidal bureaucratic structures with power centered at the top of the pyramid [45].

Making government more responsive to its citizens thus can achieve several ends. It furthers the realization of our basic value of democracy. It provides necessary feedback for constructive political and social change. It serves to avert major societal disruption and subsequent large-scale violence.

How then can we enhance government responsiveness? The following strategies are meant to be suggestive rather than exhaustive.

1. Self-determination

Self-determination refers to the right of a people to choose its own government. Facilitating conditions include secret balloting by all the constituency, a choice of candidates representing the prevailing range of public opinion, and the absence of threat or coercion from the established power structure. To a considerable degree this ideal of self-determination has been met in this country. The growing call for decentralization of some government functions and for increased local community organization represents a heightened desire of people to determine their own fate. Notable exceptions to self-determination are slowly receding barriers to blacks voting in the South and the inability of citizens to choose directly the candidates for the office of President.

2. Effective Grievance Mechanisms

Essential to a responsive government are effective grievance mechanisms whereby communication from the people to the government is facilitated. The most widely recognized means of official feedback in this country are periodic political elections and our court system. In addition public polls, personal communications to one's congressman, mass demonstrations, and picketing are unofficial yet important means of registering grievances. Despite these practices the feeling of alienation between our people and our government still is significant. One suggested solution is for the application of an *ombudsman* to our political scene. This might counter the growing feeling among dissenters and minority group members that they are powerless to have their grievances dealt with by the establishment unless they resort to violent means of protest. The function of this office would be to impose a highly respected public official with investigatory powers between the government bureaucracy and the public [9]. Such issues as police brutality, judicial prejudice, and discrimination in the application of law at all levels of government would be subject to the scrutiny of the ombudsman, whose position would entail investigation, recommendation, prosecution, and publicity [38]. The creation of this office by the government would be taken by many as an act of good faith in attempting to increase communication with all levels of society.

3. Enforced Office Rotation

One of the surest means of preventing ossification and stagnation of a political system is by requiring periodic changing of the office occupants. The chief advantage of this practice would be the altering of the politician's priorities from primarily that of furthering his own political career to that of serving his public, since reelection would no longer be an issue. Equally beneficial would be the influx of fresh ideas and new energy. The disadvantages of enforced office rotation are that a certain amount of experience is lost, yet proponents claim that this is more than balanced by the high enthusiasm and novel ideas of the new officeholder. Such a system of enforced rotation or retirement has worked successfully in the administration of the Peace Corps and for the office of the Presidency. Why should it not be extended to state and local governments and members of Congress and the courts? Officeholders might not have to retire permanently but may be allowed to run for a different office or perhaps to run again for their original office after an interim time period. The experience of past officeholders could perhaps be utilized by offering them positions as advisors and consultants to the current governing officials.

NEGOTIATION

Negotiation is the process by which conflicting parties attempt to reach agreement through mutual discussion and bargaining over issues that divide them. The issues may be singular or plural, but in order for negotiation to take place it is necessary that each party believe he has something important to gain by reaching an agreement with the other over the issue in question. Clearly negotiation may provide a basis for increased social cohesion or for effective social protest and change. The aim of this section is to delineate the psychological factors operative in the negotiating process, with the hope of improving its efficiency and effectiveness.

Psychosocial Factors

Negotiators usually have special status or training that has led to their selection as representatives of their group. Some experiments involving small groups suggest that members tend to choose their more independent and nonconforming fellow members to represent them, possibly because these individuals are perceived as being less likely to submit to the pressures applied by the other side [4]. On the other hand, the ideal negotiator, who presents his group's case and then skillfully influences the acceptance of an agreement that reflects, inasmuch as it is possible, the conditions favorable to his own group, is not always found. Factors affecting the outcome of even the most important international negotiations may revolve around the negotiator's personal needs and idiosyncrasies, fortuitous social encounters, and momentary states of physical fatigue or ill health [34]. These factors can theoretically be minimized by more careful psychological screening of negotiators and by reasonable modifications of meeting conditions.

One problem inherent in the negotiating situation that complicates the motivation of the negotiator is the so-called traitor trap [3]. It is based on the fact that any negotiator is under significant pressure from his group to bring home an agreement which reflects the least number of concessions for the group's position. Each concession that he makes earns him the dissatisfaction of his fellow members and the accusation of unwitting or calculated disloyalty. In order to avert such an accusation, he must avoid making concessions to the other side. With his counterpart on the opposing side receiving the same pressure, negotiations can easily become deadlocked.

This process of "traitor trap" has been nicely demonstrated in group dynamics experiments performed with groups of approximately ten persons each who were involved in a human relations training program. These groups met for a half dozen two-hour sessions over three successive days to examine their own process of group formation. At the end of this period they had actually become cohesive groups having their own structure and sense of identity. All groups were then given several hours to prepare a solution to some familiar problem such as the correct approach to handling a deviant college student. The different solutions were read; after indicating familarity with opposing arguments, captains elected by each group met to seek agreement on the best solution. Discussions were held in the presence of all group members, but while group members were permitted to speak privately with their captains, only the captains could participate in the intergroup discussions.

The results indicated that in almost every case the negotiations were deadlocked. Whenever a team captain showed signs of capitulating to a reasonable argument, his fellow group members put pressure on him to stay with the group position. Even when negotiations were conducted in the absence of the group members, the captains held firmly to their original arguments. This evidence suggests that the risk of being labeled "disloyal" can significantly disrupt the efficiency of negotiators in reaching agreements [5].

Of further interest was the finding that although rival group members felt that they understood opposing positions, in all groups the members were consistently unable to identify items from rival positions as readily as from their own. Often they claimed ideas that were common to both positions as exclusively their own. Noncompeting comparison groups showed no such distortions of perception [6]. The tendency to place excessive value on their own group's solution was similarly evident when groups rated their own solutions superior to the opponent's on 46 out of 48 possible criteria [7].

Solutions to Psychosocial Problems

Various solutions to these pitfalls for negotiators have been suggested. One proposal is that nations employ hired bargainers from neutral countries, who would presumably be less subject to the "traitor trap" and to unprofessional influences. Fees for these negotiating "mercenaries" would be proportional to the number of concessions won from the other side. Under-the-counter payoffs to obtain concessions would ostensibly be prevented by the professional negotiator's need to maintain a faultless reputation if he is to stay in business [43]. In addition, the professional negotiator could be paid according to the speed of settlement, thus promoting quick concessions and early agreement. Though the professional negotiator idea has been criticized for its assumption that hired bargainers would be less responsive to external pressures and would be more competent negotiators than professional diplomats [46], it offers an interesting concept for consideration. Additional strategies for negotiation have been suggested [15]. One is the idea of multiple negotiating teams, with a reward going to the group who first reach an acceptable solution. Another idea is that of *anticipatory negotiations*, in which regular meetings are held before and after the times of crisis; this might help the problem-solving process because emotions and irrational behaviors presumably would be less during lower stress periods.

There are several other proposals that seek to develop a cooperative rather than a competitive attitude between negotiators. Instead of choosing representatives from each group to speak for their group's position, both groups might submit a list of names. From this list each would select a mixed panel of negotiators whose main commitment would be to reach an agreement. The difficulties inherent in applying such a plan are self-evident, but in a period of mutual trust such an approach might be more feasible [3].

Another suggestion stems from the evidence that opposing groups fail to hear each other's arguments very well. It is proposed that as a prerequisite for negotiations to commence and periodically throughout the negotiations, both sides should be required to state the opposition's position to his satisfaction [10].

Communication Problems

Even if these psychological mechanisms that seem to interfere with the negotiator's efficient fulfillment of his function could be minimized, there are still a number of variables that need more precise study. These include the role of language and cultural barriers, sites and media of interaction, and the relative effects of positive and threatening messages. The degree to which negotiations are rendered more difficult by linguistic and cultural differences is not easily measured, but the effects certainly are important in the majority of intergroup relations. Differences in culturally ingrained habits of thinking and reaching agreements can produce bewildering impediments to negotiation. Opponents must understand each other's definition of the situation and each other's symbols of defeat and victory in order to negotiate. Cultural attitudes of the opposing group must be grasped. These difficulties can sometimes be circumvented by employing negotiators familiar with the nuances of language and culture of the opposition [20].

The negotiation site may also influence the outcome of negotiations. If both parties are meeting in a place which is clearly more congenial to one of them, that team is likely to have a considerable advantage. This advantage stems from the dependence of the other party on the "home team" for resources required to maintain the outside negotiators during the meetings. At one level these may simply include food, lodging, and communications facilities. At another level, however, the visiting participants are dependent on their hosts for protection and security in an often hostile environment. For this reason a powerful party usually refuses to negotiate unless its terms regarding a satisfactory location are met.

Similar to the problem of the location of negotiations is the question of the medium of communication. Face-to-face meetings between negotiators are by far the most common means of conducting high-level negotiations. However, one very important crisis in recent memory, the Cuban missile crisis, was conducted via the now famous "hot line" between Washington, D.C., and Moscow. It would be interesting to explore how in the age of electronics negotiations are facilitated or impeded by the different media of electronic communications.

Other aspects of the problem of communications have been more readily subjected to systematic study. Examination of the relationship between communication and trust, for example, has been markedly benefited by the development of certain experimental games. Such games may simulate such intergroup bargaining situations as nuclear test ban negotiations. Here both sides stand to benefit from being able to trust each other, but both are fearful of doing so because the penalty would be so high if the other side should cheat and develop a significant lead in the arms race. Logically it would appear that the amount of communication and the degree of trust vary together. This has been found experimentally [29], namely, that communication of intentions and evidence of cooperativeness contribute to the establishment of mutual trust.

Whether another mode of communication, the threat, inhibits negotiations remains unclear. On one hand, there is some experimental evidence for threat offering little contribution to cooperation in negotiation [29] and for threat markedly reducing the gains of both participants [17]. However, in a slightly different experimental setting the absence or presence of a condition of threat did not seem to affect the outcome [26]. It seems that in those cases where threats have not hindered cooperation, it has been because subjects learned to use them to communicate intentions. In most experiments, however, threats have only served to decrease the efficiency of subjects in obtaining mutually beneficial outcomes.

Resolving Conflicts in the Negotiation Process

The above principles of successful conflict resolution have found application in many social and political institutions. Perhaps more than any other institution, the United Nations embodies the principles that have been examined here of nonviolent settlement of intergroup differences. The facilitation of communication between potentially hostile parties is of great importance, and the reduction of stereotyped attitudes toward rival groups, which such communication fosters, is similarly required. A random sampling of a large number of national missions indicated that 90 percent of the delegates had experienced increased informal contact with members of hostile delegations. In light of the findings that relate increased amounts of communication to trust, this function of the U.N. probably contributes to improved relations among its representatives. Here in the United States this same principle might be fruitfully applied through an ombudsman system, as previously discussed. This would increase communication between the government and dissident subgroups and very likely would lead to an increase in the intergroup trust within our society.

Another application might apply to negotiators in the field. Contemporary international negotiators are vested with considerable responsibility, and their task can be affected by a number of powerful influences including the "traitor trap," cultural and linguistic distortions, personal psychological factors, and the variable effects of positive communications and threats. Given this complex situation, it might be of significant benefit to have all participants undergo a complete orientation in the psychological aspects of negotiation to familiarize them with the kinds of influences they might experience during the negotiation process. This *role induction* for negotiators would enable both sides to have some cognizance of factors that might otherwise interfere with their efficiency at reaching an agreement.

An extension of the idea of a thorough psychological briefing for negotiators is the concept of using specialists in the behavioral sciences as negotiators. Important here would be the training in recognizing unstated assumptions and the ability to reveal the issues in relatively nonthreatening ways. One example of such an occurrence took place at Tallahassee Federal Prison in the spring of 1968, when the prison's medical officer, who happened to be trained as a psychiatrist, succeeded in staving off what might have developed into a major riot by employing techniques often used in psychotherapy [32]. With almost a quarter of the prison's five hundred inmates gathered before the administration building shouting for reforms and the warden preparing to order his armed guards to use tear gas and force to break up the demonstration, the medical officer walked out among the men and asked whether he could possibly be of some help. The generally favorable but confused responses made it clear to him that the group had developed neither clearly defined leaders nor clearly conceived goals. By asking the group to select spokesmen and then asking them a number of questions, he led the group into defining a realistic act on the part of the administration that would satisfy their demands. The warden complied, and most of the men seemed satisfied. One of the group leaders, however, began quietly arousing further opposition away from the main body of men. The psychiatrist observed what was occurring and mobilized another of the group leaders, who went over and convinced the splinter group to break up. By facilitating intragroup and intergroup communication, defining issues, clearing up misunderstandings, and mobilizing positive leadership, the psychiatrist was able to help avoid an almost certain outbreak of violence. A crucial factor in this example was the genuine willingness of both sides to compromise—in this instance especially the warden, who complied with the prisoners' realistic demands.

A final application of experimental findings to the negotiation process would be the use of female negotiators. In experimental games simulating negotiations, females more than males preferred to disengage or try alternate means rather than participate in prolonged competitive interactions [26]. The validity of this provocative finding should be examined in other cultures to see whether it might not be recommended as one means of relieving the competitive elements that can stalemate negotiations.

Summary

Currently available evidence suggests that the negotiation process might be facilitated by the following measures:

1. Psychological and medical screening of negotiators to aid in selection of emotionally stable and physically healthy individuals. Further research into the personality characteristics of successful versus unsuccessful negotiators would be relevant.

2. Education of negotiators to the types of psychological influences involved in their work including experience in small group experiments, which demonstrate nicely the kinds of perceptual distortions that can occur between opponents.

3. Periodic reemphasis of the importance of discovering superordinate goals that exist between the adversaries, with a highlighting of the consequences of failing to reach agreements, including graphic reminders of the effects of nuclear weapons, riots, or other relevant phenomena of collective violence.

4. Exploration of novel negotiating techniques involving hired neutral bargaining teams, mixed panels of negotiators from both sides, competing negotiating teams, and "anticipatory negotiations."

5. Demonstration of the negotiators' ability to state the views of the opposing side before negotiations begin, as a way of avoiding the tendency to misperceive the arguments of opponents.

6. Thorough familiarization on the part of negotiators with the linguistic and cultural patterns of the opponent, including his symbols for victory and defeat.

7. Study of the ways in which negotiation sites and electronic means of communication, including computer simulation of various outcomes, can be manipulated to maximize the probability of reaching an agreement.

8. Support and development of institutions and other situations that improve communication and contact between opposing groups and their representatives under conditions which promote trust and trustworthiness.

9. Limitation of the employment of threats in the negotiation process insofar as it is possible to communicate contingencies effectively without resorting to threatening statements.

10. Investigation of the effectiveness of female negotiators versus male negotiators in light of experimental evidence suggesting a tendency for females to prefer reaching agreements rather than experience prolonged competition. Cross-cultural studies in this area would be important.

11. Exploration of ways in which behavioral scientists might contribute their specialized knowledge and techniques to intergroup negotiations, in either an advisory or participatory capacity.

12. Emphasis on the principle that stressing the availability of alternatives to violence to one's adversary will reduce that adversary's chances of employing violence to gain his ends.

NONVIOLENCE: "SOUL POWER"

Nonviolence is a type of response to social conflict that has existed for at least two and a half millennia and is taking new forms in this century. When successful in achieving social change, it brings victory to those who employ it while simultaneously inhibiting violence and demoralizing their opponents. A proponent of nonviolence [16] explains the conviction from which it arises: "Commitment to nonviolence must not be based on patient acquiescence of intolerable conditions. Rather it stems from a deeper knowledge of the self-defeating, self-corrupting effect of lapses into violence." Nonviolence is not a passive act nor an act of weakness but a very active effort to defeat an opponent who relies on superior destructive power. It requires the pitting of all one's courage and initiative against the adversary along with discipline in standing firm for one's beliefs.

Types of Nonviolence

The idea of nonviolence is not a simple one; it has been given many different descriptions and taken different forms in action. Pacifism and nonresistance, the refusal to retaliate, are only one category of nonviolence. Other types are civil disobedience, which is lawbreaking for moral reasons, and direct action, which may include such means as boycotts, strikes, picketing, mass demonstrations, and resignation of office in the name of conscience. The most complete inventory to date of nonviolent methods is being provided by Gene Sharp [40], who distinguishes between nonviolent protest, nonviolent noncooperation, and nonviolent intervention. Under nonviolent protest he lists 36 forms of activity including parades, vigils, meetings, and emigration. Under nonviolent noncooperation he lists 72 forms of action in three subcategories: strikes, boycotts, and political noncooperation. Under nonviolent intervention he lists 16 forms of action including sit-ins, hunger strikes, nonviolent obstruction, and parallel government. Each of these forms of nonviolent action has been tested in actual situations and has yielded influence and power. Any one nonviolent campaign may use several of these methods.

Abe Fortas [19] makes an important distinction between two types of civil disobedience: breaking a law one thinks is wrong, and breaking a law to inconvenience others or to gain attention for one's cause. Breaking a law that one thinks is immoral may be the only way to bring the law to test and is a regular part of the political and legal process. However, breaking a law that in itself is unobjectionable in order to dramatize a protest carries with it the obligation of the demonstrator to accept the punishment of the law. His moral conviction gives him no immunity. At times in recent years this distinction has been lost. Subsequently there has been violent resistance to the sentences for civil disobedience in support of one's cause.

Gandhi, the most effective practitioner of nonviolence in modern times, made great use of disobedience to ordinary civil law in his protest against the British. Both his protests and submission to the penalties were carried out peacefully. According to an authority on Gandhi his principle was this: Act in a group struggle in a way conducive to long-term universal reduction of violence [33]. Gandhi's target was not the opponent but the structure of the society that had forced him into his position. He asked respect for the humanity and conscience of the adversary, who himself believes that his line of action is right. Gandhi wrote, "Man and his deed are two distinct things. Whereas a good deed should call forth approbation and a wicked deed disapprobation, the doer of the deed, whether good or wicked, always deserves respect or pity as the case may be" [21].

Part of Gandhi's method for the preparation for "soul force" is a spirit of service—offering some replacement for what one is opposing. "In a group struggle you can keep . . . the ability to work effectively for the realization of the goal stronger than the destructive violent tendencies and the tendencies to passiveness and despondency only by . . . giving all phases of your struggle, as far as possible, a constructive character" [33]. Such constructive action makes it hard for the opponent to dehumanize the participant in nonviolence.

Objections to Nonviolence

Nonviolence has been praised by many authors, but objections to it have been discussed by few. One concern is that nonviolence permits the minority to impose its will upon the majority. This appears to be true only when the majority is divided or manifests little concern over the issue at hand; also the arousal of the moral conscience of the majority may trigger widespread changes.

A second objection is that nonviolence frequently takes a long time to show effect in contrast to the usually more immediate results of violence. Success does not usually come at once; it is a tedious and tiring process. Gandhi reported that each favorable campaign aroused five responses in its adversaries successively: indifference, ridicule, abuse, repression, and finally respect. To survive four stages and miss the fifth is obviously no victory. Intense group loyalty, inner discipline, and perseverance are absolutely essential. These in turn are aided by allegiance to an inspiring leader and commitment to an ideology of nonviolence.

A third objection commonly cited is the apparent failure of nonviolence to resolve complex social issues, such as the current racial discrimination in jobs, housing, education. In this country the struggle has left the realm of constitutional rights and has entered the area of human rights. Actually, such complex social issues are unlikely to yield *readily* to *any* protest technique. We believe that the failure to resolve these complex issues represents not a weakness of nonviolence but rather a failure of its practitioners and recipients alike—the former failing to sustain and the latter to heed. Particularly in the United States the tradition of violence as a solution for social problems [39] precludes strong allegiance to an ideology of nonviolence. And without a deep belief in the power and "righteousness" of nonviolence, it is difficult to sustain oneself through a long and fatiguing campaign.

A fourth apparent shortcoming is that nonviolence is often thought to require the threat of violence for its success. The leader of a group that is using civil disobedience or nonviolent direct action may warn the oppressor that he will not be able to keep his men from violence if demands are not met. This element of brinkmanship is sometimes useful in the nonviolent effort to coerce or resist the other side. Nonetheless, the core ingredient for the success of most nonviolent tactics is a moral appeal to the conscience of the opponent. This is why Gandhi labeled his use of nonviolence "satyagraha," which may be roughly translated as "soul force" or "soul power." One's principal power of persuasion derives from activating the adversary's conscience. However, nonviolence need not be based primarily on the moral response of the opponent; other means of influence besides a pure moral appeal are also effective. Economic pressures from boycotts or strikes, or political pressures from noncooperation, overloading the system (example of draft resisters flooding the courts), and parallel government are further successful bases of persuasion.

Nonviolence and the Ruthless Opponent

It has sometimes been argued that nonviolent techniques could be effective against some, e.g., the British in India or the Americans, but would not work against more ruthless opponents. There is evidence to the contrary in the story of the resistance to the Nazis by the Norwegians. Their example is a good illustration of the practice of "nonviolent national defense" [2]. (This is not to say that nonviolent resistance cannot be used along with violent resistance.) When the Nazis invaded Norway, the country put up armed resistance for two months, but then the Norwegian government was put to rout, and a puppet government was installed, headed by Quisling. The first act of nonviolent resistance by the Norwegians was the resignation of the Supreme Court protesting Nazi decrees. Boycotts of the newly organized Nazi sports club and of the Nazi student union at the University of Oslo were the next acts of nonviolence. Both these Nazi attempts at creating organizations were demolished by complete nonattendance. There were slowdowns and sabotage in industry and refusal of trade unions to comply with Nazi demands. The clergy put up a determined and almost unanimous resistance to Nazi changes.

In 1941 the Nazis made demands on the schools, which were nonviolently opposed by both teachers and students. The decrees required Quisling's portrait to be hung in the classroom, Nazi propaganda to be included in the curriculum, and German to be the primary language at school. These requirements were all withdrawn in the face of absolute refusal to comply by teachers and the students, backed up by their parents. However, Quisling reinstated these decrees in 1942 simultaneously with a campaign to make teachers join a Nazi teachers' association. The schools were then closed for a short time to give them time to join, but no one did. Some thirteen hundred of the teachers were arrested, and over half of these were subjected to concentration camp tortures. Only thirty-two gave in. The others were sent to a village above the Arctic Circle and set to hard labor. About a month later the schools reopened, but all the teachers still refused to join the Nazi association. As a consequence of this adamant nonviolent resistance by patriotic Norwegians, Quisling gave up trying to Nazify the students, teachers, clergy, and members of trade unions. The military strategist Liddell Hart claimed that Hitler's generals found nonviolent resistance in Norway, Denmark, and Holland far more baffling than the violent resistance in other occupied countries.

Jerome Frank [20] maintains that nonviolence works best where one's adversary has superior force and claims it is directly applicable to protests in dictatorships. Speaking of a dictatorship's inevitable internal tensions and mutual suspicions, he notes that violent opposition keeps the dictatorship cohesive by supplying an object on which it can displace internal hatreds and frustrations without guilt. Conversely, nonviolent tactics intensify internal tensions by giving them no appropriate outlet and by mobilizing latent guilt feelings.

Nonviolence in America: The Montgomery Boycott

In our own country we find, as elsewhere, that each successful use of nonviolence combines different quantities of expediency, strategy, and religious or secular emphasis. Much in the current nonviolent civil rights and peace movements is kindred in spirit to the abolitionist and pacifist movements of the nineteenth century. Civil rights has roots in the labor movement of the 1930's as well, which similarly drew strength from the unsatisfied poor. "We Shall Overcome" was a song of the Appalachian textile workers, and the sit-ins were inspired by the sit-down strikes of that period.

One of the most fruitful nonviolent campaigns in the United States was the year-long Montgomery bus boycott protesting segregation in the buses. This campaign showed how organization, discipline, and training extending through the whole community is necessary to back up the commitment to change. More importantly it inspired many other successful nonviolent direct action and legal action campaigns and shattered once and for all the myth that blacks were content with their status. Riding the buses was a humiliation for blacks in the South. Often the drivers compelled blacks to get off the bus after paying their fare and to reload in the back. If the white section was full, blacks had to relinquish their seats to white passengers. Even pregnant women were required to yield their seats to white teenagers. One terrifying incident lying behind the Montgomery protest occurred early in 1955, when five black women and two children were arrested and one man was shot to death, for disobeying a bus driver's order.

The incident that sparked the boycott occurred on December 1, 1955, when Mrs. Rosa Parks refused to give up her seat and was arrested. Since she was an admired and well-known seamstress in the black community, news of the incident traveled fast. Some were readying their arsenals for retaliation. Ministers heard about these riot preparations, and Ralph D. Abernathy and Martin Luther King, Jr., hurriedly arranged a meeting of the black leaders to consider an alternative. A one-day bus boycott was decided upon. Only a few days were taken to publicize and prepare for the boycott. When the day came, there were empty buses running that normally would have been packed. Even in busy hours there were a scant number of passengers. Blacks used taxis and car pools, and thousands walked.

That same evening the Montgomery Improvement Association was formed. The name, suggesting improvement, embodied the constructive element so important in nonviolent philosophy. Young Martin Luther King, Jr., was made president of the M.I.A., and he called a mass meeting which made an enthusiastic commitment to continue the boycott. There was 95 percent participation in the boycott throughout the following year. Sympathy and respect from many whites were evidenced by increasing numbers of favorable letters to the editor and offers of rides to blacks. That year the rough element in town unexpectedly joined the churches that were centers for specific instructions in nonviolent techniques. This instruction was needed, as segregationists were arresting car pools on false charges, and waiting riders were threatened with arrest for vagrancy.

During the year three bombs were thrown at the homes of the leaders of the Montgomery Improvement Association. On one such occasion King spoke to the angry mob outside his home and asked them to "meet hate with love." When ninety blacks were indicted on an old law against boycotts, King's trial was held first. He was convicted but appealed, and the verdict was ultimately reversed.

In May 1956 NAACP lawyers filed suit to change the city ordinance which held that the buses should be segregated. The litigation ended in the Supreme Court, which decided in favor of the Montgomery Improvement Association's suit in a decree given in December 1956. At last the boycott ended.

King wrote about the reactions of both the privileged and the underprivileged to nonviolence:

When the underprivileged demand freedom, the privileged first react with bitterness and resistance. . . . So the nonviolent approach does not immediately change the heart of the oppressor. It first does something to the hearts and souls of those committed to it. It gives them new self-respect: it calls up resources of strength and courage that they did not know they had. Finally, it reaches the opponent and so stirs his conscience that reconciliation becomes a reality [27].

Psychological Factors in Nonviolence

What are the key psychological ingredients in the nonviolent process? These may be listed as conscience, incompatible response, energy release of aggression, and increased self-esteem.

The dynamism of nonviolence consists in the fact that it reduces the nonviolent person's guilt feelings (since he is not committing destructive aggression), while at the same time it activates the opponent's guilt. It is this guilty conscience of the opponent that renders him more vulnerable. But to the degree that the nonviolent person acts toward the opponent in a caring, respectful manner, not only has he brought the other's guilt to consciousness but he has made him accept this guilt. It can no longer change into blame and paranoid projection. Conversely, any threatened or actual violence by the protestor will likely be viewed as providing justification for retaliation by the opponent.

Incompatible response refers to the fact that nonviolent manner and behavior by their very nature usually inhibit a violent response. It is innately difficult to attack someone who refuses to fight back but instead voices his concern for the attacker.

It should be apparent that nonviolence is a highly active process for the participant and monopolizes and utilizes much of his aggressive energy. Nonviolence is aggressive but not destructively aggressive. This is a critical distinction. The reader will recall that there are other, more adaptive forms of aggression besides destructive aggression, and nonviolence is proving to be one of these forms. Indirect evidence for this mobilization of aggressive energy in a constructive manner comes from studies reported by Solomon et al. [44] and Pierce and West [36]. Solomon and his colleagues collected data on incidence of personal crime in three cities from various sources. For all three cities—two in the South and one in a border state—there was a decrease in aggravated assaults by blacks ranging from 20 percent to 30 percent during the "years of sustained civil rights activity" of 1961 and 1962, compared to 1960 and 1963. Such a trend was absent for aggravated assaults by whites. Pierce and West in their paper claim that among 300 "regular" sit-in demonstrators from the local Oklahoma City NAACP Youth Council there "have been virtually no manifestations of delinquency or anti-social behavior, no school drop-outs, no known illegitimate pregnancies." This the investigators attribute to a "strong conscious sense [among the demonstrators] of being able to control their own potentially aggressive feelings." These studies illustrate a further feature of nonviolence. It breaks the psychological link between masculinity and violence. For the participant there is a heightened self-esteem and sense of moral integrity.

Here then is a strategy that can claim all the benefits of violence without most of its limitations. Achievement, pride, and self-esteem are enhanced without corrupting oneself or harming others. A "danger signal" is provided to society with less stimulation of further opposition and repression. The strategy engenders group solidarity without alienating the outsider. Most importantly, when applied in a studied and patient manner, nonviolence produces meaningful social change.

Why then with these advantages is there a turn away from nonviolence among dissident groups in this country, notably the student radicals and black militants? One can only speculate. Perhaps it is because change in the majority and power structure has been too slow in comparison to the increasing awareness and expectations of the aggrieved group. It may be partly that violence promises a more speedy, visible, and understandable road to masculinity and personal pride. Perhaps it is because the mass media have concentrated on those leaders advocating violence, so that the appetites of their audience for violence are stimulated and there is a more obvious target for the white majority's anger. An additional reason for the blacks' use of violence may be that their goals are now more complex and long-range than they were a decade ago. Certainly, their move to violence is not from the failure of nonviolence, for the civil rights movement has already achieved more significant change by "soul power" than any other nonviolent effort in our national history [30].

Indeed the facts question the advocates of violence as speaking for black citizens: Nine-tenths of blacks do not approve of violence, according to a poll of a representative national sample conducted by CBS during the summer of 1968 [8]. This poll also found Ralph D. Abernathy to be the black leader most admired by 53 percent of those questioned, and he was followed by Roy Wilkins with 25 percent. This is in sharp contrast to the well-known militants and sometimes advocates of violence for "self-defense," such as Stokely Carmichael and H. Rap Brown, none of whom polled over 5 percent.

It has been proved that the power of nonviolence *can* effect change socially and politically; participants are no longer dismissed as fanatics; methods are no longer considered Indian or esoteric. Nonviolent techniques can be adapted to present settings. Measurable and visible payoffs resulting from nonviolent campaigns must be the aim. But to be effective, nonviolent tactics must capture the conscience of the American public or wield an impact on American economic and political interests, or both.

Overview

This chapter has viewed social conflict in an adaptational or "coping" framework. The presence of social conflict itself has been seen as both beneficial and deleterious, depending on its overall effects. Violence also has certain functions, but these appear to be outweighed at the present time by its limitations. In order to provide some alternatives to violence, we have named several strategies for coping with social conflict. Among those that facilitate social cohesion and control are overriding authority, group identity and pride, overlapping group memberships, and superordinate goals. Suggested strategies for effective social protest and change are measures to increase government responsiveness, the process of negotiation, and nonviolent action—"soul power." Examples illustrating these strategies have been drawn largely from our national racial crisis.

Oftentimes throughout this chapter, research findings have been generalized to circumstances beyond their original settings. While this generalization makes our comments somewhat more tenuous, we offer no apologies. The importance of the issues at stake has demanded immediate attention and sometimes premature recommendations. The need for informed action on these issues by local and national decision makers and for their further study by social and behavioral scientists cannot be stressed sufficiently.

Acknowledgment

We offer special appreciation to Mary Wilson Noyes, volunteer research assistant, who aided significantly in the preparation of this chapter.

References

1. Allport, G. *The Nature of Prejudice*. Cambridge, Mass.: Addison-Wesley, 1954.
2. American Friends Service Committee. *In Place of War: An Inquiry into Nonviolent National Defense*. New York: Grossman, 1967.
3. Blake, R. R. Psychology and the crisis of statesmanship. *American Psychologist* 14:90, 1954.
4. Blake, R. R., and Mouton, J. S. Competition, Communication and Conformity. In Berg, I. A., and Bass, B. M. (Eds.), *Conformity and Deviation*. New York: Harper & Row, 1961.
5. Blake, R. R., and Mouton, J. S. Loyalty of representative to ingroup positions during intergroup competition. *Sociometry* 24:177, 1961.
6. Blake, R. R., and Mouton, J. S. Comprehension of own and of outgroup positions under intergroup competition. *Journal of Conflict Resolution* 5:304, 1961.
7. Blake, R. R., and Mouton, J. S. Overevaluation of own group's product in intergroup competition. *Journal of Abnormal and Social Psychology* 64:237, 1962.
8. CBS News Public Opinion Survey. White and Negro Attitudes Toward Race Related Issues and Activities. Princeton, N.J.: Opinion Research Corporation, July 1968.
9. Cheng, H. Y. The emergence and specialization of the ombudsman institution. *Annals of the American Academy of Political and Social Science* 377:1, 1968.
10. Cohen, J. Reflections on the Resolution of Conflict in International Affairs. In *Proceedings of the International Congress on Applied Psychology 1*. Copenhagen: Munksgaard, 1962.
11. Coleman, J. S. *Community Conflict*. Glencoe, Ill.: Free Press, 1957.
12. Coser, L. *The Functions of Social Conflict*. Glencoe, Ill.: Free Press, 1956.
13. Coser, L. *Continuities in the Study of Social Conflict*. New York: Free Press, 1967.
14. Dahl, R. A. The American Oppositions: Affirmation and Denial. In Dahl, R. A. (Ed.), *Political Oppositions in Western Democracies*. New Haven, Conn.: Yale University Press, 1966.
15. Daniels, D. (Stanford Department of Psychiatry.) Personal communication, 1968.
16. Dellinger, D. The Future of Nonviolence. In Lynd, S. (Ed.), *Nonviolence in America: A Documentary History*. New York: Bobbs-Merrill, 1966.
17. Deutsch, M., and Krauss, R. M. Studies of interpersonal bargaining. *Journal of Conflict Resolution* 6:52, 1962.

18. Festinger, L. *A Theory of Cognitive Dissonance.* Evanston, Ill.: Row, Peterson, 1957.
19. Fortas, A. *Concerning Dissent and Civil Disobedience.* New York: Signet, 1968.
20. Frank, J. D. *Sanity and Survival: Psychological Aspects of War and Peace.* New York: Random House, 1967.
21. Gandhi, M. *An Autobiography: The Story of My Experiments with Truth.* Boston: Beacon Press, 1957.
22. Gluckman, M. *Culture and Conflict in Africa.* Glencoe, Ill.: Free Press, 1955.
23. Goodenough, W. H. *Cooperation in Change: An Anthropological Approach to Community Development.* New York: Russell Sage Foundation, 1963.
24. Hermann, M., and Kogan, N. Negotiation in leader and delegate groups. *Journal of Conflict Resolution* 12:332, 1968.
25. International Sociological Association. *The Nature of Conflict: Studies on the Sociological Aspects of International Tensions.* New York: UNESCO, 1957.
26. Kelley, H. H. Threats in interpersonal negotiations. *Journal of Conflict Resolution* 9:79, 1965.
27. King, M. L. Pilgrimage to Nonviolence. In Mayer, P. (Ed.), *The Pacifist Conscience.* Middlesex, Eng.: Penguin, 1966.
28. Le Vine, R. Anthropology and the study of conflict: An introduction. *Journal of Conflict Resolution* 5:1, 1961.
29. Loomis, J. L. Communication, the development of trust, and interpersonal behavior. *Human Relations* 12:305, 1959.
30. Lynd, S. (Ed.). *Nonviolence in America: A Documentary History.* New York: Bobbs-Merrill, 1966.
31. McNeil, E. B. (Ed.). *The Nature of Human Conflict.* Englewood Cliffs, N.J.: Prentice-Hall, 1965.
32. Miller, W. (Stanford Department of Psychiatry.) Personal communication, 1968.
33. Naess, A. A systematization of Gandhian ethics of conflict resolution. *Journal of Conflict Resolution* 2:140, 1958.
34. Nicholson, H. *The Congress of Vienna.* New York: Harcourt, Brace, 1946.
35. Pettigrew, T. F. Racially Separate or Together? (Presidential Address of the Society for the Psychological Study of Social Issues, San Francisco, Sept. 1, 1968.) *Journal of Social Issues* 25:45, 1969.
36. Pierce, C. M., and West, L. J. Six years of sit-ins: Psychodynamic causes and effects. *International Journal of Social Psychiatry* 12:29, 1966.
37. *Report of the National Advisory Commission on Civil Disorders.* New York: Bantam, 1968.
38. Sandler, A. An ombudsman for the United States. *Annals of the American Academy of Political and Social Science.* 377:20, 1968.
39. Schlesinger, A. *Violence: America in the Sixties.* New York: New Library, 1968.
40. Sharp, G. *The Politics of Nonviolent Action.* To be published.

41. Sherif, M.   *In Common Predicament: Social Psychology of Intergroup Conflict and Cooperation.* Boston: Houghton Mifflin, 1966.
42. Sherif, M., Harvey, O. J., White, J., Hood, W. R., and Sherif, C. W. *Intergroup Conflict and Cooperation: The Robber's Cave Experiment.* Norman, Okla.: Oklahoma University Press, 1961.
43. Singer, J. D.   Negotiation by proxy: A proposal. *Journal of Conflict Resolution* 9:538, 1965.
44. Solomon, F., Walker, W. L., O'Connor, G., and Fishman, J. R.   Civil rights activity and reduction in crime among Negroes. *Archives of General Psychiatry* 12:227, 1965.
45. Spiegel, J. P.   Psychosocial factors in riots—old and new. *American Journal of Psychiatry* 125:281, 1968.
46. Sullivan, C. D.   Negotiation by proxy: A critique. *Journal of Conflict Resolution* 10:383, 1966.
47. Triandis, H. C., and Davis, E. E.   Race and belief as determinants of behavioral intentions. *Journal of Personality and Social Psychology* 2:715, 1965.
48. Wolfgang, M., and Ferranti, F.   *The Subculture of Violence.* London: Tavistock, 1967.

Part **II**

CURRENT ISSUES *of* VIOLENCE *in the* UNITED STATES

6. The Choice of Collective Violence in Intergroup Conflict

Thomas E. Bittker, M.D.

That there is a holocaust coming I have no doubt at all . . . the violent phase of the black liberation struggle is here and it will spread . . . America will be painted red . . . now all black people in America will become Black Panthers in spirit . . . Now there is the gun and the bomb, dynamite and the knife, and they will be used liberally in America. America will bleed. America will suffer . . . [4].   ELDRIDGE CLEAVER

It is difficult to read this passage by an angry black militant without remorse. Those of us who wish to limit the expression of violence in our country eventually must confront the Eldridge Cleavers and examine the position that collective violence holds in their constellation of tactics. How has their use of violence evolved? Does violence have an adaptive function? Are there alternative forms of expression available to the black militant, and if so, what kinds of response should the power structure invoke to increase the likelihood that these alternatives will be employed?

I hope in this chapter to suspend that bias which views violence as necessarily deviant, maladaptive, or criminal, and to consider those instances when violence might be functional. For example, collective violence might seem to be the most productive tactical option available to an oppressed group in conflict. Although the short-term value of violence may be more than offset by its long-term consequences, it cannot be denied that in the United States violence is praticed as though it were productive. Thus the productivity of violence is very much a function of one's perspective.

Our country has known a variety of both oppressed and oppressing groups that, in their efforts to extend or limit socioeconomic enfranchisement, have resorted to collective violence. Beginning with the American Revolution in 1776, through the rebellion of Daniel Shays in 1786, through the "Irish" antidraft riots of the 1860's [3], through the battles of industrial unionism, to the recent uprisings of urban blacks and of university youths, collective violence has served as an important intergroup conflict resolution mechanism [20]. Thus the urban black militant is not unique in using violence or the threat of violence. I have, nonetheless, directed this discussion toward an understanding of collective violence as it is used by the black militant because of the particular immediacy and gravity of his dilemma. This chapter, then, reviews the function of collective violence in black militancy. It is neither an indictment nor an endorsement. Nor is it my intention to suggest that the responsibility for collective violence rests primarily with the black militant. Indeed I intend that the reader will emerge from this chapter with an appreciation of just how much collective violence is a consequence of the *interaction* between groups rather than merely the responsibility of *one* group in an intergroup conflict.

Before moving on in this discussion, I shall attempt to clarify several terms frequently used and confused in the literature on collective violence. In an effort to embrace most of the definitions previously proposed, I shall define *violence* as direct action applied to physically restrain, injure, or destroy persons, groups, organizations, or property. *Collective violence* would be group behavior leading to the physical restraint, injury, or destruction of persons, groups, organizations, or property. This latter definition would include war, revolution, insurrection as well as riot, and, frequently, riot control. *Riot* will be used here as a general term to indicate an uncontrolled violent disorder involving groups of people whose participation in the disorder may or may not include a shared sense of social, economic, or political oppression. *Insurrection* or *uprising* are more specific terms that indicate a violent disorder, at least partially planned, involving a group whose members do share a sense of social, economic, or political oppression. The word *militant* will be used to signify an aggressive combatant in a social struggle. It should also connote a sense of total commitment to a group cause. The term should not be confused with the word *rioter*, someone who participates in a violent disorder. A militant is not necessarily violent, and a rioter is not necessarily militant. Furthermore, *militancy* should not be confused with *radicalism*, which is a commitment to the overthrow of a social system. A militant may actually be seeking to enter the system rather than to overthrow it.

What follows is an examination of several elements in the choice of collective violence or its threat by the black militant. I shall first describe the characteristics that distinguish the rioter from his non-rioting counterpart. This description will stress the grievances and socioeconomic background of rioters and nonrioters. Second, I shall examine several elements contributing to the choice of violent versus nonviolent alternatives by the black militant. These elements are objectives, leadership, ideology and self-esteem, and the opposition. Third, I shall attempt to assess the degree to which the total black community has become committed to the tactical use of collective violence. Fourth, I shall examine some of the possible adaptive functions of collective violence for minority groups. Finally, I shall present a theoretical model to facilitate the understanding of collective violence involving minority groups.

The "Rioter"

BACKGROUND

According to a number of observers, the core complaints of the urban black community focus on abusive police practices, inadequate housing, inadequate education, and inadequate job opportunities. The National Advisory Commission on Civil Disorders [17] found that discrimination or white racism was the most important underlying cause of these inadequacies. Two social psychologists, Nathan Caplan and Jeffrey Paige [2], supported this impression in a carefully designed study that sampled randomly selected households in the riot-ridden areas of two of the hardest hit riot cities of 1967, Detroit and Newark. Trained black interviewers questioned male and female inhabitants above age 15 in Detroit and male inhabitants between ages 15 and 35 in Newark. They divided their sample of 673 interviews into two groups, those of rioters and nonrioters.

CHARACTERISTICS

Respondents were classified as "rioters" if they reported that they were active in breaking windows, looting, or fire bombing. Those who reported that they had stayed at home or had gone out in front of their homes to watch the disturbances were considered nonrioters. The study reported that 11 percent of the Detroit sample and 45 percent of the Newark sample identified themselves as rioters. Using their interview data, the authors attempted to distinguish rioters from nonrioters along several parameters: education, occupation, employment record, perceived job obstacles, income, age, family background, geographic region of childhood, attitudes toward whites, attitudes toward other blacks, political sophistication, and social integration (sex ratios were not included). They found that the rioters were by no means "deviants" or "riffraff." Rioters, for example, could not be distinguished from nonrioters on the basis of income. Approximately one third of each group earned incomes less than $5,000 per person in Detroit and $5,000 per family in Newark. In the words of the authors:

> The rioters are not the poorest of the poor. They are not the hard core unemployed. They are not the least educated. They are not unassimilated migrants or newcomers to the city. There is no evidence that they have serious personality disturbances. None of these factors set the rioter off from the rest of the community in a way that justifies considering him a personal failure or an irresponsible person. In fact on some pro-social items . . . the rioter compares favorably with the non-rioter or even surpasses him.

The authors did find, however, that rioters were significantly more likely than nonrioters to report the following: dissatisfaction with their jobs and an aspiration for better jobs, racial discrimination as the major obstacle to better employment, personal experience of discrimination in their work and in schools, and hatred of whites. Furthermore, rioters were almost twice as likely as nonrioters to rate blacks smarter, nicer, braver, and more dependable than whites, and to consider the United States not worth fighting for (more than 50 percent of the rioting group shared this last sentiment).

The authors conclude:

> The continued exclusion of Negroes from American economic and social life is the fundamental cause of riots. This exclusion is a result of arbitrary social barriers rather than of lack of ability or aspiration on the part of Negroes, and it is most galling to young Negroes who perceive it as arbitrary and unjust.

The Caplan-Paige study [2] provides a useful statistical description of some of the motivational elements in rioting. Their work is clear, and their conclusions have particular relevance to social scientists. Compared to his nonrioting counterpart, the rioter is unlikely to be any poorer, less educated, or, at least by gross measurements, any more likely to be emotionally disturbed. Indeed he may be a bit better off educationally. He is, however, angrier than the nonrioter; much more aware of the disparity between his social role expectation and his objective condition; much likelier to offer white racism as an explanation of this disparity; and less likely to attribute it to black biological, social, or cultural inferiority. Although this analysis has taken us a long way in determining the source of rioter disaffection, it still leaves open the question of why some have chosen rioting to express this disaffection.

Violence vs. Nonviolent Alternatives

Thomas Pettigrew [15] has outlined four conditions that he considers capable of provoking "revolt" by a minority group. These are as follows: (1) living conditions of the dominant group advance faster than those of the subordinate group; (2) the aspirations of the subordinate group advance faster than actual changes; (3) social status inconsistencies among subordinate group members increase sharply; and (4) a broadening of comparative reference groups occurs for the subordinate group.

Each of these four conditions characterizes the black citizen today. Thus, according to Pettigrew: (1) though the past few decades have witnessed rapid advances in black America, these gains have failed to keep pace with those of white America during these same "prosperous years"; (2) public opinion surveys have documented the swiftly rising aspirations of blacks, especially since 1954; (3) moreover, social status inconsistency has been increasing among blacks, particularly among the young, whose educational level typically exceeds the low-status employment offered them; (4) finally, blacks have greatly expanded "their relevant reference groups" in recent years—affluent whites and blacks are routinely adopted as the appropriate standard with which the disadvantaged compare their conditions.

These conditions constitute a near-classic case of *relative deprivation*, a condition that greatly intensifies the impatience for social change felt by a minority group.

Under these circumstances, of what value are litigation, negotiations, and two-party politics to an aggrieved group? For some these conflict resolution devices are still helpful, but for the urban black militant these alternatives offer increasingly less appeal. They seem tedious and have proved disillusioning. Perhaps more importantly these activities favor those groups with access to experienced personnel and large budgets, resources that the black militant does not sufficiently command. Without them he approaches traditional in-

tergroup encounters in a one-down position with a very small sense
of involvement and a very small "piece of the action." Lacking other
sources of power can make the power of disruption much more attractive. What then is the place of nonviolent protest? Certainly,
here is a tactic that has offered a sense of participation to many people despite their financial or technical resources. Where recently has
the American black triumphed as he did in his nonviolent confrontation with the legal underpinnings of southern racism in the early
1960's? Is the black militant turning away from nonviolence, and if
so, what is it that violence offers him that nonviolence cannot provide? To answer these questions demands considering several characteristics of black militancy: objectives, leadership, ideology and
self-esteem, and the opposition.

OBJECTIVES

First, let me consider the objectives of the urban black militant.
How do these differ from those of the civil rights worker in the
South? Recall that in the South the resistance to equality rested in an
irrational system that denied to blacks the most elementary rights of
free men—rights which had been long ago guaranteed to the white
citizen. These rights—to the security of life and property, to vote,
to free assembly, to a fair trial—were withheld in many cases by
those who legislated and who enforced the laws of the South. Other
rights, i.e., free, integrated education (affirmed by the 1954 Supreme
Court decision) and free public accommodation, had been ignored
by this same establishment. The objectives of the civil rights worker
were sharply defined. The goals were apparent, and the remedy was
equally clear—the white racists' rigid control of southern state law
and law enforcement had to be broken. In its place would be introduced more equitable federal laws and, if necessary, federal force.
As the civil rights movement dramatized the plight of the southern
black, northern legislative power came to its aid, and the Jim Crow
system began to crumble. This was the initial stage of reform, equivalent in its moral clarity to those earlier battles to ban child labor, to
obtain woman's suffrage, and to establish labor's right to organize
and bargain collectively [12].

Now a second stage emerges, one in which the problems are more
complex, one which demands administrative skills and bureaucratic
competence. It is in this second stage of reform that the traditional
civil rights movement has floundered. Rather than attempts at just
legislative change, the objectives now have become those of increasing job and educational opportunities, of improving inner-city hous-

ing, and of assuring the urban black of such services as health and police protection that would work in his behalf rather than against him. These objectives do not readily respond to the sit-in, the freedom ride, or the peace march. Nor can it be, in the words of Nathan Glazer [12]:

. . . decreed that Negroes and Whites have the same income regardless of their skills and education, or that they should have the same education regardless of their home backgrounds, or that they should have the same home backgrounds, regardless of their history, their culture, their experience.

LEADERSHIP

Among the tactical problems confronting the nonviolent practitioner in the big city, one of the foremost is the problem of leadership—the ability to command the respect and attention of both black and white communities. Nonviolence, at least as it was practiced by Martin Luther King, Jr., depended in part upon a moral appeal and required the attention of the mass media to realize the full impact of nonviolent efforts (see Chapter 5). As the more superficial evils began to crumble and more complex problems took their place, the successes of nonviolence seemed fewer and less apparent. With these diminishing successes a portion of the black community became less attentive to its nonviolent leadership. The white community had become at the same time more self-righteous—they had given up enough, it was time to slow down. But the demands of the urban black had been awakened by the successes in the South and awakened in a paradoxical fashion. What was this hue and cry about the success of the civil rights movement? How had it changed his life in the northern city? Furthermore, the impatience of the black youth had grown, as he, in the words of Pettigrew [15]:

. . . surveys the current scene and observes correctly that the benefits of recent racial advances had disproportionately accrued to the expanding middle class, leaving further behind the urban lower class. While the middle-class segment of Negro America has expanded from roughly five to twenty-five per cent of the group since 1940, the vast majority of Negroes remains poor. Raised on the proposition that racial integration is the basic solution to racial injustice, the young Negro's doubts grow as opportunities open for the skilled while the daily lives of the unskilled go largely unaffected. Accustomed to a rapid pace of events, many Negro youth wonder if integration will ever be possible in an America where the depth of white resistance to racial change becomes painfully more evident: the equivocation of the 1964 Democratic Party Convention when faced with the challenge of the Mississippi Freedom Democratic Party; the Selma bridge brutality; the summary rejection by the 1966 Congress of anti-discrimination legislation for housing; the repressive reaction to riots from the Chicago Mayor's vow to shoot looters and maim children to the New Jersey Governor's suspension of the Bill of Rights in Plainfield; and, finally, the wanton assassinations within ten weeks of two leading symbols of the integration movement. These events cumulated to create understandable doubts as to whether Dr. Martin Luther King's famous dream of equality could ever be achieved.

Thus it became necessary for the black leadership to raise the ante of provocation in order once again to capture the attention of the white American and the respect of the black man. As this occurred, many blacks directed their attention away from the "bland orthodoxy" of such men as Roy Wilkins and sought instead more charismatic advocates of the black cause, for example, "Rap" Brown and Stokely Carmichael. The Reverend Martin Luther King, Jr., who retained his own quality of personal magnetism, began to lose both his constituency and the attention of the mass media to these more radical leaders, as his demands remained unanswered by the white establishment and as his tactics, though noble, paled in contrast to the provocation of Black Power.

IDEOLOGY AND SELF-ESTEEM

What of the ideological compatibility of nonviolence to the cultural heritage of the northern black man? What function do nonviolent tactics—as compared to those of violence—serve in the self-esteem system of the northern black? Which tactic permits him to feel more self-confident and more powerful? Jerome Frank [11] suggests that the nonviolent activist, when properly trained, can derive considerable self-esteem from his activities. Robert Coles in his very compelling description of youth working in the southern civil rights movement [6] emphasizes the importance that the movement attached to developing a sense of pride and self-confidence among its workers. But Coles also describes [5] a battle fatigue syndrome that occurred among nonviolent civil rights workers. The syndrome resembled reactive depressions seen in psychiatric practice. It was characterized by feelings of exhaustion, weariness, despair, and outbursts of bitterness and rage. Often the syndrome heralded an abandonment of a commitment to nonviolence. In its place appeared a bitter disengagement or the advocacy of "a total disruptive assault upon society" [5]. Certainly, this suggests that *the work of nonviolence is tough; that it demands restraint; and that when this restraint fails, violent impulses emerge.*

VIOLENCE AND SELF-ESTEEM

To some, collective violence has appeared particularly well suited to the self-esteem requirements of the urban black. Many observers [9, 16, 19] have indicated that the contemporary interracial conflict represents, at least in part, an attempt on the part of the black to create a new self-image. All too frequently he has had to contain his hatred and rage and present the humiliating facade of docility and passivity. Against this background the nonviolent option seems conspicuously unattractive—too closely associated with past stigma, too symbolic of submission, weakness, and inferiority. In contrast, violence provides an opportunity to overcome the colonial mentality, a chance to beat the feeling of being a "nigger" [9]. Violence can be an irrevocable gesture asserting that one will no longer tolerate the humiliation of the past, that one is a man and must be respected as a man. Franz Fanon, a French-trained black psychiatrist who, in recording his observations of the Algerian revolution, became an intellectual fountainhead to the colonized black people of the world, put it this way [10]:

The group demands that the individual commit an irreversible deed. In Algeria, for example, where almost all of the men who called for the struggle of national liberation were condemned to death or pursued by the French police, confidence in a man was proportional to the degree of severity of his police case. Colonial man can liberate himself in and through violence.

Thus the act of violence commits a man symbolically to the revolutionary movement and breaks his ties with his previous life and its commitments. Fanon's observations might be credibly applied to the urban black man of this country who, like Fanon's Algerian insurrectionist, can be viewed as asserting his masculinity through arson, looting, and shooting and as finding these experiences self-liberating [9]. Presumably participation in such violence offers an opportunity to affirm one's identity, to slam the door on past humiliation, and to claim one's full manhood in a way not previously possible using nonviolent tactics.

THE DETROIT STUDY

In their analysis of the attitudes of 222 Detroit teen-age and young adult blacks, Charlotte Darrow and Paul Lowinger [9] attempted to document the degree to which activists were disillusioned with nonviolent methods. They performed their study in August 1967, within one month of the Detroit uprising.* In it they instructed 12 young blacks between the ages of 20 and 30 who had been active in the disturbances to present a structured interview to any of their black male friends and acquaintances between the ages of 15 and 30. Of the interview population most were unmarried, many were students and intellectuals, and almost all were self-described activists. Some 20 percent of them had previously participated in the civil rights movement. The sample included followers of Stokely Carmichael, H. "Rap" Brown, Malcolm X, Floyd McKissick, and Martin Luther King, Jr. The sample was divided into three age groups: 15 to 19, the 74 teen-agers; 20 to 25, the 98 "middle-aged"; and 26 to 30, the 50 "oldsters."

Among the teen-agers most were in the right grade for their age, 33 percent were entering their senior year in high school, and 12 percent were in college. Among the 20- to 25-year-olds, 70 percent had finished high school, and 14 percent had completed college. Among those over 25, 72 percent had finished high school, and 20 percent had graduated from college. This contrasts with the findings of a 1962 census of the Detroit black adult population, which included only 25 percent high school graduates and 4 percent college graduates.

The Darrow-Lowinger interviewees were better educated, younger, and more likely to be considered militant than the average Detroit black. Thus rather than a survey of the sentiments of the average black, this study assesses the sentiments held by black activists.

The activities of the interviewees testify to a considerable sympathy for the riot process. One-third of the total sample admitted to looting, using weapons, or setting fires. From the report it appears that a third of the teen-agers took part in the looting and one in twenty set fires. Among the men in their early 20's, 40 percent looted, 5 percent participated as arsonists, and 5 percent were snipers. Those older than 25 were the most restrained, less than 20 percent of this group having joined in the looting.

Furthermore, this older group also reported the largest proportion of negative feelings toward the riot (almost 60 percent) compared to 20 percent holding only positive feelings (24 percent were ambiv-

---

* The authors prefer the term uprising to riot or revolution. They consider a riot to mean "aimless behavior involving disturbances or turmoil" and a revolution to mean "the overthrow of a government by new political leadership with a new program." The collective violence in Detroit should, according to these authors, more properly be defined as an insurrection, connoting a "spontaneous insurgency of slum dwellers who feel oppressed by the political and economic structure."

alent). In contrast, 51 percent of those under age 26 held positive feelings about the riot, and less than one-fourth admitted to negative feelings. Negative feelings in this younger group arose from fear of police retaliation and disappointment, particularly among the teenagers, that "they couldn't get as much loot as they wanted" [9]. Those who felt positively toward the riot explained that it represented a successful assertion of black rights and that it provided an opportunity to retaliate against unfair merchants, usually white, or against the police.

Of the 143 interviewees who expressed an opinion, 81 agreed more with H. "Rap" Brown than with Martin Luther King, Jr. Brown received most of his support from the younger men and teen-agers— about 60 percent of this group—whereas only 40 percent of those between ages 26 and 30 agreed with him. Among the 153 subjects who offered an opinion about whether there would be another riot, 90 percent predicted that it would happen again.

Finally, the authors drew some striking, albeit controversial, impressions from their interviews:

The lack of communication between our subjects and the power structure is clear. This is no simple problem to be solved by calling a bi-racial committee. This new wave is not communicating with the Negro or the white leadership and the lack of communication is apparent in several areas. The Civil Rights Movement as we have known it is largely dead or moribund. No one denies the historical importance of Martin Luther King . . . nor questions the real achievements of the Civil Rights activities, especially in the South. But the local and national leaders of the Civil Rights Movement no longer speak for the militant segment of the Negro community we have interviewed. The new leadership is largely informal and almost entirely unrecognized in either the white or Negro establishment. The main demand of the people who answered our questionnaire is for self-government . . . and it is clear that our subjects do not regard the presence of two Negro congressmen, a Negro city councilman, Negro state legislators, Black judges and other Negro officials in Detroit as control . . . Integration . . . has become irrelevant according to our subjects . . . Better schools, jobs, police and housing . . . are not necessarily integrated schools, jobs, police and housing to our subjects.

The Darrow-Lowinger study makes no claim to represent a cross section of the black sentiment in Detroit. Their results, however, do offer some insight into the sentiment of those who may well be in the vanguard of black activism.

THE OPPOSITION

Depending in large part upon how an event in intergroup conflict is perceived and responded to, subsequent events will be more or less conciliatory. Campbell and Schuman [1] indicate that more than one-third of the more than 3,000 randomly selected urban whites interviewed in the spring of 1968 considered nonviolent demonstrations to be as offensive as riots. This finding suggests that many people are willing to have nonviolent tactics punished to the same degree as violent tactics. The interaction between the black and the white community depends very much upon how each perceives the other's behavior. Focusing on the black community, John Spiegel [19], Director of Brandeis University's Lemburg Center for the Study of Violence,* speaks of a *hostile belief system*, which, he suggests, prejudices the perspective of an aggrieved group. Black ghetto inhabitants believe that white people seek to exploit them; only under the strongest pressure, they argue, have whites enlarged opportunities for blacks. Furthermore, whites sanction the black man's daily harassment by police. Thus, according to Spiegel, the hostile belief system predicts what sort of abuse the black man anticipates from the dominant white community. In the ghetto the white community is represented most tangibly by the police [19].

POLICE PRACTICES AND GHETTO VIOLENCE

Several studies have emphasized the seriousness of perceived police mistreatment to urban blacks. In a survey of black grievances in twenty United States cities, the Kerner Commission [17] reports that police practices most commonly were cited as the most important grievance. In supplementary studies performed for this same commission by Campbell and Schuman [1], police practices proved once again a significant source of black dissatisfaction. Of the 2,800 blacks interviewed in fifteen large cities, more than one-third believed that police employ unnecessary force, make unnecessary searches, and give disrespectful treatment toward blacks. Another one-quarter were uncertain about this. Although only 4 percent of the black sample claimed direct experience with police brutality, this was four times the proportion found in the white sample. The authors observe further that:

Among both races, younger people are more likely to report and perceive police malpractice than are older people. On all items involving police excesses, men report direct experiences more often than do women. Major dissatisfaction, whether warranted or not, is thus concentrated among young males.

* Since September 1966 the Lemburg Center has been conducting research in six northern cities, directed toward elucidating causes and remedies for collective violence.

Quite probably the hostile belief system compromises the perspective of all protagonists in an intergroup conflict. For our purpose this includes the white population in general and the police as well as blacks and black militants. In a survey of attitudes among more than 1,000 white Philadelphia police officers in 1952, William Kephart [13] found that when asked what percentage of arrests in their district were black, three out of four officers overestimated the actual figures. Whereas blacks comprised about 70 percent of all persons arrested in the city, estimates of arrest rates by white officers averaged over 95 percent. Furthermore, this high expectation of black criminality held by white officers may influence the actual arrest rate by increasing the likelihood that ambiguous behavior on the part of blacks would result in their arrests.

More recently, in the spring of 1968, Peter Rossi and his coworkers [18] at Johns Hopkins University interviewed over 400 police in 15 major cities in an attempt to clarify the nature of the police relationship to the community. Part of their sample was selected randomly among officers working in predominantly black precincts. A sizable portion, however, had been chosen by precinct captains who presumably were reluctant to permit the interviewers access to their less liberal officers. Thus the sample probably was biased in the direction of those who maintain more positive attitudes toward blacks. In spite of this probable bias almost one-third of the white officers (three-fourths of the sample were white) believed that most black residents perceived the police as enemies. Almost 50 percent of the white officers believed that young adults and adolescents regarded the police as enemies. Likewise, one of four white officers held strongly negative attitudes toward the residents of their precincts. One-third of all the officers sampled did not know a single important youth leader well enough to greet him. Only one officer in six lived in the neighborhood in which he worked. Finally, the majority of white policemen attributed riots primarily to "militant agitation" and to "criminal elements" in the community.

That the hostile belief system contributes to the emergence of ghetto violence is supported by an analysis of the precipitating event in the twenty-four costliest civil disorders of 1967. Half of these grew out of a police-black confrontation. Recall further that in Watts, Newark, Detroit, Miami, and Chicago each riot began with an alleged abuse of police power [17].

VIOLENCE AND THE HOSTILE BELIEF SYSTEM

Several aspects of Spiegel's hostile belief system formulation need emphasis [19, 20]. First, the hostile belief system is a polarizing concept; as one employs the system, the positions of the two elements in conflict become almost irreconcilable. Second, extrication from the system's influence is almost precluded by the real limits confining the communication of the protagonists. In other words, the situation in which the opponents function seriously limits their capacity to avoid hostile encounters with each other. On the one hand, the black man sees the police as the most obvious manifestation of the white presence in the black community. The "cop" is, in fact, *the* representative of the white community in the ghetto and may be the only object available to the black man when other black-white communication outlets are foreclosed. Often one obeys or disobeys the law in the way one relates to police. If one does not like "cops" or what "cops" represent, there may be a great temptation to disobey the law, e.g., riot. The policeman, on the other hand, has been assigned responsibility for controlling criminal activity or, for the purposes of this discussion, for controlling collective violence. Yet other than controlling their own reactions, there is very little that the police can do to correct the conditions that are the source of this rioting. By the time police control is needed, it is almost too late to remedy a particular situation. The black man argues that police use of suppressive violence legitimates his own use of retaliatory violence. Some may reply that the police use violence not to suppress the black man but to defend the law. Of course this still leaves open the question of whether that law is being equitably applied. Furthermore, as psychiatrist Coles [7] points out, "The law which Negroes now defy once decreed them to be chattle." Whatever the facts may be about the real function of the police in the inner city, the irresponsible execution of their force obviously serves only to justify further violence on the part of the black.

Black Attitudes Toward Collective Violence

In the foregoing section I have considered some of the attitudes held by the black militant toward collective violence. To what degree do these militant attitudes represent those of his less militant neighbor, or more specifically, to what degree has collective violence, rather than its alternatives, captured the tactical commitment of the total black community? In a study performed for the National Advisory Commission on Civil Disorders, Angus Campbell and Howard Schuman [1] examined this question and reported some provocative findings. Trained black investigators interviewed over 2,800 black inhabitants in fifteen major United States cities. By means of a rigorous selection procedure known as probability sampling, they drew from enough addresses in each city to provide a sample of from 150 to 200 individuals per city. The age and sex distribution of the respondents approximated that of the urban population. Like the Caplan and Paige study [2], Campbell and Schuman's is a model of well-designed survey research: Sample groups are large, randomly selected, and representative of the population under study; interview questions are specific and uniform. Because of the rigor with which the authors approached the study, one should expect their data to provide a reliable index of the attitudes prevailing in the target population. The study offered compelling evidence of black attitudes toward collective violence:

1. Almost six out of ten blacks believed that the riots were justified responses to unfair conditions (one of ten believed the riots to have been primarily looting exercises).

2. The percentage of those who felt that the riots had benefited the black cause was half again as large as that of those who thought riots had hurt the cause.

3. More than three out of four respondents considered law, persuasion, and nonviolent protest to be "the best way for Negroes to try to gain their rights"; 15 percent advocated violence as the principal tactic.

4. More than three out of four indicated that they would "stay away" should a riot occur in their city; one of ten claimed that he would join the riot; and one of ten said that he would try to stop rioting should it occur.

5. Of those interviewed in the riot cities, 8 percent (2 percent of the full sample) acknowledged that they had taken part in past riots. Of these "rioters" six of ten indicated that they would join in again. Of those who had not participated, one in ten said that he would like to join a future riot if he had the chance.

6. Lastly, 6 percent of the sample felt so embittered toward American society as to advocate the formation of a separate black nation.

Campbell and Schuman share the impression of other investigators that self-reported rioters are usually young men. Advocacy of violence is three time as likely among those between 16 and 20. Of this group 30 percent favored violence as the primary focus to obtain full civil rights for blacks. Similarly, advocacy of violence is twice as likely among those between 20 and 30 as it is among those between 40 and 60. Men indicated willingness to participate in violent activities twice as often as women.

Although one can conclude from the evidence presented by

Campbell and Schuman that advocacy of violence is shared by only a minority of the black community, this fact is far from reassuring. The authors estimate that this 15 percent minority represents a population of half a million distributed throughout the fifteen cities studied. Furthermore, age trends indicate, albeit inconclusively, that the advocacy of collective violence is increasing in these cities. (To prove this, however, would require follow-up studies. Rather than a trend toward violence we might be observing the increased susceptibility of youth to novelty or to a form of expression that becomes less attractive with increasing age.) Finally, *more than 50 percent of urban blacks condone rioting in the setting of the ghetto or believe in its efficacy, or both.*

In their summary statement these authors [1] offer some cogent insights into the tactics and aspirations of the urban Negro:

The most important fact about those inclined toward violence is that they are not an isolated band of deviants condemned by almost all other Negroes, but are linked to a much larger group by a common definition of the problems that beset the Negro in America. . . . The use of violence as a form of protest has special meaning for Negroes at this point in history. The sudden outbreak of mass violence in the inner cities of the nation probably astonished the black population as much as it did the white . . . [yet] most Negroes see the riots as mainly protest, partly or wholly justified, and they are more likely to think them helpful to the Negro cause than hurtful. . . . The word "protest" is a key one . . . [for] revolutionary terminology . . . is misleading when one considers the meaning that most Negroes attach to the disturbances. Like the Montgomery bus boycott, the sit-ins, and the marches on Washington, to most Negroes the justification of the riots lies in their character as dramatic protests against racial injustice. They are louder and they are more dangerous, but their purpose is much the same. . . .

We must mention one other significant note in these data. There seems to exist in the Negro community a desire for cultural identity that is neither violent nor separatist in character. It expresses itself in the desire for knowledge of Negro history, in an interest in African culture and language, and in the concern to be openly and proudly black. While it may sometimes occur in forms that seem impractical, on the whole it appears to be a positive impulse toward racial identity which may in the long run contribute substantially to a more genuinely equal relationship between the races.

Value of Collective Violence

I turn now to an examination of the adaptive value of collective violence. Much of the theoretical work on the uses of violence has been performed by Professors Lewis Coser [8] and H. L. Nieburg [14]. Borrowing heavily from their work, I have attempted to delineate collective violence, as it could be employed by minority groups, into five functions: (1) direct utility, (2) self-actualization, (3) a danger signal, (4) a catalyst to other modes of communication, and (5) an instrument for group cohesiveness.

DIRECT UTILITARIAN FUNCTION OF VIOLENCE

Violence is one of several options available to a group trying to "get the job done." Generally, but not uniformly, a group will experiment with other alternatives before resorting to violence in accomplishing its end. All too often, however, the violent alternative is employed prematurely. This may occur as a consequence of the following: the equating of violence with personal heroism, the absence of sufficient group cohesiveness to sustain other options, or the appearance that violence may require less discipline—for example, it readily discharges frustration. In addition, violence may seem to be both the most direct means of getting the job done and the means involving the least danger of compromise. It is most likely to occur prematurely when an outside force is perceived to be threatening the annihilation of a group or when that force is perceived to be so unthreatening that the risk of retaliation is minimal. Finally, using violence to get the job done will occur when it seems to be the only means to achieve an important goal and when the importance of that goal outweighs whatever risks occur secondary to the use of violence.

VIOLENCE AND SELF-ACTUALIZATION

Self-actualization is defined here as the process through which man realizes his potential. The process occurs in a social matrix. Thus although the individual may be endowed with the potential for various forms of expression, it is ultimately the interaction between the individual and the environment that will determine which form will be used.

The self-actualization hypothesis suggests that some men effectively are prevented from using legitimate channels of self-expression. When this occurs, as it does frequently in the ghetto, violence may offer an alternate road to achievement. Whereas opportunities for upward mobility in important dimensions of this society's status system—ethnicity, education, income, employment—seem nil or negligible, the succcessful exercise of violence has historically been a road to achievement for poor youth. This is particularly true among adolescent gangs. Recently this road has provided expression for a variety of talents. The black gang may evolve into a political coalition that has cultivated organizational skills and verbal eloquence as well as the ability to apply force.

VIOLENCE AS A DANGER SIGNAL

Seeing violence as a danger signal presumes several things: (1) Social dysfunction will be attended to only when its existence can be communicated by those suffering the dysfunction to those who can remedy it. (2) Violence is one of many forms of intergroup communication. (3) Of all forms of intergroup communication, violence, at least in this culture, is most likely to elicit a response from the group receiving the communication. (4) Violence is most likely to be employed when other forms of communication have failed to elicit the desired response. Thus violence is a signal so drastic that it cannot fail to be perceived by men in power who previously have been inattentive to other forms of communication and who have not proven conspicuously sensitive to social ills.

When used as a danger signal, violence represents political intimidation. Implicit in this mechanism is the expectation that governing elites must attend to more benign forms of communication unless they are willing to take on a violent confrontation. It does not preclude the possibility that dissident leaders will attempt to co-opt unplanned violence—for example, rioting precipitated by an abuse of police power—and use this violence to reinforce their demands for reforms. If they retain a genuine constituency among the rioters, these leaders can be instrumental in calming their constituents and in attenuating the riot. Spiegel [20] has observed that in the early phase of rioting, when police are first confronted by angry ghetto inhabitants, the riot can be cooled by inviting militant leaders to present their grievances to important urban political officials. In this manner the rioting process can be short-circuited by sanctioning other forms of communication, like negotiation. One must emphasize, however, that the use of this device will only continue to be effective so long as dissidents trust the parties in the negotiations—their own leaders and the mayor or his representatives—and believe that negotiations will yield meaningful reform.

VIOLENCE AS A CATALYST

Next is the consideration of violence as a catalyst. In this case potential violence or the threat of violence opens up communication options to dissident groups that would not otherwise be available;

it represents the power to disrupt and, as such, catalyzes dialogue. Rather than simply signaling that "something is wrong" in a social system, collective violence, when used as a catalyst, specifically enhances the stature of an aggrieved group in conflict and *increases* the likelihood that a dialogue will occur between that group and the community power structure.

These catalytic effects act most characteristically to enhance the stature of the more responsible elements of the militant leadership. Communication in this case is rather complex because it involves three groups: the "responsible militants," the "irresponsible mob," and the "establishment." The responsible militant presents an implicit or explicit threat of violence unless concessions are granted to him by the establishment. It is assumed that both the power structure and the militant wish to avoid a violent encounter. The former does not wish to dissipate its energies in the suppression of a violent insurrection. Nor does it wish to suffer damage to goodwill images or to community property that would emerge from a violent protest. Similarly the militant may not wish to provoke the repressive countermeasures engendered by violent tactics, nor may he wish to risk the inevitable leadership upheaval likely to occur when collective violence runs amok. Classically the catalytic function of violence has been used by nonviolent leaders. In this form the leader pleads for concessions, threatening that without them he would lose control of the movement to more "radical" advocates. But the device can be used equally well in obtaining the objectives of militants more willing to employ tactical forms of collective violence. Many militants, including Malcolm X and Eldridge Cleaver, have employed the threat of violence in an attempt to gain concessions from city power structures. Among both types of leadership, violent and nonviolent, the message is identical: "You have been dealing with the wrong people; you must *deal* with *us;* otherwise, we will lose control of or unleash our people."

It must be emphasized that the catalytic effect of potential or threatened violence can only operate if the threat of violence seems credible. A leader cannot be caught too often crying "wolf." Consequently, violent demonstrations, usually against property, tend to occur in order to maintain both the status of the militant leader and the dialogue between the leader and the city power structure.

VIOLENCE AND GROUP COHESIVENESS

The cohesive function of violence has two aspects: (1) the effect collective violence has on its practitioners and (2) the effect on the recipients. Recall that the study by Lowinger and Darrow [9] suggests that many militants felt an increased sense of racial pride as a consequence of participating in a riot. Perhaps cohesiveness is a manifestation of attitudinal consistency. For instance, if an insurgent endangers himself in behalf of a group, he is subsequently more likely to look upon that group as something for which endangering himself is worthwhile.

As for the recipients of violence, a group under attack probably becomes more cohesive in order to defend itself. The threat of violence by black militants serves this cohesive function well by provoking police reprisals, which may in turn reinforce the militants. First, police violence tends to validate the hostile belief system of the militants by offering tangible justification to their interpretation of social reality, for example, "cops are fascist pigs." Second, white violence increases cohesiveness among black militants by providing an object on which they can, with a minimum of guilt, displace otherwise divisive internal hatreds and frustrations. Third, police violence further enhances militants' strength by attracting to their ranks those black moderates who often become its unwarranted recipients. "Riot control" can readily become neighborhood control, increasing the likelihood that police violence during a riot will affect bystanders as well as agitators. The nonviolent bystander, whether moderate or militant, having been stung by police nightsticks, mace, or bullets, becomes increasingly receptive to the persuasion of his more violent brother. Police violence, furthermore, produces martyrs to the militant cause, many of whom may not have been actively involved in the militant movement at the time of their martyrdom. One must also keep in mind that in similar fashion black violent provocation can consolidate the antiblack posture of the white community. In short, violence pushes people into opposing groups, each of whom sees the other as an enemy. *The perception then of an increasing threat to group survival facilitates intragroup cohesion.*

Collective Violence by Minority Groups: A Theoretical Model

In an attempt to synthesize the foregoing discussion, I propose a model for understanding collective violence in the black community. With some modifications this model should be useful in understanding collective violence as it may be employed by other minority groups—students, under-class whites, Mexican-Americans, and American Indians.

Collective violence, in this instance in black communities, will emerge, although not quite sequentially, from the following conditions.

1. To a significant degree, the black American occupies a social class that has only limited access to the advantages accruing to other classes or groups in a community—advantages such as adequate employment, housing, and education [17]. Hence many blacks comprise an under-class—a social group not sharing sufficiently in the experience of upward mobility and blocked from the prerogatives of full citizenship. In the case of the urban black, that blocking force is perceived as racial discrimination [2].

2. Poor living conditions such as those occurring in the ghetto or inner-city slum serve as an omnipresent reminder of the black's perceived exploitation by the white community. Likewise the police are perceived as the occupying force of this white community, who function to control the black man rather than to work in his behalf [1, 17].

3. In turn, police see themselves for the most part as alien to the black community. Many of them view agitation for black rights as unjustified and view riots as the handiwork of criminals or subversives [18].

4. Interaction between police and ghetto dwellers is potentially explosive. Communications are compromised by what Spiegel calls the *hostile belief system,* as each party to the interaction focuses on the most negative aspect of the other party's communication, thus confirming its hypothesis that the other party is a pernicious force. Responses become progressively more defensive, which results in less possibility for conciliation and greater potential for violent conflict [19, 20]. In this way each side comes to see its cause as justifying violence.

5. Alternatives to collective violence—litigation, negotiation, two-party politics, and nonviolent protest—although successful in some instances in the past, have become increasingly tedious and disillusioning for a sizable minority (currently about 15 percent) of the black community [2]. Most of these alternatives demand expertise and finances that this militant minority does not sufficiently possess. In addition, these alternatives are perceived both as having yielded little improvement in the grievances of this group and as having failed to awaken community power structures to the intensity of the needs of the urban black man.

6. The promises of the civil rights movement, together with the mass media, especially television (the universal appliance of the ghetto), have awakened and heightened the expectations of the urban black. They have increased his awareness of the disparity between his aspirations and his condition [11]. The failure of the promises, combined with the awareness of their potential fulfillment, results in the anger-producing phenomenon of dashed hopes (see Chapter 4).

7. Young, relatively well-educated men become most sensitive to the disparity between their aspirations and their actual conditions. They have, in addition, been quickest to dismiss the utility of nonviolent alternatives in fulfilling these aspirations and have been quickest to perceive, or be seduced by, the apparent effectiveness of collective violence [1, 9]. Pettigrew [15] has observed that the "most significant fact about this 'newest new Negro' is that he is relatively released from the principal social controls recognized by his parents and grandparents." Pettigrew identifies these restraints as an extended kinship system, a conservative religion, and an acceptance of the inevitability of white supremacy. That the northern black is more likely to feel free from these traditional social constraints may explain, in part, the greater frequency of and propensity for violent protests among northern versus southern blacks. Furthermore, recent changes in urban conditions, although small, may be more visible in the South, thus serving as a temporary palliative to black distress.

8. Traditional roads to self-fulfillment such as education require years for payoffs to occur, if they occur at all. This is true of all upwardly mobile groups. What seems conspicuously lacking among black youth, however, is the confidence that these traditional roads will yield rewards. The cynicism emerging from past disappointments has become increasingly oppressive. Violence, in contrast, seems to provide a quick means to self-fulfillment for ghetto youth. It provides a sense of competence that is neither constrained nor thwarted by the inhibitions which the youth confronts when he undertakes other forms of self-expression. Furthermore, violent tactics may reinforce the participant's sense of personal potency and offer him a chance to overcome a legacy of humiliating compliance [9, 10].

9. Thus an ideology or romance of violence has emerged, which partly because of tactical realities and partly because of needs for self-esteem has captured a sizable constituency among urban blacks. This ideology lowers the threshold of provocation.

10. Current conditions such as overcrowding, "long, hot summers," and insensitive police practices conspire to further lower this threshold and, particularly in the case of police practices, often become the immediate precursor to collective violence [17].

11. Finally, collective violence or threatened collective violence has short-term adjustive potential that warrants consideration. Collective violence may represent some combination of the following: (1) direct utility in getting the job done, (2) temporary self-actualization or aggrandizement, (3) a danger signal that awakens a previously inattentive establishment to the needs of an aggrieved group [8], (4) a catalyst to dialogue between the aggrieved group leadership and the establishment [8], and (5) an instrument for group cohesiveness. Indeed it is the potential combination of immediate valued effects that makes violence a tempting means for an aggrieved group to resolve conflict.

SHORTCOMINGS OF COLLECTIVE VIOLENCE

Yet the shortcomings of collective violence cannot be ignored. Many of these are well known. Some warrant particular emphasis. Collective violence is, first of all, a polarizing tactic that yields not only cohesiveness within groups but also increases hostility and suspicion between groups. Once employed, the possibility of restraint or reconciliation is considerably reduced. If unrestrained, collective violence can yield human misery of a magnitude not attending other communication options, and it risks functional extinction for the weaker group in a violent encounter. Finally, learning theory indicates that as violent behaviors are practiced, they become learned; and as they become learned, they become increasingly relied upon in subsequent encounters (see Chapter 3). Thus the most unfortunate repercussion of collective violence is the continuation of the violent process itself.

One might at this point want to inquire, "What function does collective violence serve that the nonviolent alternative could not better serve? Couldn't nonviolent protest also be employed as a danger signal, a catalyst to dialogue, a builder of self-esteem, or a means to group cohesiveness?" In response one must acknowledge that although nonviolent tactics may serve these functions well, they demand, unlike collective violence, a strong leadership, a unified and disciplined following, a coherent ideology, and a responsive adversary—in this case a white community willing to relinquish power. *With time, as these conditions are met by urban militants, we can anticipate an increase in the use of nonviolent alternatives.* At present, however, this development seems unfortunately remote or, at any rate, one that will be very difficult to achieve in the foreseeable future. Dr. Jerome Frank [11], a self-acknowledged advocate of nonviolence, has observed that:

While not all the participants in a nonviolent campaign need to share the leader's philosophy, it is questionable whether such tactics can succeed in the total absence of a sustaining ideology because the temptation to abandon them as soon as they appear not to be working is very strong. The present growing resort to violence in the American civil rights struggle suggests that nonviolence cannot be maintained in the absence of allegiance to a leader who is sustained by an ideology . . . non-violent action probably cannot succeed as a set of tactical maneuvers unsupported by ideas, and it will probably also fail if based on ideology without discipline. . . .

Conclusions and Recommendations

What responses might the behavioral scientist invoke to facilitate the use of nonviolent rather than violent alternatives by an agrieved minority like the urban black community?

Several issues demand careful consideration. First, it would be valuable to *know* rather than to speculate what impact collective violence has on individual self-esteem, intragroup cohesiveness, and extragroup resistance to change. It would be equally important to study the effect on urban black attitudes of such reforms as increased intergroup exposure, increased community control, improved housing, broadened education and job opportunities, and so forth. To obtain this information would require well-designed prospective studies without which it would be extremely difficult to identify attitudes and behavior trends. In particular, it would be nearly impossible to relate conclusively such stimulus factors as riots or reform policies to the responses that these factors would elicit in a community.

Second, white and integrated communities, as well as black communities, should be the objects of social research. To date, the balance of investigations of interracial problems have focused on black people and black communities. This reflects an unstated bias on the part of behavioral scientists that changes among blacks will yield resolution of interracial conflict. Such an approach may reflect so-called institutional white racism in scientific endeavors. Investigations should emphasize understanding the origins of racism and the development of a strategy to decrease interracial tensions. Explorations need to be made at the interface areas between blacks and whites, e.g., integrated schools, with a view toward distinguishing successful from unsuccessful intergroup coping processes.

Third, active recruitment and training of black behavioral scientists would serve to broaden considerably the perspective and activities of the behavioral science community.

Fourth, in the wake of recent strident cries for black separatism, it unfortunately is easy to forget that a substantial majority of both *black and white Americans* favor integrative rather than separatist solutions to interracial problems [1, 15]. To date, the balance of social research indicates that *sustained* increase of interracial contact provides a successful device both for reducing interracial suspicion and for increasing interracial acceptance [15]. In contrast, racial separation has shown to be a cause rather than a remedy for interracial conflict.

Integrative solutions are least likely to work in the ghettos of our largest cities, but most blacks reside outside these large central cities, in small to middle-sized cities and rural towns, where the opportunities for integration strategies are considerable [15]. A successful integration effort would require tax support as well as broad metropolitan cooperation. Such an effort is far from impossible and, indeed, is urgently needed.

In our largest metropolitan areas, where total integration remains a very long-term objective and where the specter of collective violence is a recurrent possibility, exclusive commitment to integration solutions or to community enrichment programs (including self-determinism) will not suffice. Efforts must be focused exclusively neither on total integration (a vain hope in the short run) nor on programs of community self-determinism (certain to increase rather than decrease interracial animosities). Rather the objective should be a "both-and" rather than an "either-or" approach—both integration and community enrichment rather than simply desegregation or separatism.

At the conclusion of his cogent analysis of separatist assumptions, Pettigrew cautions [15]:

Our . . . examination . . . leads to one imperative: the attainment of a viable, democratic America, free from personal and institutional racism, requires extensive racial integration in all realms of life. To prescribe more separation because of discomfort, racism, conflict, or autonomy needs is like getting drunk again to cure a hangover. The nation's binge of *apartheid* must not be exacerbated but alleviated.

Thus we must commit our resources to a combined strategy of integration and community self-determinism if we wish to remain a pluralistic society and reduce collective violence. To this I would add that the hour is late—the longer we defer our commitment, the more difficult the solution will become.

It should be clear by now that our faith in laissez-faire social mobility has been misplaced—it alone has not relieved the despair of urban blacks and other minorities. Other solutions must be tried. It is in catalyzing and guiding the development of these solutions, many of which will be truly "social experiments," that the behavioral scientist can prove most useful. No longer can he permit himself to be merely an observer of human events. Increasingly his energies should turn toward translating information into action. Nowhere is the need for his contribution so urgent as in the control of human violence.

Acknowledgment

The author is deeply indebted to Professors David N. Daniels and David A. Hamburg of the Department of Psychiatry of Stanford University for their thoughtful assistance in the review and preparation of this chapter.

References

1. Campbell, A., and Schuman, H.   Racial Attitudes in Fifteen American Cities. *Supplemental Studies for the National Advisory Commission on Civil Disorders.* Washington, D.C.: U.S. Government Printing Office, 1968.
2. Caplan, N. S., and Paige, J. M.   A study of ghetto rioters. *Scientific American* 219:15, 1968.
3. Clark, D.   Urban violence. *America* 118:728, 1968.
4. Cleaver, E.   Requiem for nonviolence. *Ramparts,* May 1968.
5. Coles, R.   Social struggle and weariness. *Psychiatry* 27:305, 1964.
6. Coles, R.   *Children of Crisis: A Study of Courage and Fear.* Boston: Little, Brown, 1967.
7. Coles, R.   Maybe God will come and clean up this mess. *Atlantic* 220:103, 1967.
8. Coser, L. A.   *Continuities in the Study of Social Conflict.* New York: Free Press, 1967.
9. Darrow, C., and Lowinger, P.   The Detroit Uprising: A Psychological Study. In Masserman, J. (Ed.), *The Dynamics of Dissent.* Science and Psychoanalysis, vol. 13. New York: Grune & Stratton, 1968.

10. Fanon, F. *The Wretched of the Earth.* New York: Grove Press, 1963.
11. Frank, J. D. *Sanity and Survival.* New York: Vintage, 1968.
12. Glazer, N. The new left and its limits. *Commentary* 46:31, 1968.
13. Kephart, W. *Racial Factors in Urban Law Enforcement.* Philadelphia: University of Pennsylvania Press, 1957.
14. Nieburg, H. L. Uses of violence. *Journal of Conflict Resolution* 7:43, 1963.
15. Pettigrew, T. F. Racially Separate or Together? (Presidential Address of the Society for Psychological Study of Social Issues, San Francisco, Sept. 1, 1968.) *Journal of Social Issues* 25:45, 1969.
16. Poussaint, A. A Negro psychiatrist explains the Negro psyche. *New York Times Magazine*, Aug. 20, 1967.
17. *Report of The National Advisory Commission on Civil Disorders.* New York: Bantam Books, 1968.
18. Rossi, P., Berk, R., Boesel, D., Edison, B., and Groves, W. Between White and Black: The Faces of American Institutions in the Ghetto. In *Supplemental Studies for The National Advisory Commission on Civil Disorders.* Washington, D.C.: U.S. Government Printing Office, 1968.
19. Spiegel, J. P. The Social and Psychological Dynamics of Militant Negro Activism: A Preliminary Report. In Masserman, J. (Ed.), *The Dynamics of Dissent.* Science and Psychoanalysis, vol. 13. New York: Grune & Stratton, 1968.
20. Spiegel, J. P. The nature of the riot process. *Psychiatric Opinion* 5:6, 1968.

7. Violence in the Mass Media

Alberta E. Siegel, Ph.D.

Americans have long wondered whether the violence that pervades our mass media in this country—our comic books, newspapers, movies, and television shows—may spill over into our behavior toward each other. This question has been raised about the penny dreadful, the tabloid newspaper, the lurid comic book, the dime novel, the radio crime serial, and more recently about television. Whenever a group discusses the stain of violence on our social scene, someone is bound to ask whether we should blame the media. Is there a link between our high rate of homicide and the endless stream of brutal Westerns and ugly crime shows that are mass produced in our television and movie studios?

The question is raised so persistently and so earnestly that it deserves careful consideration from social scientists. I am especially interested in the impact of the media on the young child, and as a child psychologist I am able to discuss violence in the mass media in the context of what is known about how the child experiences his world and learns to live in it and cope with its challenges. This discussion must begin with a consideration of how the child takes in experience and draws lessons from it.

Modes of Receiving Information

Mammals rely on sense organs for information. Impressions reach the brain only after being mediated by either touch, smell, vision,

This chapter is a revision of a paper, The Effects of Mass Media Portrayals of Violence upon Interpersonal Relations, prepared in November 1968 for the National Commission on the Causes and Prevention of Violence.

hearing, taste, and so forth. For each species particular senses are especially vivid and capable of transmitting detailed information.

Human beings gain information from several senses but are particularly attuned to certain senses. In comparison with the dog, for example, the human is not especially attuned to smell. Rather, man gains most of his information from looking and hearing.

Vision and audition are not dominant at birth in man, but rather they assume their dominance as the child matures. Early in human life the proximal senses are most important to the human—the baby communicates with his environment via modalities like touch and taste. He makes choices on the basis of how something feels or tastes. Very quickly in the development of the child, however, the distal senses—vision and audition—assume dominance over the proximal. This fact is important for our understanding of how a human child learns to be a useful and contented member of his social group.

Processes of Social Learning

A continuing task of every human group is the socialization and enculturation of its young. For a society to survive, the infants born to its members must survive, and they must acquire the habits and beliefs and values of the society's members. Every society is organized to assure the survival of at least some of the infants born into it. Through countless formal and informal techniques it socializes these youngsters into its way of life. In teaching the young child, the adults in the society rely on all his sensory equipment. The adult "reaches" a child and educates him by every communication mode available to that child.

We do not know what a child would be like if he grew up apart from any human society; there is no well-documented instance of the occurrence of this, and on the face of the matter such an event seems unlikely. The human infant's survival depends almost entirely on intelligent and devoted ministrations to him by other persons. These ministrations occur in the context of an emotional bond between the adult and infant, which calls forth socializing efforts from the adults and learning efforts from the child.

Although every society has some formal program for socializing its young—some program of education, religious instruction, inculcation of values through exhortation, and so forth—most socialization occurs informally, in the context of day-to-day living. Thus the child learns to walk not usually because anyone has taught him but because informally he has been encouraged to acquire the skills of walking. Speech is learned the same way—it is not common for individuals in a society to make a formal effort to teach a child to speak, but rather they provide him with countless examples of speech, which he learns through observation and imitation.

The child's motivation to learn about how to behave in his society depends largely on his wish to please other people, especially those who care for him; his wish to gain acceptance and love from them; his wish to gain the material rewards that are contingent on acceptable behavior; and his wish to gain mastery over his environment. My task here is not to consider these motivations in detail but instead to consider how the child gains information from his environment about how to act in accordance with these wishes.

TRIAL AND ERROR, REWARD AND PUNISHMENT

From the first days of life the child makes many responses. Some of these result in pleasure for him, and others bring pain. His behavior is shaped by these experiences of reward and punishment, and through trial and error he learns which behaviors on his part are likely to be rewarded and which likely to be ignored or punished. From earliest infancy behavioral science research shows that infants are capable of learning from this process and that the learning is important.

OBSERVATION AND IMITATION

But the child is not stranded on a desert island in his learning. He need not learn everything for himself, by the tedious and painful processes of trial and error. He may also learn by drawing on the successes and failures of others around him, by observing how they behave and what works out well for them.

The child uses all his senses in learning about his social group and its customs. When a young child sits at night at his tribe's campfire, taking in adult narratives of the tribe's bravery and accomplishments, every sense is active. He hears the story the adult is telling; he sees the adult's gestures and facial expressions; he feels the warmth of the campfire and the warmth of the other bodies near him; he smells the fire, the other people, the dampness that presages rain later in the night.

Anyone who observes young children carefully will be impressed by how much of their time is spent in passive observation of other people. Although it is true that the child of one or two years is a bundle of energy, constantly on the go, it is also true that he is a devoted watcher, a looker-on. In fact observation and imitation probably constitute his principal mode of learning at this age, supplanting trial and error in importance. Like other primates ("monkey see, monkey do"), the young human is a watcher and an imitator, relying on vision for information about how people behave, and then incorporating this visually transmitted information into his own way of behaving.

It is customary to say that primitive man transmitted his culture from generation to generation through an oral tradition, meaning that older people spoke, and the younger people listened. But it is inexact to say that only oral speech was involved in cultural transmission. In fact the child learned about the tribe's culture not only by listening to talk about it but also by observing its enactment. For example, a youngster learned the dances of his tribe by observing them and not principally by spoken instruction in dance movements. He learned how to hunt by watching the skillful performance of talented hunters and not merely by listening to disquisitions on the arts of maiming and killing. Thus not only listening but also all the other sensory modes of receiving information are used by the youngster in learning about the people around him, how they live, what they do, and what they believe.

SPOKEN INSTRUCTION

There are several "universals" in children's social learning. Universally, in all cultures, children learn by trial and error, and they learn by observation and imitation. It is also true in all human groups that children learn from spoken instructions. All human groups have the ability to speak a language, and all normal children in a society learn to understand and speak the language used by the adults in that society. Over the face of the earth and over long stretches of time, human beings have developed many different languages. Although different groups can not understand each other's speech in the Tower of Babel, what is common to all men is the use of some spoken language. An oral tradition of cultural transmission depends on the existence of a language for the representation of information, and all cultures have language.

The human infant is not born with the ability to speak. There is no instance of a newborn using language. Throughout the first year of life communication between adult and infant occurs without the aid of language—the mother conveys information to her infant by touching, suckling, frowning, smiling, cooing, cuddling. Although she may speak words to him and may have the impression that these words are "getting to" him, in fact, it is usually the tone and inflections of her voice rather than her words that are meaningful to the infant. Toward the child's first birthday he begins to understand some of the words spoken to him, and in his second year he begins to speak a few words. His understanding of spoken language grows rapidly in the second and third years of life along with his ability to produce meaningful sounds. By age four or five the human child typically has a working grasp of the language of his cultural group. From then on he is capable of learning from its oral tradition. Now he can learn not only through observation and imitation but also through verbal conceptualization. The child whose brain does not mature in a way enabling him to learn to understand and to speak language is seen in any society as atypical and deviant. In all human groups this ability to employ language emerges in the first four or five years of life.

GRAPHIC REPRESENTATION

Most human social groups have supplemented their spoken language by a graphical representation of objects or ideas. Sketches, paintings, and various signs have been used to stand for certain objects or concepts. Cave paintings, sand paintings, etchings on bark, carvings in stone and bone, and so forth are used to preserve information and to transmit it across the generations. There is thus a visual tradition that supplements the verbal transmission of culture.

WRITTEN INSTRUCTION

Only a comparatively few cultural groups have gone beyond graphical representation to more abstract ways of encoding and transmitting information visually. A written language is such a system. The signs in the language are not graphic representations but instead are symbols, which by convention are understood to represent some object or idea. Those human groups that have developed a written language have benefited enormously. It is the cultural groups with writing that have had an advantage in competitive situations, have developed complex technologies, have expanded their geographic control, have achieved economic development, and so forth.

In all cultures in which writing exists, it is used to preserve information about the group's values, history, beliefs, and religion. It is used to supplement the spoken tradition in socializing the young. Thus in a human group that has a written language, it is possible to educate the young not only by relying on their ability to observe and imitate and on their ability to understand spoken language but also by relying on their ability to learn and to use the written language. The child who can read is able both to learn about the history of his civilization over many centuries and to acquire a detailed understanding of his group's technology.

We who live in the United States in the latter half of the twentieth century are so accustomed to book learning that it is easy for us to forget how specialized this form of learning is and how insignificant in the sweep of human experience. Most human beings in the history of the world have been totally illiterate, and even today literacy is not characteristic of the majority of the inhabitants of the world. The ability to employ a written language is "power," and that power has been preserved for privileged groups. In the medieval period, for example, only the nobility and the clerical groups had the ability to read and write, and, in fact, among the nobility it was only the males who had this ability. In modern times literacy has been shared by the nobility and the clerics with the middle class. In the early nineteenth century in the United States, it was expected that white males would learn to read, but good reading ability was not expected of most females, and slaves of both sexes were not expected to be able to read. Only later in the nineteenth century was literacy expected of both males and females among the whites and an effort made to teach reading to the freed slaves and to their children.

The ideal of universal education of the young is a twentieth-century notion of Western man, and only in Western civilizations has it been implemented. Even today four years of schooling is the minimum requirement in many Western nations, and many youngsters leave school as soon as they achieve that minimum. The United States is quite unusual in the total range of human historical experience in its stress on literacy for all its youth and in its insistence that youngsters remain in school well into the second decade of life. And even we, with our heavy stress on education, have not achieved universal literacy among our people. Adequate schooling is not available to our total populace. Where it is, school problems are common among grade school children, and dropping out is common among adolescents. Both represent our failure to teach literacy adequately.

Thus in the United States we are still implementing the revolution in social learning that was launched by the development of a written language and subsequently by the development of printing. We are still at work at the task of instructing all our people in the skills of deriving information from the printed word.

At the same time our society has plummeted into an era in which the printed word is no longer the only mass medium of communication. New ways of transmitting information from one human to another have been developed, and our children are learning from these new media of communication at the same time that they continue to learn from spoken communication and from the printed word. In their social learning our children rely not only on trial and error, observation and imitation, and spoken instruction, as have all children through history and throughout the world, but they also rely on other sources of learning.

The Media, the Senses, and Information Transmission

The media of communication differ in the perceptual modalities to which they appeal and in the amount of training that is necessary before they can be used. Thus *personal spoken communication* is perhaps the primary human medium of communication. It appeals to audition and secondarily to vision (lip reading), and the training needed to understand it is given universally to all children in the early years of life.

Graphic communication, through drawings, sketches, etchings, appeals to vision. When it is directly representational, only a little training is needed to understand it.

Written communication appeals to vision also. Extensive training is needed to understand it. As is noted above, that training has in the past been offered only to selected human beings. Moreover, the production of written communications has in times past been a slow process. Until the invention of printing, a written communication could be reproduced only laboriously by a human copier. In the medieval period many individuals devoted their lifetimes to copying texts. With the invention of printing, mass production of printed texts became possible, and thereafter the written (printed) word became increasingly important in human affairs. Yet it took centuries for our society to develop the means to benefit from the invention of printing, and only by the late nineteenth century and early twentieth century did we have the technology to support this invention—the ability to produce paper, to produce printing machines, to distribute printed paper rapidly and widely, and so forth. And only by that period did we have a mass base of consumers able to benefit from this technology—people who could read and understand the printed word. Only then did the printed word become increasingly important to mass culture.

The twentieth century has witnessed the invention and promulgation of several new modes of communication.

One of these, the *telephone,* appeals exclusively to audition. The special appeal of this mode is that it enables contact between individuals who are not within hailing distance of each other. The telephone is an extension of the ear. Very little training appears to be needed for its use, although there are folk tales about adult immigrants to America who could never learn to use the telephone effectively, who never got over the habit of shouting into the receiver, and who were preplexed by the babble in the receiver. It is notable that infants are fascinated by telephones and that young children go through a period when they appear to understand the speech that they hear through the phone receiver but do not respond to it. (Every doting parent has had the experience of telling his 2-year-old to "say hello to grandma" and of then standing by with growing exasperation watching his child listen mutely to grandmother's voice saying "Hello, Danny," and "Are you there, Danny?") By age 3 or 4 the child is able to carry on the give-and-take of a telephone conversation. The school-age child is an accomplished telephone user, and by adolescence the telephone seems to be almost the perferred mode of social interaction.

Radio is another modern medium that appeals exclusively to audition. In contrast to the telephone it is a one-way rather than a two-way system, putting the communications receiver in a totally passive role. (The recent renaissance of radio has occurred in part because of "call-in" techniques that remove the listener from that passivity, and which use the telephone to make radio into a two-way communications system.) Radio contrasts with the telephone also in fidelity, being capable of transmitting a very wide range of sounds with high fidelity, so that it may be used for music as well as for human speech. Essentially no training is needed to enable an individual to receive radio communication, and very little skill is required to operate a radio. Children are able to receive radio communication as soon as they are able to attend to sounds, and many mothers find that their young infants are soothed by music from radio or by an announcer's mellifluous tones. Children are able to comprehend spoken communications by radio almost as soon as they can understand face-to-face speech. There is a difference in favor of personal speech because in face-to-face speech the spoken word is augmented by detailed nonverbal communications that accompany and reinforce it. The child gets the message not only from the words but also from the speaker's facial expression, body position, and so forth. These modalities are absent from radio, and for this reason radio is less effective than a personal speaker. By age three or four, however, children are "tuned in" to radio, and in years past it was a preferred communications medium for many school-age children. Just as their mothers listened to the soap operas during the morning and early afternoon hours, school-age children listened to their serials during the late afternoon and early evening hours.

Comic books are a form of visual communication, although they have esthetic appeal through touch and smell as well—most adults are able to remember how the books felt and how they smelled as well as what they looked like. Their central device is redundancy between the verbal message and accompanying graphic message, which is typically vivid and simple. The books hold some appeal for children who cannot read at all, an indication of how much is communicated directly by the pictures. Their central appeal is to the partly literate reader, child or adult, and for this reason the comic book format has been widely imitated—for instance, in manuals to train hard-core unemployed workers and in appeals to voters in underprivileged communities. In contrast to the telephone and the radio, the comic book has almost no appeal at all to the infant and young child, and children become interested in this format only after they are relatively mature and sophisticated as communications-receivers, in their fifth year and later. Another contrast between the telephone or the radio and the comic book is that the pacing of the former is beyond the receiver's control; the radio listener cannot adjust the rate at which the announcer or comedian speaks. But the comic book reader can control the pace at which the information on the page comes to him. Adults who watch children read comic books are struck by the children's absorption, their deliberateness in plodding from square to square, their turning back to pages for re-reading, and their return to the same comic book for another exposure on another day.

The wax *recording* was also a permanent embodiment, this time of an auditory rather than a visual message. Despite initial low fidelity, records won a wide audience, and they continue to be a popular form of mass communication. As with the comic book the consumer has wide control over this medium—the child can play the same record over and over. Very young children can listen to records, but their access to them is controlled by the difficulties in playing them. The task of getting the needle into the groove is too difficult for a child until he is three or four years old. Special records for children have a wide audience among the young, and of course records for adolescents are the mainstay of the recording industry.

The *film* was a dramatic innovation in communication technology. Like the comic book and the record, and in contrast to the telephone and the radio, it involves the permanent embodiment of a message. Film provides a means of recording, preserving, and transmitting visual images that is infinitely more faithful to the source than any comic strip could be. The silent movie appealed exclusively to vision but did so in a way that had much greater impact than that of the earlier visual media—print, graphics, and the comic book. This impact occurs because of the film's fidelity to its source and because of its minimal reliance on words to transmit meaning. Further, the film embodies motion, and the human visual system is especially attuned to the perception of motion. The audience for a silent film does not need to know how to read in order to enjoy the film, though that ability is necessary for understanding the subtitles. As with comics the subtitles in a silent film are largely redundant with the visual information. Children respond to and enjoy films from a very young age. Their access to films has been controlled by the economics of the motion picture industry rather than by any constraints in their own sensory or intellectual endowment. The expense of owning and operating the film projection equipment, the need for a darkened room in which to show the film, plus the expense of renting commercial films, all combined to keep movies in commercial theaters, with access blocked by an admissions booth collecting tolls. The importance of the box office in controlling access by the young to films is attested by the ingenuity of youngsters in dreaming up ways to circumvent it and also by the fact that many American youngsters habitually spent all of their weekly allowances at that box office during the heyday of the movies.

The printed page became a mass medium of communication only when the system of education created a mass audience of readers. Only then could books and newspapers become the "first wave" of the *mass* media of communication. This first wave required the sophistication of being able to read the printed word. Radio, comic books, records, and silent films were the "second wave" of the modern communications media. They were techniques of communication that required little sophistication on the part of the receiver. Unlike books and newspapers these media did not require reading ability of their audience. Each technique in this second wave was beamed to one sense modality—radio and records appealing to audition, and comic books and silent movies to vision.

The "talkie" was such a major innovation that it deserves to be thought of as the "third wave." Here is a medium that reaches both vision and audition simultaneously, that provides an integrated appeal to eye and ear. The members of the audience for a talking film need no special training nor special skills; they need only the capacities for visual information-processing and for sound-decoding, which are universally characteristic of the human species. Just by being a normal member of the human race, and by having the price of admission to a theater, one is able to receive communication from *sound motion pictures*. The communication from sound films comes to us in the senses that are most acute and discriminating—seeing and hearing. The sound motion picture seemed to be "the ultimate" in mass communication, and it seemed so not only to the masters of hyperbole who were paid to advertise Hollywood. There was some talk about adding scents to the stimuli being emitted by the golden screen so that the audience would be stimulated olfactorily as well as visually and auditorily, but the talkies were so satisfactory that this proposal to replace them with smellies never got off the ground. Refinements on the movies—wider screens, curved screens, three dimension, color, stereophonic sound—were but minor embellishments on the basic technique of reaching the viewer's brain through both eye and ear with a vivid and integrated message. Children were delighted by the talkies, usually preferring them to any other medium of communication. Even the youngest child could be held in rapt fascination by a movie, and the amount of information children learned effortlessly from films was prodigious. As with the silent films, limitations on children's use of movies were external to the child, created by the technology and the economics of the movie— the need for a darkened room, expensive equipment, and money to rent the expensive film.

These limitations were bypassed rapidly by the next major innovation in mass communication, *television*. Like the movies, television beams simultaneous signals to both eye and ear. But unlike movies, TV does not require a darkened room, expensive equipment, nor rental payments. In our national economy the TV receiver is cheap, and TV programs are free. There is no admissions booth standing between the child and the TV screen; his access to TV is limited only by his ability to switch on the set, and most children can do that as soon as they can stand, i.e., by the end of the first year of life.

And the TV program is often "live" rather than "canned"—the TV viewer watches an event a split second after it occurs, rather than waiting for film to be developed, printed, and shipped to a theater. These differences between movies and TV justify our calling the advent of TV a separate wave in the development of mass communications.

Several trends are evident in the history of the development of techniques for transmitting information to the human senses.

One trend is diminishing reliance on written symbolization. To enjoy a book, one had to be a skilled reader. To read a newspaper, one needs less skill. Even less reading ability yet was needed for access to comic books and to silent films. And no reading ability at all is needed to be able to get the message from sound movies, radio, records, and TV.

A second trend is the integration of appeals to several senses. The early media reached one sense principally, but the newer media reach two senses simultaneously with an integrated message. The two senses that movies and TV reach—vision and audition—are the senses most highly developed in man, those on which he relies most heavily for gaining useful information from his environment. Further, movies and TV embody motion. In the deployment of attention the human visual system is especially vigilant to movement.

A third trend is toward rapidity of communication. In the days when the only way to get information across distances was to send a courier with a hand-written document, information traveled slowly. The invention of printing signaled the development of faster means of communicating across space, but generations passed before the supporting technology developed enabling use of printing in the production of newspapers. Simultaneous transmission of information is achieved by the newer media—radio, telephone, and television—with only a split second elapsing between the occurrence of an event and the apperception of it by the communications-receiver at a distant spot.

Fourth, there is a trend toward increased fidelity in communication techniques. The fidelity of a communication is the closeness of its correspondence to the event itself. The correspondence between the printed word *fire* and an actual fire is very low, but the correspondence between a color film about a fire and the actual event is much closer. One can almost feel the heat and smell the charred remains, though, in fact, neither temperature nor scent is being conveyed by the film. Today's telephone is a much higher fidelity instrument than its predecessors, but still the correspondence is not exact between the voice one hears over the telephone and the voice of that person when he is in the same room with the listener. Radio has higher fidelity than the telephone, and today's radio is notably higher in fidelity than its ancestor of fifty years ago. Similarly phonograph records and tape recordings have improved audio fidelity over the years. The color movie is, like the color TV set, more "hi fi" than its black and white counterpart.

What is the social significance of these trends? I have shown that with technological innovation the mass media have become (1) less word-bound, (2) more multisensory, (3) faster in transmitting information, and (4) of higher fidelity. Do these changes have any meaning for the lives of the people the media reach? Do the technological changes alter the social role of the media?

Fidelity, Vividness, Credibility, and Authenticity

Every member of a society must learn about that society, its values, and its habitual ways of behaving. All children achieve this learning through trial and error, through reward and punishment, through observation and imitation, through spoken instruction, through attending to graphic representations. In addition, children in literate societies like ours learn about their society and its culture through written instruction. To what extent are children likely to learn also from the even newer media—from radio, movies, and TV? I have reviewed the characteristics of these media, showing how they reach different senses and how accessible they are to children. Now it is important to consider how much children and adults learn from these media.

Fidelity is an engineering concept, readily definable in terms of the correspondence between an event and its reproduction by a communications medium. More interesting to the social scientist than a medium's fidelity is its credibility—the credence that is attached to what it communicates. The social scientist wonders how credible, believable, compelling, or authentic the medium is—he leaves preoccupation with fidelity to the hi-fi buff.

The mass media have historically been used for two main purposes. One purpose is to entertain, and the other is to inform.

Every medium has been used for both purposes. The book provides entertainment, for example, in the form of novels, poetry, and albums of photographs; and it provides information in the form of textbooks, encyclopedias, biographies, histories. Radio entertainment comes in the form of comedy skits, radio dramas, and the like; and information is distributed by radio in news reports, bulletins about traffic conditions, weather reports, interviews. Comic books have been used principally to entertain, but also the comic format has been adapted for political propaganda and in how-to-do-it manuals. The film provides entertainment in dramas, comedies, and musicals, but its capacity to inform has been exploited as well, in instructional films, documentaries, news films. TV spans both entertainment shows and informational presentations such as news reports. And the newspaper contains crossword puzzles, comic strips, horoscopes, and humor columns as well as columns of news calculated to inform. So the distinction between entertaining and informing does not rest on which medium is being considered—every medium is used in both ways.

The distinction between entertaining and informing is important because it is linked to the distinction between fantasy and reality, between fiction and truth, between romance and history. In making this distinction, I am not suggesting that only entertainment has esthetic value or that all informational presentations are unentertaining and boring. It should be obvious that so-called entertainment can be boring and unesthetic and that informational presentations can be pleasurable, absorbing, exciting, disgusting, and profoundly moving.

We all believe that presentations meant to inform should be authentic. A factual error in an encyclopedia is harmful to the reputation of that publication. A distortion of fact in the news columns of a newspaper can provide the basis for a libel suit and public demands for a retraction. A textbook is judged by the accuracy and completeness of the information it conveys to the student reader. A historian's account of a sequence of events is judged above all by its authenticity, and the notion of changing history to make it conform to ideology or political convenience is abhorrent to our tradition.

On the other hand, for presentations meant to entertain, authenticity is not usually thought to be an issue. We do not criticize or reject a comic strip about spacemen because the rockets portrayed in it move faster than any known propellant could power them. A soap opera is relished no less if in real life it would be impossible for a human to endure such an unending succession of melancholy reversals and still retain the liveliness and attractiveness of its radio characters. A comedy skit may be improved, not debased, if a comedian wears outsize shoes, a necktie like none ever seen off a vaudeville stage, a zany hat. We do not reject a children's story because it claims that all the characters will live happily ever after. Part of the creativity of fiction is the use of fantasy, imagination, dramatic distortion, and the like.

In short, we grant poetic license not only to the poet but also to the novelist, the comic strip artist, the soap opera dramatist, the comedian, the children's fiction writer, the TV dramatist. We do not grant poetic license to the educator, news broadcaster, reporter, biographer, historian, or encyclopedist.

The distinctions between fact and fiction, between history and romance, between news and entertainment, between reality and fantasy, are old distinctions. They antedate all the media, including print. Sophisticated and literate adults find these distinctions both useful and relatively easy to apply. They can be applied to each of the media—to the textbook in contrast with the novel, to the news broadcast in contrast with the war movie—but in making this distinction, one may be in danger of ignoring the authenticity or credibility that inheres in that medium.

For the intellect of the child, and for the less sophisticated aspects of intellect that adults share with children, there may be another distinction. Perhaps each medium of communication has its own *intrinsic* authenticity or credibility, and perhaps this feature lends itself indiscriminately to all the communications from that medium.

At the outset it seems plausible that this intrinsic authenticity is simply identical with the fidelity and the vividness of the communications. We have already defined fidelity as the psychophysical correspondence between the communication and its source. The *vividness* of a communication is defined in terms of the senses to which it appeals.

Since vision and audition are the primary modes of information processing in man, a medium that appeals to these senses is especially vivid. Thus it would be possible for the average housewife to locate the vegetables she wishes to buy in the supermarket solely by smell, since each vegetable has a distinctive fragrance. And through relying on smell and touch she could choose the particular vegetables that correspond to her standards of freshness and crispness. But no normal housewive selects vegetables this way, since it is so much more efficient for her to rely on vision in locating the wares she wants.

Furthermore, media that appeal to more than one sense are more vivid than those reaching only one. The most vivid media in the present array are those that appeal to the two most efficient senses, vision and audition. Thus I have already argued that talking movies and TV are in a class by themselves as effective media; this is because of their vividness as here defined.

A medium's intrinsic authenticity is a joint function of the medium's vividness and its fidelity. While both print and film appeal solely to vision, film has more intrinsic authenticity than print because its fidelity is higher. Similarly, though black and white film and color film likewise appeal solely to vision, color film is more authentic because its fidelity is higher. If a communication technique is both vivid and of high fidelity, as is the color film (a high fidelity representation reaching the two most important senses) or the color TV image (for which the same characterization holds), then its intrinsic authenticity is especially high.

The central point is that certain media present messages that seem to be de facto true or valid. Because of the characteristics of the medium the presentation on that medium comes across as authentic. Our judgment as to its authenticity or credibility does not rest on the sophisticated apparatuses of mature intellect, but rather on simple apparatuses that adults share with children. We may "know better," but still there is a part of us that gullibly accepts the vivid evidence of our senses. The psychologist might apply the term *face validity* to describe the intrinsic authenticity of a TV presentation. The vividness and fidelity of a presentation provide an implicit internal validation of its authenticity.

The quality of inherent authenticity that I am attempting to define here is the quality of film which makes it not quite appropriate for a musical comedy. Every film fan has had the discomfiting experience of being unable to enjoy and "get involved in" a musical precisely because the film does not come across as fantasy. It is difficult to believe that an enactment is not real when it comes to you in living color. This makes it difficult to accept the unreal actions of the characters in a musical—breaking into song while embracing, tap dancing down a factory assembly line.

The success of the animated cartoons in portraying fantasy, on the other hand, rests precisely on the fact that they circumvent the inherent authenticity of photography.

When movies and TV are used to report and inform, their quality of inherent authenticity, based on their high fidelity and their vividness, works to impress the news on the viewer in a forceful and compelling way. Most observers of our contemporary social scene are struck by how significant TV news reporting is in affecting the public's involvement in political issues, understanding of current affairs, and preferences among public figures. Through TV coverage of a national catastrophe and its aftermath, the tragic assassination of our President in 1963, a single mood of shared grief and mourning was sustained and augmented in the entire American population.

A typical comment on the impact of TV news reporting is the one made by a newspaper reporter [18] in his by-lined account of the 1968 presidential election contest in rural Iowa. He noted that the farmers whom he interviewed seemed less centrally preoccupied with the political issues immediately affecting their livelihood and their communities than they were with those they had learned about through TV and the other mass media:

Other issues have become so overriding as to obscure the farmer's problems, even in his own mind. Through some miracle of modern communication and repetition, the farmer lives in rural solitude and dwells upon crime-filled city streets, fiery demonstrations, bloody riots, bearded campus protestors, the frustrating war in Vietnam. And all indications are that those are the images that will fill the farmer's mind when he walks into the voting booth November 5.

Today the commonplace observation that TV news reporting influences people's conceptions of reality and thus their behavior, as exampled by the reporter's comments quoted above, is beginning to be joined by observations that TV dramatic shows may have the same effect. Many thoughtful observers of the contemporary scene note that the same TV set that brings news into the living room is also bringing realistic dramatic presentations. Russell Baker [1], in commenting on the nation's response to the assassination of Senator Robert F. Kennedy, noted the mixed emotions that were evoked by the fact that information about this event came to the viewer on the same set that purveys entertainment and sports:

Gradually, grouped together around the social center of the TV screen with its humdrum evocation of the shared boredom of idle evenings and endless Sunday afternoons, we struggle to suppress the horror.

Perhaps the fact that news and entertainment appear on the same medium is blurring the distinction between fact and fantasy. This was suggested by Clive Barnes [8] in a review of a new play on Broadway when he remarked that its playwright is

against the moral blindness that permits millions of people to treat [the war in Vietnam] as a kind of spectator sport to be watched on TV until we are no longer completely sure whether we are seeing our sons and brothers being killed on a newsreel or a few Hollywood actors biting the dust on the Late Late Show.

Again, we must consider the possibility that the inherent authenticity which characterizes TV is lending credibility to fictional presentations. George Willey, a newspaper columnist who writes about television, has raised his own doubts [34] about the distinction between reality and the producers' make-believe: "The growing concern is that what they make, many believe." He argues that the problem with violence in the mass media is not that it is emotionally upsetting or esthetically displeasing but that it is accepted as a representation of the way things really are. In one column [35] he reviewed the difficulty that TV producers have encountered in attempting to edit violence from TV programs already in production. His example is a producer who cut out some of the gorier aspects of a violent scene—a lady sniper fires a rifle at a young man driving through Black Rock town.

What will not be seen . . . is a part of the same sequence which had been filmed in the original version: a close-up shot of the windshield shattering and the young man, face bleeding, collapsing over the steering wheel. This, of course, is missing the point altogether. The objection to violence is not directed so much to the effect of violence but to the constant use of violence and the implicit suggestion that it should be anticipated wherever one goes.

This account bears on one response to the assassination of Senator Kennedy, an effort by the television and advertising industries of the United States to cut down on the amount of violence beamed over the airwaves. Other comments on that effort also touched on the topic under consideration—the blurred distinction between reality and fantasy. For example, a newspaper column [11] related that the Association of National Advertisers was urging its members to select television scripts that avoid excessive or unnecessary violence. The column concluded:

Yesterday an agency media guy made a valid point about television violence. "What do you do about the news programs?" he asked.

The same intuition was the basis for a by-lined column [22] that appeared after the Democratic Convention in Chicago in August 1968 with TV coverage of violent clashes between police and demonstrators. The columnist wonders whether the campaign against violence in TV programs, which started after the killing of Dr. Martin Luther King, Jr., and Sen. Robert F. Kennedy, has suffered a setback because of the riots at the Democratic National Convention.

All three networks have been seriously examining ways of diminishing violence in dramatic entertainment and in children's cartoons partly as a result of the widespread belief that television's example can influence the impressionable for good or evil. But the way network spokesmen look at it at the moment there isn't much point in cutting out the shooting in a Western or the pistol-whipping in an underworld drama if the viewer can switch to a news program and see citizens and the police locked in a bloody real life no-holds-barred conflict.

The argument imputed to the network spokesmen in this report makes sense only if one lumps together both fictional and news presentations in evaluating their effects on behavior.

No doubt the internal cues as to a communication's authenticity are important. A television presentation identified on the screen as news, and discussed and commented on by a man called a newsman, provides internal cues that its photographs of mayhem and destruction are to be understood differently from similar photographs identified as drama.

But the comfortable and well-understood old distinction between truth and fiction is blurred by a medium that presents truth and drama alternately, in the same frame, with the same sharp fidelity, and with the vividness that only a medium appealing to eye and ear simultaneously can invoke. The intuition is now widely shared that both fact and fancy have a certain *inherent* authenticity when presented on TV.

Media Content, Social Learning, and Violence

Is social behavior affected by the media? Do children who have grown up sustained by a diet of TV fare behave differently from the way that they would if TV did not exist?

These questions lie at the heart of our current concern about the media and violence. They are not easy to answer. Serious and disinterested observers differ as to how to frame the best answer on the basis of our current knowledge. Observers with a stake in the media capitalize on our present ignorance to draw reassurance that the profitable status quo is benign.

Human social behavior is learned. Much of the learning occurs through trial and error, through reward and punishment, especially in the earliest years of life. It does not seem likely that TV and other noninteractive media play much role in such learning, since they cannot provide differentiated feedback to an individual depending on the specifics of his behavior. Whether an infant is crying or quiet, awake or asleep, hungry or full, walking or sitting, behaving well or mischievously getting into trouble, the TV set drones on and on, uninfluenced by the infant's behavior. Such an unresponsive communications system does not enter readily into the trial and error learning occurring through reward and punishment.

But much human social behavior is learned also through observation and imitation. Increasingly as the years pass, children acquire the ability to model their behavior after behavior that they have observed, and this ability seems to be independent of rewards and punishments. To explain a child's behavior, we inquire about what observational learning opportunities have been available to him— "Where in the world did he learn to do *that?*" We know that children observe TV. Do they also imitate what they observe on TV?

The inherent authenticity of TV and movies makes it easy to believe that they do. Children understand TV presentations as being authentic and credible and assume that the world is really the way it appears on these representations. So it is natural for them to take the behavior they observe on TV as a model for their own. An amusing illustration of this [26] comes from Britain:

Presenting a resolution urging the Government to consider a code of conduct to guide people responsible for selecting television programs, Fred Armstrong [a member of the Rural District Councils Association, speaking at its annual conference] said that during one half-hour program the word "bloody" had been used 30 to 40 times.

Was it surprising, he asked, when a 6-year-old boy told a woman in a shop she was a "bloody silly old moo" because his favorite candy was sold out?

Although Americans might differ with this Briton as to the seriousness of the behavior he described, most would agree with him that the child probably did indeed learn from TV, and that his use of the forbidden word "bloody" probably resulted from his watching shows in which it was used by characters he subsequently imitated. At the other extreme is another account [23] of imitative behavior in Britain, this time about a 12-year-old boy who was found dead at his home in Leicester, in the English Midlands:

Television chiefs issued a warning to millions of youngsters today after an inquest on a boy who died while imitating his masked and cloaked hero, "Batman" . . . His father . . . told the inquest yesterday he thought his son, hanged while wearing a homemade Batman-style outfit, had been leaping from a cabinet in the garden shed when his neck caught in a nylon loop hanging from the roof. The inquest verdict was misadventure.

After the inquest [the father] said that he hoped the Batman show would be taken off British television. "It is far too dramatic and hair-raising," he said. "It encourages children to attempt the impossible." A television company spokesman said:

"We regret that the death of Charles Lee should be attributed to his viewing of Batman. Young viewers are cautioned that they should make no attempt to imitate Batman's activities.

"Before each episode young viewers are reminded that Batman does not in fact fly and that all of his exploits are accomplished by means of his secret equipment."

How are we to think about this event? In what sense is TV responsible for this young man's violent death? Is this 12-year-old's imitative behavior in the same category as the 6-year-old's remarks about "a bloody silly old moo"?

Not only children imitate TV dramatizations. Adult behavior may also be imitative.

On December 13, 1966, the National Broadcasting Company presented a filmed drama [14] entitled "The Doomsday Flight."

The plot of the film centered on the placement of a bomb on a transcontinental airliner. . . . The plane emerged safely because it landed at an altitude above that at which the bomb was triggered to go off. The supposed suspense lay in tracing the deranged man who kept teasing officials with information on his deadly act.

Even while the film was still being beamed to home TV sets, a bomb threat—a hoax—was telephoned to one United States airline. Within twenty-four hours of the show four more had been phoned. Within the week following the show eight such hoax calls in all were received by various United States airlines [15]. These eight hoax bomb threats in one week equaled the number of such calls that had been received in the entire previous month, according to the Federal Aviation Agency [25].

Before the date that the film was shown on TV, the Air Lines Pilots Association had urged NBC to keep the program off the air in the interest of air safety [24]. They advised NBC that experience had shown that "the mentally unstable are highly responsive to, and easily provoked by, suggestion." The pilots indicated that they feared the program could cause an irrational person to commit an act of sabotage. Telegrams were sent by the president of the pilots' association to the author of the script, to an NBC vice-president, to the West Coast publicity director for NBC, and to the producer of the film at a Hollywood studio. When no response was received from any of these officials, another representative of the pilots' association telephoned another NBC vice-president in a further attempt to convince the network to call off the program.

These efforts by concerned pilots were unsuccessful, the TV drama was sent out to home screens, and the feared rash of bomb hoaxes did ensue. Fortunately, there is no record that any bomb was in fact placed on any plane in the period following the screening of this realistic bit of TV fiction. Unfortunately, there is no information on the identities of the individuals who translated screen behavior into acts in their own lives. Their ages and their social histories are not known, nor whether they were "disturbed," unstable, or impulsive. Probably some of them were. Many such individuals do exist in our society, and they must be considered in any appraisal of the effects of the media.

For many years black citizens have been objecting to the stereotyped representations of blacks in the mass media. They have resented the fact that blacks were almost always portrayed in subordinate and menial roles, as servants, shoeshine boys, field hands, and ne'er-do-wells. They have felt that these condescending portrayals would influence the way Americans felt about black people, including the way black Americans would feel about themselves. This argument rests on the assumption that people accept and believe the fictional representations in the media. The depth and seriousness of the objections of black citizens lends seriousness to this assumption. It has not been sufficient to reply "But it's only a story" or "That's only fantasy." Even the media men themselves have finally accepted the validity of this argument, and serious efforts are now being made to portray blacks in dignified and admirable roles, to represent in the media the true variety of the human condition among black as well as white Americans. They have taken seriously the notion that for some Americans the media constitute their only acquaintance with blacks and that therefore it is important for the media portrayals to be fair and realistic (see Chapter 6).

Should we also take seriously the notions that for many Americans the media constitute a major source for acquaintance with violence and aggression and that these persons learn about these phenomena and how to deal with them from the media?

Several research studies have been addressed to this question. One study [31] examined the influence of violence in the mass media upon children's role expectations. An effort was made to study how young children understand the role of taxi-driver—a role that was chosen for study because there are not already widespread stereotypes about taxi-drivers in our society (as there are about American Indian warriors, policemen, schoolteachers, or used car salesmen). One group of second graders heard a series of radio dramas about taxi-drivers. In each "thrilling episode" the taxi-driver got into trouble with another person and handled that trouble by being violently aggressive against him. A second group of children in the same grade heard a series of radio dramas about taxi-drivers that differed from the other series only in their endings. In this series the endings were not violent—instead the taxi-driver found a constructive way to resolve the problem.

To determine whether the children's reality conceptions about taxi-drivers had been influenced by these fictional presentations, the researcher gave each child a newspaper test. The child was shown a copy of the local newspaper published and read in his community and was asked to explain what a newspaper is. Only those children who understood that a newspaper reports reality were included in the final analysis of the results of the study. Each of these children was asked to tell how certain newspaper stories came out. The first news stories presented to the child concerned current local news—the current weather, the fact that Lincoln's Birthday was approaching and that it would be a school holiday. Then the child was read putative news stories about local taxi-drivers and was asked to say how they came out. One of these news stories told of an episode very similar to one the children had heard enacted in a radio drama. The children who had heard the violent endings to the radio drama gave very different responses to this "newspaper" story than did those who had heard the nonviolent endings. The responses were categorized according to how much aggression the child attributed to the taxi-driver in completing the newspaper account. In this Pennsylvania community taxi-drivers are helpful and friendly, so it is not surprising that the children who had not heard the violent radio dramas tended to finish the news story in a way that attributed no aggression to the taxi-driver (in two-thirds of the cases) or only intermediate aggression to him (in the other one-third). The children who had heard the violent series, on the other hand, apparently thought that taxi-drivers in their own town would behave in the same way as the fictional taxi-drivers in the radio dramas, for half of them finished the news account in a way that attributed "high" aggression to the local taxi-driver, and only one-third attributed no aggression to him.

This small study would need to be duplicated with various children, various roles, and various media before we could know how to generalize from its findings. In the meantime it warns us that we are not being fantastic when we suggest that the distinction between reality and fantasy may be blurred for normal young children.

A striking series of studies by Professor Albert Bandura and his colleagues at Stanford University have demonstrated that children learn aggressive behavior from TV and that they enact this behavior in their play under suitable circumstances. In earlier studies [4, 5] Bandura had already shown that children will imitate the specifics of aggressive behavior they observe in an adult. He and his colleagues then conducted a study to determine whether children will imitate aggression they observe in a film as readily as they will imitate aggression they observe performed by a real-life adult in the same room with them [6]. The children he studied were 96 nursery school children, ranging in age from less than 3 to nearly 6, with an average age of 4½. He assigned the children arbitrarily to four categories. A child in the first category, the Real-Life Aggression condition, was brought to a playroom and given some materials to play with at a small table. After the child settled down to play, an adult in another part of the room began playing with several toys, including a mallet and a five-foot inflated plastic Bobo doll. The adult was aggressive toward the Bobo doll in highly novel and distinctive ways and performed each of these aggressive acts—like pummeling the Bobo on its head with a mallet—several times in the course of the session. The child, of course, observed this aggressive adult behavior occurring in his presence. A child in the second category, the Human Film-Aggression condition, was brought to the same playroom set to playing with the same toys, and then shown a color film on which the same adult model displayed the identical sequence of novel aggressive behaviors to a Bobo doll. In further contrast a child in the third category, the Cartoon Film-Aggression condition, was shown a cartoon film produced for the study, showing an adult costumed as a cat, playing against a fantasyland backdrop of brightly colored trees, butterflies, and so forth. In this film the cat performed the same aggressive behaviors against the Bobo doll as had been performed by adult models in the other two conditions. Finally, children in the fourth category, the Control condition, were reserved as a comparison group, with no exposure to aggressive models in the course of the study.

Immediately after having one of the experiences described above, the child was taken to an anteroom containing a variety of highly attractive toys. The experimenter told him he might play with them, but once he had gotten involved in doing so the experimenter purposely frustrated the child by saying she had decided to reserve the toys for some other children. She indicated that instead he could play with some toys in yet another room. They went to that room where the adult busied herself with paperwork at a desk while the child played with his toys. These included toys typically used in aggressive play and others associated with unaggressive activities. Among them was a Bobo doll and a mallet. The child played for twenty minutes, while his behavior was observed and scored by judges watching through a one-way mirror from an adjoining room.

The main prediction of this study was that children who had observed adult aggression prior to being frustrated themselves would be more aggressive in their subsequent play than would the "control" children who had also been frustrated but who had not observed any adult aggression just before that experience. This prediction was confirmed. The average total aggression score for the control children was 54, while the average was 83 for children in the Real-Life Aggression category, 92 for those in the Human Film-Aggression category, and 99 for those in the Cartoon Film-Aggression category. The differences among the three experimental conditions are not statistically significant, but all three averages are significantly higher than the average score for the control children.

The second prediction was that the aggression of the children who had observed adult models would be imitative. The child's behavior during the play session was scored as to whether his aggressive acts were imitative, partially imitative, or nonimitative. An imitative act was one that directly copied the adult behavior the child had seen earlier, with the child exhibiting the very acts he had observed or speaking the very words the adult had spoken. It was found that in the Real-Life and Human Film categories, 88 percent of the children exhibited varying degrees of imitative aggression, and in the Cartoon Film condition 79 percent did so. Thus not only were these children more aggressive altogether, but even more importantly the character of their aggressive behavior was closely modeled on the character of the aggressive behavior they had observed in adults, whether live or on film. Scores for imitative aggression were significantly higher for the children who had observed models than for the control children, and the same was true for scores of partially imitative aggression. Indeed, some children became virtually carbon copies of the adult models in the aggressive sequence they exhibited in their own play. On the other hand, aggressive gun play was displayed equally by the various groups. This is an example of aggressive behavior that had not been modeled by the adults in the experiment.

For our purposes this study holds special interest not only because it demonstrates that children mimic the aggressive behavior of adults, whether they observe this behavior in the flesh or on film, but also because it demonstrates that the mimicking occurs equally to realistic films and to cartoon-like films. The fantasy-reality distinction on which adults pin so much hope seems to have little significance for the bright middle-class preschool children Bandura and his colleagues studied.

One reason that Bandura's work is so widely respected by other psychologists is that conclusions from it do not rest on a single study. Rather he has conducted a series of investigations over the years, using different children and different films. Each study adds to the strength of the conclusions we can draw.

A second study [7] meriting close consideration here used nursery school children whose ages ranged from 3 to 5 years, with an average of just over 4 years. They were assigned at random to different categories. A child in the first category was taken to a playroom where the adult experimenter worked at a desk while the child watched a five-minute film projected on a TV console. This film concerns two adult men, Rocky and Johnny. At the start of the narrative Johnny is playing with his highly attractive collection of toys. Rocky asks to play with some and is refused. Rocky then behaves aggressively toward Johnny and his possessions, enacting a series of highly unusual and distinctive aggressive behaviors while making hostile remarks. (The purpose of employing unusual and distinctive acts of aggression in this series of studies is to enable observers to distinguish imitative acts of aggression in the child's subsequent play from other more stereotyped acts common to the play of many children.) Rocky is the victor as the result of his aggressive behavior, and "the final scene shows Johnny seated dejectedly in the corner while Rocky is playing with the toys, serving himself generous helpings of 7-Up and cookies, and riding a large bouncing hobby horse with gusto. As the scene closes, Rocky packs the playthings in a sack and sings a merry tune" as he departs with the swag. A commentator announces that Rocky is the victor.

Another film was used as well in this study, similar at the start with the other one, and also involving aggression between Rocky and Johnny, but rearranged in sequence so that the aggressive behavior shown by Rocky results in his being severely punished. "Rocky is thoroughly thrashed by Johnny. As soon as he succeeds in freeing himself, Rocky flees to a corner of the room where he sits cowering, while Johnny places his toys in the sack and walks away. The announcer comments on Rocky's punishment."

After viewing one of these films, a child was taken to a playroom for a twenty-minute play session that was observed and scored by judges behind a one-way vision screen. This room contained some toys similar to those in the film, and others as well—the latter being present to avoid loading the dice. The child's imitative aggressive acts and his nonimitative aggressive acts were recorded.

The total aggression scores of the children in the Aggressive Model-Rewarded category were 75, which is significantly higher than the total for children in the Aggressive Model-Punished category: 53. In contrast children who had seen neither film but who simply were brought to the playroom for a twenty-minute play session had total aggression scores that were intermediate: 62.

Most of the aggression was not sufficiently close to that exhibited by Rocky and Johnny to be called imitative, but the imitative aggression that was observed occurred more commonly among the Model-Rewarded children than among the Model-Punished children, and both showed more imitative aggression than the controls, who had never observed the distinctive adult behaviors.

After the play session was over, each child was asked to evaluate the behavior exhibited by Rocky and Johnny and to select the character he preferred to emulate. Among the children who had seen Rocky emerge the victor because of his aggressiveness, 60 percent preferred him, only 5 percent preferred Johnny, and 35 percent voiced no preference. Among those who had seen Johnny triumph despite Rocky's aggressiveness (the Aggressive Model-Punished category of children), 20 percent preferred Johnny, 20 percent preferred Rocky, and 60 percent had no preference.

Surprisingly, almost without exception the children who said they preferred Rocky as a model were nonetheless critical of his behavior. They preferred him despite his infamy, siding with the winner: " 'Rocky is harsh, I be harsh like he was,' 'Rough and bossy,' 'Mean,' . . . 'Rocky beat Johnny and chase him and get all the good toys.' 'He come and snatched Johnny's toys. Get a lot of toys' . . . 'He was a fighter. He got all good toys' " [7]. Bandura and his co-authors comment on this finding that successful villainy may outweigh the viewers' value systems, noting that their experiment involves only a single episode of aggression that was rewarded or punished, whereas

> In most televised programs, the "bad guy" gains control over important resources and amasses considerable social and material rewards through a series of aggressive maneuvers, whereas his punishment is generally delayed until just before the last commercial. Thus children have opportunities to observe many episodes in which antisocially aggressive behavior has paid off abundantly. . . .

Noting that immediate rewards are much more influential than delayed punishment in regulating behavior, the authors argue that "the terminal punishment of the villain may have a relatively weak inhibitory effect on the viewer."

The two studies just described demonstrate that young children imitate the specific acts of aggression they have observed in the behavior of adults on films or TV. This imitation occurs whether the dramatic presentation is realistic or fantasylike. Imitation is enhanced if the aggression brings rewards to the adult who is observed, and it is minimized if the aggression brings punishments.

A third study by Bandura, more recent and thus less well known than the two already reviewed, confirms again the finding on imitation. But it is somewhat more ominous in its implications, for it shows that from watching TV, children acquire the capability of performing imitatively many more acts of aggression than they spontaneously exhibit—that children learn more from TV than their behavior reveals.

The 66 children who participated in this third study [2] were again of nursery school age, averaging just over 4 years old. They were assigned at random to three categories—Model Rewarded, Model Punished, and No Consequences. A child in the first category began his participation by watching a five-minute TV show in which an adult exhibited distinctive physical and verbal aggressive behavior toward a Bobo doll. In the closing scene of the Model-Rewarded film, a second adult appeared, bearing an abundant supply of candies and soft drinks, informed the model that he was a "strong champion," and that his superb performance of aggression clearly deserved a treat. He then gave the model various desirable foods; and while the model consumed these, he continued to describe and praise the model's feats.

A child in the Model-Punished category saw a TV performance

that was identical to the above in its initial sequences but which concluded with a second adult's reproving rather than praising the model:

"Hey there, you big bully. You quit picking on that clown. I won't tolerate it." As the model drew back he tripped and fell, and the other adult sat on the model and spanked him with a rolled-up magazine while reminding him of his aggressive behavior. As the model ran off cowering, the agent forewarned him, "If I catch you doing that again, you big bully, I'll give you a hard spanking. You quit acting that way" [2].

Finally, a child in the No Consequences category saw a TV performance involving only the initial section of the above film, the part showing the adult model aggressing against the Bobo doll in novel and vivid ways.

Each child was then observed in a ten-minute play session while alone in a room containing a variety of toys, including some like those used by the adult model on the film. Judges observed through a one-way screen and recorded the occurrence of imitative aggressive responses.

Then the experimenter returned to the playroom, bringing an assortment of fruit juices and booklets of sticker pictures to be presented to the child as rewards. She then asked the child to "Show me what Rocky did in the TV program," "Tell me what he said," promising to reward the child with a picture of his own drawing for each imitation he performed.

The findings from this study have to do with how much imitative aggression each child performed spontaneously in play in the ten-minute session as compared with how much imitative aggression he showed himself capable of performing when offered an incentive to do so.

As might be expected from the earlier studies, the children in the Model-Rewarded and the No Consequences categories mimicked the adult model in their own free play, doing so more frequently than those in the Model-Punished category. Again we have a demonstration that children imitate aggression they observe adults display on TV, and again we have the finding that punishment of the adult in the TV show serves to inhibit the children's tendency to imitate spontaneously.

Even more important is the finding that when requested to imitate the adult's behavior and offered an incentive for doing so, each group of children performed more imitative acts of aggression than had been performed spontaneously in free play. This showed that the children were capable of more imitative aggression than they had initially shown. Further, those who had seen the model punished could imitate his aggressive acts just as efficiently as could those who had seen the model rewarded and those for whom no consequences for adult aggression had been included in the TV film. Most remarkable of all, the girls in this study, like the girls in the other two, had exhibited less imitative behavior in their own free play than the boys had; but when offered an incentive for imitating aggression, they mimicked essentially as many aggressive acts as the boys did for the incentive.

Thus this third study of Bandura's shows once again that children learn to perform the behavior they observe. Of what they learn, some sequences are exhibited spontaneously in their play, but other sequences can be elicited if the setting is right. This is equally true whether the observed behavior was condemned and had painful consequences, was rewarded and had positive consequences, or was neither rewarded nor punished and had no known consequences. The study clearly indicates that the observed consequences of behavior have some influence on whether the child will spontaneously copy that behavior in his own play but none on whether he retains the capability of exhibiting the behavior when offered an incentive for doing so.

A related study [3] deserves brief mention. The participants were 72 children, aged 6 to 8, from a lower-middle-class neighborhood. Every child saw the same TV film, a four-minute color film showing an adult performing a series of novel acts with various toys. For example, when he first came on stage, the adult had his right hand cupped over his eyes. Later he tossed bean bags at a target, but instead of standing erect and doing so in the usual way, he bent over with his back to the target and tossed the bean bags at it through his legs.

Children were assigned randomly to three categories. Some simply observed the film. Others were instructed to verbalize every action of the model as they watched the actions unfold on the TV screen. Those in the third category engaged in competing symbolization, counting aloud while they watched the TV film: "1 and a 2 and a 3 and a 4 . . ."

Each child was then taken to a room containing the toys the adult had used in the film. The experimenter asked him to demonstrate every one of the model's behaviors he could recall. She praised and rewarded with candy each correct matching response, of which 38 were possible. Further, she prompted the child with a standard set of cues, asking him to show the way the adult behaved in the opening scene; to demonstrate what the adult had done with the dart gun, the Bobo doll, and the bean bags; and to portray the adult's behavior in the closing scene.

The children did very well in mimicking the adult they had just observed on TV. Those who had simply watched the four-minute TV show were able to reproduce an average of 14 sequences of behavior they had observed on the show. Not surprisingly, those children who had verbalized the sequences as they watched the same film could reproduce even more—an average of 17. And as expected, competing verbal activity interfered with the child's retention of the TV film content—the children who had counted aloud during the film could reproduce only 9 of the sequences afterwards.

Again we have a demonstration of the child's marvelous powers of observation and retention, his ability to remember and subsequently to mimic behavior he has observed. Such demonstrations have interested other psychologists, and a number of them have conducted studies [19, 30] providing independent confirmation of this phenomenon. What is especially significant about these studies is their concern with the child's *behavior*, his *actions*, what he *does*. There are many questionnaire studies and interview studies providing reports about what people say they think and say they might do or not do, but the studies reviewed here are distinctive in providing reports on what people actually do. There is now considerable evidence to make us dubious about the trustworthiness of what people say to interviewers or mark on questionnaires and to convince us of the complexity and the indirectness of the relation between verbalization and behavior. This evidence makes us turn with special interest to studies that are concerned with behavior rather than verbalizations, like those just reviewed.

Conclusions

Every civilization is only twenty years away from barbarism. For twenty years is all we have to accomplish the task of civilizing the infants who are born into our midst each year. These savages know nothing of our language, our culture, our religion, our values, our customs of interpersonal relations. The infant knows nothing about communism, fascism, democracy, civil liberties, the rights of the minority as contrasted with the prerogatives of the majority, respect, decency, ethics, morality, conventions, and customs. The barbarian must be tamed if civilization is to survive. Over the centuries man has evolved ways of accomplishing this.

Our methods of taming or *socializing* the barbarian hordes who invade our community every year rely on the remarkable learning abilities of these small savages. The infant learns by reward and punishment—by trial and error—and throughout the ages man has capitalized on this ability by rewarding infants for acceptable behavior and punishing them for unacceptable behavior. The infant develops a close attachment to one or two persons who care for him and meet his needs. Because of this he desires to conform to their wishes and expectations; throughout the ages man has capitalized on the infant's propensity to make attachments by assigning special educative responsibilities to mothers and fathers. The young child learns through observation and imitation. Throughout the ages man has provided opportunities for young people to learn from their elders in apprentice relations—the girl learning housewifery by watching her mother, the boy learning farming skills by working alongside his father, the youngsters learning hunting skills by observing the skilled hunters. The young child learns through language—through spoken instruction—and throughout the ages man has capitalized on this skill by talking to children about the social group, extolling its values and ideals, relating legends, telling tales, gossiping, sermonizing, lecturing, conversing, explaining, scolding, moralizing. The young child learns from graphic representations, and throughout the ages man has capitalized on this ability by creating pictorial representations of the culture, its religious symbols, its heroes, its workers. All these age-old techniques of socialization have enabled man to teach most of the young barbarians how to behave as members of the group.

In the modern era these techniques refined throughout the ages continue to be very important. But they have been joined by others whose impact is less well understood. At first the new methods of teaching were available only to the privileged few. Thus the method of teaching through written instruction reached only those who had been taught to read and who could gain possession of the rare scripts. As the technology of printing and of distributing printed materials advanced, more and more individuals had access to the printed word, and more and more were taught the literacy skills needed to gain meaning from print. Thus the printed word became of some importance in socializing the young. Any educated person is impressed with the extent of this importance. Perhaps, therefore, it is worthwhile to remind the reader, an educated person, that the ability to read is acquired late in the child's life, long after his basic social learning has been accomplished. Furthermore, the ability to read efficiently and with understanding comes even later. The child is well advanced before he is so skillful in reading that the printed page can modify his behavior or alter his beliefs.

The newest forms of communication circumvent this difficulty. As I have discussed, they are meaningful to the illiterate as well as to the tutored. The most powerful of these new forms, movies and TV, communicate with the individual not only through his eyes, as print does, but simultaneously through his ears as well. And the most powerful of all, TV, accomplishes this feat in the individual's own home, bringing into that home instantaneous reports of events in the world around him, not only in his neighborhood and city, but in his nation and other nations.

The fact that we do not think of the new media as being instructors for our young does not affect their teaching ability. Although it is not governed by a board of education, TV does teach. We think of radio, movies, and TV as entertainment, but, in fact, children learn efficiently from them. Our media-saturated college students, born eighteen or twenty years ago just as TV was coming into prominence, get their kicks from playing Trivia [32], "a campy game of inconsequential questions and answers about radio, TV, movies, comic books, and popular songs" in which the effectiveness of these media as teachers is demonstrated by the young people's ability to answer questions like "Who was Bob Hope's radio announcer?" "What was the consolation prize on 'The $64,000 Question'?" and "Who was the singer of 'Come on-a My House'?" A Trivia Contest was held at Columbia University in 1967, with teams from Princeton, Yale, Pennsylvania, Barnard, and other elite schools battling it out, and with the winner receiving a trophy while a chorus sang the Mr. Trivia song—"There he goes, think of all the crap he knows." The proud winner declared, "You have to get your basic training from the time you are 6 until perhaps 12 or 13," and credited his success to "my garbage-filled mind."

The new media speak directly to the child's two best developed senses, conveying a reality that is not very different from the other realities he experiences. It is precisely the direct correspondence between reality and the TV representation of reality—with no need for reliance on verbal labels, for verbal encoding and decoding—that makes TV so powerful.

Children in this country spend many hours a week watching television. They begin watching at a very young age, and they are faithful to the set on weekdays and weekends, throughout the summer as well as during the school year, with the result that at age 16 the average American child had spent as many hours watching TV as he has spent in school classes. Is it a fair bet that the two sources of information have affected his social learning equally?

Perhaps, but one might give odds to the TV. For the child turned to the tube at a younger and more impressionable age, and he attended the TV school on his own initiative and volition, not because of the combination of social pressures, parental expectations, and truancy laws that enforce school attendance. One hears a great deal about school dropouts but very little about TV nonattenders. The ability of TV to hold its audience voluntarily better than our schools can hold their students may tell us something about TV's superior effectiveness as a communicator and thus as a teacher.

What is this electronic teacher teaching the child? The *Christian Science Monitor* completed a survey of TV programming six weeks after the assassination of Senator Kennedy. In 85½ hours of programming in prime evening hours and on Saturday mornings, 84 killings were observed. Both acts of violence and threats of violence were recorded [28].

The survey found that the most violent evening hours were between 7:30 and 9, when, according to official network estimates, 26.7 million children between the ages of 2 and 17 are watching television.

"In those early evening hours, violent incidents occurred on an average of once every 16.3 minutes. After 9 P.M., violence tapered off quickly, with incidents occurring once every 35 minutes," the paper said.

"In the early evening, there was a murder or killing once every 31 minutes," the survey reported. "Later, once every two hours."

Everything that social scientists know about human learning and remembering tells us that this carnage is being observed and remembered by the TV audience. If children can remember and reproduce 14 or 15 sequences of behavior from one of Bandura's amateurish four-minute films, how much do they remember from hour after hour of professionally produced TV?

The fact that a student can recall the singing commercial, "Use Ajax (boom, boom), the foaming cleanser," when playing Trivia does not mean that he *will* use that foaming cleanser when he grows up and has to scour his toilet bowl. Similarly, the fact that children watch TV "pictures of mayhem, mugging, and murder" [12] does not mean that they *will* perform comparable acts of violence in their own lives. This is obvious from our crime statistics, which show that children are among the least violent of our citizens and that violence is most characteristic of the adolescent and young adult male.

But television time is sold to sponsors on the conviction that although the Ajax ad won't guarantee that the viewer will buy the product, it raises the probability that he will. And social scientists would simply make the same claim for filmed or televised violence, whether fictitious or real. Viewing the carnage doesn't guarantee that the viewer will go forth and do likewise, but it raises the probability that he will.

Media spokesmen [20] make much of the fact that as yet social scientists have no convincing proof for this hypothesis. They minimize the fact that the evidence for it is accumulating year by year and at an accelerating rate. They also ignore the fact that there is no convincing social scientific evidence for or against most of our social practices and policies.

To this argument one is tempted to reply, "Media man speaks with forked tongue." For the television industry exists and reaps its profits from the conviction that television viewing does affect behavior—buying behavior.

The evidence that we do have indicates that film and TV are profoundly educative for their viewers, teaching them that the world is a violent and untrustworthy place and demonstrating for them a variety of violent techniques for coping with this putatively hostile environment.

Whether this message is beamed as fact or fiction, it is accepted by young children. They incorporate in their own potential behavior patterns the sequences of adult behavior they observe on TV, including aggressive sequences.

Whether they will ever employ these aggressive behaviors in their interpersonal relations depends on many complex factors. Obviously, every individual is capable of more different behaviors than he has occasion to display. Many of us remember our high school French, and although years pass without presenting us with any occasion to speak French, we continue to retain some capability of doing so when the occasion does arise. The analogy to TV violence is not exact, for TV as a school for violence enrolls adult viewers as well as high school students and has them in class for many more hours than any French teacher ever did. When the occasion arises that seems to an adult to call for violence, he does not have to cast his mind to his high school classroom but only to last night's or last week's thrilling episode.

What else will he remember from that episode? There was a

murder every half hour during prime viewing time on 1968 network TV. How many instances were there of constructive interventions to end disagreement? What other methods of resolving conflict were exampled? How many instances of tact and decency could an avid televiewer chronicle during the same hours? How often was reconciliation dramatized? How many adult acts of generosity were provided to children for modeling? What strategies for ameliorating hate were displayed? How many times did the child viewer see adults behaving in loving and helpful ways? What examples of mutual respect did he view? What did he learn about law and order? How many episodes of police kindness and considerateness did he see? How frequently did the glow of compassion illuminate the TV screen?

Recommendations

POSITIVE AND CONSTRUCTIVE
ROLES FOR THE MEDIA

Because the mass media of communication have such great powers of informing and persuading, they have an opportunity to play a constructive and helpful role in our troubled society. There is a growing realization of these possibilities in current trends toward more inclusive treatment of black Americans in the media, and it is to be hoped that there will be further developments in the effort to present black citizens as real people rather than as stereotypes. Series are being developed in which thoughtful and fair coverage is given to the routine work of those individuals whose job is maintaining law and justice—district attorneys, policemen, judges, and so forth. College administrators are among today's beleaguered heroes, with their commitment to open dialogue and to fairness to students at a time when some students are expressing themselves in the strident rhetoric of violence and with a self-righteous moralism; and these heroes and the effectiveness of their patient techniques could be the focus of media presentations. At a time when Americans are increasingly concerned about pollution of their environment, media presentations could inform us about the engineers and inventors who are at work on new technologies that avoid contaminating our air and water. Local school boards are hard-pressed to meet the needs of today's students in the face of resistance to increases in property taxes and of resentment about the behavior and dress of some students. Media coverage of school board meetings might aid citizens in understanding the complexities of current issues of educational policy and practice.

It is better to light a candle than to curse the darkness. We need to have alternatives to the present twaddle in entertainment and news. We need to have demonstrations of new and better ways to entertain and inform the public. The Ford, Carnegie, Russell Sage, and other foundations are supporting innovative efforts to improve the media, to devise new forms. These efforts are laudable and should be extended.

REDUCTION OF EMPHASIS
ON VIOLENCE IN THE MEDIA

The reader need hardly be told that on the basis of my reading of the research evidence, I recommend a reduction in the emphasis on violence in the media. There should be a lessening of the glorification of toughness, aggressiveness, and combativeness. This recommendation does not apply merely to the gory, shocking, or revolting representation of violence. Indeed if actual violence is to be presented, candor compels that its ugliness and gory results be explicit. A bloodless killing is a deception of the worst sort. What is of greatest concern about the present representation of violence in the media is not its goriness but rather the likelihood that children will learn from it that the world is a hostile, punitive, and untrustworthy place and that people often take recourse to violent acts in order to resolve conflicts.

CORPORATE INDEPENDENCE OF THE MEDIA

At present one of the most effective forms of social control over one medium is criticism from another medium. The concern of Broadway producers over newspaper reviews is legendary. Reviewers who publish in magazines are enormously influential in determining sales of books. The most articulate critics of TV have spoken through newspaper columns. TV promotion of a book can enhance its sales. A new movie becomes known through TV coverage and newspaper publicity.

Criticism and praise are to be encouraged, and we need to recruit discriminating and thoughtful individuals into the role of reviewer. The independence of the reviewer must be maintained.

The long-term trend in this country's economy has been toward the development of ever larger and more inclusive industries. Giant corporations develop through acquisition of competitors or through forcing competitors into financial exhaustion. This trend is now apparent in the media industry, with radio corporations purchasing book publishing houses, magazine publishers purchasing newspapers, and so forth. The citizen must view these media conglomerates with concern. When a magazine publishing house also owns a newspaper, can we expect disinterested coverage of that magazine in that newspaper? The tendency toward monolithic corporate ownership and control in the media may signal the end of intermedium criticism, which is at present one of the most effective forms of social control of the media. Strict limits upon single control of multiple communications media are greatly needed.

PROFESSIONALIZATION OF THE MEDIA

Responsibility for the treatment of violence rests with the individuals who publish newspapers, operate TV stations and networks, manage radio stations, write newspaper copy, broadcast news reports, write TV scripts. The exercise of this responsibility to meet the highest needs of the society requires ethical concern and sensitivity on the part of media participants. If judgments about violence were easy to make, then a handbook of rules could be written, with detailed guidelines. The judgments are not easy, and, therefore, they must be made by informed individuals with a moral concern for the society they serve.

Whenever the members of a particular vocation have it in their power to influence all of society, for good or for evil, the society requires that these individuals adhere to professional standards. Their behavior is not left to the guidance of the profit motive alone but instead is guided also by professional ethics. The druggist is not free to sell the drug with the highest profit markup but instead is ethically bound to fill the prescription written by a physician with whom he has no business relation. The surgeon is not free to advise the operation that is most convenient for him to perform but instead is constrained to advise the surgical procedure that will benefit his patient most. Any individual whose power is recognized belongs to a guild which constrains the exercise of that power. It is time to recognize the power of the media and to insist that professional standards guide the exercise of that power.

We have examples of professionalization in vocations whose power has long been recognized—lawyers, teachers, doctors, nurses, social workers, pharmacists. A man's success in law, education, or medicine is judged basically according to how well he meets the highest aspirations of his profession.

Not just anyone is permitted to set himself up as a lawyer, teacher, or doctor, but instead individuals aspiring to these professions must first go through careful and arduous educational preparation. The credential to practice is awarded only to those who are successful in this education and who meet standards for the profession that are legally defined. In the education of a professional, attention is given to the ethical and social issues he will face in practicing his calling.

Once an individual has gained entry to a profession, his behavior remains under the "social control" of his colleagues and, in addition, is subject to some legal controls. Other members of his profession observe his behavior and assure themselves that it meets professional standards. Each profession has its own internal methods for assuring the ethical conduct of its members. Some of these are formal, but most are informal. The methods include both rewards and punishments, in great variety. An individual member of a profession may offer tactful and respectful criticism to a colleague, who is bound to listen carefully to it. A man's work comes under the scrutiny of senior colleagues, who are in a position to change his assignment. Colleagues may publish criticism of a man's work in journals read by other colleagues. Especially meritorious work is recognized by awards, medals, editorial praise, citations. Leaders in a profession, those who have earned the respect of their colleagues, are appointed to the most sensitive and responsible positions in the profession—to national committees, editorial boards, offices in professional societies, advisory councils, executive committees, hospital boards, and so forth. Promotion within a profession occurs only after review by colleagues, and it constitutes recognition for professional accomplishment. Ethics committees are made up of professional peers to whom frank violations of ethical standards may be reported. In the most serious matters the law stands behind a profession's ethical standards, and any member of a profession may be sued for grossly unprofessional conduct.

Like the doctor or the lawyer, the media man is in a position in which often the easiest thing to do, or the most profitable thing to do, is not the act that will bring most benefit to society. The media man is in a position of social power, and with that power we must insist on the exercise of social responsibility. Professionalization of media employees will be a step toward that end.

The clients of the media include the advertising industry and the sponsoring industries. They are in a position to use direct monetary rewards to mold the behavior of the media. The clients of the media include also the public, and their ability to use the leverage of the profit motive is less clear. The appropriateness of exclusive reliance on that motive must be questioned. Professional standards should also motivate the media.

So long as profit-making constitutes the basic criterion of success in the media, ethical responsibility to the society is likely to be slighted or even ignored. The professionalization of media employees could well raise the standards of television, movies, and radio. Newspaper journalism has been moving toward professional status in the past few decades, with the growth of schools of journalism in universities and with the rise of reporting standards in newspapers. It is not evident that in other media the trend toward professionalism has progressed very far. Professionalization of media work along the lines defined above—required educational preparation, standards for membership in the profession, the use of social controls, the development of a code of ethics—would include the development of ethical standards within the media for the treatment of violence, both fictional and in the news. Professionalization of the media employees will help assure adherence to ethical standards.

INDIVIDUAL MORAL RESPONSIBILITY
OF MEDIA PARTICIPANTS

The persons who work for the media have some personal responsibility for the treatment of violence. Here I am speaking of their individual moral accountability as human beings in contrast with their professional responsibility as members of the media professions, the topic of the recommendation above. Certain entertainers and broadcasters have felt this personal responsibility and have publicly avowed that the standards they will apply to their own behavior are higher than those currently prevailing in the industry. They have indicated that they will not participate in media presentations which glorify violence and cheapen human life. One TV producer published a statement in a trade newspaper shortly after the murder of Senator Kennedy [29]:

In the name of John F. Kennedy, Martin Luther King and Robert F. Kennedy and my family, I make this solemn pledge:
I will no longer lend my talents in any way to add to the creation of a climate for murder. I call upon all who read this to join me in refusing to write, direct, produce, act, or participate in any way in the shaping of any "entertainment" that celebrates senseless brutality, aimless cruelty, pointless and violent death.

Within three days of its publication the author, Jerry Paris, had obtained 350 signatures to this statement from members of the entertainment industry [36].

A similar trend has occurred with respect to cigarette advertising, with certain celebrated performers (Doris Day, Lawrence Welk, Tony Curtis, and others) refusing to participate in media presentations extolling cigarettes [33].

Such individual declarations of conscience are admirable, and the individual performers and producers who make them and live by them deserve our respect and support.

PUBLIC EXPRESSIONS OF CONCERN
ABOUT MEDIA VIOLENCE

To a limited degree the media are sensitive and responsive to the expressed concerns of the public. Individuals who are concerned about the way violence is highlighted and glorified in media presentations can capitalize on this sensitivity by communicating with the presidents and top executives of the major networks, film companies, newspapers, and magazines.

An editorial in a leading magazine for women [21] asserted that

Women can stop the outpouring of violence and sordidness on our television screens and in the motion-picture theatres. Supposedly, television and the movie industry give the public what it wants; i.e., sexual brutality, depravity, sadism, and everything else that contributes to human desensitization and violence. If this is the case, American women should be loud and clear in letting television and movie executives know that such bilge is most certainly not what they want.

The editorial went on to give the names and addresses of the network presidents and of the president of the Motion Picture Association of America.

Unfortunately, to date there apparently is no massive public outcry:

It is not clear whether in fact there have been sustained and insistent protests to the media executives from the general public. One network head, who asked to remain anonymous, said there was no question that educators, intellectuals and many political figures felt strongly about the violence issue but that the volume of complaining mail from average viewers was negligible [17].

This suggests that the public has not yet been sufficiently aroused to launch an effective campaign of letters to media executives. Such a campaign would be useful.

SELF-REGULATION BY THE MEDIA

As a result of the concern many people feel about excessive emphasis on violence and sex in the media, there have been some efforts at self-regulation by associations of owners. Thus newspaper owners, film producers, and TV networks have set standards for their own products and have monitored these products to determine their conformity to these standards.

Since 1930 the motion picture production code has specified the limits of taste in American movies. The code's seal of approval has occasionally been withheld from a film, and monitoring of films by code representatives has led to changes in films before they were released with that seal. The industry has been reluctant in its support of this self-regulation: "The chief proponents of classification have always been the parent groups, and the strong opposition, apart from the theatre owners, has come from the member companies of the Motion Picture Association itself" [38].

The motion picture industry launched a new system for classifying movies late in 1968. It is meant to alert exhibitors and the public about whether or not a film is appropriate for immature audiences [9, 10, 37]. The decision depends in part on the film's treatment of violence and aggression. Ratings are assigned by the staff of the Motion Picture Association of America's Code Administration according to the following classification: G (suggested for general audiences), M (for adults and mature young people), R (restricted; persons under 16 not admitted unless accompanied by a parent or guardian), or X (those under 16 not admitted). Acceptance of this code by the exhibitors has been facilitated by their recognition that youngsters under 16 are not a financially lucrative sector of the film audience, since they pay reduced admission rates and yet occupy as much seating space as do adults. Moreover, the X rating is an objective certification of the salaciousness of the product and thus may attract many adults who would not otherwise attend the film; ticket sales to them will make up for any losses from the juvenile market. A Warner Brothers executive commented on the X rating given to one of his firm's films by noting that "They asked us to make some cuts, but we decided to go ahead and take the X rating and make some money" [10].

Self-regulation in the TV industry has been less effective than with the movies, in part because TV shows usually are monitored only after they are shown on the public airwaves.

Self-regulation need not inevitably be meaningless and self-defeating. Efforts at internal monitoring and regulation belong in the panoply of techniques aimed at improving the media. The current widely publicized efforts of the TV networks to "tone down violence" [13, 27, 39] are commendable, however belated. In combination with professionalization of media employees, self-regulatory boards and codes could be especially effective.

But the nation's experience to date has been that the media have used self-regulation primarily as a technique of warding off outside criticism and censorship and of placating aroused public opinion rather than as a reliable and powerful technique of improving and maintaining the quality and dignity of their productions. With the passage of the years films have become increasingly preoccupied with themes of violence, brutality, and pornography. In TV content there has been the same historical trend toward more and more reliance on violence and sex. In the light of these trends it would be extremely unwise to rely exclusively on self-monitoring, however persuasively and vociferously media spokesmen may plead for this approach to regulation.

RECOGNITION FOR EXCELLENCE

There are many occasions when the media perform outstanding public service. Such occasions deserve explicit recognition, as a reward and as a statement of standards.

Colleagues within the media have systems of awards. The Pulitzer awards, for example, have provided valued recognition for excellence in journalism as well as in history and literature. Within the film industry there are the Oscar awards. These have their counterpart in the television industry in the Emmy awards.

Several publications routinely evaluate films, advising their readers about the suitability of various films for different audiences. This is done by *Parents'* magazine, by *Film Reports* (the publication of the Film Board of National Organizations, which includes such organizations as the American Jewish Committee, the American Library Association, the Daughters of the American Revolution, and the Protestant Motion Picture Council), and by *Consumer Reports.*

The National Catholic Office for Motion Pictures and the National Council of Churches join together each year to give awards to the films they consider the best of the year. An indication of the sophistication of their taste appears in the 1968 selections: "Rachel, Rachel" and "The Heart Is a Lonely Hunter."

Among the independent groups of citizens who attempt to maintain a "watchdog" role over the media industry are several religious groups, including the National Catholic Office for Motion Pictures; the Broadcasting and Film Commission of the National Council of Churches; the Television, Radio, and Film Commission of the Methodist Church; the Office of Communications of the United Church of Christ; and a lay group in the South known as Christians for Responsible Entertainment.

FEDERAL SUPERVISION

An analysis of the possibilities for governmental surveillance, supervision, and control of the media is beyond the scope of this chapter. Some possibilities are currently under active consideration within the legislative and executive branches of the federal government.

The Federal Communications Commission was established at a time when the media were fewer, simpler, and less powerful. Possibly the FCC is no longer sufficiently large, powerful, and well-staffed to represent the public interest. There are proposals for a cabinet-level Department of Communications.

All proposals for federal action to regulate the media must recognize the constitutional guarantees for freedom of speech and freedom of the press. Efforts to arrive at a reasonable system to protect the public interest in constitutionally acceptable ways are hampered by the intransigence of the media industry. For example, a proposed plank in the 1968 platform of the Democratic Party called for a specific condemnation of television for depicting violence in entertainment. The same plank made an appeal to the FCC to apply its powers to revoke or renew broadcasters' licenses in order to compel responsible behavior from broadcasters with regard to violence [16]. The entertainment industry mobilized strong objections to this plank, and eventually only a much-diluted version was accepted.

It must be noted that political personalities are dependent on the media for their survival, under present-day modes of campaigning via the newspaper and TV. This dependence does not put politicians in a good position to speak out against what the media industry has defined as its self-interest.

Summary

This chapter presents a selective discussion of violence in the mass media and its probable effects on the lives of our children. The discussion centers on man's learning abilities and how the media interact with these. It emphasizes that certain media—film and television —have an intrinsic appearance of authenticity and that "entertainment" on these media is now serving to teach children and adults that the world is a violent and untrustworthy place in which the most effective way to cope with conflict is to employ aggression and violence.

No attention has been given to the possible "cathartic" effect of watching violence in the media. This has been the topic of considerable research, and at present there is no convincing evidence for the belief that a person is "purged" of violent impulses through vicarious experiences of violence. Some of the relevant research on "catharsis" is reviewed by the authors cited in the final section of this chapter's list of references. The positive evidence we *do* have centers on how vicarious experiences enhance learning. Indeed television and films can be said to teach the ABC's of violence.

Nor does this chapter dwell on the evidence concerning the great amount of time children and adults spend watching TV, attending movies, reading various printed media, and so forth. Again, the reader is advised to turn to the general references for information on this widely investigated set of topics.

Recommendations emerging from this chapter center on (1) positive and constructive roles for the media; (2) reduction of emphasis on violence in the media; (3) corporate independence of the various media, with firm avoidance of monolithic control by media conglomerates; (4) professionalization of the media; (5) individual moral responsibility of media participants; (6) public expressions of concern about media violence; (7) self-regulation of violent presentations by the media; (8) recognition for excellence in media presentations; and (9) investigation of the possibilities for federal supervision.

References

1. Baker, R. Observer: Nightmare out of the attic. *New York Times*, June 6, 1968. P. 46.
2. Bandura, A. Influence of models' reinforcement contingencies on the acquisition of imitative responses. *Journal of Personality and Social Psychology* 1:589, 1965.
3. Bandura, A., Grusec, J. E., and Menlove, F. L. Observational learning as a function of symbolization and incentive set. *Child Development* 37:499, 1966.
4. Bandura, A., and Huston, A. C. Identification as a process of incidental learning. *Journal of Abnormal and Social Psychology* 63:311, 1961.
5. Bandura, A., Ross, D., and Ross, S. A. Transmission of aggression through imitation of aggressive models. *Journal of Abnormal and Social Psychology* 63:575, 1961.

6. Bandura, A., Ross, D., and Ross, S. A. Imitation of film-mediated aggressive models. *Journal of Abnormal and Social Psychology* 66:3, 1963.
7. Bandura, A., Ross, D., and Ross, S. A. Vicarious reinforcement and imitative learning. *Journal of Abnormal and Social Psychology* 67:601, 1963.
8. Barnes, C. Theatre: Heller's "We Bombed in New Haven" opens. *New York Times*, Oct. 18, 1968. P. 36.
9. Canby, V. Movie ratings for children drawn up. *New York Times*, Oct. 8, 1968. P. 1.
10. Canby, V. For better or worse, film industry begins ratings. *New York Times*, Nov. 1, 1968. P. 41.
11. Dougherty, P. II. Advertising: Putting a damper on violence. *New York Times*, July 12, 1968. P. 38.
12. Ernst, M. Quoted by Gent, G. Human life seen as devalued by violence in the mass media. *New York Times*, Sept. 17, 1968. P. 78.
13. Gent, G. CBS to examine role of violence. *New York Times*, June 11, 1968. P. 76.
14. Gould, J. TV: "The Doomsday Flight." *New York Times*, December 15, 1966. P. 95.
15. Gould, J. TV: A bomb backfires. *New York Times*, December 16, 1966. P. 95.
16. Gould, J. Democratic platform came near condemnation of violence on TV. *New York Times*, Sept. 2, 1968. P. 37.
17. Gould, J. U.S. plans inquiry on possible health hazard in TV violence. *New York Times*, Mar. 6, 1969. P. 77.
18. Kneeland, D. E. Pocketbook issues secondary in rural Iowa. *New York Times*, Oct. 18, 1968. P. 34.
19. Kuhn, D. Z., Madsen, C. H., and Becker, W. C. Effects of exposure to an aggressive model and "frustration" on children's aggressive behavior. *Child Development* 38:739, 1967.
20. Loftus, J. A. CBS man doubts violence theory: Tells panel studies fail to establish links to TV. *New York Times*, Oct. 17, 1968. P. 87. [This is an account of the testimony of Joseph T. Klapper before the National Commission on the Causes and Prevention of Violence.]
21. *McCall's*. Editorial. July, 1968. Reprinted in advertisement in *New York Times*, June 20, 1968. P. 80.
22. Musel, R. Chicago violence on TV outstrips make-believe programs. *Palo Alto Times* (Cal.), Aug. 30, 1968. P. 12.
23. *New York Times*. Young Britons told not to copy Batman. Aug. 25, 1966. P. 42.
24. *New York Times*. Air bomb threats follow TV drama. Dec. 15, 1966. P. 1.
25. *New York Times*. TV show blamed by F.A.A. for rise in bomb hoax calls. Dec. 21, 1966. P. 69.
26. *New York Times*. Children in Britain, 13 to 14, called rulers of the TV set. July 17, 1967. P. 12.
27. *New York Times*. ABC acts to curb violence on shows. June 14, 1968. P. 81.

28. *New York Times.* 84 killings shown in 85½ hours on the 3 networks. July 26, 1968. P. 29.
29. *Palo Alto Times* (Cal.). TV violence to get careful look. June 11, 1968. P. 22.
30. Rosekrans, M. A., and Hartup, W. W. Imitative influence of consistent and inconsistent response consequences to a model on aggressive behavior in children. *Journal of Personality and Social Psychology* 7:429, 1967.
31. Siegel, A. E. The influence of violence in the mass media upon children's role expectations. *Child Development* 29:35, 1958.
32. *Time.* Fads: Triviaddiction. Mar. 10, 1967. P. 69.
33. *Time.* Tobacco: They will not puff. Mar. 14, 1969. P. 93.
34. Willey, G. Does happy ending justify violence? *Palo Alto Times* (Cal.), June 10, 1968. P. 22.
35. Willey, G. Editing out violence poses problems. *Palo Alto Times,* (Cal.), Oct. 8, 1968. P. 16.
36. Windeler, R. Hollywood turns against violence. *New York Times,* June 17, 1968. P. 45.
37. Windeler, R. Hollywood is preparing a broad film classification. *New York Times,* Sept. 21, 1968. P. 27.
38. Windeler, R. As nation's standards change, so do movies. *New York Times,* Oct. 8, 1968. P. 41.
39. Windeler, R. NBC is dropping 2 violent cartoons. *New York Times,* Nov. 25, 1968. P. 94.

Selected Readings

Berkowitz, L. *Aggression: A Social Psychological Analysis.* Chap. 9, Violence in the Mass Media. New York: McGraw-Hill, 1962.
Friendly, F. W. *Due to Circumstances Beyond Our Control.* New York: Vintage, 1967.
Himmelweit, H. T., Oppenheim, A. M., and Vince, P. *Television and the Child.* London: Oxford University Press, 1958.
Larsen, O. N. (Ed.). *Violence and the Mass Media.* New York: Harper & Row, 1968.
Maccoby, E. E. Effects of the Mass Media. In Hoffman, M. L., and Hoffman, L. W. (Eds.), *Review of Child Development Research,* vol. 1. New York: Russell Sage Foundation, 1964.
McLuhan, M. *Understanding Media: The Extensions of Man.* New York: McGraw-Hill, 1964.
Schramm, W., Lyle, J., and Parker, E. B. *Television in the Lives of Our Children.* Stanford, Cal.: Stanford University Press, 1961.
Skornia, H. J. *Television and Society.* New York: McGraw-Hill, 1965.
Wertham, F. *A Sign for Cain: An Exploration of Human Violence.* Chap. 10, School for Violence: Mayhem in the Mass Media. New York: Macmillan, 1966.

8. Firearms Control and Violence

J. Christian Gillin, M.D.
and Frank M. Ochberg, M.D.

O f all forms of violence, violence by gun currently is among the issues causing the greatest concern in this country. The shots that killed President John F. Kennedy, Dr. Martin Luther King, and Senator Robert Kennedy aroused the nation and have compelled us to look for meanings, causes, and steps for preventing further violence. In particular the role of the gun in our national life has become a matter of widespread concern. A highly emotional controversy over gun legislation developed and is not over yet, even though new federal legislation has been passed. In this chapter we shall examine some statistics of guns and gun abuse, we shall review certain aspects of the gun laws, and we shall consider the dilemma of the legislator as he considers laws regulating firearms. We shall look at the part played by guns in homicide and suicide, and, finally, make specific recommendations about guns. In the companion chapter that follows this one, the arguments for and against gun legislation will be outlined and discussed in order to provide greater under-standing of the psychological and social issues involved in the gun law controversy.

Gun Statistics: Twentieth Century United States

In 1967 someone was shot to death somewhere in the United States on the average of once every twenty-five minutes. Altogether, guns were involved in the deaths of over 21,000 civilians [6]. These

241

were 7,700 homicides, 11,000 suicides, and 2,800 accidents. Of the 76 police officers slain in the line of duty, 71 were killed by firearms [5]. Guns were also used in 71,000 armed robberies and 55,000 assaults.

A high proportion of homicides, suicides, and crimes involve guns. In 1967 about 63 percent of all homicides were shootings [5], and three-quarters of these were done with handguns. Nearly one-half of all suicides were accomplished with firearms [18]. More than three out of five armed robbers carried guns [5].

Considering the prominent role played by guns in our history and our mass media, it is surprising how little we know about them. We do not even know accurately how many firearms there are in the country. Estimates range from 50 million to 200 million [8]. In a careful study of this question, Arnold Kotz [10] of the Stanford Research Institute estimated that there are 115 million privately owned guns, or more than two guns for each male in the country between the ages of 14 and 65. He found that gun sales have been increasing sharply, rising in 1967 to an estimated 4.5 million firearms sold domestically and 1.2 million more imported. Whatever the actual figures, the populace is, to say the least, well armed. A Harris Survey [6] conducted in April 1968 found that over half the homes in the country have at least one gun. A significant proportion of these firearms are not intended primarily for sporting activities. According to a nationwide survey conducted for the President's Commission on Law Enforcement and the Administration of Justice [14], 37 percent of the people interviewed said that they keep a gun "for protection."

For whatever reason it is owned, a gun can of course be lethal, whether by intent or accident, whether aimed at one's self or another. How severe is the problem of gun deaths in this country? Figure 5 shows the rates of deaths by suicide, homicide, and fatal accident committed with guns since 1913.

The curves for the suicide-by-gun rate and the homicide-by-gun rate are roughly parallel to the total suicide rate and total homicide rate [18]. Note that there has been a significant reduction in death rates since the 1920's and 1930's. The figures are not worse now than ever before, in contrast to some alarmist reports. The homicide rate was high throughout the "Golden Twenties" and Prohibition era, while the suicide rate rose sharply with the Depression. Deaths by gun accident have gradually fallen. Though federal laws regulating firearms were passed in 1934 and 1938, the reduction in death rates probably cannot be attributed entirely to these laws. In general the

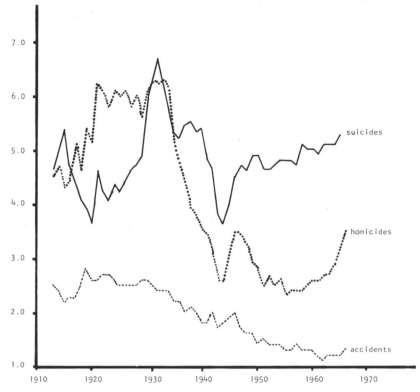

FIG. 5.   Rates of gun deaths in the United States per 100,000 population, 1913–1966 [1, 10]

homicide rate rises with prosperity, while the suicide rate increases with economic depression [9]. Medical and surgical advances in the 1930's and 1940's may account for the drop in homicide and overall gun death rate during these decades. Herbert A. Bloch and Gilbert Geis suggest that "many persons who formerly might have died from crimes of violence are now saved on operating tables, and their assailants are charged with assault with intent to kill rather than with murder or manslaughter" [4]. Many factors influence these death rates including war and peace, the effectiveness of law enforcement, and social conditions.

Notice, however, that these rates have been increasing steadily over the last decade, particularly for gun homicides and gun suicides. The rate of gun homicide, for example, increased more than 50 percent in the last eleven years. The use of guns in crime has been increasing as well. Since 1964 guns in aggravated assault increased by 76 percent, in armed robbery by 58 percent [5].

Figure 5 illustrates another important point. Over the past thirty-five years many more people have killed themselves with guns than have been murdered with guns. Discussions of whether or not there is a gun problem often focus exclusively on crime, neglecting self-inflicted and accidental deaths and injuries resulting from gun wounds. At times more people killed themselves intentionally with guns than were murdered by all methods combined [18].

Gun Statistics: United States Compared with Other Nations

Though the problem of gun deaths is not as severe now as it was thirty years ago, the recent trends are reason for concern. There is even more reason for concern and dismay when the United States is compared to other advanced nations. This is seen in Table 1, which compares deaths due to firearms in fourteen countries.

TABLE 1. Deaths due to firearms in fourteen countries, total number and rate per 100,000 population

COUNTRY	HOMICIDE		SUICIDE		ACCIDENTS	
	Number	Rate	Number	Rate	Number	Rate
U.S A. (1966)	6,855	3.5	10,407	5.3	2,558	1.3
Australia (1965)	57	0.5	331	2.9	94	0.8
Belgium (1965)	20	0.2	82	0.9	11	0.1
Canada (1966)	98	0.5	609	3.1	197	1.0
Denmark (1965)	6	0.1	48	1.0	4	0.1
England, Wales (1966)	27	0.1	173	0.4	53	0.1
France (1965)	132	0.3	879	1.8	252	0.5
German Fed. Repub. (1965)	78	0.1	484	0.9	89	0.2
Italy (1964)	243	0.5	370	0.7	175	0.3
Japan (1965)	16	0.0	68	0.1	78	0.1
Netherlands (1965)	5	0.0	11	0.1	4	0.0
New Zealand (1962)	4	0.2	39	1.7	6	0.3
Scotland (1963)	8	0.1	20	0.4	13	0.3
Sweden (1966)	14	0.2	192	2.5	20	0.3

The United States leads these other countries in not only homicides by gun but suicides and accidents by gun. To say this another way, if the United States had the same gun homicide rate as Japan, our 1966 death toll would have been 32 instead of 6,855 [10]; if our suicide-by-gun rate were the same, only 196 persons would have killed themselves with a gun instead of 10,407. Our homicide-by-gun rate is 35 times that of Germany, Denmark, England, and Scotland, and 7 times that of Australia, Canada, and Italy. The suicide-by-gun rate is more than twice that of Sweden and 5 times that of Denmark. The only other nation in the chart with a comparable accidental death rate by gun is Canada, and ours is 30 percent higher than hers.

Thus there is ample reason to believe that the United States has a problem with gun deaths at this time. Not only are increasing numbers of persons dying from firearms, but a comparison of the United States with other advanced nations is deplorable.

The Gun Law Controversy

Public concern about gun abuse has generated a raging controversy about stricter gun laws, and many legislators have found themselves caught between the arguments and political pressures of proponents and opponents of stronger gun control laws. In the congressional elections of 1968, the controversy may have played a part in the defeat of Senator Clark and Senator Morse, who favored stronger laws, and in the reelection of Senator Church, who opposed them.

Most legislators favor laws promising to reduce crime and needless deaths. But in attempting to assess the effectiveness of past gun legislation before passing new laws, they have found themselves in a dilemma because most of the evidence has been inadequate. Few good studies have been done. With little reliable data for or against gun laws, most legislators have had to choose between advocating strong legislation in the face of a determined, organized opposition or opposing it at a time of public concern about guns, crime, and law and order.

Opponents of gun legislation have cited a statistical study done by Alan S. Krug [11]. Krug, formerly an economist at the Pennsylvania State University before going to work for the National Shooting Sports Foundation, compared the thirty-six states that regulate the acquisition or carrying of firearms with the fourteen states without any regulation. There was no statistical difference in rates of homicide, robbery, aggravated assault, or total serious crimes. To conclude from this study that gun laws fail to reduce gun abuse, however, would be absurd. The study did not take into account, for example, the strength of the law or the zeal with which it is enforced. And it raises a more basic question in our own country, where most of the licensing legislation has been left to the states rather than the federal government. For what can a city or a state with strict laws hope to accomplish if its neighbors have lax laws or if there are easy ways of circumventing the law? Massachusetts, for example, with relatively strict laws, recently studied concealable weapons used in crime within the state. The police found that 87 percent of the captured weapons had been obtained in other states [14]. Another example is the city of Detroit, which requires registration of handguns. Following the riots of 1967, gun ownership increased markedly, and the police found that many unregistered handguns had been obtained in nearby states [10]. While local laws may help keep firearms out of undesirable hands, their effectiveness is limited if acquisition of guns is easy and unrestricted nearby.

Although there are an estimated 20,000 laws regulating firearms in this country, until recently there were only two federal laws of importance, the National Firearms Act of 1934 and the Federal Firearms Act of 1938. The first, aimed at the gangsters of the 1930's, imposed heavy taxes on the transfer of certain fully automatic weapons, sawed-off shotguns, mufflers, and concealable weapons, excluding, however, pistols. The second, aimed at manufacturers and dealers, prohibited interstate transport of guns to convicted felons and fugitives from the law. In a discussion of these laws, the *Harvard Law Review* in 1967 concluded that there were serious problems with both of them and that they had probably failed to keep firearms out of the hands of criminals [7]. For example, the Federal Firearms Act of 1938, while attempting to license dealers, does not require either a verified identification or a notarized affidavit from the applicant for a dealer's license. In 1964 less than half the licensees were estimated to be bona fide dealers [7].

Following the assassination of Senator Robert Kennedy, Congress did pass the first major gun legislation in thirty years, contained in two bills, the Omnibus Crime Control and Safe Streets Act and the Gun Control Act of 1968. Taken together these acts prohibit the mail-order sale of firearms and ammunition. They also prohibit the over-the-counter sale of firearms to out-of-state residents (except where contiguous states may permit this), to juveniles (under 18 for rifles and shotguns, under 21 for all other firearms), to convicted felons, to drug users, to mental defectives, and to those committed to state mental hospitals. In passing these laws, Congress nevertheless rejected President Johnson's request for gun registration and licensing of all gun owners. Congress concentrated its attention on gun acquisition rather than gun ownership. It ignored guns already in private hands.

Among the states there is marked variation in gun laws, though for the most part the laws are relatively lax [1, 8]. Only two states, Hawaii and New Jersey, require registration of all guns, and only eight states require a permit for the purchase of a handgun. In the remaining forty-two it is possible to purchase a pistol or rifle without a permit of any kind.

It is interesting to note the experience of New Jersey, whose strict law became effective in August 1966. During the 22-month period that ended May 31, 1968, police granted 94,221 permits for firearms and denied 1,659 applications. About 75 percent of the denials were for criminal records, including offenses such as first degree murder, rape, burglary, breaking-and-entering, and sex crimes of various types [16].

Despite our new federal laws, many other modern countries have much more stringent firearms laws [17]. In Japan private ownership of guns is completely prohibited. In Germany gun permits are required and are issued only to registered hunters and members of shooting clubs. France requires police permits for the purchase of handguns and military rifles. In Sweden it is necessary to demonstrate a need for a gun and a knowledge of its use before purchase. In Great Britain both civilians and the police have been essentially disarmed. Certification is required from the local police before even a long gun can be purchased. In a recent three-year study, of 400,000 criminals arrested, only 159 were carrying guns.

A most interesting and important comparison is between the United States and Israel—interesting and important because Israel has pioneering ideals and unsettled frontier areas (indeed, expanding frontiers) and is bellicose. "Yet one rarely hears about gun violence except in military encounters" [12]. There are an average of from 20 to 30 murders per year, mostly family "crimes of passion," which are performed mainly by methods other than shooting, e.g., stabbing. The incidence of armed robbery is also low. Although there may be a number of causal factors associated with the low incidence of homicide in Israel, one of likely importance is the restriction on private ownership of firearms. Licensing of the potential owner and an acceptable reason for wanting a gun are prerequisites to gun ownership. About 80 percent of the requests are turned down for lack of a sufficient reason to have a gun. Criteria for "sufficient reason" are particularly stringent for dwellers in urban areas. Ammunition also is restricted. Clearly the Israeli example shows that defense of one's country, maintenance of liberty, and a pioneering spirit do not require free access to guns.

All these countries have lower rates of deaths from guns than we do. This suggests, of course, that strong laws are effective, but again, a rigorous, comprehensive, comparative study has not been done. This comparison with other countries also raises the question of whether our so-called strong laws are really strong enough to be effective. Canada, France, Germany, Sweden, and England all require registration of either the gun or the owner or both, while only two of our states require registration of all guns.

At the present time, therefore, the legislator finds the hypothesis that strict firearms laws reduce gun abuse to be neither proved nor disproved. The question is obviously an enormously complicated one. Many other factors besides legislation influence rates of homicide and suicide. For example, homicide rates are affected by historical tradition, population density, and economic trends. There clearly is sufficient evidence, however, to warrant consideration and further study of strict firearms laws. In particular we need to know whether legislation that reduces the prevalence of guns in a community also reduces the number of homicides, suicides, accidental deaths, and crimes by firearms.

Guns and Homicide

Already there is evidence suggesting that elimination of firearms would reduce the homicide rate, even though other methods for committing murder might be attempted. This is suggested by the frequency with which firearms are used to commit murder, by what we know of the motivation of most murderers, and by the relative lethality of the gun.

As mentioned earlier, most murders in the United States are accomplished by shooting. In 1967 F.B.I. statistics showed that 48 percent of murders were done with handguns, 6 percent by rifle, 9 percent by shotgun, 20 percent by cutting or stabbing, 9 percent by personal weapons (e.g., hands, feet), and 8 percent by other means (e.g., club, poison). During the period 1962 through 1967, 58.2 percent of murders were by use of firearms [5].

Of equal importance is the nature of murder. There is a common notion, perhaps fostered by mystery movies and detective stories, that most murders are premeditated or associated with crime. The facts support the opposite interpretation. In a study of homicide in Chicago, Frank Zimring [19] of the University of Chicago Law School found that 82 percent of murders occurred in situations in which the motivation appeared to be ambiguous, short-lived, or impulsive. Typically, homicides occurred during arguments over domestic matters, alcohol, money, or children. A majority of murder victims were relatives, lovers, or friends of the murderer. Few of the attackers appeared to have a "kill-at-any-price" motive. In most gun homicides the murderer did not exhaust the capacity of his weapon, and in 70 percent of the gun murders the victim was wounded with only one shot. In addition very few of the murderers were involved in criminal activities at the time of the murder: Only 12 percent of the murders were associated with robbery and only 3 percent with teen-age gang disputes.

Other data support this view of murder. F.B.I. statistics in 1967 [5] show that almost 3 out of 10 criminal homicides occur within the family unit and that 1 out of 10 results from romantic triangles or lovers' quarrels. Four out of 10 were the direct result of arguments outside the family and not involving romantic triangles; in the majority of these cases, the individuals were acquainted prior to the fatal act. Only about 1 out of 5 homicides was a known or suspected felonious killing.

Further support comes from a comparison of aggravated assault and homicide made by Alex Porkorney [13] in Houston between 1958 and 1961. Aggravated assault is defined as an unlawful attack by one person upon another for the purpose of inflicting injury. Since assault and homicide were similar in almost all aspects studied—the place, age of participants, race, time of day, day of week—the author concluded that it may be matter of chance that an assault becomes a homicide. Unfortunately, he did not study the weapons used.

Granted there is much yet to be learned about the motivation of the murderer, but in many cases the intent to kill does not appear to be single-minded. There frequently is an element of impulsivity, and in such cases the lethality of the weapon may be the difference between a murder and a barroom brawl or a lovers' quarrel. In the Chicago study Zimring [19] found that guns were about five times more likely to kill the victim than knives, the next most commonly used murder weapon. For every 100 reported knife attacks, an average of 2.4 victims died, while for every 100 reported gun attacks, an average of 12.2 victims died. The differences could not be accounted for by the location of the wounds, the circumstances under which the attack took place, or by what was known or inferred about the seriousness of the attack. Even though more persons were attacked with knives than guns, more people died from gun attacks.

Apparently many murders result from a combination of three factors: impulsivity, the lethality of the weapon, and availability of a lethal weapon. Firearms certainly rank high on lethality and availability. Every effort should be made to reduce their access to persons likely to act impulsively. It is reasonable to believe that there would be fewer deaths by homicide if the prevalence of firearms were reduced. While the amount of domestic violence might not be reduced, the number of deaths might be. Moments of temper need to be settled by less lethal means.

Firearms always have been regarded as a means of violence. Is there any evidence that they act as an impetus to anger? In reviewing a series of laboratory experiments on children and college students, Professor Leonard Berkowitz [3] of the University of Wisconsin concluded that guns do act as aggression-eliciting stimuli. Whether or not they were angry to begin with, subjects who saw or handled guns in the psychology laboratory were more likely to be aggressive afterward than those who did not. For example, children who were given a toy gun to play with were more likely to knock down a playmate's blocks than those children who chatted quietly with adults instead. We do not know whether this effect occurs in real life outside the psychology laboratory. One wonders, however, whether the presence of a gun in the home makes for more arguments or even more murders. Is a family who arms itself really "safer"? While its ability to protect itself against robbers may be increased, the risk of an accident, suicide, or murder may also be increased.

Guns and Suicide

Although there is some evidence suggesting that the homicide rate would fall if guns were better controlled, it is difficult to know what influence, if any, is played by guns on the suicide rate. Virtually no research has been done. Now that "psychological autopsies"—detailed investigations of suicides by psychiatrists and psychologists—

are becoming routine, perhaps we shall learn more about factors determining the method of suicide as well as when and how the individual obtained the means to do it.

Aside from the high incidence of gun suicides, it is known that men are about twice as likely as women to use a gun to commit suicide; in 1966, 56 percent of male suicides were by gun, while 28 percent of female suicides used that method [18]. Guns are also a very sure way of attempting suicide, very few persons surviving an attempt with firearms. With guns, with jumping from a high place, and with hanging, the point of no return is reached almost instantaneously once the attempt is started.

In evaluating patients' suicidal potential, psychiatrists regard access to a gun as an ominous sign. It is common practice to advise family and patients to dispose of lethal weapons. One function of psychiatric hospitalization is to separate suicidal patients from available weapons of self-destruction. Such precautions undoubtedly save individual lives. In a moment of drunken despair or sullen anger, a depressed person may reach for a pistol and end in a few seconds a misery that might otherwise abate in a few days or weeks.

High-Risk Groups

Most people act on impulse from time to time. Such behavior is not usually a sign of mental illness or emotional instability. Psychiatrists and psychologists, however, have been impressed that there are some people who are highly likely to act on irrational or unconscious impulses. This type of impulsive behavior may be termed "acting out" and has been described by Freud, Fenichel, Greenacre, and others [2]. Acting out can be of tragic proportions when the deed is destructive and irreparable, extreme examples being homicide and suicide (see Chapters 11 and 13). A disturbed and impulsive person may pull a trigger to discharge tension and anxiety without having given any rational thought to the consequences of his act.

One of the functions of the psychiatrist who sees people in acute distress is to assess the risk of impulsive destruction and to take precautionary measures. We have learned to ask about the availability of a gun to a person who appears potentially violent or self-destructive. We consider the risk of homicide or suicide greater when a gun is available, especially if it is included in the patient's homicidal or suicidal fantasies. Though we may ask patients to give up their weapons, there are few legal means of separating such individuals from their guns other than by involuntary commitment proceedings. The Uniform Firearms Act of Pennsylvania makes it illegal to transfer a firearm to any person of "unsound mind," and psychiatrists are being asked to judge persons to whom this term might apply [15]. It must be emphasized that as long as general gun ownership is permitted, a history of mental illness or psychiatric hospitalization per se is not sufficient reason to prohibit gun use. Most murderers are not mentally ill in the traditional sense, and most mentally ill individuals are not homicidal or suicidal. The evidence in Chapter 11 clearly shows that released mental patients are a relatively nonviolent group. A description of the "preassaultive or prehomicidal" person is given in that chapter. The group of potentially impulsive gun abusers must be carefully distinguished from the population of mentally ill people as a whole.

An interesting comparison is afforded by the study of personality characteristics of negligent hunters in the Minnesota Hunting Casualty Study of 1953 [1]. Ninety-three hunters who were involved in shooting accidents that year were interviewed and given psychological tests, including the Minnesota Multiphasic Personality Inventory. Of these men 95 percent were judged negligent and were characterized as "relatively insensitive to the normal inhibitions that keep most of us out of trouble." The remaining 5 percent were not negligent and did not differ from the norm in personality structure. Hunters who caused one shooting accident were 100 times more likely to cause another as the average hunter was to have his first accident. Young hunters constituted an extreme high-risk group. Fifteen-year-olds led all other ages in causing accidents. Ten years later the NRA reported that teen-agers (15 through 19) were only 7 percent of the hunting population but accounted for 45 percent of the accidents.

In addition to the impulsively destructive person, the insensitively negligent person, and minors who use guns, the group of citizens at high risk to misuse firearms includes the alcoholic (Chapter 11), certain types of drug abusers (Chapter 12), and some brain-damaged persons (Chapter 1). More research and detailed study are necessary to identify, understand, and help the dangerously impulsive or insensitive citizen. However, it is particularly difficult to study this potential gun abuser when guns are unregistered and owners are unlicensed.

Conclusions and Recommendations

The availability of guns increases the probability of their tragic misuse. The United States has more available guns than ever before in its history and less legislative control of firearms than other advanced nations. Too many Americans are dying from gun wounds. And, in the case of homicide, these are "ordinary citizens" shot by "ordinary citizens," most often their relatives, friends, or loved ones —not madmen, rioters, or professional criminals. As physicians, we believe that guns are a hazard to health and that the United States has a gun-death problem. As citizens, we decry the extensive use of guns in crime and civil disorder but are even more concerned about impulsive and accidental gun deaths at home. As psychiatrists, we also hope that gun licensing and registration will be enacted to facilitate our research on the potential gun abuser. The need for future research is clear. We must learn the relationship between the number of guns in a population and the number of deaths and crimes associated with guns. We need to know the natural history of a gun: what happens over the years when a gun is bought for hunting, "plinking," or self-protection, and what happens to the family who owns it. And we need better means of identifying those who can handle guns safely and those who cannot.

We therefore recommend the following:

- Registration of all guns
- Licensing of all gun owners
- Education and advertisement of the risks of gun ownership, with emphasis on descriptions of the types of persons and situations most commonly associated with gun-deaths
- Research, as outlined in this chapter
- Restriction of guns to high-risk groups: Licenses should not be granted to minors, alcoholics, drug addicts, seriously brain-damaged and feebleminded persons. The large class of impulsive, preassaultive personalities should not own guns, but more work is needed to accurately define and delimit this group. Persons convicted of violent crimes and crimes involving firearms are in a high-risk group and should not be licensed.

This is an age of tension and rapid change. Men hope for stability and security—some find comfort in the possession of a gun. But at a time of civil turmoil with an accelerating civilian arms race, further private arming becomes maladaptive, causing more harm than it prevents.

Acknowledgment

We thank Dr. Rudolf Moos, Mrs. Alma Kays, and Mrs. Vivian Gordon for their helpful suggestions and assistance.

References

1. Bakal, C. *The* [sic] *Right to Bear Arms*. New York: Paperback Library, 1968.
2. Bellak, L., and Small, L. *Emergency Psychiatry and Brief Psychotherapy*. New York: Grune & Stratton, 1965.
3. Berkowitz, L. Impulse, aggression and the gun. *Psychology Today* 2:18, 1968.
4. Bloch, H. A., and Geis, G. *Man, Crime and Society: The Forms of Criminal Behavior*. New York: Random House, 1962.
5. Federal Bureau of Investigation. *Uniform Crime Reports, 1967*. Washington, D.C.: U.S. Government Printing Office, 1968.
6. Firearm Facts. Compiled by Criminal Division, United States Department of Justice, July 16, 1968.
7. Firearms: Problems of control. (Unsigned.) *Harvard Law Review* 80:1328, 1967.
8. Harris, R. Annals of legislation: If you love your guns. *New Yorker*, Apr. 21, 1968.
9. Henry, A. F., and Short, J. F. *Suicide and Homicide*. Glencoe, Ill.: Free Press, 1954.
10. Kotz, A. Firearms, Violence and Civil Disorders. Stanford Research Institute Project MU 7105, July 1968.
11. Krug, A. The relationship between firearms licensing laws and crime rates. Congressional Record, vol. 113, part 15. July 25, 1967. P. 20060.
12. Meisels, M. Guns and the Israeli. *Jerusalem Post*, July 8, 1968. P. 8.
13. Porkorney, A. D. Human violence: A comparison of homicide, aggravated assault, suicide and attempted suicide. *Journal of Criminal Law, Criminology and Police Science* 56:488, 1965.
14. The President's Commission on Law Enforcement and Administration of Justice. *The Challenge of Crime in a Free Society*. Washington, D.C.: U.S. Government Printing Office, Feb. 1967.
15. Rotenberg, L. A., and Sodoff, R. L. Who should have a gun? Some preliminary psychiatric thoughts. *American Journal of Psychiatry* 125:841, 1968.
16. Sills, A. R. (Attorney General of New Jersey). Statement Before

Senate Subcommittee on Juvenile Delinquency, U.S. Senate, 90th Congress, June 26, 1968.

17. Tydings, J. Brief Summary of the Firearms Problem in the U.S.A. Personal communication, June 1967.

18. U.S. Department of Health, Education and Welfare, Public Health Service, National Center for Health Statistics. *Vital Statistics of the United States*. Washington, D.C.: U.S. Government Printing Office. Various annual reports from 1913 to 1968 were consulted.

19. Zimring, F. Is Gun Control Likely to Reduce Violent Killings? Unpublished study, Center for Studies in Criminal Justice, University of Chicago Law School, 1968.

9. The Gun Law Controversy

ISSUES, ARGUMENTS, AND SPECULATIONS
CONCERNING FIREARMS LEGISLATION

David N. Daniels, M.D., Edison J. Trickett, Ph.D.,
Mary M. Shapiro, B.A., Jared R. Tinklenberg, M.D.,
and Jay M. Jackman, M.D.

I n the preceding chapter, the existence of a firearms problem is documented clearly. In 1967 more than 21,000 United States citizens died from gun wounds. Violence by gun is not simply a problem of crime control. It is a serious health problem that includes homicide among friends and relatives, suicide, and accidental shootings. Yet "in no major nation in the world is the sale, possession, or use of firearms so free as it is in the United States" [23]. Few issues have produced such great public and legislative controversy as those relating to the manner and degree of legal control over the sale and use of guns. Even the frightening recurrence of assassinations, while contributing to the emotional fervor of gun control arguments, has led to relatively little federal legislation.

Against the backdrop of arduous legislative struggle and the rising rates of gun deaths, we undertook the analysis of the issues and arguments in the gun law controversy. Our goal is to increase understanding of the controversy so that realistic firearms legislation can be enacted. We also hope that our analysis will promote rational examination of the broader issue of violence and subsequently further understanding among groups.

To accomplish these ends, we first review and analyze public opinion and the nature of groups favoring and opposing firearms legislation. Since most groups claim to support a positive program of effective legislation, defining the sides of the controversy is not easy.

257

The most apparent dividing line is over the issue of registration and licensing. Hence we define the proponents of "strong" gun legislation as those who at least favor registration of firearms, or licensing of owners, or both. Opponents are those who do not favor such licensing or registration. In this section we also discuss how "single-interest" groups, such as the National Rifle Association, function. Then we review and classify the array of arguments given by opponents and proponents. Wherever possible, we state the assumptions upon which arguments are based so that future studies may assess their validity. Next, we present the psychological and social issues associated with the various arguments. Often these are covert or implicit, hence our analysis here is speculative and interpretive. Then we present some views from other lands, particularly in relation to the assassinations of the Reverend Martin Luther King, Jr., and Senator Robert F. Kennedy. Finally, we discuss the implications and conclusions of our analysis and review. Here we make specific recommendations for resolving the gun law controversy and show how this controversy reflects the broader struggle for a more tolerant and peaceful nation. In this highly charged area of gun control, we have continuously tried to examine our own moral and political biases; and though no pretense is made at being impartial, we attempt throughout to be accurate in analysis and fair in interpretation. Our interest is to resolve conflict and reduce violence, not to indict and polarize.

Public Opinion

For assessment of public opinion we have relied heavily upon the Gallup Poll. It provides a stratified sample that approximates the United States population and measures a variety of demographic characteristics. Because this poll also supplies information about the standard error of measurement associated with differing sample sizes, it has the additional advantage of providing a way to compare the percentage responses of two groups to determine whether they differ significantly from each other.

The Gallup Polls and Political Indices we reviewed date back three decades to 1938. The sum total of these many polls is both dramatic and consistent. One poll [11] in March 1938 asked the question "Do you think all owners of pistols and revolvers should be required to register with the government?" In response 84 percent of a national sample answered yes, and 16 percent no. Two years later the respective percentages to the same question were 80 percent and 20 percent [11].

Polls [22] since 1959 have asked the question "Would you favor or oppose a law which would require a person to obtain a police permit before he or she could buy a gun?" In all these polls at least 68 percent of a national sample favored such a law. "A January 1967 Gallup Poll disclosed: 70 percent of the persons in a survey believed 'laws concerning rifles and shotguns should be more strict'; 75 percent believed 'a person should not be able to send away for a gun through the mail'; 73 percent were 'for a law which would require registration of a rifle or shotgun'; and 85 percent were 'for a law which would require registration of a handgun'" [17]. Thus at least 68 percent of a national sample (and more often about 75 percent) representative of the American people has favored more stringent gun registration or licensing laws. Indeed a September 1959 poll [49] indicated that 59 percent of the people would support legislation that *outlawed* all handguns except those intended for police use.

Demographic breakdown of polls taken in February 1965 [22] and September 1967 [21] demonstrates that political affiliation, educational background, and level of income do not significantly differentiate those in favor of registration from those opposed to it. Certain consistent and statistically significant differences do appear, however. Women favor registration of guns more than do men. The September 1967 poll [21] further indicates that those in white-collar or professional and business occupations favor registration more than do farmers. Consistent with the occupational division is a rural-urban difference. People living in towns of population less than 2,500 are less favorably disposed to registration than are those living in cities of 500,000 or more. Geographically, the East repeatedly favors gun registration more than do all other sections of the country.

Two other findings are of great interest. Though gun owners are less enthusiastic about registration than those not owning guns, a February 1965 poll [23] indicated that 60 percent of gun owners favored a law requiring a police permit before a gun could be bought. Finally, an August 1967 poll [24] indicated that both blacks and whites agree on the registration of guns.

Generally speaking, demographic differences regarding gun registration involve a rural-urban distinction and a related occupational one. While specific implications about these differences will be presented later, it is important to note here that even though some groups favored gun registration more than did other groups, the polls showed that at least 60 percent of all groups favored registration. Thus as evidenced by the Gallup polls, over the past decade *all* groups, including gun owners, have supported the registration or licensing of guns. Nonetheless, there are identifiable groups who favor or oppose strong gun controls.

Interest Groups in the Gun Law Controversy

A wide variety of groups for an equally wide variety of reasons take sides in the controversy over gun legislation. For example, those who oppose strict gun controls are politically, psychologically, and sociologically a "mixed bag." In the "black ghetto" the Black Panthers see arms as necessary for survival and registration as equivalent to "surrender" or acquiescence to an intolerable and unjust situation. To quote Black Panther Eldridge Cleaver [13]: "We are going to keep our guns to protect ourselves from the pigs [police]." Similarly one issue for the political right is protection, but here the gun is protection against the criminal and subversive [36]. Yet for most of these varied subgroups, the issue of gun control is but one facet of a number of legislative and social issues of concern. Hence their concern with gun legislation may wax or wane as other important matters occur.

But special interest groups, ones with a primary focus on a specific issue or goal, are another matter entirely. As we shall show, having a vested interest in a particular issue can result in a much more durable and powerful impact on the legislative process.

PROPONENT GROUPS

Interest groups with a primary concern for enacting strong gun control laws were until recently virtually nonexistent. The National Council for a Responsible Firearms Policy (NCRFP) [6, 17] is a small group formed in 1967 with prominent men as directors, such as New York Mayor John Lindsay, Dr. Karl Menninger of the Menninger Foundation, and author Cleveland Amory. It is said to have fewer than 100 members, no full-time staff, and very little money. After the assassination of Robert Kennedy another group, the Emergency Committee for Gun Control, was formed by former astronaut John Glenn, Jr., with the assistance of the NCRFP[6]. Another response to the assassination of Robert Kennedy was the formation of Womanpower-in-Action [59], whose purpose is to help reduce violence in America. Mary K. Harvey, a senior *McCall's* editor, directs this group, and *McCall's* magazine has provided much of the initial support. As part of its effort Womanpower-in-Action favors strong legislation. In addition, a number of knowledgeable organizations without special interest endorse strict firearms legislation. These include the American Bar Association, the International Association of Police Chiefs, the National Association of Citizens Crime Commissions, and the President's Commission on Crime [16, 26.]

OPPOSITION GROUPS

The opposing groups constitute an effective block to strong gun controls despite the expressed opinion of a large majority of the American people. These groups include several diverse organizations: industry organizations, various wildlife groups, and the National Rifle Association (NRA) [17, 26]. Although these groups often are called the "gun lobby," neither they nor any proponent groups are legally considered as lobbies. The industry organizations include the National Shooting Sports Foundation (NSSF), "an organization of about 100 manufacturers, dealers, magazines and organizations with interests in sports shooting" [17], and the Sporting Arms and Ammunition Manufacturers' Institute (SAAMI), "a trade association of nine of the largest makers of guns and ammunition" [17, 26]. Some wildlife groups and conservation organizations also oppose strong gun control legislation. Among these organizations are the National Wildlife Federation and the 15,000-member Wildlife Management Institute, both of which receive considerable support from firearms and ammunition manufacturers [17].

While both industrial organizations and wildlife groups add to the economic and popular influence of opposition groups, by far the most visible and powerful group consistently opposing strong gun control legislation is the National Rifle Association (NRA). The NRA is well organized, large (1,040,024 members as of September 30, 1968), and well financed (approximate operating budget of 5.7 million dollars in 1967) [2, 42, 43]. While the NRA did not have ethnic, rural-urban, or socioeconomic data in relation to membership, it readily supplied us with the membership data broken down by states [43]. The total NRA membership represents approximately half of one per cent (.52 percent) of the nation's population. Analysis by states shows that the Pacific and Mountain states have the largest proportion of NRA members. The average for these states is .72 percent of their population. The South Central Atlantic and Southeastern states have the lowest proportion of NRA members, .38 percent and .40 percent, respectively, of these states' population. Mississippi NRA members make up only .29 percent of the state's population. The remainder of the states—the Central, Northeastern, North Central Atlantic states—vary moderately around the national average of .52 percent. Massachusetts is relatively low at .37 percent NRA membership, and Michigan relatively high at .70 percent. These data are congruent (but not identical) with the aforementioned public opinion data except for the NRA underrepresentation in the South, which perhaps can be accounted for by a relative lack of Negro members. Thus the NRA is stronger in hunting and Western states as well as in rural and farming areas.

The NRA's activities include encouraging hunting and recreational shooting, training in safe gun use, marksmanship training, gun competitions, and acting as the "foremost guardian of the American tradition and constitutional right of citizens to 'keep and bear arms'" [2]. The NRA claims to support a positive program of firearms legislation [2, 42], which includes banning "destructive devices" such as bazookas and antitank guns, increasing penalties for crimes in which firearms are used, banning handguns from minors, and requiring statements of eligibility in ordering handguns through the mails. Registration of guns or licensing of owners is not part of this program.

THE NRA AS A SPECIAL INTEREST GROUP

There are several factors contributing to the NRA's efficacy in blocking strong firearms legislation. Often these relate to its role as a special interest group and can be described as follows.

First, the NRA clearly is a single-interest group. Its existence depends entirely upon firearms-related issues. This single-purpose nature, with ideological agreement centering around a common important goal (in this instance of maintaining relatively unrestricted access to several kinds of guns), facilitates commitment and united action. This may result in a willingness to oppose actively any legislative candidate who favors gun controls, irrespective of his other stands. On the other hand, those lacking the intense single interest in the issue of firearms legislation are less likely to vote for or against a candidate on the basis of this issue alone. In this situation the prospective legislator may feel that voting with the majority will gain him very little, while voting against the special interest group will hurt him a great deal.

Second, the NRA's organization and resources allow it to sustain an effort over time. This can be a crucial factor in influencing the legislative process, since the organization with sufficient resources to

follow proposed legislation through the entire committee and hearing process has a decided advantage. For instance, the NRA's
"lobby" can generate mail from its constituency nearly at will during all phases of the legislative process. NRA Secretary Frank C.
Daniel's claim [17] that "perhaps half a million [letters to congress-
men] would not be too far off" serves to indicate the potency of the
NRA in this regard. The NRA's ability to sustain influence helps to
account for the pattern of favorable and unfavorable congressional
mail on gun legislation subsequent to the tragic deaths of John Kennedy, Martin Luther King, Jr., and Robert Kennedy. In each instance initial mail favored stronger gun controls. As time passed,
however, the organized "anti" group sustained its level of mail input,
thus reversing the ratio of pro and con mail.

Third, the unequal geographic distribution of the opponents to
strong gun controls serves to enhance the NRA's influence. The poll
and NRA membership data cited previously indicate that rural areas
and Mountain and Pacific states contain proportionately more opponents of firearms legislation. Because the legislators from these rural
areas tend to retain their positions, they consequently acquire positions of congressional authority and influence, which afford them
many more opportunities to block firearms legislation.

Fourth, the NRA, as is so with special interest groups in general,
influences members and others sympathetic with its cause by disseminating information, some of which is informational and some propa-
gandistic. Through its official publication, the *American Rifleman*, the
NRA has urged its members to write their congressmen opposing
specific bills, while providing members information about these bills
that contains omissions and distortions [26]. One of the most crucial
misunderstandings fostered by the NRA is that of equating gun control with the *banning* of all guns, a proposal suggested by none of
the current bills. The highly emotional nature of the gun control
issue, reflecting that basic ideological and psychological issues are at
stake, contributes to the acceptance of distorted and one-sided arguments by those wanting to believe them. Indeed an official NRA
representative testifying before a congressional committee against a
particular bill made the remarkable admission that he had not even
read the bill [26].

Our intent here is not to ignore the positive contributions of the
NRA. In fact the NRA literature in general is restrained, as is partially indicated by the strict adherence of its advertising policy to
the law. Our concern is to point out that on some occasions the
NRA has disseminated information which misrepresents proposed

legislation and arouses fears of restrictions and false beliefs about pending legislation, which in turn obscure the critical social issue of violence and its reduction. Accurate information is crucial in creating rational dialogue about the issues in gun control.

SUMMARY

Many diverse groups comprise the less than one-third of the population who oppose strict gun control laws. Their motivational patterns and the social milieu in which these attitudes develop differ greatly, and, consequently, they see firearms legislation in diverse ways. However, the successful blocking of strong legislation is in large part due to the unofficial NRA "gun lobby." The NRA's efficacy can be attributed to its status as a powerful special interest group, the relative lack of organized proponent support, the intensity of feeling unifying its members, the positions of congressional authority held by those favorable to the NRA point of view, and the NRA's ability to keep the "cards and letters" coming from members.

Arguments in the Gun Controversy

The task of classifying and analyzing the arguments over gun controls is complicated by at least three features of these arguments. First, the arguments take a polymorphous form, naturally leading to some apparent inconsistencies. For instance, the National Rifle Association stresses the growing need for armed protection while presenting statistics showing that guns are playing a decreasing and relatively minor role in crimes and deaths in general [2, 42]. Similarly the NRA urges that police should not be empowered to register or regulate guns, but at the same time it advocates stronger law-enforcement procedures [2, 42]. Arguments of proponents also range over large expanses and contain inconsistencies. An NRA analysis [3] of Carl Bakal's book [6] favoring firearms legislation states that Bakal distorts many facts, uses slander, and resorts to "guilt by association." For example, Bakal writes of Charles Whitman's 1966 Texas tower shooting spree as "the worst mass murder in our Nation's history" when in fact it is not. The NRA points out [3] that several instances of airplane bomb plantings killed more than twice the sixteen murdered by Whitman.

Second, various proponents and opponents of gun control legislation selectively present an array of statistics favorable to their positions, the total effect of which is to baffle the reader [2, 26, 32, 56, 58]. One opponent [32] indicates that Switzerland, a low-crime country, requires all males ages 20 to 50 to keep a military weapon in their homes, but he fails to state that detailed registration of all firearms and ammunition is also required [6, 26]. NRA statistics cite the "low rates" of gun deaths resulting from accidents, the decreased rates resulting from homicide compared to the 1930's, and the lack of correlation between gun control laws and these rates. Yet they fail to make comparisons with rates of gun deaths in other countries or to emphasize recent upward trends in rates of killings [42]. On the other hand, proponents are likely to stress the positive effects of gun legislation—for example, New York's Sullivan Law [26]. They also stress the total number of Americans killed by guns, 795,000 since 1900 [6, 56], and cross-cultural data showing much lower rates in other advanced countries [9, 26, 56]. Proponents, however, deal inadequately with the fluctuations in death-by-gun rates (see Chapter 8).

Third, there is considerable overlap among arguments. In some instances one argument merges into another, and there are variations upon themes. In our classification following, most similar arguments are placed contiguously. The order does not reflect relative importance or frequency, since both vary greatly depending upon the source of information. All categories presented are considered important. For each category we present the formal arguments of both opponents and proponents. We leave discussion of psychological and social issues and their interpretation to the next section.

The arguments over firearms legislation can be divided into six categories: rights and fairness; protection, security, and availability; punishment, justice, and prevention; effectiveness and consequences; economics and conservation; and recreation and sport.

RIGHTS AND FAIRNESS

A recurrent argument from those opposing gun legislation [2] is that gun controls of any kind infringe upon the basic American freedom and right to bear arms, as specified [14] in the Second Amendment: "A well-regulated Militia being necessary to the security of a free state, the right of the people to keep and bear Arms shall not be infringed." Since the courts have held that the Second Amendment applies to a well-regulated militia, not to individuals, there seemingly is no legal constraint against gun legislation as provided by the Second Amendment [6, 26]. However, of late the constitutionality of strong gun legislation has been challenged on other issues. For instance, although the issue is not yet decided, the Fifth Amendment recently has been invoked concerning the right not to testify against oneself for possessing guns [14, 23].

In addition to purely legal considerations, the infringement argument takes other forms: Restrictive legislation is an effort ultimately to disarm sportsmen and law-abiding citizens; and restrictive legislation would lead to further encroachment upon individuals' rights by large and powerful state and federal governments. Furthermore, the issue of confiscation, which arises in several contexts and which opponents regard as a major infringement on their rights, is a factor in the opposition to proposed regulatory legislation imposing only licensing and registration. Whatever their reasons, those fearing confiscation and discrimination have a legitimate fear. Many proponents would like to see a disarmed citizenry, ideally eventually to include the police. Fears of discrimination likely have a realistic basis too. Licensing requirements inadvertently could result in several forms of discrimination: against the rural citizen and sportsman because of the inconveniences of registration; against the small dealer because dealer fees in effect might make it economically infeasible for the rural store owner to operate; and against minorities because they are more likely to have discriminatory arrest records and less police protection.

On the other hand, proponents of strong gun laws respond to the restriction and loss of rights argument by pointing out that the increasing use of guns in crimes and homicides simply makes strong gun laws a necessity for the preservation of citizens' rights. Although unnecessary restrictions on the individual are to be deplored in a free society, it is argued that in our complex urban society some traditional freedoms must be relinquished for more important rights, such as the freedom of safe movement in crowded cities. Since we already require the taxation, restriction, or registration of many items—such as automobiles, boats, and drugs—registration of guns would not constitute an infringement of an individual's rights per se but only an inconvenience.

One writer [40] even envisions a new Bill of Rights to supplement the old one, an important aspect of which would be repeal of the Second Amendment: "The right of people to bear arms shall be promptly, effectively and permanently abridged by Congress, which shall confiscate all weapons, including those used by police: violation of this law shall be punishable by exile."

Two other points are sometimes made by proponents in connection with rights. First, the will of the majority (since the majority favor strong regulations) is put forth as a "rights" argument [17]. Second, a lack of uniformity in the many differing state laws serves to discriminate against the state with the more restrictive law. Edward Kennedy [16] pointed out this fact in an address to the 1967 annual meeting of the NRA when he said that it was unfair to the citizen of Massachusetts when those whom the laws of Massachusetts deprive of guns can obtain guns in neighboring states having few restrictions.

Thus the rights and necessity argument has more than technical legal implications. It merges into the arguments concerning protection and security and involves basic political and ideological issues concerning even the way of life in the United States.

PROTECTION, SECURITY, AND AVAILABILITY

Perhaps the real bedrock issue for opponents, especially in urban areas, is that guns are seen as protection against attacks on the nation, the community, groups with which one is identified, or on the self. The gun stands for personal protection and security against life-threatening dangers and destructive evil forces, whatever these forces might be—criminals, drug addicts, rapists, Communists or other subversives, mental patients ("kooks"), rioters, police, or racists. In a number of instances the theme of self-defense has taken the form of arming collectively, as in the case of both the Minutemen and the Black Panthers.

The rationale for these protection and security arguments again differs, depending on the locale and the motivation of those involved. One prominent rationale is that gun laws are feared because they could lead from initial registration to discrimination and finally to confiscation of all guns[26, 58]. With regard to national security, restrictive legislation, it is feared, would hinder the protection of our country from tyrannies of the right or left. An extreme rationale for this fear is given by Harry L. Graham [17], legislative representative of the National Grange: "If it ever became possible that a rebel government of some kind might by armed force take over the United States, they would know exactly who owned firearms and what kind they were." The example of Nazi Germany is offered as proof of this point, since the Nazis allegedly used registration lists to systematically disarm their victims [32]. However, Bakal [6] claims that there is no historical evidence that this was so, that if a dictatorial power really wants to get the populace's guns, it sends its men from house to house without regard for any lists. The ultimate premise of this "rebel government" rationale seems to be a "you never can tell" assumption. Because refutation of this kind of rationale rests on negative evidence, this type of "logic" is essentially irrefutable. The fact that a rebel government has not taken over the United States in the past does not absolutely ensure that it will not happen in the future, no matter how remote the possibility. Consequently, the only empirical evidence that could absolutely answer this question would be provided only if and when a rebel government *did in fact* take over the United States.

In another vein, since handguns are not particularly effective military weapons, their confiscation would not be nearly as serious (from the standpoint of military defense) as current legal restrictions on automatic weapons, bazookas, grenades, and the like. One could argue that defense-minded citizens should be permitted to arm themselves with these more effective weapons. Furthermore, the belief in the necessity and effectiveness of a militia-type military organization can be questioned. Militias tend to have high desertion rates, poor discipline, and inferior training compared to full-time regular troops. For instance, the belief in the efficacy of militias has been viewed as "a dangerous illusion that almost cost us the Revolution" [6].

The concern with protection and security is focused not only on threats to national security. Many arguments relate to the internal problems of this country and the individual safety of citizens. A fear expressed by many people revolves around a concern that police protection is insufficient. The NRA's official publication, the *American Rifleman*, has advocated arming and training women in the use of firearms as protection against "burglars and marauders" [2, 57]. Also, a regular feature of the magazine, the "Armed Citizen," is based upon the opinion that "law-enforcement officers cannot at all times be where they are needed to protect life or property in danger of serious violation. In many such instances, the citizen has no choice but to defend himself with a gun" [2]. In addition the NRA points out how its shooting program strengthens national defense by training potential and actual soldiers in weapon usage.

Although an armed citizenry often is assumed to provide greater protection than an unarmed citizenry, data presented in Chapter 8 indicate that such an armed citizenry is not without its costs and that there is a relation between firearms availability and murder. For instance, Zimring's work [60], discussed in the preceding chapter, demonstrates impressively the greater potential deadliness of serious gun assaults compared with equally serious assaults with knives. Furthermore, advocates of strong gun laws [8, 26] suggest that even the

mere presence of a gun may encourage, tempt, and even incite violence. As J. Edgar Hoover [7] put it, "Those who claim that the
availability of firearms is not a factor in murders in this country are
not facing reality."

Thus for proponents a particularly important point is that the potential dangers of armed individualized protection may outweigh the
benefits it offers in our congested, urban society. These dangers include harm to innocent bystanders, accidental shootings, and the increased danger of impulsive violence, which accounts for over 80
percent of homicides (see Chapter 8). Proponents argue that the
balance between these dangers and the benefits of individualized
protection has tipped. An armed citizenry is viewed as losing whatever utilitarian value it may once have had. The current escalation in
gun acquisitions menaces public safety, including that of the police.
In vicious circle we see more killings, greater polarity, and further
gun acquisitions. Indeed between 1963 and 1967 firearms sales increased 132 percent [20].

Therefore proponents of stronger legislation suggest that even
with realistic dangers the method of protection must be questioned.
An armed citizenry may not be the best answer for those citizens,
especially in urban areas and changing neighborhoods, who are increasingly concerned with rising crime rates and civil disorders. Nor
may it be the best cure for the understandable national anxiety over
law and order. Proponents claim that strong laws would keep states
from being flooded by the unchecked and irresponsible influx of
guns [58] and that police could make arrests for illegal possession
before more serious crimes could occur. To some, reducing the
availability of guns would extend to disarming police, but this position is not generally offered for serious consideration [40, 48]. However, there is some support for the possibility of restricting off-duty
police from carrying guns [53]. At the very least, it is argued, guns
should be kept from high-risk groups: minors, "accident"-prone
sportsmen, mentally defective and brain-damaged persons, felons,
and others with a previous history of violence. Similarly laws may
differentiate among types of firearms. There is reason to treat handguns more restrictively than long arms, since handguns account for a
much higher proportion of homicides and play only a small role in
recreation. As put by a spokesman [15] for the Wildlife Management Institute, "America's sportsmen object to treating rifles and
shotguns in the same manner as handguns, when they know that the
latter are susceptible to the greatest misuse by criminals, addicts, unstable persons, and others."

PUNISHMENT, JUSTICE, AND PREVENTION

Opponents of strong firearms legislation state this argument in several ways: Guns don't kill people, people kill people; when guns are outlawed, only outlaws will have guns (because they steal them anyway); crime is not associated with guns but with such social factors as population density, population composition, economic status, and police effectiveness; and stern punishment for gun crimes will deter others from committing similar offenses [2, 32, 42]. To quote Representative R. L. Sikes (Democrat, Floriaa) [18]: "It is not the firearms that are purchased legally that are the cause of trouble, but that [sic] it is the guns obtained through illegal channels by the criminal element that are at the root of the problem. The statistics reported by the Metropolitan Police Department support this strongly." Though criminals do purchase weapons from legal sources [26], gun registration and the feared confiscation (a type of unilateral disarmament) are viewed as a futile way to control possession of guns by criminals, since criminals are seen as irresponsible lawbreakers. As viewed by Representative Dingell (Democrat, Michigan) [15]: "The threat to our society today is not the weaponry of crime, but crime itself. Lawbreakers are not more apt to abide by laws governing possession of deadly weapons than they are to abide by general criminal laws." Indeed one report [39] interprets restriction upon the law-abiding private citizen as encouraging crime: "A potential burglar is more likely to break in if he can be sure that the victim is unarmed."

As further support for the "people kill people" argument, the NRA and others have pointed out that none of the recent assassinations would have been prevented by gun legislation [2, 58]. There is, however, an ironic twist to the killing of Robert Kennedy. The gun allegedly used by Sirhan Sirhan was originally purchased by a white man for protection after the Watts riots in the summer of 1965. In time the gun passed through others' hands on the way to Sirhan [47]. In this way the instrument of one man's presumed defense became the very instrument of the killing of another American.

Associated with the "punishment as prevention" argument is advocacy of swift and stern justice, which at the very least should include more vigorous application of existing laws. Indeed enforcement of existing firearms legislation "has been less than vigorous" [17]. For example, a Treasury Department official indicated [17] that he knew of only one conviction in thirty years under the section of the 1938 law prohibiting mailing firearms to the eight states with gun permit requirements. However, the advocacy for strict enforcement sometimes takes the form of recommending stronger and even cruel punishment of criminals who have used guns as a deter-rent to others [2, 26, 42]. Hence stern punishment is seen as the cure, even though its effectiveness remains undocumented. Further-more, the issue is complicated by the fact that more than three-fourths of homicides and two-thirds of criminal assaults occur among family and friends, i.e., are not committed by "hardened" criminals [26, 58]. Since most of these are unpremeditated and im-pulsive homicides, further doubt is cast upon stern punishment as an effective treatment (see Chapter 8).

In contrast, proponents of strong gun controls see prevention or prophylaxis rather than punishment as most important. First, since availability is considered a factor in gun deaths, proponents advocate intervention before a gun is likely to be used. As indicated, guns could be kept from high-risk groups.

Second, the proponents argue that increasing crime rates and the "breakdown of law and order" represent symptoms, not causes. For opponents of gun laws, illegal gun usage is the cause; it requires getting tough and cracking down on the irresponsible criminal and hoodlum elements. For proponents, illegal use of guns is a symptom; it requires looking for underlying problems and rectifying social wrongs. It is suggested further [52] that "the legal justification for the use of deadly force against a felony suspect is based on the prec-edent that at one time all felonies were punishable by death. But today few crimes call for the death penalty." In this way shooting suspects becomes an unjustifiable act in itself.

While the two positions often become polarized and representa-tive of tenaciously held ideologies, they are not necessarily incom-patible. One can advocate simultaneously strong consistent law en-forcement, the restriction of gun availability, and the reduction of frustrating social conditions.

EFFECTIVENESS AND CONSEQUENCES

Opponents of firearms legislation claim an interest in effective procedures to reduce gun deaths: "The issue is not one of guns ver-sus no guns. Rather it centers on various kinds of approaches that are necessary and can be taken to best accomplish the goals that are sought" [15]. One opponent view presented thus far suggests en-forcing strong laws against criminal use of guns. Another view sug-gests armed citizens as an effective deterrent. Indeed the *Manion Forum* [36] expressed the view that the citizen without a gun is guilty of "turning the Nation over to a bunch of criminals."

But the effectiveness argument as put by opponents to stricter legislation states that laws falling short of confiscation simply will not work because registration and licensing alone would still leave firearms available to irresponsible individuals—the criminal and impulsive killer alike. Then, since nobody wants excessive restriction of individual freedom in our society, restriction must be warranted by clear evidence before further controls are imposed upon the private citizen, evidence which opponents feel is currently lacking [39]. Furthermore, opponents claim that registration and licensing procedures would be difficult to enforce and cumbersome to administrate. More problems would be created than cured. Possible consequences could include a blackmarket in guns and ammunition, difficulties in interstate transfer of weapons by hunters and sportsmen, and excessive federal regulatory authority. The latter presumably could result in use of the laws by the executive branch of the government in ways never intended.

To counter the argument that evidence warranting restrictions is lacking, proponents present the aforementioned data connecting increasing gun deaths to availability and data comparing this country's alarmingly high death-by-gun rates with those of other advanced countries (see Chapter 8). Although these data are not confirmatory, proponents feel that they do provide positive evidence warranting restrictions. In addition they feel that the benefits resulting from even such a partially effective law would outweigh any such burdensome consequences as enforcement and administrative difficulties, extension of governmental authority, personal inconvenience, and increased monetary costs. However, any potential legislation should of course consider and safeguard against these and other potential inadvertent consequences.

ECONOMICS AND CONSERVATION

The effectiveness and feasibility arguments of opponents merge into economic issues. The economic costs involved in gun control legislation must be measured against the benefits accrued in reducing violence. Opponents argue that the licensing and registration of 50 to 200 million firearms located in more than half of American homes would be extremely costly, as would enforcement of strict gun laws. All these costs, opponents claim, would go for undetermined and perhaps minimal benefits. Well-documented cost estimates for licensing, registration, and enforcement of uniform and strict laws are not readily available. However, New York Mayor John Lindsay in a press release [35] stated that licensing could run to more than 6 million dollars in New York City alone or about 20 dollars per owner. Good decision-making is hampered considerably by the lack of realistic cost estimates and enforcement procedures; enacting legislation without an adequate budget to implement and enforce it renders any legislation meaningless.

Perhaps, argue the opponents, it would be wiser to spend our limited tax revenues on more important social and cultural factors associated with violence. It is argued that violence by firearms must be compared with other forms of violence in our society. In 1966 there were 53,000 people killed by automobiles, and roughly 50 percent of these deaths were associated with the use of alcohol. Thus, say opponents, if the objective is to reduce deaths, further restrictions on automobile use, better highways, and control of alcohol abuse should receive priority over gun control [39]. However, compared to the greater number of automobile drivers, gun users proportionately cause more deaths [6].

Another economic argument revolves around potential economic losses to various groups. The year 1967 saw approximately 400 million dollars in firearms, ammunition, and shooting accessory sales and 1.5 billion dollars in "side" expenses such as transportation, lodging, and food [6]. Opponents argue that the red tape of registration and licensing [50] and the "inevitable" firearms confiscation would damage this substantial firearms and shooting industry. The money generated by hunting, which represents a sizable portion of income and revenue in western hunting states, would be reduced [26]. In 1967 the cost of approximately 20 million hunting licenses and permits represented nearly 80 million dollars [6]. (NRA data for 1968 [43] number hunting licenses at 14,685,732, still a substantial number and fourteen times the NRA membership.) If the revenues now obtained from these hunting license fees and sales taxes on guns and ammunition were reduced, other means of supporting conservation programs and outdoor recreation would have to be found. Furthermore, some even claim that a reduction in hunting could lead to a problem in wildlife control [2, 55], ignoring the fact that conservation and wildlife control could be achieved by other means.

The figures stated above indicate that economic arguments are important. It is no wonder that opponents of gun legislation, for example, the NRA and the National Shooting and Sports Foundation, are supported extensively by gun and ammunition manufacturers [26]. Nor is it surprising that mail-order restrictions are supported by United States firearms manufacturers, since most mail-order guns are foreign imports [26]. In a similar vein, it is of interest to note how economic considerations unite some conservation groups, such as the American Wildlife Federation, with such shooting groups as the NRA. Western states having a large influx of affluent hunters each year are loath to see legislation passed that might have the effect of reducing the number of hunters. Thus practical economic issues may in fact be very important determinants of some opposition to strict gun controls. In this case removing the fear of economic loss may be more relevant and important to some than offering a host of other reasons.

RECREATION AND SPORT

Many of those who are opposed to strong gun legislation are concerned about being restricted and deprived of healthy outdoor life, the hobby of gun collecting, family recreation, and the fellowship associated with hunting and target shooting. In general this argument is a straightforward concern for the continuation of recreational activities enjoyed by many Americans. Articles in the *American Rifleman* reflect the interest in hunting, outdoor life, and relationships between fathers and children. For instance, an article in the *American Rifleman* [2] entitled "Happiness Is a Warm Gun" convincingly depicts a close father-son relationship centering around shooting. While concern is directed toward teaching gun safety to eager children, other important, unmentioned concerns include the possible thrill of shooting something and the different meanings that guns and death may have for children, issues raised in the following section. Worth stressing again is the fact that while current gun legislation would cause inconvenience, it is not intended to curtail the recreational aspects of shooting. Furthermore, shooters' present willingness to obtain hunting licenses and permits at considerable cost and inconvenience stands in contrast to the resistance to having guns registered or owners licensed.

Psychological and Social Issues

The foregoing analysis of formal arguments clearly indicates that there are important psychological factors and social forces operating in the gun controversy. Indeed the selective presentation of data (sometimes entirely out of context), the contradictory and inconsistent presentation of data, and the very vehemence of presentation bespeak the emotional quality of the controversy. The ridicule and hostility implicit and sometimes explicit employed by both sides imply strong emotions about guns and gun legislation [2, 6, 7, 16, 17, 26]. While opponents have been called a "minority of Americans, spurred on by the propaganda of gunrunners" and "paramilitary fanatics and extremists" [16], proponents have been called "do-gooders," "fanatics," and "extremists determined to destroy what we know and treasure as the American way of life" [17].

The emotional fervor, including even the language of violence, pervades the gun controversy, discloses psychological and social issues, and betrays the irrational as well as the rational forces at work. These must be examined if the resistances on both sides are to be understood and modified and effective legislation worked out. Our analysis here centers on six themes: the changing way of life, guns and fears, guns as symbols, violence—good and evil, the phenomenon of loss, and trust versus mistrust.

THE CHANGING WAY OF LIFE

While the urban population is increasing at the rate of over 10 million a decade, the rural population remains about the same. Consequently, the country is presently over 70 percent urban [41]. Both sides of the gun controversy see the social change accompanying this urbanization as a central issue. Among the many ramifications of our changing society that opponents abhor is the relative loss of the so-called frontier or rural way of life. Opponents view gun legislation as symbolizing further encroachment upon individual liberty and traditional individual self-reliance—a fettering to which they respond "don't fence me in." For opponents a crucial aspect of the national identity is being taken away by an ever-expanding federal government. Even keeping guns away from juveniles (a well-documented high-risk group) is depicted as depriving young Americans of a national tradition [6]. The disappearing frontier-life values may explain two of the few opinion poll factors that differentiate those Americans more likely to oppose firearms restrictions from other Americans: farming and rural residency.

The meaning of guns is quite different in rural and urban areas. In the urban center guns are more likely to be seen as protection (whether against potential looters or murderers or against the police). In rural areas, however, guns are a more integral part of growing up. Giving a child a gun at a certain age is a natural and accepted norm. On a farm there may well be a feeling of family unity built up around the hunting of small game and protecting the farm or garden from animal predators. Because guns have been such a long-standing and integral part of rural life and their presence associated with sport, enjoyment, and family unity, it is understandable that opposition should arise to a law that is perceived as an intrusion.

But to advocates of strong legislation the frontier way of life as we know it with its emphasis on self-reliance and individualism has been asphalted over and developed away by our complicated modern society. Guns thus are considered an anachronistic vestige of an earlier era. As K. E. Meyer [40] put it:

. . . the authors of the Bill [original Bill of Rights] lived in a rural society innocent of metropolitan thrombosis, of sonic boom, and color television, and of the F.B.I. The first ten Amendments are not redundant; they are simply incomplete. We need to affix an additional ten to take contemporary account of our rights—our civilized rights—which are menaced by a transformed society which would surely have astonished and probably appalled Thomas Jefferson.

One needs only to review the pro and con arguments to see how the theme of a changing way of life is reflected in the politics of legislation and in the strategies for coping with rents in our social fabric. An irony here is that our new affluent economy makes it more possible than ever for every citizen to defend himself with his own gun, a value of old traditional America. Furthermore, one even could experience the new United States as being an urban and suburban jungle, just as dangerous and lawless as the frontier woods, and hence requiring just as much self-reliance.

One further ramification of social and cultural change is the stake people have in maintaining the status quo. An impression we have is that some opponents of legislation would like the controversy over firearms legislation to disappear so that they could be left alone to pursue their other interests—hunting, shooting competitions, gun collecting, and the like. Because these interests and the associated economic interests of the gun and hunting industries can be vital to those directly involved, they naturally defend the status quo. Surely the NRA, in common with other large organizations and special interest groups, has a stake in perpetuating itself and its perceived self-interests. These self-interests need not serve simply to maintain the status quo, however. One way for the NRA to gain new meaning in this time of rapid change would be for it to function as the national registration and licensing agency, should strong gun laws be enacted.

GUNS AND FEARS

There are many potential dangers confronting man that evoke feelings of fear and helplessness, both rational and irrational. Unfortunately, several factors combine to make the fears behind the gun controversy particularly potent. First, the dangers associated with personal or group safety are core fears in man, potentially ever present. These fears are often ambiguous, difficult to remove, poorly understood, and only partially based in reality (that is, they combine rational and irrational elements).

Second, given these circumstances, the sense of personal danger and feelings of helplessness to do anything about it can produce intense and sometimes poorly conceived reactions. Almost anything that will reduce the fear may be utilized or adopted. For instance, if one believes the proposition that a gun *might* offer protection, the proposition can be readily transformed into "a gun *does* offer protection," hence providing a potentially false sense of security. In this way the gun can represent the equalizer, making up for feelings of insecurity and inadequacy in the face of danger. This phenomenon probably accounted in part for the run on gun shops during the 1965 Watts riots [6], when people trying to purchase guns actually stood in lines. Over 4,000 guns were sold in a single day, of which just 37 allegedly were sold to blacks. People thus arming themselves for protection are not likely to hear the pleas of law-enforcement officials stressing the dangers one takes in possessing a gun for self-protection. In addition, if an individual tends to be the impulsive type, then the likelihood of his misusing a gun becomes even greater. The problem is that the gun represents an effective coping strategy in the mind of the person acquiring it, even though there may be other strategies for dealing with perceived personal threats—for example, nonresistance when confronted by a person with a gun, irrevocable property insurance, and better police protection.

Third, abhorrence or fear of guns can reflect difficulties with one's own destructive or violent feelings. This may underlie the apparent inability of some proponents of strong controls to understand or empathize with sportsmen and traditionalists [7, 26]. The abhorrence may be reflected in ridicule and contempt directed at gun enthusiasts or even in the wish to confiscate all weapons and exile violators [40] (next to death and torture, ostracism is possibly the most cruel punishment). Yet for others the fear of guns can represent legitimate abhorrence of violence and acute recognition of the potential violence in our culture and ourselves. Once again, when hidden yet basic personal concerns are at stake, rational arguments alone are likely to fall on deaf ears. Someone who winces at the sight of blood should not be expected to see pleasure in the sport of "gunning down" animals, called hunting. On the other hand, hunters would reject as unsatisfactory the recommendation of some of the control proponents that all shooting should be done with a camera.

GUNS AS SYMBOLS

Embedded in the "guns and fears" theme is the excess of meaning attributed to guns. The protection attributed to guns can be extended so that guns represent symbols of strength and manliness. Guns are associated with acts of heroism and bravery. For instance, NRA members receive distinguished fighting medals, and "standing up for your rights" is advocated in the gun literature [2]. Eldridge Cleaver [13] clearly implies that guns represent manliness with regard to the Black Panthers. Hence from the psychological perspective guns variously symbolize a source of power, pride, control, independence, strength (the "equalizer" for feelings of inferiority or inadequacy), manliness, virility, potency, and the male sex organ [6, 58]. Gun advertisers know and play upon these symbols [2]. Similarly the converse is implied: Fear of guns can represent cowardliness, submission, weakness, dependency, a disregard for the American way of life, and the like. In the extreme case the abhorrence of guns can mean the inability to deal with one's own aggression and potential for violence.

The point is that guns clearly can and do have symbolic meanings which make their use additionally attractive, or abhorrence unusually intense. This is not to say that either gun proponents or opponents in general have psychopathological tendencies; rather, guns can and do represent these qualities in our particular culture and to a pathological degree for some of us. Nonetheless, intense symbolic representation may account for descriptions of Americans as "addicted to guns" or absorbed in a fascination "to an often passionate degree" [6]. We believe that alternate sources of self-esteem, pride, and proof of strength and manliness would tend to diminish attachment to guns as a source of these important qualities.

Guns also are a symbol of killing and death. To the sportsman there is unquestionably joy in the successful hunt [2, 6]. Whatever its source, there is an excitement, a joy, a thrill associated with the kill. But the wish to kill or destroy and the pleasure and excitement in so doing can occur in some and are seldom discussed except in reference to obviously "mentally deranged" criminals and psychiatric patients. Yet these people certainly are not the only ones with whom to be concerned when it comes to assessing the emotional impact and meaning of recreational shooting and hunting. What, especially, are the ways that shooting activities affect young children? Are friendship bonds and healthy fun the sole effects on children? Or for some children are there additional, less healthy consequences of shooting and hunting? Certainly the meaning of these activities varies greatly with the personality of the child and the surrounding circumstances. This is an area of concern and inquiry generally overlooked by behavioral scientists as well as by the arguers for and against gun legislation. We think that this matter deserves urgent attention.

VIOLENCE — GOOD AND EVIL

Closely related to guns as a symbol of killing is the way guns may personify the evil of violence. From one perspective the entire gun controversy symbolizes the issue of coping with violence in a changing world. For some proponents the wish to restrict guns, whatever the reasons they offer, is not the primary goal. The primary goal, the bedrock issue, is the eradication of violence [7, 10, 26]. Hence, for some, guns simply represent instruments of violence and destruction. As such they evoke dread and anguish rather than excitement and joy. In England, killing the unarmed bobby is not considered "cricket"; in the United States police are becoming "fair game." Killing a policeman has become acceptable behavior in the eyes of some of our citizens. In the eyes of more of our citizens, killing an escaping felon, executing a condemned criminal, and waging war on our enemies are all acceptable forms of behavior. This use of guns is accepted as a legitimate social action. But for those for whom violence symbolizes evil, such killing may *never* be acceptable, no matter what the justification or ends. To them the ends can never justify the means if the means are violent.

While the multitude of threats to important aspects of the self or group encourage violence by gun, a number of psychological mechanisms permit the acceptance of deliberate violent behavior as good. The ability to attribute unacceptable aspects of the self to others allows one to perceive evil and violence as "his, not mine,"—as his wish to injure me. The human ability to rationalize almost any act allows one to "justly" punish that evil. Then he, the evil one, deserves to be punished by me, the good one. Thus we tend to polarize good (we) and evil (they) and to stereotype people. Law offenders often are thought of in some monolithic way as though they were all the same "hardened criminals." Yet the sometimes cruel and ruthless quality of punishment might be seen as betraying the violence within the punisher [38].

PHENOMENON OF LOSS

The theme of threatened or actual loss or violation of important aspects of the self, one's group, one's customs and beliefs, and the concrete representation of these in terms of property and territory are interwoven throughout the gun law controversy. At one time or another opponents have expressed concern with all the following losses: The American way of life is being violated, including such basic values as self-reliance. The gun, a prized possession, will be taken away and with it the personalized meanings attached to it. A crucial source of protection and security will be lost. Hunters and sportsmen will suffer inconvenience and be deprived of pleasure. Registration provides an example. To some opponents, registration may pose the threat of loss and the feared ultimate confiscation of all guns instead of mere inconvenience.

The threat of losses like these are very basic psychological concerns of all human beings. They have their roots in the dynamics of loss and separation that begin in early life and make up a number of major developmental crises. Little wonder that gun laws are resisted by those who believe that some or all of the aforementioned losses would be the result of strong gun controls. Yet little attention is given to the dynamics of loss and violation. In this instance communication among various groups could be facilitated by recognizing and dealing with the theme of loss and how it applies to different groups of people.

TRUST VS. MISTRUST

All the fears or threats of loss in the gun controversy are nurtured in large part by mistrust. The controversy virtually subsists on mistrust among individuals and groups [4, 26]. Ironically the arguments of militants of various political persuasions are very similar in their extreme degree of mistrust. They stress the dangers of subversion from evil forces (whether police, Communists, or others) and the need for individual and sometimes vigilante armed protection [13, 26, 36].

The fear that proposed gun legislation will indeed make gun ownership and use impossible and hence will leave citizens defenseless reflects this grave mistrust among groups and between individuals. Even though the proposed gun laws neither intend systematically to disarm the public nor to fulfill the so-called domino theory of gun legislation (that is, the first step to confiscation), mistrust persists. "Give an inch, and they'll take a mile" is reflected in the doubters' charge that registration alone could lead to confiscation, should a dictatorial power come into control.

Not all opponents fear a dictatorial take over. Some fear confiscation because it would deny them the use of their guns. This particular mistrust is aided by those proponents who do want confiscation of all guns and are willing to advocate the second-best alternative of registration only because confiscation does not seem feasible at the present time. Further, the advocates of confiscation implicitly reciprocate mistrust, since the need to confiscate guns may imply that those with guns cannot be trusted.

The theme of trust, or mistrust, in the gun controversy represents in microcosm the current situation in this country. The problem is how to get our people to have faith in and willingness to trust our society to protect all of its citizens. The Rightists need to feel that the government will not allow marauders to plunder and the "Commies" to take over. The Leftists need to feel that police will not bash in their heads. Blacks need to feel that the whites and the "pigs" are not going to slaughter them. The problem is how to unite our people in a desire to belong to one nation where guns are not needed for protection from one another. If trust among Americans is a valid goal, *ultimately and soon* we must face our mistrust through honest dialogue and seek ways to expand the boundaries of inclusion.

Views from Other Nations

The insights to be gained from "seeing ourselves as others see us" are a valuable tool for furthering self-awareness. An opportunity to gain foreign press opinion about the gun controversy and violence in this country arose when the Hoover Institution on War, Revolution and Peace of Stanford University held an exhibit the week of August 12, 1968, entitled "Violence in America: Views from Abroad." Selections for the exhibit were keyed to the assassinations of Martin Luther King, Jr., and Robert F. Kennedy—events that provoked a flood of emotion-laden commentary and frank opinions from the foreign press. Although the episodic nature of the materials and the selection process of the Hoover Institution probably introduced some biases into the exhibit, we judged the material to be broad in scope and generally representative. We also reviewed *Atlas*, a world press periodical. The material in it corresponded closely with the Hoover Institution exhibit.

Most countries represented in the exhibit quite understandably were concerned about the implications and repercussions that these two assassinations would have for their own people and vested interests. A Lebanese editorial [19] was concerned with exonerating the

Arabs from Sirhan Sirhan's deed: "The Arab people . . . abhor violence. They are not prone to hatred, the vilest of human passions." An African article [1] charged racism: "Robert Kennedy is dead because in the American society there exists the virus of racism that we Africans have always deplored." A South African paper [34] vindicated racism: "It [King's assassination] just goes to prove that integration only aggravates racial hatred." The Communist Chinese [51] exploited Martin Luther King's death to berate the United States generally: "The evil system of colonialism and imperialism arose and throve with the enslavement of Negroes and the trade of Negroes, and it will surely come to its end with the complete emancipation of the Black people. Fight on, heroic Afro-American brothers! Victory will certainly be yours!" Similar, though milder, comments were made by the Russians [5]. A German writer [25] asked: "What nation could understand President Johnson's plea [to reject the idea of national guilt] more deeply than this country, which knows what it means to live under the reproach of collective guilt?" Clearly the foreign press has viewed our violence through the filters of their own national concerns. Yet when we remove the chaff of their national biases, we find kernels of truth in their analyses of our violence. We shall now focus on their general themes and insights about violence in the United States.

VIOLENCE AS A NATIONAL TRADITION

This widely held view [12, 19, 37, 44, 48] takes two basic forms: the Wild West frontier theme—"A man often was his own law and he needed a weapon to enforce it" [12]; and the theme that the right to revolt is built into the Constitution—"written into the American Constitution is the right of revolution—and, historically, revolution has usually needed a gun" [48]. A view [44] related to but less extreme than that of the "constitutional right to revolt" is the belief that conflict (not necessarily violence) has been an American way of life from the very beginning. Our system of government is based on the division of power among the legislative, judicial, and executive branches. Such division leads inevitably to conflict, which in turn leads to compromise and synthesis. In our judicial system, politics, and business we have adversaries and competitors, struggling against each other for a favorable verdict, vote, or contract.

The United States is viewed as still holding to simple or extreme remedies for complex problems [44] and to excessive individual achievement, individual virtue, and self-reliance. Our violence is the result of the frontier and revolutionary spirit that never died. It is seen as proof that the United States is still an "uncivilized" nation [4, 26]. As eloquently put by an Italian writer [5], "All American literature, all American films have their roots in the epic of the lone conqueror in conflict with his environment and himself. His real wife is his pistol. A moralistic literature obliges him to use it to further Good in the battle against Evil." In the extreme, others see us as a sick, violent, and savage people, in a country where any "just" cause gives one the right to violent action. Now the Vietnam war also is blamed for an increased disregard for the sanctity of human life [31, 54].

FRAGMENTATION AND POLARIZATION OF GROUPS

Our country is seen as split into hostile ethnic factions, especially black and white, and into polarized political factions [1, 5, 27, 33, 44, 46, 51]. Robert Kennedy who took "upon himself the task of creating unity out of the split American society became its victim" [27]. The United States is a combustible mixture of many heterogeneous groups, a result of the influx of immigrants from all parts of the world [28]. Thus one view of our nation has us split into hostile, opposing racial and political factions disposed to violence and desperately in need of a unifying force.

Polarization also is viewed as a result of our increasing technology, which has led to a disintegration of our traditional and now passé cultural values. This loss of values has freed Americans but has also left us uncommitted to and uninvolved with our society. Violence shows us that we need "to forge a kind of moral assertion of values" [19].

Perhaps all the explanations of polarization could be unified under the concept—reflected in many arguments of the gun controversy— that our way of life has changed over time and will continue to change. When individuals and groups refuse to recognize these changes and to change themselves to accommodate the new way of life, the new reality, then they become removed from the mainstream of thought by standing still as the current of life flows past them.

VIOLENCE AND DEMOCRACY

The view here is that violence is a dire threat to democracy [25, 29, 44]. Can a democracy survive when minorities—even one man— resort to violence "to overthrow a point of view with which they disagreed" [29]? Somewhat related to this concern is the suspicion of conspiracy associated with the assassinations [5, 10, 24, 30, 44]. The African press [33] stated: "The Reverend Martin Luther King would not have fallen under the bullets of a fanatic if democracy had prevailed." Likewise, a German press report [25] viewed the Kennedy assassination as a blow to political harmony and survival of the democratic system. If the United States, founded on democratic principles, can be disrupted by violent dissenters, what chance can democracy have in other nations? This may be the unspoken fear.

GUNS AND VIOLENCE

In the foreign press commentary the gun per se is seen as one symbol, one facet, of a total problem of violence. Nonetheless, the press of five countries in the exhibit specifically mentioned gun controls [12, 28, 37, 45, 48]. A Japanese report [28] mentions easy availability of guns as a factor: "The ease with which all sorts and conditions of people can obtain possession of firearms is, we feel, an invitation to violent crime." One British report [48] stressed equal restriction of weapons for all groups, including the police, as "the only just way to de-escalate the spiral of violence which is threatening the whole fabric of American political life." Two foreign press reports [12, 37] compare America's present firearms control with their own highly restrictive regulations. An article from Taiwan [12] chastises us for our firearms policy, while pointing out that in Taiwan possession of firearms is not permitted except for specific purposes—for example, hunting and law enforcement. The article says, "Tempers flare in Taiwan, too, but guns are not within reach and murders are infrequent. The United States could . . . take a look at our control of firearms and profit from the example." An Israeli press report [37] takes a similar stance, as reported in the preceding chapter.

In sum, the composite picture drawn by the foreign press, while critical, is also sympathetic. Our country is seen as beleaguered by splits, mistrust, and polarization among groups. We are struggling to resolve the polarity that threatens the democratic fabric of America, handicapped by Wild West virtues, excessive fear of controls, and the long-standing but now anachronistic acceptance of violence.

Implications and Conclusions

Analysis of the firearms controversy is important because the various arguments and issues reflect in microcosm the larger controversy tormenting Americans today—the crisis of violence.

We found that both proponents and opponents of gun legislation unfortunately tend to obscure issues and perhaps damage their cases by presenting a baffling array of statistics and "facts" that are sometimes incomplete, contradictory, or taken out of context. In addition there are deficiencies in data. For instance, beyond the East-West, rural-urban, and male-female dimensions, we could not discover relevant scientific information on who holds specific views regarding what particular legislation and why.

We also found that both sides tend to back up their "facts" and statistics with distorted arguments presented with emotional fervor. This finding indicated that even irrefutable data would likely not convince some people to change their positions. Our analysis of arguments and issues in the gun law controversy shows that many interacting variables are involved besides adequate scientific proof. The controversy is "overdetermined" by ideological, political, social, psychological, and pragmatic factors. For instance, the theme of threatened loss and violation of one's being, group, beliefs, and valued symbols runs through the arguments of opponents to gun legislation. Loss of prized possessions, loss of a way of life, loss of self-reliance, loss of pleasure, and loss of protection and security are all involved and are among the basic psychological concerns of all human beings. Yet little direct attention has been given to such psychological concerns and mechanisms. The controversy over guns cannot be considered adequately without reference to the basic biobehavioral bases and dynamics of aggression. In this instance of the psychological meaning of loss, ridicule and overgeneralization about gun usage by proponents of strong legislation tend only to reinforce perceived threats.

Without attention to important psychological and social themes, the controversy is likely to go on with some saying, "Don't trouble me with the facts; my mind's already made up." Indeed many times the specific content of a proposed law seems to be irrelevant. The question "Are you or are you not in favor of gun legislation?" is asked rather than "What kinds of specific freedoms would be relinquished or gained if a particular law were passed?" Despite current deficiencies in data, much evidence does exist to support strong gun controls. The recommendations made in the preceding chapter for registration, licensing, research, education, and restrictions are the most logical conclusions to be drawn from the evidence. In addition the following deserve legislative consideration: the prohibition of off-duty policemen from carrying weapons [53], the development and substitution of nonlethal weapons for use in law enforcement and "self-protection" [52], a contractual agreement with the NRA to administrate registration and licensing procedures, and assurances to sportsmen of ready access to their chosen recreation.

However, our analysis indicates that consideration should be given to the differential impact legislation has and needs to have. This includes recognizing that guns do not mean the same thing to everybody; that important psychological themes and social factors undergird the controversy; that a rural-urban dichotomy exists; that there are high-risk groups, such as juveniles and previously violent offenders; that various weapons, such as rifles compared to handguns, have differential effects; that suicide and accidental shooting, as well as homicide, are part of the gun problem; and that legislation needs adequate resources for implementation and effective enforcement.

Furthermore, studies covering demographic, social, and psychological factors of groups holding various views are needed. Some of the questions requiring definitive answers are these: the actual protective value of a gun in specific, potentially dangerous situations like liquor store operation; the reasons for gun purchases; the actual amount of gun use by firearms owners; and the proportion and characteristics of people who keep guns compared with those who do not. These and many questions arising from assumptions made in the pro and con arguments are subject to empirical test.

If effective and *mutually* satisfactory resolution of the gun problem is to occur, differing groups need to recognize the various levels of abstraction and discourse employed, make covert or hidden issues overt, recognize both the rational and irrational components of arguments, and provide each other with substitutes for perceived threats. The unhappy alternative is increased polarity and divisiveness, which block coming together on the superordinate goal of reducing killings and violence.

Rapid change in our society brings the need for our nation to alter its methods of conflict resolution and coping with threats. In our crowded, complex, urban society we must at least question the utilitarian value of guns. Having a gun for protection very likely increases the risk of being hurt or killed. As in many other spheres of the new America, necessity forces us to relinquish some individual control and self-reliance.

Finally, we are concerned about excessive focus upon legislation as a solution to the crisis of violence. While reflecting our nation's traditional action-orientation, preoccupation with legislative control tends to obscure other basic issues of violence, individual and collective, and the choice of violence is a way to resolve conflicts and cope with social changes. Although strong gun control legislation may symbolically commit us to reducing violence and should help to reduce it, legislation alone is not the answer. We must take other steps to increase trust and unity among our people.

Acknowledgment

We appreciate the helpful assistance of Gordon Black, Ph.D., Assistant Professor of Political Science, University of Rochester, Rochester, New York.

References

1. *Afrique Nouvelle* (Dakar, Senegal). Quelle societé! [editorial] June 13–19, 1968. P. 3.
2. *American Rifleman.* Various writings from a series of four issues. Feb. through May 1968.
3. *American Rifleman.* Dodd blessed anti-gun book bears new title, little else. Sept. 1968. P. 54.
4. Arnold, M. Experts link shooting to a strain of violence in U.S. *New York Times,* June 6, 1968. P. 23.
5. *Atlas.* Talk of the world. 16:12, July 1968.
6. Bakal, C. The [sic] *Right to Bear Arms*. New York: Paperback Library, 1968.
7. Balk, A. The firearms theater of the absurd. *Saturday Review.* July 22, 1967. P. 28.
8. Berkowitz, L. Impulse, aggression, and the gun. *Psychology Today.* Sept. 1968. P. 19.
9. Brucker, H. Nation's conscience: gun-control law near adoption. *Palo Alto Times* (Cal.), June 21, 1968. P. 23.
10. Canham, E. D. The Kennedy shooting: "Nation needs deeper disciplines." *Christian Science Monitor.* June 6, 1968. P. 1.
11. Cantrill, H. (Ed.). *Public Opinion.* Princeton, N.J.: Princeton University Press, 1951.
12. *China News* (Taipei, Taiwan). Control of firearms. June 9, 1968. P. 2.
13. Cleaver, E. A letter from jail. *Ramparts,* June 15, 1968. P. 17.
14. *Collier's Encyclopedia,* vol. 15. The Constitution of the United States. New York: Crowell Collier & Macmillan, 1966.
15. *Congressional Digest.* Federal firearms control legislation. 45: 289, Dec. 1966.
16. *Congressional Digest.* Congress and the national crime problem. 46: 193, Aug.–Sept. 1967.
17. *Congressional Quarterly.* Lobbying activities. Apr. 12, 1968. P. 805.
18. *Congressional Record.* Gun laws should be for criminals. Vol. 113, no. 83, part 2. May 25, 1967. P. H6309.

19. *Daily Star* (Beirut, Lebanon).   Outcast [editorial]. June 6, 1968. P. 4.
20. *Firearms Facts*.   Compiled by Criminal Division, U.S. Department of Justice, July 16, 1968. (Based in large part on the Uniform Crime Reports, 1967, of the F.B.I., later released by the U.S. Government Printing Office, Washington, D.C., Aug., 1968).
21. *Gallup Opinion Index* Report No. 27.   Polls and the 1968 presidential election. Sept. 1967.
22. *Gallup Political Index*.   Attitudes toward gun control legislation. 1965–66.
23. *Gallup Poll*.   Public would favor police permit for gun. Feb. 7, 1965.
24. *Gallup Report*.   Negroes, whites agree on 4 plans to deal with racial problems. Aug. 27, 1967.
25. *German Tribune* [first appeared in *Die Welt*, June 10, 1968]. America's chain reaction of tragedy confounds her friends. June 15, 1968. P. 1.
26. Harris, R.   Annals of legislation: If you love your gun. *New Yorker*, Apr. 20, 1968. P. 56.
27. Hirasawa, K.   Politics in review: Need for rejuvenation in politics. *Japan Times* (Tokyo), June 7, 1968. P. 1.
28. *Japan Times* (Tokyo).   Death of Robert Kennedy [editorial]. June 7, 1968. P. 12.
29. *Japan Times* (Tokyo).   Gorton feels tragedy. June 7, 1968. P. 4.
30. *Japan Times* (Tokyo).   LBJ leads nation in mourning RFK. June 7, 1968. P. 1.
31. *Japan Times* (Tokyo).   Leaders here mourn death of Kennedy. June 7, 1968. P. 1.
32. Kane, M.   Bang! bang! You're dead. *Sports Illustrated*. Mar. 18, 1968. P. 70.
33. Kanida, T.   Ces jours-ci. *Afrique Nouvelle* (Dakar, Senegal), Apr. 11–17, 1968. P. 6.
34. Lawrence, P. S.   African thoughts on Dr. King. *Star* (Johannesburg, Union of S. Africa), Aug. 13, 1968. P. 9.
35. Lindsay, J. V.   Press Release No. 409–67, Nov. 14, 1967.
36. Manion, D.   Anti-gun laws aimed at wrong target. *Manion Forum*, Sept. 24 and Oct. 1, 1967.
37. Meisels, M.   Guns and the Israeli. *Jerusalem Post*, July 8, 1968. P. 8.
38. Menninger, K.   *The Crime of Punishment*. New York: Viking, 1968.
39. Meyer, F. S.   The right of the people to bear arms. *National Review*, July 2, 1968. P. 657.
40. Meyer, K. E.   . . . So does the Bill of Rights. *Esquire*. Oct. 1968. P. 147.
41. National Education Association, Research Division. Research Report 1966–R1, Rankings of the States, 1966.
42. National Rifle Association of America.   Various editorials, pamphlets, and speeches sent by NRA (Washington, D. C.), upon request, June 1968.
43. National Rifle Association of America.   Analysis of Director Representation. Sept. 30, 1968.
44. *Observer Review* (London).   America's tragedy: Violence. Michael

Davie reports on the self-questioning mood of a shaken society under the gunman's shadow. June 9, 1968. P. 25.

45. *Observer Review* (London). Pentagon behind U.S. gun lobby. June 9, 1968. P. 40.

46. *Observer* (London). Patriots of mankind: What the *Observer* thinks. June 9, 1968. P. 10.

47. O'Neil, P. Ray, Sirhan—what possessed them? *Life* 64:25, June 21, 1968.

48. *Peace News* (London). Oh, America! June 14, 1968. P. 1.

49. *Public Opinion News Service.* Public would outlaw all pistols except for police. Sept. 4, 1959.

50. *Reader's Digest.* Press Section: "Gun shy" [*N.Y. Post*]. June 1968. P. 22.

51. Ribao, R. Fight on, heroic Afro-American brothers! *Peking Review* (Peking, China). Apr. 12, 1968. P. 20.

52. Sagolyn, A., and Coates, J. Wanted: Police weapons that do not kill. *Reader's Digest.* Feb. 1968. P. 129.

53. *St. Louis Post-Dispatch.* Off-duty firearms [editorial]. Feb. 8, 1968. P. 4a.

54. Sakamoto, Y. Three myths of U.S. democracy. *Atlas.* Aug. 1968. P. 39.

55. Schroder, B. Gun law threat to wildlife [letter to editor]. *Palo Alto Times* (Cal.), June 21, 1968. P. 23.

56. Selover, W. C. Gunplay exceeds warfare toll. *Christian Science Monitor,* June 8, 1968. P. 3.

57. *Time.* Glory of guns; gun magazines campaign against legal control of gun sales. Aug. 25, 1967. P. 62.

58. *Time.* The gun under fire. June 21, 1968. P. 13.

59. Womanpower-in-Action. Various materials sent Dec. 1968 by Mary K. Harvey (Sr. Ed., *McCall's*).

60. Zimring, F. Is gun control likely to reduce violent killings? Unpublished study. Center for Studies in Criminal Justice, University of Chicago Law School, 1968.

10. *American Presidential Assassination*

Robert L. Taylor, M.D.,
and Alfred E. Weisz, M.D.

The political murders of John F. Kennedy, his brother Robert F. Kennedy, Martin Luther King, Jr., Malcolm X, George Lincoln Rockwell, and Medgar Evers, all within a relatively brief time period, tragically underscore the increasing threat of assassination in the United States. The phenomenon of assassination is the result of a complex interaction between the assassin and his victim, occurring in a specific social environment. Our purpose is to explore as best we can the nature of this interaction as it has transpired in presidential assassinations with a view toward suggesting possible approaches for preventive intervention. In most instances these suggested changes designed to reduce the likelihood of assassination are relevant to other areas of violence prevention as well.

Presidential assassins and their acts have been extensively studied in the past, and we have drawn heavily from these previous studies. In contrast, the possible contributing roles of the victim and the social environment have not been studied to any significant degree as they relate to presidential assassination. Here our conclusions and suggestions for intervention are necessarily more speculative. Furthermore, these conclusions are based on presidential assassinations, not on the full range of political assassinations.

Characteristics of the Assassins and Their Acts

Nine men have been involved in the eight known attempts on lives of American presidents. They were all Caucasian males ranging in age from 24 to 40. All were smaller than average in stature. With the exception of John Wilkes Booth they were unknowns, coming out of obscurity to attempt political murder. Five of the nine were born outside the United States, but all were citizens of this country at the time of the event. Marriage was attempted by four of these men but was disrupted within a short period in three instances. Striking socioeconomic deterioration occurred over the year prior to assassination in all but two instances. All made attempts with handguns except for Lee Harvey Oswald, who allegedly used an Italian rifle. Each of these men had some cause or grievance that appeared obsessional, if not delusional, in intensity. Table 2 outlines the dates and major facts of actual and attempted presidential assassinations in the United States.

THE ASSASSINS

Richard Lawrence has the distinction of being the first man to attempt the assassination of an American president. He was described as a well-behaved "loner" as a child. During the two years preceding the murder, Lawrence's family and friends noticed striking personality changes marked by unprovoked fits of laughing, crying, and violence. He had lost interest in his work as a housepainter and had started talking to himself. By the time of the attempt Lawrence's world had become a delusional one in which he believed he was Richard III of England to whom the United States owed large sums of money. Initially he felt that steamship owners were conspiring to cheat him out of his fortune, but later his delusion widened to include the Congress, and finally Andrew Jackson. He haunted the grounds of the Capitol Building seeking official support for his claim that Congress owed him money. At one point Lawrence personally accosted the Vice-President, Martin Van Buren, threatening that either he or President Jackson would fall if the money was not paid [11]. In 1835 he stepped from a crowd and fired twice at Jackson as the President was walking in a funeral procession. The first shot was fired at a distance of 13 feet. When Lawrence fired the second time, Jackson was charging down upon him brandishing his cane. The second shot was at point-blank range. In both instances the powder failed to ignite.

Following this abortive assassination attempt, Lawrence's mental derangement was so apparent to those who interviewed him that even the prosecuting attorney for the District of Columbia, Francis Scott Key, encouraged the defense to plead insanity.

TABLE 2. SUMMARY OF ACTUAL AND ATTEMPTED PRESIDENTIAL ASSASSINATIONS

Assassin	Intended Victim	Date	Outcome
Richard Lawrence	Andrew Jackson	Jan. 30, 1835	Jackson not injured. Lawrence committed to mental hospital until his death in 1861
John Wilkes Booth	Abraham Lincoln	Apr. 14, 1865	Lincoln fatally wounded. Booth killed by self or soldiers 12 days later
Charles J. Guiteau	James A. Garfield	July 2, 1881	Garfield fatally wounded. Guiteau hanged June 30, 1882
Leon F. Czolgosz	William McKinley	Sept. 6, 1901	McKinley fatally wounded. Czolgosz electrocuted Oct. 29, 1901
John N. Schrank	Theodore Roosevelt	Oct. 14, 1912	Roosevelt was wounded. Schrank committed to mental hospital, died 1943
Giuseppe Zangara	Franklin D. Roosevelt	Feb. 15, 1933	Roosevelt not wounded. Mayor Cermak of Chicago killed. Zangara electrocuted, Mar. 20, 1933
Oscar Collazo Griselio Torresola	Harry S Truman	Nov. 1, 1950	Truman not injured. Guard Coffelt killed, 2 guards injured. Torresola killed at time of attempt. Collazo wounded, death sentence commuted to life imprisonment
Lee Harvey Oswald	John F. Kennedy	Nov. 22, 1963	Kennedy killed. Governor Connally of Texas injured. Oswald assassinated by Jack Ruby, Nov. 24, 1963

John Wilkes Booth's father, Junius Brutus Booth, suffered from manic-depressive psychosis, described in some detail by Stanley Kimmel in the *The Mad Booths of Maryland* [17]. A quote from that book notes that "he was either on the heights of jubilance or in the depths of depression, and so wavered between madness and genius that no one could be certain which would predominate." John Wilkes was the ninth of ten children born to his father and Mary Ann Holmes, a woman whom Junius finally married on John Wilkes's thirteenth birthday. Out of this stormy background grew a future assassin who achieved considerable success as an actor.

In 1858 John Wilkes Booth received a series of bad reviews in the North and decided to tour the South, where he was triumphantly received. He adopted the southerners' cause and enthusiastically championed their position. However, when war broke out, he abandoned his supposed comrades for the North. He became obsessed with the idea that Lincoln was president only as the result of a fraudulent count of votes and that Lincoln's ultimate goal was to become king. At one point John Wilkes left a sealed letter with his sister in Philadelphia describing his early plan to kidnap the President. When the letter was opened months later, it proved to be rambling and in some parts incoherent.

Booth speculated aloud on several occasions that a man who killed Lincoln would win immortality. Three days prior to the assassination he became enraged when Lincoln in a public speech regretted that Louisiana had not given the franchise to Negroes, and Booth was heard to say, "Now, by God, I'll put him through!" [2]. On April 14, 1865, Booth discovered that Lincoln would attend Ford's Theatre in the evening. Lincoln's preannounced attendance at the play, combined with the irresponsibility of his guard, who spent the evening in a bar across from the theatre, made the assassin's task relatively simple. Afterward he wrote in his diary:

Our country owed all her problems to him, and God simply made me his instrument of punishment. . . . I bless the entire world [11].

Charles Guiteau's father, Luther, had a longstanding delusion that he was immortal [12]. In addition one of Charles's uncles and two of his aunts were psychotic. Several of his cousins had been committed to mental hospitals. As an adolescent the future murderer of James A. Garfield posted a notice stating, "Charles J. Guiteau, Premier of England, will deliver a lecture in St. James Hall, London" [8].

Guiteau was an odd mixture of fanatical evangelist and inadequate lawyer. In his first assigned case his defense was so confused and bizarre that the district attorney was convinced of Guiteau's insanity. In 1880, following the failure of his new lecture entitled "Some Reasons Why Two-Thirds of the Human Race Are Going Down to Perdition," he decided to shift his talents to the political arena. He produced a series of rambling, incoherent speeches supporting the Republican Party, and following Garfield's election he demanded that he be assigned an ambassadorship out of gratitude for his services. He frequently visited the White House in disarrayed clothes to press his case for a diplomatic appointment and became so troublesome that President Garfield's staff was instructed to keep him out. Two months before mortally wounding the President, Guiteau wrote Garfield a letter demanding the resignation of the Secretary of State and threatening ". . . otherwise you and the Republican Party will come to grief" [5].

On several occasions Guiteau was in position to shoot Garfield, only to change his mind at the last moment, once because Mrs. Garfield was with the President and at another time because the weather was too sultry. Finally in July 1881, as Garfield was leaving on a vacation, he walked past Guiteau in the Washington, D.C., train station. The assassin turned and shot Garfield in the back. The President lingered until September, when he died.

Leon Czolgosz was described as a quiet, shy child without friends. He never had a girl friend. Although he claimed to be an anarchist, he was never part of a formal organization. In fact, he acted so strangely at one anarchist meeting that the members thought he must be a government spy [12].

Czolgosz lost his ability to work three years before he shot McKinley. He became shy and self-absorbed. His family said that he had "gone to pieces" and later noted that he developed a fascination with the assassination in 1900 of King Humbert I of Italy. Czolgosz developed a delusion about being poisoned, refusing to let his stepmother prepare his meals and refusing even to eat food that he prepared for himself if she were present in the house [1]. At a public reception for McKinley held in September 1901 at the Pan American Exposition in Buffalo, Czolgosz stood in line with his hand wrapped in a handkerchief as though bandaged. The hand held a .32 caliber Iver Johnson revolver that shortly became the instrument of death for McKinley as the President reached out to greet the public for the last time.

On the night of McKinley's assassination John Schrank had a

vision. He saw the dead President rise from his coffin and accuse Theodore Roosevelt, the incoming President, of arranging his death. Eleven years later, chronically unemployed and wandering from place to place in the Bowery of Manhattan, Schrank reexperienced this vision, which he interpreted as a divine mandate to avenge McKinley's death. He purchased a Colt revolver and, considering himself the reluctant agent of God, set out to kill Roosevelt, who was running again for the presidency on the Bull Moose ticket. He followed Roosevelt. After twenty-four days of traveling more than two thousand miles in eight states, Schrank had succeeded in putting himself in the same city at the same time with Roosevelt on only three occasions [5]. Though the opportunity presented itself in Chicago, Schrank failed to shoot the candidate, for he feared that his act might give the city a bad name. Outside a hotel in Milwaukee Roosevelt stood up in the back of a convertible to speak. Schrank stepped out of the crowd and fired a shot into the candidate's chest. Before the bullet could enter the right lung, it had to pass through a metal eyeglass case and a folded fifty-page speech. It spent its final force in cracking a rib. After the unsuccessful assassination attempt police found among Schrank's personal papers a note which read:

Theodore Roosevelt is in conspiracy with European monarchs to overthrow our Republic. Theodore Roosevelt's unscrupulous ambition has been the murder of President McKinley to satiate his thirst for power . . . We want no king. We want no murderer. The United States is no Carthage. We will not yield to Rome [5].

Guiseppe Zangara was born to poverty in Italy and put to work at age six by his father. His resentment of authority spread outward from that time on until it became a murderous rage directed toward all heads of state. He was regarded as a harmless bachelor, so fond of solitude that on occasion he rented two adjoining rooms in order to avoid neighbors. He was particularly frightened by cold night air, which he felt intensified his chronic stomach complaints for which doctors could find no cause. Two years prior to the attempted assassination, Zangara abandoned a lucrative contracting job and traveled south looking for warm night air and health.

During the winter of 1933 in the depths of the economic depression Zangara's anarchist philosophy evolved. He began to make actual plans for assassination but couldn't bring himself to travel to the wintry cold of Washington to kill Hoover. He waited. Franklin Roosevelt was elected and soon after traveled to Florida. Zangara bought a revolver, but when he arrived at the amphitheater, he was unable to make his way to the front as planned. He panicked, jumped onto a wobbly chair, and fired five wild shots into the crowd. All five shots struck persons surrounding the President-elect. Mayor Cermak of Chicago was killed, but none of the shots struck Roosevelt.

Oscar Collazo and Griselio Torresola were members of the Puerto Rican Nationalist Party, which advocated complete independence for Puerto Rico. As a means of protesting the Puerto Rican condition, they attempted to enter the Blair House in 1950, where President Truman was staying while repairs were being made on the White House. Having purchased one-way train tickets and traveled from New York to Washington, D.C., they studied the situation and decided on tactics. The two men separated and approached the Blair House from opposite directions. They were unsuccessful in their attempt to maneuver past the guards, and in an ensuing fierce gun battle involving an exchange of twenty-seven shots in less than three minutes, Torresola was killed. Collazo was apprehended after being wounded. He was tried, found guilty, and sentenced to death. Truman later commuted his sentence to life in prison. This attempt was a carefully planned and executed effort to accomplish a political objective by murder. As such it seems quite unlike the seven other assassination attempts on the lives of American presidents, which were either hurriedly conceived or almost haphazard encounters of disorganized delusional men with their intended victims.

At the age of 13 Lee Harvey Oswald was examined by Dr. Renatus Hartogs at the request of the Bronx Children's Court. Dr. Hartogs's summary impression characterized Oswald as guarded, secluded, and suspicious. His diagnosis was incipient schizophrenia with strong paranoid overtones and potential dangerousness [15]. Oswald was consistently unsuccessful economically with the exception of his time spent in the service. His tendency toward social alienation was demonstrated most poignantly by the fact that he was the founder and sole member of the New Orleans Fair Play for Cuba Committee [14]. His marriage was unsuccessful, and by the time of the assassination he was separated.

On November 22, 1963, Oswald successfully shot and killed John F. Kennedy as the President rode through Dallas, Texas, in an open convertible along a predesignated route.* At age 24 Oswald was the youngest of all the assassins, the only one to use a rifle, and the only

* Statements concerning Lee Harvey Oswald are largely based on the Warren Commission Report with recognition that questions concerning this assassination still exist.

one to deny his involvement in the murder. After Oswald's murder by Jack Ruby, Dr. Hartogs was interviewed by *Life* magazine. He commented, "Psychologically [Oswald] had all the qualifications of being a potential assassin. Such a criminal is usually a person with paranoid ideas of grandiosity who can get satisfactory self-vindication only by shocking the entire world and not just a few people. . . ." [15].

EVIDENCE FOR MENTAL DISORDER

In every case but one there is considerable evidence to support the thesis that each assassin was severely deranged. The exception was the attempt of Collazo and Torresola to kill President Harry S Truman. At first glance their belief that killing the President would provide a spark to the faltering Puerto Rican Nationalist movement seems to be nearly delusional judgment. However, by definition, a delusion is a persistent false belief not shared or sanctioned by a group. Many of the associates of these men did share their beliefs. In addition Collazo and Torresola demonstrated a capability for cooperative planning and coordinated action not usually associated with severe emotional disturbance.

Delusions of persecution and grandeur are examples of disordered thinking most often, but not exclusively, associated with the diagnosis of paranoid schizophrenia. They have been identified in the lives of most of the assassins. Richard Lawrence believed that he was the lauded King Richard III of England. John Wilkes Booth demonstrated his grandiosity on numerous occasions, ending one diary note with the grandiloquent benediction, "I bless the entire world." Guiteau and Schrank shared with Booth the belief that they acted under divine mandate. Guiteau vehemently denied that he was insane at his trial, but on one occasion he stated, "I expect an act of God will blow this court and jury out of that window if it is necessary" [12]. Czolgosz had delusions apparently restricted to fears of poison in his food. There is evidence that Zangara's gastrointestinal complaints were delusional in nature. At age 25 an appendectomy was performed because of symptoms of pain and anorexia. The tissue specimen sent to the pathologist was not inflamed. Seven years later the autopsy following his execution failed to reveal any abnormality of the gastrointestinal tract [13].

The evidence for delusions in Lee Harvey Oswald is not entirely clear. Most people who knew him attributed his homicidal act to the desire for fame: "He had to show the world he was not unknown, that he was someone with whom the world had to reckon. . . ."

[15]. Oswald's need to bolster his self-esteem is clear. He might well have developed delusions of persecution as one means of denying the painful truth of personal failure. The paranoid individual finds some comfort in the belief that he is important enough to be persecuted. It may be an unpleasant form of recognition, but for some people delusions of persecution are preferable to no recognition at all. Blaming others for personal adversity can also be preferable to facing one's own shortcomings.

Excessive ambivalence and distractibility are traits often associated with mental illness. Although many of the assassins had brooded about their plans for a number of weeks, months, or even years, it is surprising how some were temporarily dissuaded from their intended acts by fairly minor considerations. Guiteau and Schrank were armed and in position to shoot their victims on several occasions before they pulled the trigger. Zangara would not chance the cold of Washington to kill President Hoover and might have harmlessly waited in Florida had not President-elect Roosevelt traveled to Miami. These examples provide indications that it would be worthwhile to institute administrative and physical obstacles to block the often vacillating motivations of potential assassins. Specific preventive intervention suggestions are discussed later.

Socioeconomic deterioration has been a frequent prelude to the act of assassination and is also a frequent manifestation of severe mental illness. Lawrence gave up his job as a housepainter two years before his assassination attempt. Booth was forced to space his stage appearances at longer and longer intervals because of laryngitis starting two years before Lincoln's murder. Guiteau had suffered a downhill financial course for seven years before his violent act. Czolgosz was described as a "vagabond" by his own family during the last three years of his life. Schrank inherited a $25,000 tenement but gave up work and lived in cheap Bowery rooms during the year before his assassination attempt. Zangara left a lucrative contractor's business to move to Florida several years before he shot at Franklin Roosevelt. Oswald had never been a steady worker but was not really sinking into lower socioeconomic levels. Nonetheless, his wife frequently berated him for not being able to earn a living [8].

Examples of interpersonal alienation and loneliness are found throughout the biographies of the assassins. Most remained bachelors. Those who tried marriage usually met with failure. Attempts at joining or organizing groups were usually unsuccessful, and this failure sometimes contributed to the development of anger directed toward the head of state.

Thus to a grossly disturbed person the act of assassination can represent a desperate attempt to achieve importance, reverse a downward course, and obtain retribution for imagined wrongs. Repeatedly one sees an alienated man struggling to cope and failing. To him the act seemingly provides resolution of the conflict.

DISPLACEMENT OF HOSTILITY
TO THE HEAD OF STATE

Rothstein [20] has carefully studied a series of men who were incarcerated in a medical center for federal prisoners and whose offenses included threatening the president. He later published a study drawing remarkably similar parallels between the lives of his patients and the life of Lee Harvey Oswald [21]. Rothstein observed that his patients had turned in adolescence from their unhappy families to find a family substitute such as military service, political organizations, or even mental hospitals or prisons. In this new "family" the wished-for dependency gratifications were again denied, resulting in a displacement of rage from parents onto the recently rejecting organization. If this organization was governmental, the natural focus for the anger became the chief of state. The idea of a head of state serving as a displacement object for feelings originally directed toward parents has received some support from the work of de Grazia [4], who studied the reactions of patients in analysis to the death of Franklin Roosevelt. De Grazia concluded that the head of state is a symbolic superparent ("magnamater") and a ready target for displaced feelings from real parents.

PREVENTIVE INTERVENTION

Three early assassins, Lawrence, Booth, and Guiteau, made public threats on their presidents' lives. Present laws of this country make it an offense to threaten the life of the head of state, and, because of this statute, some potential assassins have been identified before their threats resulted in violent acts [20]. Solomon [24] has noted the reluctance of physicians to consider and carefully evaluate the violent potential of emotionally disturbed patients. Patients with the diagnosis of paranoid schizophrenia should be seen as constituting a high-risk group. (See also Chapter 11, Mental Illness and Violence.) When they make statements concerning thoughts of injuring the president or other political leaders, such statements should elicit serious concern and thorough assessment.

Considering the distractibility and ambivalence that have characterized some assassins, we might assume that prevention of assassination may be aided by setting up administrative blocks, such as a waiting period between the announced intention to own, and the actual possession of, firearms. Prevention might simply depend on the passing of an impulse during the time consumed in moving through the mechanics of an administrative block. These would prove no obstacle to the thoughtful planner but could be of considerable hindrance to a man like Zangara, who wouldn't even leave the warm climate of Florida to carry out his intention of shooting President Hoover.

Role of the Assassinated

One can only speculate concerning the role of the victim in contributing to his own assassination. The fatalistic stance of victims such as Lincoln, Garfield, and both Kennedys is striking. Robert Kennedy stated a view common to these four men: "There's no sense in worrying about those things. If they want you, they can get you" [22]. On another occasion he is quoted as having said, "I play Russian roulette every time I get up in the morning. But I just don't care. There's nothing I could do about it anyway" [22]. Fatalistic speculation may be a personally comforting defense against the real danger involved in being a controversial political leader. It is as though being aware of the threat and consistently denying that the danger can be avoided make risk-taking appear less frightening.

Unfortunately fatalism may contribute to negligent, counterphobic behavior that results in creating even greater danger. John Cottrel, in *Anatomy of an Assassination* [3], documents many instances in which Lincoln exposed himself to unnecessary risks. He would ride on horseback through Washington unescorted at night, and several times returned to the White House with bullet holes in his hat. In summary, Cottrel says: "Lincoln was not merely casual about his own safety; he was downright reckless." Robert Kennedy specifically stated: "If I'm elected President, you won't find me riding around in any of those awful [bullet-proof] cars" [22]. Unnecessary exposure of presidents and presidential candidates creates situations in which potential assassins with limited cognitive abilities have less difficulty in carrying out their tasks.

PREVENTIVE INTERVENTION

Fatalistic statements and negligent self-exposure to danger have been documented for assassination victims. To what degree these findings are the result of retrospective scrutiny remains unknown. A comparison of assassinated and nonassassinated presidents contrasting their attitudes toward presidential protection might provide information that would clarify further the role of the victim in assassination.

Former French President Charles de Gaulle survived three assassination attempts over the past few years [19]. What are the various protection systems being employed? What is de Gaulle's concept of assassination? Answers to these questions could provide useful information relevant to the protection of American presidents.

"Mixing with the people" is a strongly embedded concept in the political tradition of the United States, but it has also proved to be an accomplice to assassination. More effective use of mass media represents a partial solution to the unprotected exposure of political figures. But protection is virtually impossible without the cooperation of the man to be protected. We are not arguing for a reverse paranoia that would result in the fear of an assassin at every street corner nor for the desirability of restricting public figures only to electronic communication. We do suggest that presidents and presidential candidates be prohibited by enforceable laws from close contact with large crowds in places where their presence has been publicly announced in advance.

Role of the Social Environment

SANCTION FOR KILLING

Killing is not legally or socially defined as an *unequivocal* criminal act (see Chapter 15). Capital punishment and war give qualified sanction to the taking of human life, implying that killing is sometimes a legitimate means of conflict resolution. The message is that in dealing with social issues of sufficient importance, killing is justified. When a would-be assassin is convinced of the overwhelming importance of his cause and begins to search for ways of implementing that cause, killing provides a "legitimate" answer. The role of the assassin's environment in this decision is far from clear, but it seems reasonable to assume that certain social inconsistencies may mesh with the assassin's poor concept of reality, making assassination seem a justifiable means to accomplish his goal.

In other cultures the role of homicide in politics has reached phenomenal proportions. In 1962 Friedrich [10] wrote that in the Tarascan village of Acan in Mexico, which at no time had contained more than 1,500 persons, there had been 77 political homicides in the past thirty-five years. A study of Tarascan political life would be helpful in further clarifying the role of social environment in the genesis of assassination.

GRIEVANCES AND BUREAUCRACY

In a bureaucratic system of government there are innumerable administrative hindrances that block the effectiveness with which an individual can register a complaint against a governmental agency. There is suggestive evidence that when the potential assassin faces the frustration of being unable to lodge his grievance against a government agency, he turns his wrath against the person who is the symbol of the government, the President [20]. Thus Lawrence fired on President Jackson only after unsuccessfully trying to have his claims for money heard in Congress, and Guiteau killed Garfield only after the Secretary of State refused him a diplomatic appointment. Months before President Kennedy was assassinated, Lee Harvey Oswald protested to the Navy Department that he had been wrongfully given an undesirable discharge from the Marines [14].

PREVENTIVE INTERVENTION

The ombudsman system of mediating between expanding bureaucratic government and the individual originated in nineteenth-century Sweden and now remains largely confined to the Scandinavian countries and New Zealand [6]. Ideally, the ombudsman functions as an independent and impartial arbitrator between government and individual. He is readily identifiable as a grievance receiver. In performing his service, the ombudsman may simply solicit clarification of a complaint. He often serves as an interpreter attempting to explain why a certain agency policy exists. On other occasions he may be instrumental in aiding a discontented citizen to state his complaint in an intelligible and effective fashion. The establishment of an ombudsman system would serve to intercept the delusional discontent of the disorganized complainer before it becomes directed toward the president. In those instances where the ombudsman is confronted by a person with persistent irrational complaints, unaffected by appropriate explanations, referral for evaluation of possible psychopathology and need for counseling could be made.

We are not suggesting that an ombudsman system be instituted solely as a preventive measure for assassination. This system would function as a legitimate complaint-registering agency, and in an era of dissident minorities who feel alienated from a powerful establishment, the significance of the ombudsman would extend far beyond the prevention of political assassination.

Reactions to Assassination

A large segment of the population develops hostile feelings subsequent to the assassination of an American president. Sheatsley [23] reported on the reactions of over one thousand persons surveyed immediately after the death of John F. Kennedy. Not surprisingly, three out of four "felt angry that anyone should do such a terrible deed." More remarkable was the intensity of feeling in 11 percent of those interviewed who "hoped the man who killed him would be shot down or lynched." The increased number of assassination threats around the world following John Kennedy's murder [18], the killing of Lee Harvey Oswald by Jack Ruby, and the shooting of a Jordanian grocer subsequent to Robert Kennedy's assassination lend further support to the idea that violence can be contagious.

A diverse set of studies suggests that the people most prone to overreact to an assassination are those who are already struggling with violent feelings within themselves. Most of the men hospitalized for threatening to kill presidents showed unusual amounts of agitation following President Kennedy's actual assassination [20]. Rothstein postulated that their defenses against violent action had been seriously undermined by news of the actual murder. He speculated that a person "with strong but previously unconscious homicidal and Presidential assassination impulses might also become seriously threatened by an actual assassin, and that his defenses against his own homicidal impulse might be weakened to the point of allowing him to murder the assassin, a possible explanation for Jack Ruby's behavior." Katz [16] polled a group of psychoanalysts on the reactions of their patients to the John Kennedy assassination. The patients with the greatest degree of anxiety about the event were those reported to have strong impulses to kill their fathers.

One further study provides evidence that people with negative feelings toward the victim of assassination suffer the most serious and prolonged reactions. Suinn [25] administered questionnaires to fifty college students after John Kennedy's assassination. He asked about political affiliations and about the nature and length of time of psychological symptoms. Those who had the strongest emotional reactions to the President's death were not, as might be expected, the

Kennedy Democrats but those who differed from the President politically.

PREVENTIVE INTERVENTION

The contagion of assassination may affect large groups of discontents in a population who will use the violent act as a signal to riot, loot, and kill. Such a reaction followed the death of Martin Luther King. The prevention of this phenomenon will depend on reducing the sources of chronic discontent for these population groups. However, if such an ideal were achieved, there would still remain a sizable scattering of seriously disturbed, alienated, hostile individuals who fight battles with their own delusional beliefs and who would not be pacified by social or economic reform.

One preventive effort designed to reduce the contagion of violence and aimed primarily at ambivalent, mentally disordered potential assassins would be the establishment of violence prevention centers, functioning in much the same way as the burgeoning network of suicide prevention centers. There is ample dynamic overlap between suicide and homicide. As early as 1910 Wilhelm Stekel [9] stated, "No one kills himself who has never wanted to kill another, or at least, wished the death of another." Complementing this view is Rothstein's [20] observation that potential political assassins often have strong self-destructive tendencies. Certainly the life expectancy of an assassin who succeeds in his intent is short. Of all the presidential assassins whose acts resulted in a death, only Oscar Collazo lived for more than one year.

Volunteers who are now being trained to counsel suicidal individuals could readily expand their expertise to the area of homicide prevention. A fundamental therapeutic approach with both suicidal and homicidal patients is the strengthening of boundaries that separate destructive thoughts from actions. As destructive thoughts are explored with these individuals, emphasis is placed on the idea that thoughts need not necessarily lead to action. Suicide prevention workers are already skilled at making sophisticated estimates of the seriousness of an individual's violent or self-destructive plans. Counselors would be able to help effect appropriate dispositions ranging from further supportive psychotherapy to recommendations for confinement.

The *Uniform Crime Reports* published annually by the FBI [7] note that most homicides and aggravated assaults are committed within the family unit or among neighbors or acquaintances and are not a result of planned felonies. The conclusion is made that "criminal homicide is, to a major extent, a social problem beyond police prevention." In light of this information the establishment of combined suicide-homicide-violence prevention centers, like the suggestion for an ombudsman system, would have significance far beyond the problem of presidential assassination.

Summary

A review of the literature on presidential assassinations reveals that with one exception assassins have been young men with delusional thought processes who tended toward lives of alienation and socioeconomic deterioration. The assassin's victim has often enhanced his own vulnerability by exposing himself unnecessarily. Society has contributed an inconsistent attitude toward killing as a means of conflict resolution and an inadequate system of grievance registration. Suggestions are made for studies to examine cultures where political assassination is more prevalent than in the United States and for studies of methods used to protect the lives of other world leaders. Preventive suggestions include stronger gun laws, legislation regulating preannounced exposure of presidents to large crowds, establishment of an ombudsman system for processing complaints against governmental agencies, and extension of suicide prevention centers to include homicide and violence prevention.

Acknowledgment

The authors are indebted to Barbara Baxter, Jewell Gibbs, Anne Robinson, Beatrix Hamburg, M.D., and Alberta Siegel, Ph.D., who helped in the preparation and review of this chapter.

References

1. Briggs, L. V. *The Manner of Man That Kills: Spencer—Czolgosz—Richeson.* Boston: Gorham, 1921. P. 313.
2. Bryan, G. S. *The Great American Myth.* New York: Carrick & Evans, 1940. P. 144.
3. Cottrel, J. *Anatomy of an Assassination.* London: Muller, 1966. P. 38.
4. de Grazia, S. A note on the psychological position of the chief executive. *Psychiatry* 8:267, 1945.
5. Donovan, R. J. *The Assassins.* New York: Harper, 1952.

6. *Encyclopaedia Britannica*, vol. 16. Ombudsman. Chicago: Benton, 1968. P. 961.
7. Federal Bureau of Investigation. *Uniform Crime Reports for the United States.* Washington, D. C.: U. S. Government Printing Office, 1967. P. 8.
8. Freedman, L. Z. Assassinations, psychopathology and social pathology. *Postgraduate Medicine* 37:650, 1965.
9. Friedman, P. (Ed.). *Discussion of the Vienna Psychoanalytic Society—1910, On Suicide.* New York: International Universities Press, 1967. P. 87.
10. Friedrich, P. Assumptions underlying Tarascan political homicide. *Psychiatry* 25:315, 1962.
11. Hastings, D. W. The psychiatry of presidential assassination. I. Jackson and Lincoln. *Journal-Lancet* 85:93, 1965.
12. Hastings, D. W. The psychiatry of presidential assassination. II. Garfield and McKinley. *Journal-Lancet* 85:157, 1965.
13. Hastings, D. W. The psychiatry of presidential assassination. III. The Roosevelts. *Journal-Lancet* 85:189, 1965.
14. Hastings, D. W. The psychiatry of presidential assassination. IV. Truman and Kennedy, *Journal-Lancet* 85:294, 1965.
15. Jackson, D. The evolution of an assassin. *Life,* February 21, 1964. P. 68.
16. Katz, J. On the death of the President: President Kennedy's assassination. *Psychoanalytic Review* 51:661, 1964–65.
17. Kimmel, S. *The Mad Booths of Maryland.* Indianapolis: Bobbs-Merrill, 1940.
18. *Newsweek.* The imitators. Dec. 23, 1963. P. 27.
19. *Newsweek.* Flower potshot. Sept. 14, 1964. P. 36.
20. Rothstein, D. A. Presidential assassination syndrome. *Archives of General Psychiatry* 11:245, 1964.
21. Rothstein, D. A. Presidential assassination syndrome. II. Application to Lee Harvey Oswald. *Archives of General Psychiatry* 15:260, 1966.
22. *San Francisco Examiner.* It's Russian roulette every day, said Bobby. June 6, 1968. P. 6.
23. Sheatsley, P. B., and Feldman, J. J. The assassination of President Kennedy: A preliminary report on public reactions and behavior. *Public Opinion Quarterly* 28: 189, 1964.
24. Solomon, P. The burden of responsibility in suicide and homicide. *Journal of the American Medical Association* 199:321, 1967.
25. Suinn, R. M. Note: Guilt and depth of reaction to the death of a president. *Psychoanalytic Review* 53:81, 1966.

11. Mental Illness and Violence

George D. Gulevich, M.D.,
and Peter G. Bourne, M.D.

Are mentally ill people more violent? The presumption has long existed that psychiatric patients are unusually prone to acts of violence and represent a particular threat to the safety of other members of society. This belief has been unusually prevalent in our culture for many generations. Reforms instituted one hundred years ago by Dorothea Dix, which unintentionally led to the isolation of psychiatric patients in foreboding institutions far from centers of population, did much to foster this belief. Confining deviant individuals in prisonlike seclusion encouraged the unknowing to believe that psychiatric patients were spontaneously capable of heinous crimes if not permanently restrained. In addition the remote geographical location of such institutions produced a lack of familiarity among the general population. This ignorance has inevitably led to unknowing fear, which tends to encourage the attributing of hostile intent to all those who are strange or unfamiliar. In today's society, which claims an enlightened understanding of the mentally ill, many of these old and indiscriminate prejudices persist toward all who are so labeled. These prejudices ascribe to the mentally ill a potential for violence that is supported at best only by anecdotal evidence.

The work of John and Elaine Cumming [10] has clearly demonstrated that the attitudes toward the mentally ill in our culture are deeply ingrained and strongly resistant to change. Using careful attitude surveys before and after an intensive educational program designed to alter the beliefs about the mentally ill in a small town, they conclusively showed that preexisting prejudices remained essentially unchanged. They also demonstrated that it is insufficient to assess popular beliefs merely in terms of their scientific accuracy. It is also

309

necessary to understand the function those beliefs perform for those who hold them. Such beliefs may allow us to blame the mentally ill, an already maligned and inherently defenseless group, for the prevalence of violence that is so condemned by our culture.

The purpose of this chapter is to examine not the prejudices but the available factual evidence relating to the incidence of acts of violence by those who have been designated as mentally ill. This examination will not only validate or disprove the popular concepts that relate violence to mental illness but hopefully will also indicate those factors, if any, which are closely associated with violent behavior. It is our hope that this information also will increase psychiatry's contribution in screening individuals with a potential for violence in order that violent behavior may be predicted and prevented.

Defining the Problem

In attempting to define the group of those who are mentally ill, we think two considerations are mandatory. The first is who is to be considered mentally ill. The definition could be made broad enough to include all who at any time sought psychiatric help as well as those in society who are significantly disturbed but have not received treatment. There is also the argument that people who behave in a deviant manner in that they murder, rape, or assault others are "insane," "sick," or in some way mentally ill. However, our definition of the mentally ill will be restricted to those who have been hospitalized for psychiatric problems. This restriction is made not only for reasons of simplicity but because most available data deal with the hospitalized psychiatric population. We think that limiting the population under consideration to those regarded as more seriously disturbed will produce the most meaningful testing of the proposition that the mentally ill are more violent than the general population.

The second and equally important consideration is how an act of violence is to be defined. Again we shall structure our definition in order to obtain maximum information from the data available. First, overall arrest rates that include acts of violence as well as other socially deviant behavior will be examined. Reviewing arrest rates for psychiatric and nonpsychiatric populations will give at least a partial view of the degree of violent behavior in each group. Second, crimes of violence inflicted on others, such as murder, rape, negligent manslaughter, robbery, and aggravated assault, committed by those with a prior history of psychiatric illness, will be compared with similar acts committed by the general population. This comparison will permit an even closer look at the question of whether or not the mentally ill are dangerous.

Other areas having to do with violence, while very important, will not be considered in this chapter. For instance, the act of suicide is inherently violent and considered by many in our culture as prime evidence of mental illness. Since this form of behavior has received considerable attention by numerous investigators, and since our primary concern is with the potential danger of the mental patient to the rest of society, this issue will not be taken up here. Also we have chosen to omit the so-called psychopath or sociopathic personality and others with defects in "character" formation from our analysis of mental illness and violence. Although these types of persons make up a significant proportion of violent offenders, discussion of the criminally deviant person under the rubric of mental illness is both controversial and beyond the scope of adequate analysis here (see Chapters 2 and 13).

Hence we are interested in examining the incidence of violent acts against others that are sufficiently serious to come to the attention of authorities and comparing the number of these acts committed by those previously hospitalized for mental illness with the incidence of similar acts in the general population.

Violence in Discharged Mental Patients

Let us examine some of the evidence concerning the relationships of mental illness to violence. There are several studies that have examined discharged hospital populations to see what percentage of their members engage in criminal behavior. The relative incidence of arrests associated with the discharged psychiatric population can be compared to the nonhospitalized general population. Most of these studies indicate that discharged psychiatric patients have lower arrest rates than the nonhospitalized general population.

Rappeport [29] quotes a study by Ashley done in 1922 covering 1,000 patients discharged from a state hospital over a ten-year period. Only 12 of these were arrested, producing an extremely low overall arrest rate of 1.2 percent. No attempt was made in this study to compare this arrest rate with that of the general population, nor are we given any information indicating how many arrests involved crimes of violence against the person. The same author also quotes

Pollock, who in 1938 studied the offenses committed by patients paroled from state hospitals in New York during the previous year. Offenses committed by paroled patients consisted of 26 misdemeanors and 11 felonies by male patients and 3 misdemeanors and no felonies by female patients—all this with an average daily number of 5,833 patients on parole. The rate of misdemeanors per 1,000 men on parole was 8.8, and the rate of felonies, 3.7. The rate of misdemeanors among paroled women was 1.03 per 1,000. At that time the rate of arrests per 1,000 of general population 15 years of age and over was 184.4 for men, 15.1 for women, and 99.7 for both sexes combined. The corresponding arrest rates of paroled patients were 12.5 for the men, 1.03 for the women, and 6.9 for both sexes combined. This indicates a patient arrest rate fourteen times lower than that of the general population. A breakdown of the psychiatric population's offenses reveals 29 misdemeanors, 5 felonious assaults with dangerous weapons, and 1 homicide. None of the felonious assaults resulted in serious harm. The one homicide was attributed to alcoholism. It is interesting to note how the language in even the psychiatric literature reflects our bias. Mental patients are "paroled," even though they have not committed any crime. The use of this word to signify "release" from the hospital is much less prevalent today than it was in previous decades.

Cohen and Freeman [9] studied 1,676 patients who were paroled and discharged over a four-year period (1940–44) from the Norwich State Hospital in Connecticut. The arrest rate per 1,000 for this population was 4.2 for felonies, while the arrest rate for felonies in the general population was 27. No homicides were committed by former patients, and all assaults were described as not serious. These authors also pointed out that 18.4 percent of their population had a police record prior to hospitalization, while only 5.2 percent became known to the police after discharge from the hospital. Thus the authors concluded that hospitalization apparently produces a reduction in arrest-precipitating behavior. While one cannot argue with the fact of a much lower felony arrest rate of the released psychiatric population as compared with the general population, it is difficult to accept the conclusion that hospitalization produces a reduction in arrest-precipitating behavior on the basis of the data presented. First, there was no control group. Second, it would make sense that the percentage of people initially becoming known to police in a population would decrease with age. Finally, a selective release process, with violent patients being retained for long periods of time, is likely the most important factor accounting for the above results.

Brill and Malzberg [6] studied 10,247 male patients discharged from the New York State mental hospitals over a five-year period. The overall arrest rate of the patient population was 122 per 10,000, while that for the general population was 491. The authors report that patients with arrests prior to hospitalization were the major offenders following discharge, while those with no previous arrests had a very low rate after discharge. Arrest rates among patients seem to be associated with the same social factors as seen in the general arrested population. Arrest rates were not correlated with factors of mental illness except in a negative way.

Hastings [19], in attempting to evaluate the dangerousness of a discharged psychiatric population, studied 1,638 patients six to twelve years after discharge from the University of Minnesota Hospital. He reported that no patient died by homicide, and no patient committed homicide. Similarly Brennan [5], evaluating the aggressiveness of patients in a paid work program in a Veterans Administration Hospital, reports no aggressive behavior associated with patient employment in and out of the hospital over a period covering 75,000 man-days.

What these studies report in common is that the mentally ill are much less likely to engage in criminal behavior than is the general population. In this case "mentally ill" is defined as that population discharged from a mental hospital. It would be comforting, but premature, to conclude that the mentally ill individual is markedly less dangerous and less likely to resort to violence than the general population.

Rappeport and his associates [27] have studied the problem closely using more current populations, tests of statistical significance, and more exact figures as well as corrected arrest figures for the general population. They initially studied all male patients over 16 years of age discharged from all Maryland psychiatric hospitals during 1947 and during 1957. There were 708 patients from the year 1947 and 2,152 patients from 1957. Arrest rates for these two patient populations were determined for the following five crimes, all representing felonies that are a danger to other people: murder, negligent manslaughter, rape, robbery, and aggravated assault. Arrest rates were compared of the discharged mental hospital population before and after hospitalization and of the general nonhospitalized population.

The results of this study can be summarized thus: (1) There was no clear-cut evidence that the mentally ill are to any significant extent more involved in criminal behavior than those in the general community. (2) For the offense of robbery both hospital groups had a significantly higher arrest rate than the general population. While the statistical evidence is not unequivocal, these data suggest that rape has a higher incidence of occurrence in the previously hospitalized population than in the general population. (3) Arrest rates for murder, negligent manslaughter, and aggravated assault are less clearcut but suggest that these offenses in the mentally ill occur about as often as in the general population. (4) Unlike other studies previously quoted, these data indicate that the hospital experience had no definite effect on reducing the total arrest rate. Some diagnostic groups, however, showed a change after the hospital experience. The alcoholics showed a drop in arrests, the antisocial reactions showed a marked increase, the schizophrenics showed no change. (5) There were no significant differences in the arrest rates of the two populations of mental patients in 1947 and 1957. The authors state that they would have expected the newer treatment techniques to have been reflected in this variable. (6) Alcoholics and schizophrenics accounted for the largest percentage of those contributing to the statistics because they represented the majority of the hospitalized patients.

Rappeport [28] continued his work by doing the same study on women who had been hospitalized and discharged. He utilized the same methodological approach as in the male study and the same years of study, 1947 and 1957. Some of the results are as follows: (1) The female patients reflected the general trend in the female community of committing more aggravated assaults per capita than males. The female patient population was clearly more assaultive than the general population, particularly after hospitalization. (2) Except for aggravated assault there were no significant differences in the arrest rate of the two populations from the years 1947 and 1957. According to the authors this indicated that the newer treatment techniques and psychoactive drugs developed since 1947 have not been effective in controlling this type of antisocial behavior. (3) The arrest rates for murder and robbery are lower for female patients than for the general female population, and there were no arrests in the female patient population for negligent manslaughter or rape. (4) As with the male population, alcoholics and schizophrenics account for most of the patients and therefore contribute a higher absolute number of arrests, but the alcoholics appear to have a higher arrest rate than the schizophrenics in the 1957 population.

The last two studies do not show a lower rate of arrests for released psychiatric patients, as did the previously mentioned studies.

They show rather that viewed overall, the male and female psychiatric populations reflected the same trends of criminality as found in the male and female general population. While there is no certain explanation for this difference between the Maryland studies and the ones described previously, it is our opinion that the difference lay mainly in the more sophisticated methodology of the Maryland studies, in which populations were more specifically defined, the definition of violence limited to five specific crimes, and corrected figures of arrest rates were used. The lack of difference in the arrest rates betwn the 1947 and 1957 groups for both sexes led the authors to conclude that our newer treatment techniques, including the psychoactive drugs (tranquilizers), have no effect in controlling antisocial behavior. We do not feel that this can be a firm conclusion, since the data indicate that the 1947 and 1957 patient groups have a somewhat different composition. Also the authors concede that different diagnostic criteria may have been used in these two time periods. There is no indication from the data that Maryland State Hospitals were treating more dangerous patients in 1957 than in 1947.

The intriguing fact that the female former patient becomes more assaultive than her counterpart in the general population requires an attempt at explanation. The authors offer several lines of speculation: (1) Perhaps assaultiveness as a form of acting out replaces psychiatric symptoms; (2) perhaps the hospital experience is so unacceptable and uncomfortable that previously internalized anger is subsequently externalized; and (3) perhaps hospitalization and the use of psychoactive drugs result in using less physical restraint to handle aggressive impulses. Unfortunately, there are no additional data with which to clarify the situation. Examining the differential arrest rates among the diagnoses does not reveal any diagnostic subgroup in the mentally ill population that stands out as being more dangerous than others. This is in part due to the fact that sometimes the samples from which certain statistics were derived are small.

Criminal Studies

Another perspective on the issue of mental illness and violence can be obtained by examining criminal populations for the prevalence of psychiatric disorder and type of disorder present. This retrospective approach is perhaps less valuable, since it occurs after the criminal act has been accomplished. The individual is evaluated psychiatrically, in part because of his criminal behavior; knowing that someone has committed a murder is likely to influence the psychiatric evaluation. Guze [18] studied 223 consecutive convicted felons in attempting to determine the prevalence and kinds of psychiatric disorders. In the entire group 48 percent received no psychiatric diagnosis exclusive of sociopathic personality. The remaining 52 percent received one or more of the following diagnoses: alcoholism (43 percent); drug addiction (5 percent); anxiety reaction (12 percent); homosexuality, schizophrenia, and epilepsy (1 percent each). Alcoholism in this study was shown to be associated with a family history of alcoholism and suicide and a personal history of suicide attempts, military service difficulty, fighting, and arrests. Some aspects of this study that are striking are the high incidence of alcoholism and the low incidence of psychotic disorders within a given criminal population. The same author in a follow-up study of this same population [17] revealed that the men who received a diagnosis of alcoholism had a significantly higher criminal recidivism rate than did the non-alcoholic parolees.

Bromberg [7] cites the data obtained from the Psychiatric Clinic of the Court of General Sessions in New York, where every convicted felon was examined physically and psychiatrically. This project, in effect a continuous one since 1932, examines 2,500 to 3,000 individuals per year. Approximately 80 percent of the convicted felons fall into the "normal" category, while 20 percent receive a diagnosis indicating psychiatric disorder, including psychosis, psychoneurosis, mental defective, or psychopath. The incidence of psychosis in the total convicted population varied from 2 to 2.5 percent. The value of this study is quite apparent. It examines consecutively every convicted felony offender; no selection is made to examine only those referred for examination or those who exhibit unusual behavior. The large scale of the study means that the population being considered is now in excess of 60,000 people.

Wolfgang and Ferracuti [37] in their recent book have summarized a voluminous amount of research on the psychiatric aspects of homicide and violence. They point out that homicide can be "caused" by practically any type of major psychiatric illness and that large-scale studies of criminal populations indicate that the number of psychotic persons is small, the bulk of cases being either "normal" or "psychopathic." The authors also review data regarding the incidence of criminal homicide in different psychiatric syndromes. Alcoholism, they state, can lead to homicide through its violent motor outbursts or through its persecutory or jealousy delusional components. The same authors conclude that in psychomotor epilepsy the frequency of aggression and homicide is greater than in the normal population. In addition, Chapter 1 of this book illustrates how brain disease caused by specific tumors, encephalitis, and diffuse brain damage (the *dyscontrol syndrome*) can be an important element in violent, destructive behavior.

Other authors [1–3, 14, 16, 23–26, 30, 32, 33, 35] find many, if not a majority, of homicidal individuals in their study populations to be psychotic. While this may seem to contradict the previously mentioned data, a closer look clarifies the situation. Several of these studies [14, 23, 24] start with a highly selected population rather than using any sampling or survey technique. One author [14] personally examined 66 accused murderers over a ten-year period. He found 21 percent psychotic and over 50 percent affected by alcohol at the time of the offense. Another [23] studied 100 cases in which homicide was committed while the murderer was mentally ill. Of these cases 57 percent were diagnosed as schizophrenic (psychotic). Interestingly 44 percent of the victims were family members, while most of the other victims were friends, neighbors, or work associates. Only 10 percent of the victims were strangers. It appears that mental illness increases the likelihood that the violent act will be directed against family members. In a study of 500 murderers in Great Britain, East [13] found that 32 percent of those who were deemed sane killed family members, whereas 56 percent of the insane murderers killed within the family. Growdon [15] reports that 32 percent of the victims of his juvenile population were family members. He postulates that a greater proportion of young murderers than older murderers may kill family members.

Included in the previously mentioned sources are a group of studies that deal with specific crimes and offenses [1–3, 25, 26, 30, 32, 33, 35]. This type of study is quite different from the psychiatric evaluation of consecutive felons. Studies of the sudden murderer [3, 35] will serve as an example. The authors define the sudden murder as a single, isolated, unexpected episode of violent acting-out behavior. This behavior is not well thought out and has no obvious purpose or hope for personal advantage or profit as a foreseeable result. The characteristics of 43 sudden murderers, predominantly males, were described. The sudden murderer typically came from a cohesive family with a domineering mother. Such persons maintain an extremely precarious equilibrium, being constantly preoccupied with the need to curb surges of anger. They are reluctant to reveal their feelings of hopelessness in ever becoming close and intimate with others. With a desperate hope of overcoming this sense of aloneness, the sudden murderer uses homicide as a way of settling the raging inner conflict. It is when this individual is at the threshold of developing meaningful interpersonal relationships that his fear of being rejected creates an increasing feeling of self-doubt and rage.

About half these sudden murderers had been seen previously by mental health professionals. They were usually treated for short periods of time and then discharged from treatment. The authors stress the importance of continued professional contacts with such schizoid and schizophrenic persons (the predominant diagnostic groups), even during periods of apparent adequacy. Unfortunately, there is no way of predicting from the psychodynamic material which of these isolated conflicted people will engage explosively in murderous behavior. However, the authors do indicate that the behavioral histories of the sudden murderer contrast sharply with typical histories of either the habitual criminal offender (the psychopath) or the sexual deviate offender.

The foregoing is a somewhat encouraging finding because it suggests that a thorough study of specific kinds of violent behavior may yield data about the specific individuals drawn to that behavior. For instance, analysis of a group of mothers who murdered [33] indicated that all five were seriously disturbed with a diagnosis of schizophrenia at the time of murdering their own children. They all shared a general inadequacy and inability to cope with the task of raising children, and their homicide attempts were associated with serious suicide attempts in four of the five cases. Looking at this problem by starting with the victims [1] supplements the data of the previous study. Of 46 homicides in which the victims were infants or preadolescent children, 37 were killed by parents or persons who acted as parents. Seventeen of the assailants were obviously mentally ill at the time of the crime (the authors imply that they were psychotic), and four were borderline psychotic. Again, suicide attempts were a common aftermath to the homicide. Both of the last two studies indicate that the assailant usually had a past history of psychiatric disorder or had demonstrated overtly disturbed behavior for some time prior to the crime, or both. The implication is that there are instances of murder where danger signals are given and presumably could be acted upon in order to prevent tragic consequences. These two studies lend further support to the proposition that the psychiatrically disturbed individual, when violent, is more likely to express his violence within the family circle.

The last group of studies of *selected* case samples provides thoughtful and provocative clinical material as well as indicating tentative hypotheses regarding individual motives for violence. More detailed clinical material will be found in Chapter 13. However, the data thus far do not allow us to conclude that someone defined as mentally ill is either more or less violent than his counterpart in the general population.

Violence and Alcohol

We were impressed by one aspect of the data as we reviewed, namely, the close association of excessive use of alcohol to aggressive and destructive behavior. The inhibition-releasing and judgment-altering effects of this drug have been well known for centuries, and its abuses continue to present a monumental public health problem. Although the legal status of alcoholism as a disease is repeatedly under review, it often has been classified as a mental illness with some justification. Part of the reason for alcoholism's indeterminate status is the difficulty encountered in deriving a satisfactory definition that distinguishes the pathological drinking of the alcoholic from that of the social drinker. Alcoholics have been defined [38] as:

. . . those excessive drinkers whose dependence upon alcohol has attained such a degree that it shows a noticeable mental disturbance or an interference with their bodily and mental health, their interpersonal relations and their smooth social and economic functioning; or show the prodromal signs of such development.

However, the answer to the question "Is the use of alcohol related to acts of violence?" is *yes*, whatever point on the drinking spectrum one selects. The effect of alcohol as an intoxicant, generally acting to lower the threshold for violence, is considered in Chapter 12. What concerns us here is the substantial evidence that violent behavior is more frequent among those defined as alcoholics and hence categorized as mentally ill.

Studies relating to this problem follow two general approaches. In the first the drinking histories of those convicted of felonious acts of violence are investigated, and in the second the criminal records of known alcoholics are examined. Exemplifying the former type of study is the survey [12] conducted of 2,325 new arrivals in California prisons, 29 percent of whom indicated that alcohol had been a major problem in their lives. The majority of this group had been convicted for crimes of violence. Utilizing the second method, Clark, Hannigan, and Hart [8] studied a series of 100 alcoholic felons and found a preponderance of violent crimes. The work of Wolfgang and Strohm [37] provides strong supportive evidence. In their careful and detailed study of 588 homicides over a five-year period in Philadelphia, they found that alcohol was present in either the offender or the victim in 64 percent of the cases. Although they lacked sufficient data to make accurate retrospective diagnoses of alcoholism, the diagnosis was strongly suggested in a significant number of cases. The previously cited work of Guze [18], in which 43 percent of 223 convicted felons were diagnosed as being alcoholic, adds further evidence to the belief that alcoholism as a disease is correlated with acts of violence.

Haughey and Heiberg [20], as well as Blane [4], draw attention to the distinction between alcohol as a primary factor in crime, unleashing violence in the form of assaultive and homicidal behavior, and as a secondary factor causing chronic alcoholics to act in criminal ways. The alcoholic—often poor, already a social outcast, and with little self-esteem—may more readily act in an antisocial and often violent manner even when sober.

While the question may legitimately be raised whether alcoholism should be equated with other forms of mental illness, there remains little doubt as to its correlation with acts of violence. The evidence is substantial and convincing, in contrast to that of other mental illnesses, where the data are less clear cut. Perhaps one of the more judicious uses of the time and energy of mental health professionals might be directed toward coping with the distribution, use, and abuse of this widely known and legal drug. The mass media have informed us of the tragic consequences of the use of more recently acquired inhibition-releasing and judgment-altering drugs, e.g., LSD and Methedrine. The relationships of these drugs to violence will be explored in Chapter 12. It is our opinion that the last thing man needs in the world today is extensive use of more agents to "blow" his mind.

Furthermore, a recent bulletin [34] issued by the United States Department of Transportation states that the use of alcohol was implicated in 50 percent of the traffic fatalities during the year 1967. This means that abuse of this well-known drug was involved in 25,-000 deaths.

Predictive Studies

Clearly little of what has been said relates significantly to our ability to predict, before the act, which individual will be likely to commit an act of violence. Some authors have attempted to broach this problem. McDonald [22] studied 100 consecutive threat-to-kill admissions to the Colorado Psychopathic Hospital. After a five- to six-year follow-up, three patients had taken the lives of others, and 4 patients later committed suicide. While 7 cases may not be very significant, 7 percent of the threat-to-kill group are known to have taken another life or their own. In actuality these figures may be higher, since 25 out of the original 100 patients could not be traced. In order to isolate prognostic factors in the threat group, the same author compared this threat-to-kill group with a group of convicted murderers and with a group of psychiatric patients who had threatened neither suicide nor homicide. The data suggest the following conclusions: (1) In those who threaten homicide, absence of suicide attempts indicates a higher homicide risk. (2) Prior suicide attempts indicate that the threat-group individual is more likely to kill himself than others. (3) The one distinguishing factor noted between the homicide-threat and homicide-offender groups was the incidence of attempted suicide in the threat group. Obviously homicide threats require the most careful assessment that can be provided. As with suicide, it is not correct to assume that the person who talks about it will not do it.

History of deviancy is an important factor. Robins [31] in *Deviant Children Grown Up*, shows that the best predictor of sociopathic behavior in adulthood is sociopathic behavior in childhood, and the only known nonsociopathic trait in childhood significantly related to deviant behavior was bed wetting beyond the age of 6 years.

De Leon [11] described what he calls the "preassaultive" or prehomicidal state, in which he stresses the five following points in evaluating an individual as a possible homicidal or assaultive risk: (1) Difficulty in pleasurably and constructively utilizing leisure time on off-duty hours, weekends, holidays, and periods of unemployment. Special note should be taken of any excessive use of alcohol, a recurrent theme. (2) Frequent frictional encounters with significant persons within the patient's emotional orbit such as wife, husband, lover. Particular attention should be taken of sexual partners whose relationship revolves around a prominent sadomasochistic (love-hate) axis. It is relatively infrequent for the slayer and victim to be strangers. (3) Conspicuous accounts of fistfights and other physical evidence of violence such as scars. (4) A penchant for guns and knives. (5) Age. The tendency to homicide is greatest among relatively young people, whereas older people are more prone to suicide. As de Leon points out, none of these five factors is of great predictive value when taken alone, but if a combination of them is present, the patient may be considered preassaultive. It is clear that de Leon places little or no emphasis on the traditional psychiatric diagnosis in assessing the preassaultive person but rather uses a combination of social factors, past behavior, and gross indices of interpersonal adjustment to reach his conclusion.

In a related attempt to define the predictors of violent behavior, Kinzil [21] studied federal prisoners brought before a discipline committee for fighting or assault. He compared detailed histories of 8 prisoners who were most frequently involved in violent behavior with 6 prisoners who were least frequently involved in violent behavior. Some distinguishing characteristics of the most violent prisoners were "repeated violent behavior with little provocation, frequent necessity for forceable restraint, fighting with a weapon, carrying a weapon for prolonged periods 'for protection,' and a history of violence between parents." Other hallmarks of the violent group were "serious accidents (self-perpetrated), bisexuality and hypersexuality, hypersensitivity to name calling, and history of violence to domestic animals." Some caution is necessary in extrapolating prison findings to other groups, since prison culture itself contributes to violent behavior.

In summary, of all the predictive factors associated with violent behavior, excessive use of alcohol and a history of violence are most important. The studies reviewed here show that a history of violence in childhood, fighting with weapons or using them for protection, and violence as a means of settling conflicts are all important. These studies illustrate how certain groups in our culture continue to use and teach outward-directed attack as a way of getting things done. On the other hand, in the assessment of potentially violent individuals a history of suicide attempts points toward suicide rather than homicide as a means to resolve conflict. Hence the way a person has learned to handle his own aggressive energies in the past, for example, turning anger *out* or *in*, affects how he will handle aggression in the future. Finally, the attempts to define predictors of violent behavior have yielded several important demographic, social, and interpersonal factors, namely, younger age, males, highly friction-laden family relationships, few recreational outlets, and sexual aberrations.

Conclusion

We think it is fair to conclude that an individual with a label of mental illness is quite capable of committing any act of violence known to man but probably does not do so with any greater frequency than his neighbor in the general population. Two exceptions to this might be robbery in male patients and aggravated assault in female patients. Put another way, that group of people in our society who have been hospitalized for psychiatric reasons and released do not, as a group, constitute a greater risk of behaving in a criminal or violent way than do people who have not been hospitalized for psychiatric reasons. Assuming these data do have general relevance for the entire United States population, it would certainly be unfair to direct any restrictive legislation against this group as a whole. For instance, gun control legislation directed against anyone with a history of mental illness would be discriminatory and ineffective in dealing with the issue of violence, since, according to the data we have presented, members of the general population will be *at least* as likely to engage in violent behavior as the discharged mental patient.

However, it is a reasonable and worthwhile task to attempt to identify any subgroup in the mentally ill population that is an exceptionally high-risk group with regard to future violent behavior. If this could be done through further research, specific action could be instituted to cope with that subgroup. This action, of course, could be legislative and psychiatric. Unfortunately our data, as we examine them now, prevent us from making definitive distinctions between violent and nonviolent subgroups. The closest example to such a subgroup indicated by studies cited are those people who use alcohol to alter their behavior toward violent and destructive ends. Most of us recall the unsuccessful attempt at restrictive legislation regarding alcohol, and most mental health professionals are painfully aware of the current problem with alcoholism and our minimally effective ways of dealing with it. If a preassaultive or prehomicidal state—for instance, like the one described by de Leon—can be determined, it would greatly facilitate preventive intervention.

While it is clear that we cannot as yet really predict which individual will become violent, there are signals which should not be ignored. If an individual threatens to kill another person, the threat

tal illness and homicide. *Canadian Psychiatric Association Journal* 11:91, 1966.
24. Neustarter, W. L. The state of mind in murder. *Lancet* 1:861, 1965.
25. Podolsky, E. Somnambulistic homicide. *American Journal of Psychiatry* 121:191, 1964.
26. Podolsky, E. Children who kill. *General Practice* 31:5, 1965.
27. Rappeport, J. R., and Lassen, G. Dangerousness arrest rate comparisons of discharged patients and the general population. *American Journal of Psychiatry* 121:776, 1964.
28. Rappeport, J. R., and Lassen, G. The dangerousness of female patients. A comparison of the arrest rate of discharged psychiatric patients and the general population. *American Journal of Psychiatry* 123:413, 1966.
29. Rappeport, J. R., Lassen, G., and Hay, N. B. A Review of the Literature on the Dangerousness of the Mentally Ill. In Rappeport, J. R. (Ed.), *Clinical Evaluation of the Dangerousness of the Mentally Ill*. Springfield, Ill.: Thomas, 1967.
30. Revitch, E. Sex murder and potential sex murder. *Diseases of the Nervous System* 26:640, 1965.
31. Robins, L. N. *Deviant Children Grown Up*. Baltimore, Md.: Williams & Wilkins, 1966.
32. Smith, S. The adolescent murderer: A psychodynamic interpretation. *Archives of General Psychiatry* 13:310, 1965.
33. Tuteur, W., and Glotzer, J. Murdering mothers. *American Journal of Psychiatry* 116:447, 1959.
34. U.S. Dept. of Transportation. *Alcohol and Public Safety Report*. Washington, D.C.: U.S. Government Printing Office, 1968.
35. Weiss, J. M., Lamberti, J. W., and Blackman, N. The sudden murderer: A comparative analysis. *Archives of General Psychiatry* 2:669, 1960.
36. Wolfgang, M. E., and Ferracuti, F. *The Subculture of Violence*. New York: Barnes & Noble, 1967.
37. Wolfgang, M. E., and Strom, R. B. The relationship between alcohol and criminal homicide. *Quarterly Journal of Studies on Alcohol* 17:411, 1956.
38. World Health Organization, Expert Committee on Mental Health (Alcoholism). Report on the Second Session, October 1951. P. 15.

12. Drug Use and Violence

Jared R. Tinklenberg, M.D.,
and Richard C. Stillman, M.D.

Man's use of drugs dates from at least 4,000 B.C., when the process of wine-making was inscribed on an Egyptian tomb [28]. The association of drugs and violence has been recorded since at least 150 B.C., when Polypious described the Gauls' drinking habits. After a victorious battle Gallic soldiers would celebrate by drinking whatever intoxicating beverages were available but then would sometimes start fighting among themselves with occasional loss of life and loot. Mohammedan tradition describes Satan at the first planting of grapes. Satan watered the ground with peacock's blood, sprinkled the leaves with ape's blood, and drenched the grapes first with lion's blood and then with the blood of swine. According to the story the first sips of wine make man like a peacock—animated, vivacious, with heightened colors. When the fumes of liquor rise to the head, he is gay and gambols as an ape. But when drunk, he becomes as a lion—ferocious, easily angered, and prone to assault. When extremely intoxicated, man is like a swine groveling on the ground and falling asleep.

Alcohol, however, is just one of the drugs that man has used to alter his consciousness and to provide a means of "coping" with the problems of life. Opium, cocaine, hallucinogenic mushrooms, and herbs have been used throughout history in many of man's activities, including some of his violence. Marihuana has been a common intoxicant in certain countries since before the time of Christ, although only in the last decade has it become popular in the United States.

In recent years the variety and amount of drugs used have increased rapidly. Today's newspapers suggest that the use of illicit drugs has become widespread among junior and senior high school students. Systematic studies such as those recently completed by Blum and associates [5] support these statements. Physicians in hospital emergency rooms give grim testimony to the increasing number of young people who require treatment after taking an unknown quantity of an unknown drug in an attempt to achieve altered awareness. Many observers in Vietnam describe the ready availability of marihuana, and some claim its use is spreading among our young fighting men despite stringent restrictive measures.

But before indicting the youth of our society, let us hasten to add that increased drug use is one phenomenon which easily crosses today's generation gap. Mass media commercials condition all age groups to think that drugs are a quick and easy solution for insomnia, "nerves," "blahs," or the "blues." One recent survey [29] of American families found an average of thirty different drugs per household, most of these used primarily by adults. Thus many people seem to be using drugs as a chemical way of coping with the pressures and frustrations of today's world.

Although we do not discuss in detail the reasons why people take drugs to affect their feelings and behavior, the major reasons for the extensive consumption of these drugs relate to one theme of this book—the attempt to cope with one's environment. The reasons for taking altering drugs, whether to relieve unbearable tension or frustrations, "get high," or improve performance, are all related to attempts to adjust (improve one's temporary state) or cope (improve the outcome of some longer-range goal). However, drug abuse of whatever kind represents an inadvertent failure in coping (or even in adjusting), just as much reactive violence does.

Although some drugs have the potential to reduce violence, other drugs predispose the user to outbursts of violent behavior—behavior that becomes increasingly dangerous for both the individual and society. This chapter will discuss the relations between contemporary drug use and violence from the standpoint of how drugs may either enhance or reduce violence. For our purposes we use the term *drug* to mean any substance that when physically taken into the body can produce a temporary or permanent change in a person's neurophysiological functions, thoughts, feelings, or behavior. Our focus will be on the users of the amphetamines, marihuana, and alcohol. Our discussion, however, will also include LSD and other mind-altering drugs, barbiturates, opiates, and tranquilizers. Much of the information in this chapter comes from our clinical observations of drug users, from systematic research at Stanford University involving the effects of marihuana on human subjects, and from review of the scientific literature. Although we describe sociological data from large groups of people, our major emphasis will be on factors influencing the behavior of the individual drug user.

Drug Use and Violence: A Model

We propose that violence in association with drug use results from the *interplay* of both drug and nondrug factors. The drug factors include such parameters as pharmacological properties, dosages, modalities of use (oral, injection, or other), frequency of use, and long-term cumulative effects. We describe nondrug factors in terms of psychosocial interactions. Crucial elements in these interactions are the significant people in the drug user's environment and the expectations about what will happen when a particular drug is used. These expectations are derived from a number of sources including the personalities of the individuals involved; recent life events; and the physical, interpersonal, and social milieu in which drug use occurs [52]. For example, when a drug user who characteristically believes that other people are trustworthy interacts with a group of people who expect that a given drug induces peace and tranquility, violence is less probable. Such interactions necessarily vary over time and are interdependent, so that a change in one element is likely to influence other elements.

In part, we shall use the cybernetic model of anger and attack, developed by Melges and Harris in Chapter 4, to identify which

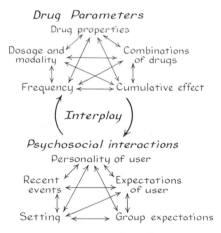

FIG. 6.   The interplay of drug and nondrug factors

specific drug and nondrug processes enhance potentials for violence. The emphasis will be on the three main conditions of this model involved in the breakdown of the appraisal process and hence in the transformation of anger into attack: (1) taking only the present view, (2) taking only the personal view, and (3) taking action as a goal in itself. In Chapter 4 these concepts were discussed in detail, so only the pertinent points will be repeated here.

People who focus intensely on the *present* often have impaired ability to utilize past experiences and consider future consequences of their behavior. Such individuals are predisposed to acting impulsively on present, here-and-now stimuli and, if angry, may attack without pausing to consider future consequences or alternatives. When an individual takes only a *personal* view, any seeming interferences by others with his plans and activities likely will be construed as a significant threat. Restraints on activity intending to remove these threats are minimal because other people are considered unimportant and are viewed only as impediments to be overcome. The third condition, taking *action* as a goal itself, focuses on the rewards intrinsically involved in taking action. Attacking may elicit the positive feeling of *doing something* rather than remaining stultified and inactive; it may engender the satisfaction of righting an imagined or real wrong; and it may give an increased sense of belonging to a group that values action. In addition, attacking may relieve the unpleasant tensions associated with feeling angry or the experience of having no influence over what is happening.

The following sections will use these three conditions in describing how the individual drug user is influenced by the interplay between patterns of drug use and psychosocial interactions. Specific attention is directed toward interplays that enhance the generation of anger and the transformation of this anger into attacking behavior.

Amphetamines

Amphetamines are drugs classified as central nervous system stimulants. Their effects include increased alertness, wakefulness, and physical activity; enhanced performance in a wide variety of tasks; and reduction of appetite. They are used extensively for a variety of purposes including weight control, sustaining activities such as studying or driving, and for inducing altered states of awareness. There are different types of and a variety of names for amphetamines, such as "methedrine," "crystal," "speed," "benzedrine," "bennies," "pep pills," and others. Amphetamines are usually taken orally but may be injected intravenously or intramuscularly, sniffed through the nasal mucosa, or absorbed through other skin surfaces.

ASSOCIATIONS WITH VIOLENCE

"Speed Kills" has been a popular inscription on buttons and bumper stickers in the Haight-Ashbury district of San Francisco, an area reputed to be the illicit drug capital of the world. In this "hip" world *speed* refers not to automobile velocity but to methamphetamine and its pharmacological properties that accelerate many types of activities. *Kills* emphasizes the death and violence associated with methamphetamine usage. Although this slogan illustrates the contributions of the drug itself in generating violence and neglects other important variables, it does summarize a widespread belief. This belief is held by residents of the Haight who have been participants and observers in extensive, uncontrolled experimentation involving a wide variety of drugs. These same people are exceedingly tolerant about drug usage in general and yet come to this negative conclusion about methamphetamine.

Experienced law officers, mental health professionals, and others who have frequent contacts with chronic methamphetamine users have reached similar conclusions about the frequency of violent behavior in certain groups of amphetamine users [8, 38, 46]. Common anecdotes emphasize the extreme unpredictability of these people. For instance, violent assaults result from such slight irritations as pencil tapping. Although extensive data are not yet available, initial reports from the San Francisco area suggest a very strong association between amphetamine abuse and crimes of violence [14]. However, with people who use amphetamines in different psychosocial settings, the associations between assaultiveness and the use of the drug are less apparent. For example, people who occasionally use low doses of amphetamine for weight reduction or truckers who infrequently use low doses for driving do not seem especially predisposed to violent behavior. In addition, there are clinically well-recognized, legitimate uses of amphetamines that paradoxically decrease tendencies toward violence in individuals with certain brain disorders. Amphetamines are occasionally helpful in reducing destructive outbursts in brain-damaged and hyperactive children.

Thus one pattern of amphetamine use is associated with violent, assaultive behavior, and yet the very same drug given under medical supervision and usually in lower doses can be helpful in reducing violent behavior. This contrast illustrates that the behavior of drug users is multidetermined and influenced not just by the drug but also by dosage, setting, and other contributing factors.

DRUG FACTORS AND PATTERNS OF USAGE

Several pharmacological properties of the amphetamines directly enhance probabilities of violence. These drugs induce a generalized increase in muscle tension, in a person's energy level, and in physical activity. Amphetamine users frequently comment, "I have to *do* something, I can't remain still." When such tendencies for action are curbed or thwarted, anger easily follows. Given these increases, assaultive action (in accordance with the third cybernetic condition) may intrinsically reward the individual by relieving pent-up tensions, including the heightened tension in the body musculature.

The pharmacological properties of amphetamines also contribute to the other two conditions in the cybernetic model for the transformation of anger into attack. These other two conditions are taking only the present view and taking only the personal view. Increased focus on the present results from amphetamine-induced tendencies toward hair-trigger, almost reflex responses to a wide variety of stimuli. In this "stimulus-bound" state there is a marked decrease in ability to delay responses. Focus is by necessity only on the immediate present, as the rapidity of response precludes recalling past experiences or considering future consequences. Thus possible inhibitions of assaultive behavior are less operative, and attack becomes more likely. In addition, amphetamines increase awareness of many previously unnoticed sensory cues. This increased awarenesss can be interpreted by a user as his becoming the unique, *personal* recipient of more information from his surroundings. These sensations may be increasingly distorted, so that more stimuli are perceived as referring only to the user. In the extreme case the blatantly psychotic methamphetamine user believes that all events refer to him in a personal way; all sights and sounds have special meanings just for him. Any interference with this paranoid, self-referential world is liable to be interpreted as a personal affront, with the result that anger and attack become more probable.

These assault-enhancing properties of the amphetamines are more apparent in certain specific patterns of amphetamine consumption. One such pattern is a repetitive series of intravenous injections known as a "run." A run entails self-administered injections of usually unknown amounts of methamphetamine, commonly called "speed" or "crystal," at variable intervals for several days to a week or more.

Immediately after each injection, called "shooting" or "mainlining," the user experiences a generalized pleasurable feeling termed a "flash" or "rush." A few minutes later the user feels invigorated and driven toward physical activity. For the next few hours the amphetamine user is alert and frequently performs repetitive mechanical tasks such as kneading beads or fondling trinkets. After several hours, however, the user experiences the gradual onset of irritability, vague uneasiness, and uncomfortable aching sensations throughout his body. To avoid these discomforts and recapture the pleasure of the initial rush, the user is impelled to take another dose. In this way the repetitious pattern of methamphetamine use is fostered by the pharmacological, "up-down" properties of the drug. Throughout this run the individual is continuously awake and often engaged in purposeless activities or in attempts to get more methamphetamine. Bodily needs are frequently ignored, as the user neglects eating or drinking and roams outdoors without adequate clothing. This sequence is commonly terminated only by total physical exhaustion or complete depletion of drug supplies. At the end of a run the user experiences an exacerbation of uneasiness and aching sensations throughout his body and demonstrates extreme irritability and unpredictability. These discomforts may be reduced somewhat by barbiturates or other sedatives. *It is during this period of "coming down," particularly after a prolonged run, that the user is most prone to assaultive behavior.*

After coming down the individual usually sleeps solidly for one to three days, awakes with a ravenous appetite, and then after a day or two of stabilization may start the cycle again. These runs frequently are augmented with other drugs, such as heroin, cocaine, or barbiturates. Whatever the variation of the run, associations between the long-term use of intravenous amphetamine and violent behavior persist.

When amphetamine use has been of shorter duration, or at less frequent intervals so that there is a smaller total cumulative consumption, associations with assaultive behavior are less pronounced. Smith and Meyers [46], who conducted an extensive study of methamphetamine users in the San Francisco area, did not observe increased assaultiveness in people who use intravenous methamphetamine only on weekends. Similarly they did not record increased violence among people who were having their first few experiences with speed. In contrast these initial trips were sometimes characterized by inappropriately friendly and generous behavior, such as giving away money and possessions to total strangers. Our observations of novice methamphetamine users do include examples of assaultive behavior, but such episodes seem to be indiscriminate attempts at relieving unexpected, frightening perceptions rather than purposeful attempts at harming others.

The different rates of violence in long-term users as compared with short-term or infrequent users of methamphetamine are striking. In our opinion this difference is clearly indicative of a cumulative amphetamine effect that predisposes the user toward assaultive behavior. We have observed in long-term users progressive deterioration of their ability to control their own behavior. This impairment may be severe and may result in sudden destructive acts, which the users may *recognize* as inappropriate but feel unable to curb. Recognition of this impairment may be frightening to "speed freaks" and sometimes generates feelings of futility and despair over the loss of their ability to direct their own behavior. A frequent comment from these chronic heavy users of methamphetamine is that "Speed burns out your brain."

Because of the dangers associated with long-term use of methamphetamines, the question of addiction assumes great importance. The evolution of novice users into frequent or compulsive users of methamphetamine often is quite rapid, particularly when the user relies extensively on the intravenous method of taking the drug. This progression is accelerated among people who describe themselves as unhappy, depressed, without hope for future improvement, and thus stymied in a miserable present. Speed offers temporary respite from these feelings, but unfortunately the transiency of the relief requires frequent doses of increasingly greater amounts to produce the same effects. In our opinion this pattern of increasing drug dependency closely resembles the classical addiction syndrome ascribed to heroin and other "hard narcotics."

PSYCHOSOCIAL INTERACTIONS

The pattern of speed use just described occurs not in the controlled isolation of a laboratory setting but rather in the context of complex social and psychological forces. We emphasize the interactional nature of these forces to underscore the fact that the behavior of the drug user is influenced by many simultaneously occurring forces operating over time. Smith and Meyers [46] illustrate the interacting social and psychological factors that contribute to assaultive behavior among amphetamine users. They describe much violence as a culmination of ongoing encounters between assailant and victim that center on the buying and selling of methamphetamine.

Fraud in such transactions is common; the realities of the enterprise make deception easy to accomplish and difficult to detect. Quantities of drugs are readily disputed, as the standard unit of measure, a spoon (a teaspoonful), is difficult to assess accurately. In addition, the quality of drugs varies widely depending on the source and amount of adulteration ("spiking") with other ingredients. Thus when a buyer does not achieve the expected drug effects, the ensuing dashed hopes frequently result in anger. The user can easily feel realistically or unrealistically that he has been victimized ("burned").

Action Orientation

Important group expectations operating among these drug users compel the burned individual to attain retribution. "Making things righteous" is a common expression among methamphetamine users and refers to the extreme value placed on revenging all real or imagined wrongs. The user must comply with such expectations or risk loss of status and his sense of belonging with his peers. In addition, individuals who do not retaliate are acceptable targets for overt ridicule, scorn, and sometimes brutal scapegoating. Thus retribution is common and often takes the physical form of beatings and stabbings, sometimes even shooting. Similarly the targets of such assaults are expected to retaliate, and the cycle of assault inducing more assault continues. In short, taking action as a goal itself predominates in the psychosocial interactions of chronic methamphetamine users and further enhances the activating characteristics of the amphetamines.

Present Orientation

Excessive focus on the present becomes another theme in the psychosocial interactions of people who continue to use methamphetamines. The novice speed user may maintain some ties with his past, perhaps by occasional communication with his parents or old friends. But these bonds tend to wither as drugs encroach upon other areas of his life. Similarly, with regard to the future, the neophyte methamphetamine user may maintain some long-range goals and continue his education or vocational training. But the sustained performances that are necessary for successful accomplishments in these areas are incompatible with prolonged methamphetamine use. The user is unable or unwilling to pursue such endeavors and commonly "drops out." His concerns increasingly narrow into the immediate present of procuring and using drugs as he becomes separated from the past and unconcerned about his future. Any interference with these single-minded pursuits becomes an overwhelming threat, as his life has few other sources of satisfaction or meaning. Thus assaultive behavior becomes more probable as the inhibitions to immediate action that usually come from recalling past experiences or considering future consequences are minimized.

This present-oriented focus of the chronic user *centers* on a system of drug supply that is distinguished by instability and transiency. Part of the instability is intrinsic to most illicit drug activities and results from the attrition of people involved who are arrested or who flee to avoid arrest. Further attrition occurs when individuals become ill from needle-transmitted hepatitis and other diseases or are killed in drug-related criminality. Additional instability results from the continual flux in sources of speed. In most areas of the United States there are a number of methamphetamine manufacturers ("chemists") because methamphetamine can be easily produced. The required ingredients are readily obtainable, and the procedure for chemical synthesis is easily mastered even by people without specialized training. Thus distributors ("dealers") and users are not limited to doing business with a few sources of drugs. Competition is fierce, and switching "brands" is common, so that long-term arrangements between a given buyer and seller in this system of free enterprise are unusual. Transiency in the methamphetamine market also is generated by the high geographical mobility of all parties. The chemical apparatus necessary to produce speed is easily transportable. Furthermore, methamphetamine factories are frequently moved to avoid detection by law enforcement officials, rival chemists, and dissatisfied customers. Users can travel widely without concern of being without drug supplies because they know that since most areas have multiple sources, "contacts" can easily be found. The transiency of these psychosocial interactions makes the past and future less important and predisposes the user to a present-oriented view of life. This view is enhanced by the pharmacological properties of the amphetamines, which, as previously described, induce an increased focus on the present.

Extreme transiency in the world of methamphetamine users enhances the prevalent code of getting and doing what you can in the present and not expecting anything from the future. The uncertainty and unpredictability in the lives of these people is in striking parallel to the developmental history of sociopaths, people prone to criminal acts, described by Melges and Bowlby [34]. (See also Chapters 2 and 13.)

Personal Orientation

Taking only the personal view also is manifested in the psychosocial interactions of the chronic methamphetamine user. He focuses on procuring and using *his* drugs; any interference with these activities becomes a significant personal threat. Cooperation in the world of speed is rare because each user expects others to be concerned only with *their* personal goals. Consideration of others' concerns is a deviation from group expectations, so that showing concern may receive negative reactions. Often such consideration is mistakenly identified as indicating homosexual tendencies. Trust is unusual because of the expectation that others will either not take into account the user's concerns or will perhaps exploit the user for their own ends. Smith and Meyers [46] describe how suspiciousness determines certain procedures of the methamphetamine market. For example, transactions involving significant amounts of speed are usually conducted in a neutral setting such as a public restaurant rather than in a private apartment where one party could set up an ambush. The hypervigilance that develops among users who live amidst this intense distrust is often manifested by the carrying of concealed weapons. As illustrated in Chapter 8, the immediate availability of weapons further increases the probability of violence.

An additional aspect of taking only the personal view is that assaultive behavior among methamphetamine users commonly involves individuals who are acquaintances. With acquaintances, personal expectations are at least implicitly involved. Such expectations are vulnerable to frustration and disappointment. These thwarted expectations are likely to be interpreted, perhaps even correctly, as personal affronts. Anger is generated, and violent retaliation for such personal insults becomes more probable.

A final and not surprising phenomenon that is associated with extensive amphetamine use is the development of paranoid reactions [13, 16, 28]. These paranoid reactions range from unfounded suspiciousness and hostility to overtly psychotic reactions characterized by hallucinations and persecutory delusions. Paranoid psychotic reactions are associated with violent behavior.

As with most drug-behavioral relations, the associations between amphetamines and these paranoid reactions are complex and multidetermined. Some observers emphasize that these reactions occur mainly in people who already manifest personality tendencies for paranoid behavior [7, 22, 57]. Other clinicians maintain that this phenomenon is primarily influenced by the drug effects of amphetamines per se and that the user's personality predisposition is less crucial [13]. One report [27] claims that intravenous administration, as compared with oral or other modalities of intake, increases the probability of paranoid reactions.

We believe that an "either-or" focus on any one element results in the neglect of other crucial contributing factors. Our experience indicates that predisposing personality trends toward paranoid behavior, pharmacological properties of amphetamines (particularly methamphetamine), and the intravenous modality of intake are all important contributing factors to the development of paranoid reactions. But these factors must be considered as operating in conjunction with other crucial elements over a period of time. These critical elements include the individual's ability to organize coherently the experiences he is having and to maintain control over his behavior. In turn, these processes are greatly influenced by whether people in the immediate environment are perceived by the user as enhancing or impeding his ability to cope with his surroundings. When the user begins to doubt his own abilities to influence events that are significant to him and has the expectation that others will not consider his concerns, paranoid behavior and associated violence become likely.

These themes of distrust, retribution, and violence are in marked contrast with the relatively peaceful patterns of life in the Haight-Ashbury area of San Francisco before the widespread introduction of intravenous methamphetamine during the summer of 1967. Until that time marihuana and LSD were the illicit drugs in vogue, and violence was rare. However, as speed use increased, assaultive outbursts became more common. Marihuana- and LSD-using "flower children" became alarmed at such attacks and fled the Haight-Ashbury, sometimes to establish communes in nearby areas where they could live with less fear of violent disruption. This exodus of one group of illicit drug users to avoid other drug users illustrates the importance of carefully differentiating the psychosocial factors in drug use.

SUMMARY

Throughout this section we have described a number of factors associated with amphetamine abuse that contribute to anger and assaultive behavior. One factor is the acute effect of amphetamines to enhance the tendency to take physical action quickly and to decrease inclinations for a mediating pause to consider future consequences. A long-term cumulative result of intravenous methamphetamine abuse is the impairment of impulse control, which increases

the potential for sudden, unpredictable outbursts of destructive behavior. However, the fact that low doses of amphetamines can be
used in certain supervised settings with beneficial effects, including
the reduction of aggressive outbursts, illustrates the importance of
considering the multiple determinants of any given drug effect.
Specific psychosocial factors among chronic abusers of amphetamine
interact to increase chances for violence. The long-term speed user
often develops an intensely personal perspective and becomes suspicious and distrustful of all others. The instability and transiency of
the methamphetamine scene encourages the user to get what he can
in the present, as future rewards are too uncertain. Powerful peer
pressures operate among methamphetamine users to demand that an
individual right any wrong and obtain revenge if cheated or abused
by others. A high prevalence of concealed weapons among users
adds further potential for violence. Additional assaultive tendencies
are generated by the high instance of paranoid reactions that develop
among chronic users. Thus there are a number of drug and nondrug
factors involving chronic methamphetamine users which combine
and interact to transform anger into attacking behavior.

Marihuana

Marihuana is a crude preparation of the resin from Indian hemp,
Cannabis sativa. This resin contains the active ingredients in marihuana, chemicals called tetrahydrocannabinols (THC). The concentration of THC in any given amount of marihuana varies widely
according to such factors as where the hemp is grown; how it was
cultivated, harvested, and cured; and what parts of the plant are
being used. THC also can be made synthetically, although the chemical procedure is difficult and costly.

The classification of marihuana is debated by experts and confusing to everyone else. Although marihuana is regulated under narcotic laws, its pharmacology differs significantly from heroin,
opium, cocaine, and other drugs controlled by these laws. Marihuana
has been categorized as a hallucinogen, a mild stimulant, or a mild
tranquilizer. We prefer the term *psychotomimetic* to emphasize the
dominant changes in thought, mood, and perception as compared to
marihuana's other effects [23].

The usual effects of low doses of marihuana include altered perception of sounds, colors, spatial configurations, and other sensory
phenomena. Disorders of time perception also occur. Thoughts

come more rapidly than usual, and it becomes difficult to focus on one task. Memory is somewhat disordered, and the coherent recall of events occurring a few minutes previously may be difficult or impossible. Moods tend to be pleasant and at times euphoric. These phenomena are not experienced in a continuous, predictable fashion but instead are usually episodic "highs," interspersed with periods of normal mental functioning. These highs may be experienced as abrupt jumps in levels of awareness or as being slowly swept away from usual perceptions, as if the person were on a slowly revolving wheel. There is usually a decrease in physical activity and inability to perform physical tasks that require sustained efforts.

Marihuana presently is not used for medicinal purposes, although there is some research exploring its possibilities as a mood elevator or tranquilizer. Usually marihuana is smoked, but it may be consumed as "tea" or mixed into confectionaries or other foods. Marihuana has different names in different parts of the world. In the United States these include "Mary Jane," "pot," and "grass."

ASSOCIATIONS WITH VIOLENCE

Many observers claim that present-day usage of marihuana in the United States is seldom associated with violence. Our clinical and laboratory experiences support that general assertion but with certain specific qualifications. One qualification stems from the fact that the tranquilizer effects of marihuana can be suppressed by the users. People who are on the verge of assaultive behavior usually are not deterred by marihuana. For example, a delinquent gang preparing to do battle is unlikely to be pacified by pot.

Another qualification, by our studies, is that higher concentrations of THC often induce aberrant behavior. Tendencies toward assault become more probable than with the low doses usually taken by smoking in nonlaboratory settings. These high concentrations of tetrahydrocannabinols are seldom found in the natural products used in the United States, and the more potent synthetic forms of THC are not available to most users. However, these more potent forms could become more obtainable and thus more troublesome in the future.

A third limitation to our statement that marihuana usage is seldom associated with violence comes from the small group of people who react idiosyncratically to very low doses of marihuana with frenzied overactivity and indiscriminate violence [49]. Despite widespread myths to the contrary, these "bad trips" or "bummers" occasionally do occur, even in people with no predisposing psychiatric difficulties who take marihuana in pleasant, supportive settings with experienced "guides." This again illustrates the principle that the same drug and dose can lead to very different behavioral responses in different people.

During a bummer the user feels inundated by a myriad of sensory cues from his environment, and subtle changes in perception become gross hallucinations. Thoughts intrude so rapidly that the individual is unable to direct his thinking and feels he is losing control over his mind. He experiences various degrees of anxiety to the extreme of stark terror as he may feel trapped and endlessly suspended in these processes. Some individuals feel the only way out of their maelstrom is to take action indiscriminately; others threaten or attempt physical assaults on people they mistakenly perceive as blocking escape from the dilemma.

A final qualification focuses on associations between long-term marihuana users and violence. Extensive marihuana consumption in the United States has not been prolonged enough to make inferences. Conflicting reports are obtained from other parts of the world where more potent marihuana than that usually available in the United States has been consumed for centuries. Some observers in these areas describe long-term users as extremely lethargic and unmotivated toward any activity including the exertion required of violence. Others associate chronic marihuana consumers with loss of impulse control and increased propensities for violence if provoked. The need for extensive investigation is clear.

DRUG FACTORS AND PATTERNS OF USAGE

Specific pharmacological effects of marihuana contribute to the usual tendencies toward nonviolence in users. The most predominant among these is the THC effect to retard taking action of any kind. Marihuana, after an initial stimulating effect, usually induces pronounced lassitude with a marked decrease in physical activity. With higher doses most people desire nothing more strenuous than to sit or lie motionless. Marihuana induces variable amounts of muscular weakness and inability to sustain physical efforts, and thus capabilities for assaultive behavior are decreased [24]. The common expression describing the results of marihuana as "being stoned" summarizes these sensations of demobilizing lethargy. These action-inhibiting pharmacological effects are in marked contrast to the amphetamine effects that are associated with invigoration and increased tendencies toward physical action. We maintain that any tendencies toward violence among marihuana users are deterred primarily by the inactivating characteristics of the drug.

Although marihuana enhances the other two conditions of the cybernetic model that predispose a person to attack—taking only the personal view and only the present view—there is usually marked inability to maintain attention on any given task. Thus interactions with other people are usually fragmented, and the sustained encounters usually required for assault are less probable. Although there is an increase in present focus with marihuana, the marihuana user is less likely to feel rushed or constrained as contrasted with the amphetamine user. In addition, there are a number of psychosocial factors that tend to inhibit violent behavior in marihuana users.

PSYCHOSOCIAL INTERACTIONS

Until recently marihuana usage in the United States was almost exclusively confined to some Mexican-American laborers, inhabitants of black and Puerto Rican ghettos, jazz musicians, and members of a few isolated bohemian groups. Because some individuals in these groups were characterized by high rates of assaultive behavior, marihuana was assumed to be a cause of violence, although no satisfactory studies were conducted to test this widespread belief.

Our limited experience with drug users from lower socioeconomic classes suggests an opposite tendency. Drug users who use mainly marihuana seem less inclined to violence than their counterparts who prefer other drugs such as alcohol or amphetamines. Besides the previously described pharmacological factors that inhibit assaultive behavior, a crucial role in inhibiting violence is played by the expectations of lower-class marihuana users that one should be cool and mellow, not angry and violent. Important peer status is obtained by remaining cool and aloof regardless of the irritation or stress of the circumstances. Users who respond to threats with physical action and assaultiveness violate group expectations and are likely to be excluded from the group [6]. Thus the psychosocial expectations are diametric from those of the speed scene, where premium is placed on actively defending one's esteem and honor at any cost.

The use of marihuana has changed significantly in the last few years by spreading from the ghettos into the mainstream of our society. Blum and associates in their excellent two volumes, *Society and Drugs* and *Students and Drugs*, document these changes [4, 5]. Marihuana has become prevalent among students, young military personnel, and particularly among people who profess a "hip" life philosophy. In certain parts of the United States, marihuana usage has infiltrated the Establishment to include bankers, lawyers, businessmen, and others. In most of these groups marihuana consumption is planned in advance and includes such predictable features as comfortable surroundings, dim lights, pleasant music, and food. The participants are usually acquaintances or close friends, and the psychological atmosphere is one of tolerance and trust. In this comfortable setting the user has a peer-supported and sanctioned opportunity to indulge in private perceptions and thoughts. Social interaction with others is not necessary, and each user can achieve the goal of a good high without depending on others. Thus when each user "does his own thing" with minimal expectations of others, the opportunities for anger-producing frustrations are decreased.

Among marihuana users premium is usually placed on feelings and sensual experiences. Intellectual processes and behavior that could be scrutinized and appraised by others are usually considered less important. Thus with value placed on subjective experiences that cannot be evaluated by others, the user's self-esteem is less vulnerable to degradation by others, and personal affronts become less likely.

In addition, middle-class marihuana users follow the ghetto tradition of strong reinforcement for *not* taking impulsive action. Premium is placed on "not getting hassled," that is, upset, regardless of frustrations or interferences from others. People who are assaultive or who take other action that might attract the attention of police are usually excluded from the group. Thus these factors combine to inhibit taking assaultive action.

SUMMARY

The use of marihuana is associated only infrequently with violence. There are, however, certain circumstances in which assaults become more probable. These circumstances include idiosyncratic reactions in susceptible people, high concentrations of THC, and perhaps the long-term, excessive usage of marihuana. More commonly the interplay of drug and nondrug factors among marihuana users actually inhibits assaultive behavior. Most of this inhibition stems from the interplay of action-reducing drug effects with the pronounced tendencies among marihuana users toward inaction regardless of circumstances.

Alcohol

Alcohol refers to a group of beverages including distilled spirits, wine, and beer that contain ethyl alcohol along with other ingredients. Alcohol is usually classified pharmacologically as a central nervous system depressant, although recent works suggest that this description is overly simplistic [10]. The effects of alcohol on human behavior are well known to most people and include variable amounts of anxiety reduction, a decrease in ability to perform most physical and mental tasks, and changes in the user's characteristic behavior patterns.

In this section we first shall examine evidence for the association between assaultive behavior and the consumption of alcohol. Then we shall explore the particular interactions of alcohol users that are involved in processes culminating in violence. Much of this information is derived from Blum's comprehensive reviews [2, 3]. (See also Chapter 11.)

ASSOCIATIONS WITH VIOLENCE

Throughout history people have suspected that the use of alcohol increases the probability of violent behavior. Contemporary cross-cultural studies demonstrate the frequency with which the use of alcoholic beverages is regarded as a dangerous custom [25]. Even today women in some primitive tribes of the South African jungles hide all the spears and other weapons before tribal drinking bouts.

Systematic studies provide strong support to these widespread beliefs associating alcohol with violence. In a comprehensive investigation of 588 criminal homicides, alcohol was present in 55 percent of the offenders [54]. In a survey of nine studies on the role of alcohol in murders, the median of people who had taken alcohol prior to committing murder was 54 percent [31]. Three more recent investigations [19, 21, 51] associated alcohol with about 50 percent of the homicides studied.

The use of alcohol has also been linked with forms of violent behavior that did not result in homicide. In one investigation [44] alcohol was detected in 91 of the 100 people arrested for assault, assaults with deadly weapons, and carrying concealed weapons; alcohol was also present in 83 percent of the cases involving a nonfatal shooting. The prevalence of alcohol in suicides and in violence resulting from motor vehicle "accidents" has been repeatedly demonstrated [2, 32, 39, 47, 58]. Industrial, home, and leisure-time accidents have also been associated with alcohol [2, 47].

Similar findings are described in people with a history of frequent and excessive alcohol consumption. In one series 59 percent of those arrested for assault and robbery and 26 percent of those arrested for murder were known to be "heavy drinkers" by the Alcoholics

Anonymous classification [33]. Another study found "alcoholics" (no definition given) committing 39 out of 76 murders and 13 out of 30 episodes of assault with wounding [15]. In a series of men under the influence of alcohol at the time of their crimes, over 50 percent had histories indicating heavy alcohol use and involvement in violent crimes [1].

From the available evidence we conclude that alcohol is indeed often associated with violence. However, since the use of alcohol is so widespread, we must carefully differentiate which interactions of alcohol users increase chances for violence and which do not.

DRUG FACTORS AND PATTERNS OF USAGE

When assaultive behavior occurs in association with alcohol, there is a tendency to focus on such pharmacological causes as the release of inhibitory centers in the brain. But these pharmacological explanations are poorly documented and probably less important than generally assumed.

One drug parameter that is correlated with assaultive tendencies is the dose of alcohol. Figure 7 is derived from a study [44] of 211 people arrested for crimes of violence (excluding sex crimes). Although inferences must be limited by lack of control data, the larger percentages of arrests at higher urine alcohol levels suggest that as-

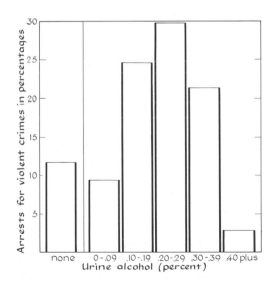

Fig. 7. Percentages of total arrests for violent crimes (excluding sex crimes) associated with different urine alcohol levels [44]

saultive tendencies increase with increasing doses of alcohol. Very high levels induce coma (or death), obviously making violence less probable or impossible.

The drug factors of frequency and chronicity also are implicated in violence as discussed previously. Further studies are necessary to delineate the exact contributions of these parameters.

PSYCHOSOCIAL INTERACTIONS

In systematic studies involving the effects of alcohol on aggressive behavior in humans, group expectations played important roles [48]. Many people expect that aggressiveness and loss of control will increase with intoxication. These expectations implicitly enhance taking action by partially absolving the individual of personal responsibility for his behavior while under the influence of alcohol. "I would never have done that if I hadn't been drinking" is an acceptable explanation for assault, which shifts the onus onto alcohol and away from factors within the person or group that might have inhibited violence.

Another factor associated with alcohol use that enhances assaultive behavior is taking only the present view. This present orientation has been described in people who habitually use alcohol to excess. They are usually concerned with immediate gratification and have difficulties in sustaining long-range goals. Gliedman [20] concludes his review with, "Alcoholics seem to live in an extended present unaffected by past or future." Several systematic investigations [40, 43] support these clinical notions. One study [45] using matched groups of alcoholics and social drinkers demonstrated that alcoholics had less extensive and less coherent perspectives about future events. Another investigator [18] found that people who habitually use excessive alcohol are deficient in the capacity to extend themselves mentally into the future. In these people the tendencies toward a present orientation occur when not drinking as well as when drinking. In addition, low doses of alcohol in "normal" volunteers increased performances of immediately rewarded tasks despite the possibility of future punishment [50]. These studies show an increased tendency to act on the impulse of the present moment and a decreased consideration of future consequences. If angry, such people would have an increased propensity to attack.

Another theme associated with alcohol and violence is the frequency with which individuals involved in a violent interaction have had an ongoing personal relationship. In over 80 percent of all homicides involving alcohol, the victim and offender are relatives, lovers, or close personal friends [55]. In such personal relations expectations of the other develop, which increase the risk of being thwarted or unfulfilled. Consequently, the potential for ensuing dashed hopes, anger, and possible attack is raised. By contrast, less is expected of strangers, and thus frustrations are less likely to be taken as personal affronts.

The specific encounter between the offender and victim that culminates in assaultive behavior also follows predictable patterns. Violence is unusual in initial phases of these encounters. Instead there is a series of interactions consisting of events that enhance anger and possibilities for attack. This series of interactions often begins as an animated discussion, escalates to an angry argument, and then explodes into an assault. The significance of this interactional process is that at least *two* people are involved, either one of whom has the potential for reducing violence by disengaging at *various* points during the encounter. When violence is a culmination of such interactions, it is only after a series of opportunities for de-escalation of anger were not utilized by either party.

Although we have focused on the role of alcohol in the assailants, there are also significant associations between alcohol and the victim. In one comprehensive study of 588 homicides [56], 53 percent of the victims had been drinking, frequently with their ultimate killer. Other observers [42, 53] detected alcohol in up to 87 percent of the homicide victims examined. In addition to being less able to defend themselves physically against assaults, alcohol-using victims probably have impaired ability to perceive warning cues that the other's expectations are being dangerously thwarted. Because of their own focus on the present and on their own personal concerns, the victims are less inclined to modify their behavior in order to abort an assaultive culmination to a potentially dangerous series of interactions.

A final association between alcohol and violence is the physical method employed in homicidal interactions. In the most comprehensive study available [54] alcohol was involved more often in homicides resulting from sustained violence such as repeated stabbings or beating than with homicides from one shot or one blow. Again, the assailant had options to cease his attack but instead persisted in his assault to the exclusion of the consequences of his act and considerations of the victim.

In summary, alcohol frequently is involved in the entire process of violence from the initial relationship of the two principals to the final assault. In comparison to the other drugs we have examined in detail, alcohol is associated less frequently with violence than is methamphetamine but much more frequently than is marihuana.

LSD and Other Psychotomimetics

The *psychotomimetics* are drugs that, in proportion to their other effects, induce marked alterations of normal thoughts, perceptions, and moods. The most common drug of this class, marihuana, has been discussed; this section will focus on more potent psychotomimetics which include lysergic acid diethylamide (LSD), mescaline, psilocybin, dimethyltryptamine (DMT), and phenylcyclidine (Sernyl). Of this group LSD is the most common and will be discussed as a representative example.

LSD is one of the most potent drugs known to man. The ingestion of one-millionth of an ounce, barely visible to the naked eye, will produce noticeable effects in most people. These effects have become widely known through sensationalized reports in the mass media. The effects of LSD include somatic changes of dizziness, weakness, nausea, and blurred vision; perceptual alterations with distorted time sense, visual aberrations, and heightened auditory acuity; and psychic symptoms of rapid changes in mood, depersonalization, distortions in body image, and dissociation of oneself from external reality. As outlined in Hollister's informative text, *The Chemical Psychoses* [23], these effects usually occur in a sequential pattern. The somatic changes come first, then the perceptual alterations, and finally the psychic changes, although there often is considerable overlap among these three phases. LSD and other potent psychotomimetics have been touted as enhancing creativity, for improving interpersonal sensitivity, as an adjunct for various kinds of psychotherapy, and as an aid for many other kinds of human endeavors. However, extensive studies have failed to confirm these enthusiastic claims. To date, creditable scientists know of no beneficial effects from these drugs.

ASSOCIATIONS WITH VIOLENCE

LSD and other potent psychotomimetics seldom are associated with assaultive behavior. The user's attention usually is directed inward toward his own experiences, and the external events that might elicit anger usually have little significance. However, severe panic reactions (bummers or bad trips) and other untoward effects are

more common with these potent drugs than with the milder marihuana. During these panic states sporadic, unpredictable episodes of
anger and violence do occur. But because the user's perceptions are
distorted and planning abilities are impaired, he usually is not as dangerous as he otherwise could be. More frequent is accidental self-
injury or death resulting from fantasies of unusual powers such as
being able to fly or being invulnerable to moving automobiles.

DRUG FACTORS AND PSYCHOSOCIAL INTERACTIONS

LSD and other potent psychotomimetics impair coordination and
the performance of most physical activities. Weakness and lethargy
may be pronounced, further inhibiting any tendencies to take action. The user experiences continuous changes in his thought patterns, which make it difficult or impossible for him to maintain a
focus on an intensely personal or present view. These pharmacological effects usually interact to reduce the probability of violence.

However, as with marihuana there are occasional bad trips and
other adverse reactions with this group of psychotomimetics. Again,
widespread myths to the contrary, there is no way the user can
guarantee himself a tranquil trip by establishing appropriate surroundings or getting in the right frame of mind. LSD users report
having hundreds of good trips with pleasurable and ecstatic experiences, before inexplicably having a bummer replete with a demonol-
ogy of monstrous perceptions, undiluted horror, and occasional assaultive outbursts. These unexplainable bummers occur at all dose
levels but are more common with high doses. Unfortunately, accidental overdoses can easily occur because the purity of LSD varies
widely and is impossible to determine except in specialized laboratories. Also the extremely small amounts of drug in each dose require
skillful measurement, which again is seldom available in the illicit
marketplace.

Furthermore, some chronic LSD users demonstrate a pattern of
what we call "cumulative bummers." These individuals commonly
experience a series of good trips, then for unknown reasons have a
bummer. Thereafter, they become increasingly predisposed to unpleasant effects with LSD. Good trips become less frequent, and bad
trips more common. Often this group of chronic users persists in
taking LSD despite these unpleasant experiences in futile attempts to
recapture the good trips they formerly had. This phenomenon is
probably associated with the laboratory finding of Hollister [24] in
which LSD subjects demonstrated selective recall. While under the
influence of LSD, these subjects would describe a mixture of pleas-

ant and unpleasant sensations. But after recovering from the effects of the drug, they would selectively report the more positive aspects of their experience.

Finally, there is a disturbing incidence of other untoward effects in LSD users. Prolonged psychotic reactions and "flashback" phenomena have been demonstrated in both occasional and chronic users. Flashbacks are sudden, unexpected perceptual distortions and bizarre thoughts of an LSD trip that occur after the pharmacological effects of the drug have terminated (perhaps months or years since the last ingestion).

SUMMARY

Although violence may be associated with flashbacks, psychotic reactions, and cumulative bummers, more commonly the predominant fear and anxiety preclude assaultive behavior. Thus, in general, LSD and other potent psychotomimetics have minimal associations with violent behavior. The violence that does occur usually accompanies the panic of an untoward reaction, is poorly enacted, and is often self-directed.

Opiates

Heroin, morphine, and opium are all members of a group of drugs known as the opiate alkaloids. These drugs are usually classified as narcotics and are used medically for their analgesic properties. Addiction to these drugs has been a continuing problem in the United States for over a century. Heroin is usually the preferred drug among today's narcotic addicts and goes by such names as "H," "smack," and "junk." Other drugs in this category, which at present are less common sources of addiction, include codeine, methadone, and demerol. Most of these drugs can be taken in a variety of ways: Heroin is commonly injected or sniffed, opium smoked or ingested, and morphine injected.

ASSOCIATIONS WITH VIOLENCE

Opiate users come from very diverse groups. In some of these groups violent behavior is prevalent; in others, violent acts are rare. The evidence to date suggests that in none of these groups is the probability of violent behavior substantially increased by opiate use. This evidence refutes the widespread public belief that the use of "hard-core narcotics" inevitably leads to criminality and violence. It has been the experience of several investigators, particularly in England where narcotics are legally obtainable, that many addicts are capable of leading useful, law-abiding lives provided they can maintain themselves with a legitimate supply of these drugs. In this country such supplies cannot be obtained legally. Illicit sources are expensive; $100 a day or more may be required to sustain the habit and prevent the extremely unpleasant mental and physical withdrawal symptoms. Many opiate users do not have the legitimate income to handle such a costly enterprise and thus turn to criminal activities, particularly crimes against property. Available evidence indicates that although force and violence occasionally are involved in such activities, nonviolent behavior predominates.

As with users of most illicit drugs, the opiate user is likely to have contact with a variety of criminals. Although the economy of opiate distribution and marketing is well regulated and tranquil in comparison to the methamphetamine scene, violent disputes over such issues as territorial rights (who is going to be the dealer for the area) do occasionally occur. Such violence may of course involve nonusers as well as opiate addicts.

Opiates also contribute to self-destructive violence in the form of accidental overdose or suicide. Although we have not been able to find precise figures, opiates are probably involved to a much lesser degree in suicide attempts than are either alcohol or the barbiturates. One other condition of opiate use, the withdrawal sydrome, has implications for violence and will be discussed in the following section.

DRUG FACTORS AND PSYCHOSOCIAL INTERACTIONS

The acute pharmacological effects of the opiates include relief of tension and anxiety, decrease in physical drive, drowsiness, and analgesia. Some users experience a sense of well-being and euphoria, but other individuals, particularly if they are not anxious or in pain, experience distinct unpleasantness from the opiates. Most authorities agree that these acute effects reduce tendencies toward violence; as Brill [9] states, ". . . in themselves opiates have a sedative value; they hold back rather than incite aggressive action. . . ."

The chronic effects of opiates include quite different results. Opiates have considerable addictive potential. Addiction, however, does not invariably result from repeated use of opiates; individual susceptibility, peer pressures, and so forth, play crucial roles. Opiate addiction has long been ascribed to minority groups among the urban poor, although they by no means have a monopoly. Among occupational groups physicians have by far the highest rates of addiction, perhaps because of their easy, unsupervised access to these drugs. In recent years there has been a dramatic increase of opiate usage among drug-oriented, middle- and upper-class youths. In *Students and Drugs* Blum and associates [5] document this trend but add that so far there are no reports of increased violence or full-blown addiction among these youths. The diversity of these three groups—the urban poor, physicians, and affluent middle- and upper-class students —again illustrates the importance of nondrug factors in determining patterns of drug use.

The painful withdrawal syndrome following cessation of long-term opiate consumption is an important factor in perpetuating the use of opiates. This syndrome includes restlessness, irritability, shaking chills, and uncontrollable muscular agitation and twitches. The addict's concerns are on the very personal focus of quickly getting more drugs to avoid these discomforts. During withdrawal the addict becomes intensely oriented on his urgent need to avoid the discomfort and is less aware of the future consequences of his continued drug abuse. A sense of desperation may be felt if drug supplies seem unobtainable. Anger and assault may occur if the addict feels that others are intentionally withholding the desired drugs from him. In addition, when such people are armed, the muscular agitation associated with withdrawal increases the possibility of unintentional shootings.

These increased propensities for anger and assaultive behavior during the withdrawal phase seem to occur in many of the different groups of opiate addicts. English treatment centers have reported destructive outbursts from their middle-class addicts who come for maintenance doses; similar uncooperativeness has been described for morphine-addicted physicians [37, 42]. Thus such tendencies for violence cannot be wholly ascribed to psychosocial interactions; drug factors must be considered.

One recent pattern of opiate use that may have implications for violence involves the modality of intake. Some opiates, particularly heroin and morphine, are used by addicts as "needle drugs," that is, injected intravenously. These drug users are more likely to take other types of drugs intravenously as well. In the San Francisco Bay area this means they are more likely to inject drugs, including methamphetamine, that, as previously described, increase the probability for assaultive behavior. The association between the modality of drug consumption and subsequent patterns of drug use has historical precedence. The Chinese ingested opiates for centuries without significant addiction problems. In the seventeenth century, the Portuguese introduced tobacco smoking, and soon opiates were consumed using the "new" modality of smoking. Subsequently addiction became widespread.

SUMMARY

Although users of the opiates are not associated with a generalized increase in violence, there are specific situations, particularly during drug withdrawal, in which users do become more inclined toward assault. In addition, opiate users are likely to be drawn into the criminal world where violence is inherent. In recent years the opiates are being used by more young people. The implications of this trend are unclear, but judging from the history of opiates, benefits to the user or society are unlikely.

Barbiturates and Other Sedative-hypnotics

The sedative-hypnotics are synthetic drugs that are classified as central nervous system depressants. Their usual acute effects include muscular incoordination, slurring of speech, changes in mood, decreased activity, and drowsiness or sleep. They are widely used for such medical purposes as the treatment of insomnia, seizure control, daytime sedation, and for anesthesia. However, they increasingly are being used illicitly for obliterating or altering awareness, often in combination with illicit use of such drugs as methamphetamine. We shall discuss the barbiturates as a representative example of this group, as they are the most common. Barbiturates, classified as "downers" among drug users, are known by a variety of names usually related to the appearance of a common trade brand. Such names include "yellows" (Nembutal), "red devils" (Seconal), "blue heavens" (Amytal), "rainbows" (Tuinal), and others. These drugs are usually ingested orally but may be injected.

ASSOCIATIONS WITH VIOLENCE

When the sedative drugs are used under proper medical supervision, their calming and soothing properties usually suppress violence, particularly with severely agitated and disturbed people. However, there are occasional episodes of paradoxical excitation and associated assaultive behavior with these drugs. This excitation seems to occur more readily when the drugs are used by people who are prone toward violence in a nondrugged state. Some drug users ingest barbiturates, become surly and drowsy, and then inject a stimulant such as methamphetamine or cocaine. In our experience and according to Smith and Meyers [46], these people develop extreme predilection for anger and attacking behavior. These conditions where sedatives are associated with violence, although apparently on the increase, are still unusual. In general, sedatives suppress more violence than they enhance.

However, in the area of self-destructive behavior, barbiturates and other sedatives clearly pose a major health problem. Barbiturates are currently the most frequent means of suicide among American women and account for over three thousand known deaths a year in this country. The actual incidence of barbiturate use in suicide is impossible to establish, as some suicides go unreported or undiagnosed. In addition, there are accidental deaths resulting from the combined use of barbiturates and alcohol, neither of which by itself would have proved fatal. Both drugs have depressant effects on the brain that can potentiate each other and produce cessation of breathing. Other barbiturate deaths may accidentally occur because of the drowsy condition following an initial dose, during which additional doses may be taken unintentionally.

The associations between sedatives and automobile accidents are poorly understood at this time. Because sedatives and alcohol share many common physiological effects, sedatives perhaps are involved in accidents in a pattern similar to alcohol. Accordingly, the association of sedatives with accidents would be heavily dependent on dose, individual drivers, and other factors.

Although we have focused our discussion on barbiturates, we expect that as the use of other sedatives becomes more widespread, similar problems will emerge. A recent example is provided by glutethimide compounds (Doriden), which was initially marketed as a safe, nonaddicting sedative. Subsequent reports indicate that, as with barbiturates, the untoward effects of addiction, withdrawal complications, suicides, and involvement in automobile accidents do occur with Doriden.

DRUG FACTORS AND
PSYCHOSOCIAL INTERACTIONS

As one would expect, the sedatives generally reduce tension and activity, so that incipient assaultive or disruptive behavior is less likely to occur. In most people the hypnotic (sleep-inducing) effect usually takes place soon after ingestion, reducing tendencies toward taking action of any kind. However, as mentioned, some individuals respond in a paradoxical fashion with increased irritability and activity, particularly if they have been taking high doses for some time. These people may demonstrate sudden outbursts of assaultive behavior, particularly if provoked.

On repeated use of most barbiturates tolerance develops, so that increasingly larger amounts of drugs are required to produce the desired effects. Some individuals become dependent on barbiturates and need to ingest twenty-five times the daily dose to get the same effect as would a nondependent user. Even when only four or five times the usual daily dose is consumed, symptoms of anxiety and tremulousness will occur if withdrawal is attempted. Withdrawal symptoms may become severe and include dizziness, muscular twitches, convulsions, unpleasant persecutory hallucinations, and occasional full-blown paranoid reactions characterized by inappropriate hostility and assaultive behavior. Even death may occur during withdrawal. This syndrome has been compared with delirium tremens following withdrawal from alcohol. One author [17] speaks of "barbiturism" to underscore the similarities between addictive potentials and withdrawal effects of alcohol and barbiturates.

SUMMARY

The barbiturates and other sedatives provide a complicated picture with respect to violence. If properly used, they are helpful in suppressing the tensions and frustrations that may give rise to anger and assaultive behavior. However, they can evoke irritability and unpredictable assault in some instances: in paradoxical reactions, in high doses, in combination with other drugs, and during withdrawal when addiction has occurred. Barbiturates are clearly involved in many suicides in the United States. Their role in automobile accidents is not well defined but may be similar to that played by alcohol.

Other Drugs and Delirium

Many other drugs, in addition to those discussed, are sometimes associated with an abnormal behavioral condition, resulting from general impairment of brain function, called delirium. This condition is characterized by changing levels of awareness to surrounding events and by decreased ability to maintain attention on any specific task. In addition, there are variable amounts of mental confusion including difficulties in maintaining time-space orientation and transient memory defects, particularly for recent events. Judgment and appraisal of the environment may be impaired. These impairments in mental function often are associated with temporary changes in normal neurological functioning, for example, incoordination and changes in reflexes. Although delirious conditions are similar in many respects to the effects of psychotomimetic drugs such as LSD, they differ in that psychotomimetic drugs seldom induce disorientation or neurological change. The delirious state is caused by a large number of agents that impair brain function, such as toxic illness, high fever, dehydration, starvation, and a wide variety of drugs. Delirium, whatever the cause, sometimes is associated with assaultive behavior even in people who are not usually prone to violence.

Excessive amounts of bromides, belladonna alkaloids, and most other drugs used for tranquilization or sedation can be associated with delirium. These compounds are readily available to most people either by prescription or as over-the-counter proprietary preparations. A few people react idiosyncratically with delirium to the routine use of such common drugs as sulfa, penicillin, or even aspirin. Delirium can also result from sniffing or inhaling glue, various aerosols, volatile solvents, kerosene, or gasoline.

Fortunately, delirious individuals, even when assaultive, seldom have sufficient control over their behavior to endanger the lives of others as often as one might expect. More commonly their outbursts result in social disruption, property damage, or self-harm. The wide spectrum of agents available to produce such delirium precludes extensive preventive measures other than continued education on the hazards and recognition of this phenomenon.

Drugs and the Prevention of Violence

Throughout the centuries man has turned to drugs for the relief of distress, for altering awareness, for facilitating social encounters, and for many other reasons. Thus it is understandable that man now turns to drugs in his quest to curb violence. At present, however, there are no drugs available that selectively prevent assaultive behavior without severely affecting most other activities. The development of such a drug, if possible, would be exceedingly difficult because of the diversity of forces that may contribute to the generation of violence.

Still, there are some circumstances where drugs are helpful in reducing assaultive behavior. The best example is the use of phenothia-zine-type tranquilizers (Thorazine is one of the best known) in re-ducing violent outbursts in severely disturbed, psychotic individuals. The pharmacological properties of these tranquilizers induce a marked decrease in aggressiveness and assaultiveness while still per-mitting the individual to continue other activities. However, the usefulness of these drugs has not been demonstrated in curbing the violence of those people who are prone to assaultive behavior but who are not psychotic. Such people are likely to find the sedation and other action-inhibiting effects of these drugs unpleasant and will usually discontinue them unless they are under close medical super-vision. Thus the prophylactic use of such tranquilizers is of limited value in reducing violence, because the people to whom they might be most helpful are unlikely to use them consistently. Similarly the nonphenothiazine-type tranquilizers and the sedative-hypnotic drugs have limited use in preventing violence. In easily angered individuals with poor impulse control, near-anesthetic doses are required to curb assaultive outbursts. However, these drugs may reduce agita-tion and distress in the initial stages of anger and thus preclude fur-ther escalation of the anger. Also since the tranquilizing effects of some of these drugs have been extensively touted by mass media advertising, many people have learned to expect soothing sedation. When such sedation is expected, it is more likely to occur.

Drugs delivered from a distance to uncooperative individuals via aerosols, gases, and such projectiles as dart guns, are limited by a number of considerations. Agents that control violence by inflicting painful disability may incur the long-range consequences of escalat-ing violence by increasing antagonism and polarization between the parties involved. Drugs that curb assaultiveness by acting directly on the nervous system, such as tranquilizers, sedatives, and various "nerve gases," are hazardous. Their effectiveness is very dependent on such variables as the size and susceptibility of the recipient. A dose that would control the assaultive outburst of a large man might prove injurious or lethal to a smaller man. Despite these present limi-tations the use of these drugs for violence control is preferable to inflicting further violence by using guns or clubs. In addition, future technological advancement may produce chemical agents that are less likely to incur harmful side effects. However, such drugs are unlikely to provide a panacea for controlling violence; the preven-tion of violence by the means of education, frustration reduction, and conflict resolution will continue to be essential.

Implications

In the preceding sections of this chapter we have reviewed what presently is known about associations between drug users and violent behavior. Most available information is from descriptive studies; in many areas there have been no systematic investigations of any kind. Understanding the issue is further complicated by rapid changes in the amount and variety of drugs available to the user, patterns of drug consumption, and crucial psychosocial variables. When the limited knowledge about drugs and drug users is contrasted with the extensive use of drugs, the urgent need for systematic research becomes clear. Several implications for further research merit explicit emphasis.

An important implication for future investigation is the range of different behavioral responses that result from varied doses of the same drug. Although it is tempting to observe the behavioral effects of a given drug dosage and infer similar behavior at all dose levels, such inferences are likely to be inaccurate. For example, in our experiments low doses of marihuana were usually associated with peaceful lassitude, but high doses in the same individual under identical conditions sometimes evoked frenzied paranoid reactions [36]. Similarly in one study [58] on drinking and driving behavior, different levels of blood alcohol were associated with different accident probabilities.

Figure 8 is partially derived from this study. The estimated number of drinks is a rough guide in which a drink refers to one cocktail, five ounces of table wine, or one bottle of beer. The cited number of drinks is the minimum for an average-sized person (150 pounds). More drinks would be required to achieve a given blood level if the drinker were heavier, absorption were delayed by food in the stomach, the drinking took place over a prolonged period of time, and so forth. The "relative probability" represents the increased chances that a drinking driver would have an accident as compared to a nondrinking driver.

The small dip between arrows *a* and *b* illustrates that in this study different doses of the same drug, alcohol, are associated with opposite behavioral probabilities. At the dose levels of arrow *a*, small additional amounts of alcohol *decrease* the chances of an accident, when all drivers are considered. But when blood alcohol is at the level indicated by arrow *b* or higher, more drinks "for the road" markedly *increase* the probability of an accident. The graph is discon-

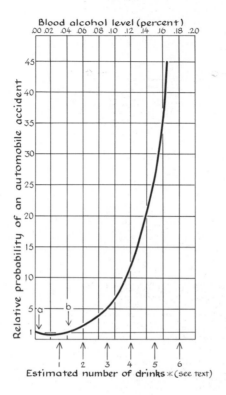

Fig. 8. The relative probability of being involved in an automobile accident according to different blood alcohol levels [58]

tinued at 0.17 because the number of drivers beyond that level was too small to make statistical inferences.

Another implication results from the fact that various people respond differently to the same doses of the same drug. Low doses of marihuana usually induce passivity and lassitude, but the same low doses, in a few people, are associated with aggressivity and assault. Low doses of alcohol in most people are accompanied by slight changes in mood and level of tensions; in a few people the same low doses bring on the poorly understood clinical entity of "pathological intoxication" with its associated violent outbursts. Two additional factors that may influence different responses are the age and developmental level of the drug user. For example, the effects of a given drug dosage on a 12-year-old youth differ from the effects on a 32-year-old adult. A 12-year-old is struggling with many developmental and physiological changes. Such factors make the youth more susceptible to adverse effects of behavior-altering drugs [3]. The previous examples illustrate the importance of dosage factors in affecting the behavior of drug users.

In the previous sections we usually discussed each group of drugs as if they were used only one at a time. In reality, issues are more complex, since the use of drug combinations is common. These combinations may be ingested or injected all at once or be used tandemly. One combination that seems particularly to predispose an individual to assaultive behavior is the use of barbiturates followed by intravenous methamphetamine. Virtually no systematic data about such combinations of drugs have been obtained, despite their prevalence and widespread association with violence.

Consideration also must be given to the interactions of nondrug elements that contribute to generating assaultive episodes. For example, we indicated that with chronic users of intravenous methamphetamine the interactions of three nondrug elements significantly contribute to the potential for violence: (1) a psychological milieu of intense distrust, (2) group expectations that any insults or inequities be avenged, and (3) the prevalence of concealed weapons among amphetamine users.

The interplay of drug and nondrug factors necessarily complicates investigation into the behavior of drug users. Laboratory research is limited by the difficulty of replicating crucial social and psychological variables. Naturalistic studies are appropriate but require extensive effort and careful attention to research design. One model for investigating drug users in a natural setting is provided by the well-designed study of drinking and driving cited previously [58]. In this study systematic data, including breath analysis for alcohol, were obtained from drivers who were involved in traffic accidents. The same data were collected from a control group of nonaccident drivers selected randomly at the times and locations at which previous accidents had occurred. Thus the control group constituted a "population at risk" who were engaged in the same behavior, driving, as the accident drivers and theoretically were at equal risk to be involved in an accident. Similarly, in the study of the associations between methamphetamine use and violence, controls could include a population at risk group. This group would be nonviolent speed users who had been exposed to situations that evoked assaultive behavior in other speed users. Crucial psychosocial factors could be explored, and the pharmacological factors would not be overly emphasized.

Conclusions and Recommendations

This chapter has described some of the violence associated with different groups of drug users. Long-term users of intravenous methamphetamine are frequently involved in assaultive behavior. In addition, amphetamines are linked with the development of paranoid reactions that enhance probabilities for assault. By contrast the current social use of marihuana in the United States is usually characterized by passivity, lassitude, and nonviolence.

These extremes illustrate the varied probabilities of violence associated with the use of different drugs. Violence results from an interplay of drug and nondrug factors that include type of drug, dosage, modality and frequency of use, personality of users, age of the users, expectations of peers, and availability of lethal weapons. The Melges-Harris cybernetic model developed in Chapter 4 regarding anger and the transformation of anger into attack is utilized to organize these diverse elements into a coherent framework.

The public, however, tends to focus exclusively on drug factors and to minimize the contribution of other factors in the behavior of drug users. This focus is limited to inappropriately specific "bad" drugs, such as opiates and marihuana, when in fact any behavior-altering drug—for example, "good" drugs like tranquilizers—can be used abusively. In sufficient amounts almost any drug can cause impairment of judgment and coping processes, which in turn can increase the likelihood of indiscriminate behavior including violence. Furthermore, the period of withdrawal from these drugs after prolonged use is a particularly dangerous time, since the immediate need state of the individual inclines him toward an exclusive present and personal orientation and hence toward violent action. Unless the entire spectrum of psychosocial and drug factors in drug use is considered, important contributions to violent behavior will be missed or ignored.

The discrepancy between the extensive use of drugs in our society and the lack of information about their effects is striking. We consider this discrepancy a mandate for extensive, systematic investigation of drugs and drug users. In general, we advocate a cautious approach toward unsupervised use of marihuana and other drugs where information about idiosyncratic reactions and long-term effects is meager. Our cautious stance results from the consideration of such drugs as tobacco, which had widespread use for decades before the long-term consequences of increased lung cancer and heart disease were "discovered."

Based upon our current knowledge concerning the relations between violence and drug use, we make the following recommendations.

First, our educational programs should teach the dangers and harmful effects of specific drugs, the patterns of drug use, and the appropriate and safe use of drugs. These programs need to include students at all levels, their parents, teachers, and professionals involved in the mass media.

Second, severe restrictions on the availability of basic ingredients for methamphetamine and closely related amphetamines are indicated, as these drugs are frequently associated with disturbed and violent behavior. Further efforts to curb illicit amphetamine use also are needed. Similarly, current data indicate that restrictions should be increased against driving after drinking. On the other hand, at least from the standpoint of violent behavior, there is no justification for the present heavy penalties imposed on marihuana users in this country. Continuing revisions of legal sanctions are necessary as more information becomes available.

Third, as indicated previously, increased research into drug effects and drug users is an urgent need. These investigations should include the factors and drugs that decrease as well as increase tendencies toward violence. Current restrictions on research with marihuana and some other drugs affecting behavior severely impede the understanding of the relationship between drugs and behavior and should be modified.

As drugs have been an integral part of our past, all evidence suggests they will be an important part of our future. Therefore, our long-range adaptation must include learning more about the drug parameters and psychosocial interactions of drug use. Wise application of such knowledge is required if we are to minimize the violence and other harmful effects associated with specific drugs.

Acknowledgment

We appreciate the helpful contributions of Mrs. Barbara Baxter, Mrs. Rachelle Marshall, and Mrs. Mary Shapiro.

References

1. Arai, N., Iijima, Y., and Nimura, T. Prevention of juvenile offenses. *Bulletin of the Police Scientific Crime Detection Laboratory* 23:145, 1962.

2. Blum, R. H.   Mind altering drugs and dangerous behavior: Alcohol. *Task Force Report on Narcotics and Drug Abuse*. Washington, D.C.: U.S. Government Printing Office, 1967.

3. Blum, R. H.   Drugs and Violence. A consultant's report prepared for the National Commission on the Causes and Prevention of Violence. Stanford, Cal., 1969.

4. Blum, R. H.   *Society and Drugs*. San Francisco: Jossey-Bass, 1969.

5. Blum, R. H.   *Students and Drugs*. San Francisco: Jossey-Bass, 1969.

6. Blumer, H., Sutter, A., Ahmed, S., and Smith, R.   *ADD Center Project Final Report: The World of Youthful Drug Use*. Berkeley, Cal.: University of California Press, 1967.

7. Breamish, P., and Kiloh, L.   Psychosis due to amphetamine consumption. *Journal of Mental Sciences* 106:337, 1960.

8. Bridges, C. (Director of Criminal Statistics, Department of Justice, State of California).   Personal communication, Jan. 3, 1969.

9. Brill, H.   Misapprehension: Drug addiction. *Comprehensive Psychiatry* 4:150, 1963.

10. Carpenter, J. A.   Contributions from psychology to the study of drinking and driving. *Quarterly Journal of Studies on Alcohol*. (Suppl.) 4:234, 1968.

11. Clark, J., Hannigan, H., and Hart, J.   Alcoholism, a parole problem: A statistical study of 100 male felons paroled from Sing Sing Prison to the New York City area during 1962. *Current Projects in the Prevention, Control, and Treatment of Crime and Delinquency* 6:353, 1964–65.

12. Cohen, S.   Pot, acid and speed. *Medical Sciences* 19:31, 1968.

13. Connell, P. H.   *Amphetamine Psychosis*. Maudsley Monograph 5. London: Chapman & Hall, 1958.

14. Currie, N. (Director, Narcotics and Dangerous Drug Division, San Francisco).   Personal communication, Jan. 3, 1969.

15. Derville, P., L'eppe, P., Lazarini, H. J., and Derville, E.   Statistical indications of a possible relationship between alcoholism and criminality: An inquiry in the Bordeaux region. *Revue Alcoholisme* 7:20, 1961.

16. Ellinwood, E. H.   Amphetamine psychosis: 1. Description of individuals and process. *Journal of Nervous and Mental Diseases* 144:237, 1967.

17. Fort, J.   The problem of barbiturates in the U.S.A. *Bulletin on Narcotics* 16:17, 1964.

18. Foulks, J. D.   Stability of Temporal Orientation of Diagnostic Groups. Paper presented at Southeastern Psychological Association Convention, Atlanta, Ga., Apr. 13, 1967.

19. Gillies, H.   Murder in West Scotland. *British Journal of Psychiatry* 111:1087, 1965.

20. Gliedman, L. H.   Temporal orientation and alcoholism. *Addictions* 3:11, 1956.

21. Guttmacher, M.   The Normal and the Sociopathic Murderer. In Wolfgang, M. (Ed.), *Studies in Homicide*. New York: Harper & Row, 1967.

22. Hampton, W. H.   Observed psychiatric reactions following use of

amphetamine-like substance. *Bulletin of the New York Academy of Medicine* 37: 167, 1961.

23. Hollister, L. E. *Chemical Psychoses.* Springfield, Ill.: Thomas, 1968.
24. Hollister, L. E., Richards, R. K., and Gillespie, B. A. Comparison of tetrahydrocannabinol and synhexyl in man. *Clinical Pharmacology and Therapeutics* 9:383, 1968.
25. Horton, D. The functions of alcohol in primitive societies: A cross-cultural study. *Quarterly Journal of Studies on Alcohol* 4:199, 1943.
26. Isbell, H., Gorodetzsky, G., Jasinski, D., Claussen, U., Spulak, F., and Korte, F. Effects of trans-tetrahydrocannabinol in man. *Psychopharmacologia* 11: 185, 1967.
27. Kosman, M. E., and Unna, K. R. Effects of chronic administration of the amphetamines and other stimulants on behavior. *Clinical Pharmacology and Therapeutics* 9:240, 1968.
28. Leake, C. D. *The Amphetamines.* Springfield, Ill.: Thomas, 1958.
29. Louria, D. B. *The Drug Scene.* New York: McGraw-Hill, 1968.
30. Lucia, S. P. *A History of Wine as Therapy.* Philadelphia: Lippincott, 1963.
31. MacDonald, J. M. *The Murderer and His Victim.* Springfield, Ill.: Thomas, 1961.
32. McFarland, R. A. Alcohol and highway accidents: A summary of present knowledge. *Traffic Digest and Review* 5:30, 1964.
33. McGeorge, J. Alcohol and crime. *Medicine, Science and Law* 3:27, 1963.
34. Melges, F. T., and Bowlby, J. Types of hopelessness in psychopathological process. *Archives of General Psychiatry* 20:690, 1969.
35. Melges, F. T., Tinklenberg, J. R., and Fougerousse, C. E. Paranoid delusions—possible mechanisms. In preparation.
36. Melges, F. T., Tinklenberg, J. R., Hollister, L., and Gillespie, H. Cannabinols (marihuana extracts) and time sense. In preparation.
37. Modlin, H. C., and Montes, A. Narcotics addiction in physicians. *American Journal of Psychiatry* 121:358, 1964.
38. O'Connor, M. (Supervisor, Federal Bureau of Narcotic Enforcement, State of California). Personal communication, Jan. 3, 1969.
39. Palola, E. G., Dorpat, T. L., and Larsen, W. R. Alcoholism and Suicidal Behavior. In Pittman, D. J., and Snyder, C. R. (Eds.), *Society, Culture, and Drinking Patterns.* New York: Wiley, 1962.
40. Park, P. Problem and Role Differentiation: A Study in Incipient Alcoholism. In Pittman, D. J., and Snyder, C. R. (Eds.), *Society, Culture, and Drinking Patterns.* New York: Wiley, 1962.
41. Pittman, D. J., and Gordon, C. W. Criminal Careers of the Chronic Drunkenness Offender. In Pittman, D. J., and Snyder, C. R. (Eds.), *Society, Culture, and Drinking Patterns.* New York: Wiley, 1962.
42. Sapira, J. D. The narcotic addict as a medical patient. *American Journal of Medicine* 45: 150, 1963.
43. Schnadt, F. W. A Study of Alcoholic Personality. Unpublished Ph.D. thesis, Washington University (St. Louis, Mo.), 1950.
44. Shupe, L. M. Alcohol and crime. A study of the urine alcohol concentration found in 882 persons arrested during or immediately after

the commission of a felony. *Journal of Criminal Law and Criminology* 44:661, 1954.

45. Smart, R. G.   Future time perspective in alcoholics and social drinkers. *Journal of Abnormal Psychology* 73:81, 1968.

46. Smith, R., and Meyers, F.   *The Market Place of Speed*. Berkeley, Cal.: University of California Press. In press.

47. Spain, D. M., Bradess, V. A., and Eggston, A. A.   Alcohol and violent death. A one year study of consecutive cases in a representative community. *Journal of the American Medical Association* 146: 334, 1951.

48. Takala, M., Pihkanen, T. A., and Markkanen, J.   *The Effects of Distilled and Brewed Beverages*. Helsinki, Finland: The Finnish Foundation for Alcohol Studies, Publication 4, 1957.

49. Tinklenberg, J. T., and Melges, F. T.   Marihuana maelstroms—adverse reactions to marihuana. In preparation.

50. Vogel-Sprott, M. D.   Alcohol effects on human behavior in reward and punishment. *Psychopharmacologia* 11:337, 1967.

51. Voss, H. L., and Hepburn, J. R.   Patterns in criminal homicide in Chicago. *Journal of Criminal Law, Criminology and Police Science* 59:499, 1968.

52. Weisz, A. E. (Stanford Department of Psychiatry). Personal communication, 1969.

53. Wilentz, W. C.   The alcohol factor in violent deaths. *American Practitioner and Digest of Treatment* 4:21, 1953.

54. Wolfgang, M. E.   *Patterns in Criminal Homicide*. Philadelphia: University of Pennsylvania Press, 1958.

55. Wolfgang, M. E. (Ed.).   *Studies in Homicide*. New York: Harper & Row, 1967.

56. Wolfgang, M. E.   Victim Precipitated Criminal Homicide. In Wolfgang, M. E. (Ed.), *Studies in Homicide*. New York: Harper & Row, 1967.

57. Young, D., and Scoville, W. B.   Paranoid psychosis in narcolepsy and possible danger of benzedrine treatment. *Medical Clinics of North America* 22:637, 1938.

58. Zylman, R.   Accidents, alcohol, and single cause explanations: Lessons from the Grand Rapids Study. *Quarterly Journal of Studies on Alcohol*. (Suppl.)4:212, 1968.

13. *Case Studies of Violence*

George F. Solomon, M.D.

Thⁱhis chapter describes three individuals whose violent acts were related to mental disturbances. It complements other sections of this book, especially those chapters dealing with mental illness and violence, the relationship of drugs to violence, psychodynamics of aggression, anger and attack, and the relationship of gun control to violence. There is also a concluding recommendation section on treatment of the violent offender.

Grossly manifest psychopathology, especially psychosis, often gives clues to mental mechanisms that may operate more subtly on an unconscious level in less obviously disturbed persons, and indeed to some extent in all of us. The selection of these particular cases (who are not "typical" murderers, if there be such) was also related to their availability for psychiatric study. The first case is that of "senseless" shootings of strangers by an individual with a long history of antisocial behavior while under the influence of drugs. His "irrational" act can be at least partially understood in terms of overwhelming unconscious guilt. The second case, in contrast, is that of an overcontrolled individual with a history of mental illness and of interest in guns, whose shooting a stranger reflected a sudden breakthrough of repressed hostility. The third case is presented in much more detail because of the availability of rich autobiographical material and of a tape recording of the actual murder. It shows the role of provocation and desperation and the difficulties inherent in the concepts of responsibility and intent. Whenever possible, minimally edited direct quotations are utilized. Identifying information is of course disguised.

The reader should keep in mind the complex medical, social, psychological, and developmental issues making up the etiology of violence; the role of the availability of weapons in destructive acts; the nature of previolent behavior and communication that might have been heeded in order to prevent these tragedies; and the question of legal responsibility. The reader might try to empathize with the killer's dilemma by trying to understand how the act of murder may have been an attempt at conflict resolution in the face of provocation, improverishment of coping strategies, impairment of rational thinking, and feelings of desperation and rage. Hence the purpose of this chapter of case histories is to demonstrate with concrete and tragic examples the many elements of violence discussed throughout this book.

A Roving Sniper

Rick Anderson is a 28-year-old, white, married male who was found not guilty of murder by reason of insanity (toxic psychosis secondary to amphetamines). He had killed one woman and wounded three other people, all strangers, during two shooting sprees three days apart.

Rick has a long history of antisocial behavior. There were many, many arrests for a variety of offenses, especially the use and selling of narcotics, burglary, and drunkenness. Rick described some of his arrests as "harassment." He admitted that he had always exploited others. In his drug sales he was a "bum artist," a person selling bad drugs, and he had a notorious reputation as such. He carried a gun most of the time. Rick had a thirteen-year history of drug-taking. However, for the first nine months of his marriage, which had taken place two years prior to the crime, he had not taken drugs. He claimed that for a year prior to his arrest he had been taking 60 to 70 amphetamine tablets a day because stimulants "relieved me of feelings." Whenever he got into difficulties, Rick would turn to his father and would become enraged if Father did not help. Rick described his need for immediate gratification. "When I didn't get what I wanted right away, I would get in such a rage I would vomit." He was never able to express any tender feelings, which he occasionally felt, because he considered tenderness unmanly and because he was hesitant to place himself in any position of vulnerability. Often when he had become fond of a woman, he would break off the relationship. He did not feel part of any group, even drug groups. His first close friendship was formed in a hospital for the criminally insane. (This friend subsequently made an armed escape from the maximum security institution and murdered a hostage.)

Rick had always liked guns. About a year prior to the shootings, he picked up a hitchhiker who invited him home ostensibly to make a drug deal. They "rolled some joints," drank wine mixed with gin, and "dropped a roll of bennies." Rick's host showed him a .38 caliber pistol that had been stolen from a police officer, and Rick immediately determined to own it. "I've always had a thing about guns ever since my father got me a rifle when I was thirteen. That was the only time before I ever shot anything alive, a rabbit, and I cried like a baby when I saw what I had done." Rick offered eighty dollars for the gun but was turned down. "I decided I was going to get it even if I had to beat him over the head." The host went out for a moment. Rick took the gun and left. This emotionally highly valued, twice-stolen gun subsequently became the murder weapon.

During Rick's childhood his father was absent from the home much of the time and did a great deal of gambling. When the father felt guilty about neglecting his son, he would buy him gifts. Rick was jealous of his two-year younger brother. When Rick was 7, he threw a ball into the street for his brother to chase, purposely exposing him to danger. The brother was hit by a car and subsequently was unconscious for thirty-one days. After this "accident" Rick ran into the house in a rage and tore up the beds and broke things. He felt more neglected after his brother came home from the hospital, since his mother spent even more time with the brother. About this time his mother started drinking and became more neglectful of all the family. When Rick was 12 years old, he found his mother in bed with a policeman, who subsequently gave him gifts as a bribe for silence. The second time he observed his mother with this man, he told his father, who seemed quite indifferent. Shortly after this event his mother abandoned the family.

When Rick was 15, his mother returned. Shortly after her return, while drunk, she approached him sexually. Although there was no overt sexual contact until later occasions, he became quite disturbed at the initial attempt at seduction. "It blew my mind." Rick's first crime was committed that night. He broke into a jewelry store with a hammer and stole costume jewelry for his mother, which she accepted. From this point on, his antisocial behavior increased and his drug history began. Rick was horrified by but unable to free himself of his sexual desires for his mother. Often he would encourage her into drunkenness so that sexual relations would occur. Following each of these episodes he would become enraged, which often resulted in a tantrum.

Rick's first marriage, at age 18, was to a girl of 16. They were separated several times and finally divorced while he was in prison for burglary at the age of 20. He feels that his mother's meddling ruined the marriage. While in jails and prisons, he participated in homosexual acts, which resulted in continuing concern about homosexuality. Approximately two years prior to his last offense, Rick married a woman eight years his senior. He was quite jealous of her three children by a prior marriage, finally insisting that they be sent to her former husband. Their own child was five months old at the time of the snipings. With the birth of this child there was a crisis. Rick was continually beset by murderous impulses toward the child.

On a holiday evening after having gotten "loaded" on alcohol, barbiturates, and marihuana, Rick left his father's home and proceeded to a liquor store, where he bought more gin. He went home and picked up his gun and started driving. At first, as he drove, he shot at windows aimlessly. Later he saw a young woman getting into her car. He shot at her and went home after shooting out a few more windows. In the morning he read in the newspaper that a woman getting into her car had been killed and that her boyfriend had been arrested for murder. Rick told his wife that he thought he had killed a woman, but she said he must be imagining things. He continued heavy amphetamine intake. Three days later he took his gun and started driving. "I saw two older women in a car and decided to shoot them. I thought I'd really be accomplishing something. I followed them on to the freeway. I emptied a clip into their window." He was passed by a newspaper truck, the driver of which looked at him. "I thought, 'Why is the guy looking at me?'" Rick then shot into the truck, wounding the driver. Next he drove off the freeway, followed by the truck, reloaded and emptied the gun into the truck, which drove on. Continuing to drive, Rick saw others he wanted to shoot, but there "was never an opportune moment, always another car in the way or something." "It was anyone I saw, for example, a kid of 15 or 16. Then I saw this guy walking, made a U-turn and called, 'Hey!' He came up to the car and I shot him. I told him I was sorry and started crying. I went home. Throughout these shootings there was no anger; there were no feelings." When the police arrived, having traced his car, Rick denied recall of his crimes. "When it was over, I had a feeling of intense excitement, but it didn't really register that I had shot people."

When I first examined him, Rick appeared calm, composed, and lacking in anxiety, guilt, or any real remorse. It almost seemed as if he felt his victims succumbed to the normal risks of life. He appeared to represent a classic picture of the psychopathic personality —a person characterized by hedonism, impulsivity, selfishness, shallowness of emotion, an inability to learn by experience, lack of meaningful interpersonal relationships, and needs for immediate gratification. In spite of a history of head injury at age 20 (when hit with a blackjack by a policeman) and the relatively common finding of a mildly abnormal electroencephalogram without evidence of any localized or specific lesion, there was no clear evidence of organic brain damage or of epilepsy elicited during the hospitalization that followed his trial. (Electroencephalographic abnormalities do not necessarily have clinical significance.) The elements of the acute organic brain dysfunction induced by drugs, which had been manifested by confusion, disorientation, perceptual distortions, and ideas .of reference, had cleared. Likewise, Rick did not show evidence on mental examination of a schizophrenic thought disorder, which would have been manifested on mental examination by loose, illogical associations of ideas, difficulties in abstract thinking, primitive logic, and idiosyncratic ideas or delusions.

In spite of the clinical picture presented of an "emotionless" psychopath during subsequent interviews conducted largely for the education of students and staff, I sensed intuitively that Rick was somehow deeply troubled. I confronted him with this impression, at which point he requested to talk with me privately. With wracking sobs, head buried in his hands, he told of his incestuous relationship with his mother. "It's so horrible; it's so horrible! How can I tell you?" He went on to report that he had come to the realization that his child represented living evidence of his incestuous relationship with his mother, since his mother and wife were confused in his mind, and since he had conscious fantasies of his mother during intercourse with his wife. He stated that he took drugs to block these horrible images from his mind. Then "I just had no feelings about what I was doing."

COMMENT

The case of Rick Anderson demonstrates many of the complex issues involved in murderous and seemingly senseless attacks. He had an extremely unstable childhood. He experienced repeated abandonment by both parents. Even when his parents were present, they showed grossly inconsistent and impulsive behavior. He himself showed destructive, uncontrolled violence at an early age. Like his mother he turned to the use of addicting drugs. In his case these included alcohol, amphetamines, and barbiturates—all of which tend to erode inner controls and judgment. Furthermore, in the repeated instances of sexual relations with his mother, he learned to use alcohol deliberately to dissolve her conscience and perhaps his own as well. Drugs thus became a means to remove guilt and to provide forbidden satisfactions.

From yet another point of view Rick Anderson may represent the "criminal out of a sense of guilt," whose unconscious self-condemnation motivated punishable behavior. Guilt over incestuous behavior was profound and led to massive repression of the superego (conscience) with the appearance of apparently guilt-free psychopathic behavior. However, the underlying punitive vengeance of the conscience broke through. The "senseless" shootings of strangers, unaccompanied by conscious emotion, can be seen as a defense against and a displacement of strong, murderous impulses toward the wife-mother figure and the child who represented living proof of incest.

The prolonged use of massive amounts of amphetamines no doubt contributed to the impairment of control, of judgment, and of contact with reality. Drugs were utilized to avoid conflict and suppress painful thoughts and impulses, but they served rather to create new conflicts and to interfere with repression and control.

Rick's case demonstrates how seemingly senseless attacks can at least be understood. The unstable childhood; poor parental models; strong, unacceptable, yet poorly controlled sexual and aggressive impulses; and "mind-blowing" drugs—all contributed to the killings. Even the possibility of prior brain damage cannot be excluded as a contributing factor. Certainly Rick showed what has been emphasized repeatedly in this book—the important relationship between violence and conflict resolution. Rick's behavior leading up to his violence—in fact, much of his behavior—could be seen as adjustive, that is, behavior providing immediate relief and effect. Yet his behavior revealed a gross failure to cope and a total lack of long-range purpose.

A Shy Killer

Wesley Glover is a 52-year-old, single, white man, who has been hospitalized for seven years since he shot a motorist who did not stop to render him aid. In the hospital Mr. Glover has been quiet, relatively withdrawn, and cooperative—"putting in time," as he stated it.

Wesley always has been a shy, solitary person except as a child, when he was somewhat rebellious, especially toward his father. He was the eldest of five children. When he was 11, his mother died after suffering from cancer for two years. Although he admitted a sense of loss, Wesley did not cry at her death. "I never cry."

Subsequently Wesley was placed in an orphanage, where he was continually in trouble for rebellious behavior until removed by his father a year later. He entered the Navy at age 24. During this time he had the only real friend of his life.

Wesley's illness became manifest while in the service. One day three officers came to the engine room and adjusted some valves of which Wesley was in charge. He became angered and disturbed. He was taken to the hospital, where he assaulted five medical corpsmen. This was his only episode of violence. He believed that the officers were plotting against him and was diagnosed as suffering from paranoid schizophrenia. He received a psychiatric discharge. On four subsequent occasions in 1948, 1951, 1958, and 1959, Wesley had recurrences of his paranoid psychosis. Each psychotic break came on suddenly with no apparent reason.

Wesley always lived alone, most recently in a hotel room. On weekends he would see his family or go hunting. During the week he attended boxing and wrestling matches alone. His major recreation, however, was shooting on the rifle range. He belonged to a local rifle club and to the National Rifle Association. He had received his first rifle from his father at age 11, with which he shot squirrels and rabbits. "I just like to shoot." Later on he did indoor target shooting and some hunting with both shotgun and rifle. He was an excellent marksman.

Just prior to the murder Wesley had obtained a new, high-powered rifle by mail order. He had worked the previous week and had not been noted to be disturbed. On the weekend of the killing he went to a cousin's home in the country in order to test out his new rifle. The family noted no disturbance. On his way home Wesley took a back road in order to shoot his rifle some more. His car became stuck in the mud. An elderly couple stopped to render assistance and noted that his speech seemed wild, threatening, and irrational. They left and got in touch with the police. However, shortly after they left the scene, a pickup truck drove by and did not stop. Wesley shot and killed the driver.

In the hospital Wesley was noted for his imperturbability. "I never get annoyed."

COMMENT

Wesley Glover illustrates the difficulty in predicting the emergence of psychotic violence. On occasion a killer can be a quiet, compliant, unassuming, withdrawn person. Yet some childhood rebelliousness, one previous breakthrough of rage, several psychotic episodes, and a preoccupation with guns (the symbolic significance of which in terms of power, strength, or masculinity can only be speculated) were features that distinguished this man, whose long-term adjustment was otherwise that of a "garden variety" schizoid nature. Wesley was overcontrolled, yet he was too fragile to maintain this control over augmented hostile impulses. He had few devices or outlets with which to cope with his emotions.

While the precipitating incident may seem trivial, it nonetheless provided some classic elements inducing anger: an annoying frustration in a planned action and an apparent inability to solve the interrupted plan quickly (see Chapter 4). In addition, Wesley's inability to express or apparently even feel emotion deprived him of the usual signal function of emotion. Feeling and action likely were poorly distinguished in this man. Thus to a rigid, "unfeeling," and somewhat fragile person like Wesley Glover, a relatively small frustrating incident can serve to release rage of psychotic proportions. Then the immediate availability of a loaded gun contributed to the violent "solution."

Finally, it is important to recognize the specificity of behavior involved. Violent behavior is determined by multiple factors differing in configuration. In contrast to Rick, Wesley was overcontrolled rather than grossly undercontrolled, and he was anything but a "psychopath" in his usual style of life.

A Tape-recorded Murder

The case of Frank Bedsloe, a husky, intelligent, soft-spoken, 33-year-old ex-Marine sergeant, is most unusual in that the murder of his former wife's husband and the immediately antecedent events were tape-recorded. Laurie's third husband, Joe Levy, was an electronics engineer and had "bugged" the living room in order to obtain evidence against Frank for his failure to pay child support. Shortly following the murder Frank became mute and withdrawn, a condition clinically called catatonia. Complex questions around the issue of responsibility were raised at his trial, some of the testimony at which was based on a "truth serum" interview.

Frank was the seventh of eight children of a very poor Oklahoma family. His difficult birth was unattended (raising the question of possible brain injury). As a toddler, Frank put everything he could into his mouth, a symptom of emotional disturbance called "pica," reflecting a "starvation for love." From the age of 15 months to 4 years he suffered convulsions, which occurred again at the age of 10 in conjunction with a high fever and shortly after he had been hit on the head by his father.

Frank was a "good child," and he always felt afraid and ashamed because of it. But much of his history is best told through his autobiographical notes, which starkly and vividly describe his life.

A boy should be brave. Try as I would, I could never measure up to what my parents expected. I remember feeling rejected, hurt, and confused. Most of the time I was told, "Stop asking silly questions." "Go and play." "Don't bother me now; I'm busy." "Good boys don't ask questions like that." After a while, I stopped asking questions, so the only way I could find anything out was to work it out for myself. There was no one I could turn to. I felt lost and lonely. My father worked in the oilfields and as a cotton picker and was seldom at home. My mother took in washing to help keep food on the table. Even so, I remember once I was so hungry I stole some potato peelings from a neighbor's garbage can. I felt very ashamed of it.

Some of my early memories are of my sisters beating me up. I was a weak, sickly child, small for my age until 12, so it was easy for them. They clobbered the hell out of me. Usually nobody touched one of them. I would always be the one to get the spanking. I remember a lulu of a spanking once. My sisters and I found a fifty-cent piece in a mattress that was airing. We were ecstatic and went to the movies. My older brother's girl friend claimed she had lost fifty cents, and, after furious questioning, my mother started spanking us to make us tell the truth. We were spanked with a willow switch until there were no tears left. We couldn't even speak any more; only dry sobs would come.

I certainly had a fouled-up idea of what a man should be. As a child I was taught that boys don't cry, don't show emotions, don't have feelings. What a mistaken idea! One day when I was about four, I didn't have anything to sleep in, and my mother decided I would wear one of my older sister's dresses. That was a horrifying idea. I cried and screamed and begged Mother not to make me wear the dress. I even tried to put on dirty trousers and wear them to bed. She spanked me, put the dress on me, and put me to bed. I knew I was the bad one around the house. But what had I done; what was I supposed to do; what was I supposed to be; why was I being punished? Boys don't act like girls; boys don't wear girls' clothes. How do boys act; are they always wrong like me?

Another important factor was my parents' inconsistencies. Many times I was told a boy acted certain ways, but when I acted that way, I was wrong. Father and Mother promised things and then went back on their word. The time my father sold my horse, after telling me he wouldn't, knocked the props from under me. My mother told me boys don't act like girls, but then she made me do girls' work. I hadn't done anything, but I was bad, bad, bad. When I tried to talk to my parents, I was shoved aside because boys aren't important. It hurt so bad to see my sisters held and loved when it wouldn't have been right to hold and love me. Oh, well, I guess boys aren't supposed to want these things. They never touched me. They used to be angry at me for getting sick. I always had the idea I was feeling bad because I was in the way. I was always afraid of new situations.

After giving much thought to the matter, I'm left with three overall impressions of my childhood: that of being always afraid and confused, that of being mostly alone with no one to talk to, that of being spanked and beaten by my sisters. I stayed pretty much to myself in school. The boys in my class didn't want to play with me because I couldn't do the same things they could. The majority of my playmates were from lower grades. One day, waiting for the bus after school, a boy a little smaller than I hunted me up and kept jumping on my back. I asked him several times to leave me alone. I couldn't get away from him. If I were sitting down or standing up, he would come up behind me and jump on my back. I got him down and started choking him. Finally, two big boys pulled me off of him. That scared me so much that I would go to almost any length to avoid a fight thereafter. I was afraid that I had inherited my father's temper and troublemaking nature.

I suppose I had the usual confused, mixed-up feelings as an adolescent. The only difference—that is, if it is different—was that there was nobody I could talk to or confide in. I worked most of the time and had no close school friends. The few times I tried to talk to my parents about, for instance, going to dances or dating girls, they made fun of me. (Actually, I think I denied that sort of feeling for the most part.) My sister and I would get up at four o'clock in the morning and do the chores before school. One of the milk cows was a beautiful, coal-black half-Jersey, half-Brahmin. She was nervous and scared around people. When my Dad tried to milk her, she fought and refused to drop her milk. He lost his temper, started beating her with a two-by-four. She was so afraid, and all he would do was beat her.

One day we went to town to do some shopping. Daddy headed for the nearest tavern. He was really tying one on, drinking everything and anything. We were afraid to ride with him when it was time to go home, but he made us. Mother was in the car with Daddy. He hit her a couple of times on the drive. The car was weaving all over the highway. He stopped to try to buy more liquor, and, when the owner of the store refused to sell him any, he really blew his stack. He came storming out of the store, jumped into the car and almost ran head-on into a Greyhound bus and a diesel truck as we roared off on the wrong side of the highway. About a quarter of a mile farther on, he was driving much too fast to negotiate a 90-degree left-hand turn. We ran off the road into a ditch. I got a deep cut on my back. Daddy hit Mother again before he got out of the car. My glasses had been knocked off, and I couldn't see. He kept hitting Mother until he wandered off in a drunken stupor. It took three hours for the ambulance to get there. Mother was groaning in pain all the time. I wanted to help her and stop the pain, but I was helpless. I was responsible, and I couldn't do anything. It was my fault, and I couldn't do anything. Mother was mumbling and delirious. I had almost decided to try and borrow a gun and shoot Daddy so he couldn't hurt her anymore when she said, "Frank, don't kill him." I was surprised and thought maybe I was imagining it when she said again, "Don't kill him." She was groaning, mumbling, and delirious the rest of the way to the hospital.

My parents' life consisted of work and more work. I used to feel that the only reason they wanted me was I brought home money. When I was around fourteen, fuzz started growing around my face. When I was standing in front of the mirror wondering if I should shave, I was trying to think of a way to ask my father if I could use his razor. Mother came in and started laughing at me and ridiculing me. God, that hurt. It seemed that I was supposed to be a man, but every time I tried to do what I thought a man was supposed to do, I was made fun of. When she told my father, he laughed too.

After high school Frank joined the Marine Corps, where he rose to the rank of first sergeant. While stationed in the South, Frank met and married Laurie. (During his drug interview it came out that the meeting took place in a brothel.) They lived together for five months before their marriage and remained together for two years until he was sent overseas in 1959. Two daughters were born to the marriage, and there was a third by Laurie's first husband. During the defendant's overseas absence of eighteen months, he had difficulty in maintaining communication with Laurie. On the day of his return from overseas he suspected infidelity. Laurie admitted the extent of her infidelity, involving three separate affairs. Frank assaulted his wife and then made a suicide gesture, superficially lacerating his wrists.

During the separation that ensued there were continual disputes about seeing the children. On one of Frank's visits to the children, Laurie picked up a .38 revolver.

She pointed it at my stomach from about ten or twelve inches away. I couldn't believe it, but her knuckles were white; the trigger was partly pulled. I saw the hammer move back a little. There was wild, cold murder in her eyes. God, that hurt! She said, "You had better get out of here," in a cold, feelingless voice. It would have been kinder of her to shoot. I can think of nothing that hurts as bad as seeing murder in the eyes of one you love and would die for. But there's no mistaking that look. For one who hasn't seen it, there is no way to describe it. For one who has seen it, there is no mistaking nor forgetting it. I thank God that I was so tired and so numb and my feelings were so dull that I was unaware of the full depth of the hurt.

Subsequently Laurie married Joe Levy, a prosperous engineer. There were continual disputes with Frank over child-support payments. The children were well taken care of because of Mr. Levy's relative affluence. Evidently for Frank to make regular child-support payments meant to accept the reality of his loss of the children and Laurie, with whom he remained obsessed. In turn, the Levys were using financial demands to control Frank and express hostility toward him. During this period of time there was some evidence of inappropriate behavior, for example, Frank's appearing for a domestic military flight dressed in full battle gear.

On the day of the murder Frank went to pick up his daughters for an outing. As had occurred on his visit the previous week, a hidden tape recorder was operating in order to document for court presentation Frank's delinquency in child support. A dispute transpired between Frank and his ex-wife and her husband regarding Frank's failure to keep up with child-support payments. Mr. Levy, perhaps because of the recording of the conversation, maintained a fairly reasonable tenor throughout most of the transaction. However, he kept assailing Frank on a cognitive level, rationally confronting him with the consequences of his not keeping up with child support and reminding him of his commitments, as the following excerpts from the tape recording indicate. (The tape recording had been turned over to the district attorney by Laurie, who had expressed the hope that it would help put Frank in the gas chamber. The district attorney made the tape available to me under court order at the request of Frank's defense attorney.)

FRANK: If I keep making these payments, I will be in no position to help the children later. I have two choices. If I pay the . . .

JOE: You don't have a choice! That's an obligation. The choice is not yours. It has already been decided by the court.

FRANK: This is awfully hard for me to come up here and see someone I consider my wife.

Up to this point Joe Levy was setting limits on the alternatives available to Frank. Now he became very angry and screamed:

JOE: Listen, all I need is to hear about one more remark like that out of you, and I'll flatten you! Do you understand that? Laurie is not your wife, and you had better damn well understand that, Bedsloe! Now what else do you have to say—real quick?

In addition to Levy's intimidation and attack on Frank's core belief that he was still married, Laurie kept interjecting herself into the conversation in a sarcastic, provocative manner, assaulting and undermining him on an emotional level. She continually belittled and humiliated Frank:

LAURIE: Will you please be quiet! You're in my house, and I'd like to say something. You made a big point about my having spent this "lavish" amount of child support on men. The last man I went with made fourteen hundred dollars a month and hardly needed your piddily little bit of child support. I'm getting very weary of your coming into my house with your filthy mouth. Whenever you come up here and speak, we all get irritated and disgusted.

FRANK: You said that I saw the children in June and July. My "seeing them" consisted of seeing them twice through a screen.

LAURIE: That was your fault. You always would bring along your greasy, ugly, brutish friends.

JOE: Let's cut it out in the next fifty or sixty seconds because I'm getting tired of it. When are you planning to bring the children back?

FRANK: I'll have them back before midnight Sunday.

LAURIE: I think we should have a definite time.

Further bickering followed about the time the children should be returned. Laurie objected to each proposed arrangement.

JOE: Are you coming up to date on your payments?

FRANK: I can't until next week. The money is not in the bank.

LAURIE: I don't trust you. I never trusted you. Now you've had your little scene. You'll hear from us by Monday or Tuesday about court, definitely.

This statement likely served further to erode whatever inner controls Frank still had intact, for he now pulled out his service revolver, which he had taken from its usual place in the glove compartment of his car.

JOE: What did you pull a gun for?

CHILDREN: [*Screaming*] Go, go!

JOE: You pulled a gun on me here in my house? Bedsloe, don't frighten the children, for God's sake!

LAURIE: Get out of here, Frank!

The children continued pathetically screaming and pleading. Frank, usually solicitous of them, seemed oblivious to their distress and entreaties.

LAURIE: Frank, get out of here!

JOE: Laurie, take the children. For God's sake, go!

FRANK: [*Calmly*] Since I had to pull this, I'm afraid it's not enough this time.

At this moment Frank shot Joe Levy four times in the chest while Laurie and the children fled from the house. It took the victim about twenty minutes to die. Approximately five minutes after the shooting Frank called the police, using a remarkably flat and unemotional tone as he had in all his comments. He then waited quietly for about ten minutes, during which time the victim was having gruesome death rattles as air was sucked through the chest wounds. Frank called the police again. They arrived during this call, and Frank warned headquarters to radio the officers not to break in. However, the police forced their way into the house. Frank spoke briefly to the officers and was taken into custody, shortly after which he became mute.

Being unable to stand trial, he was taken to the hospital for the criminally insane, where with antipsychotic medication over a course of about three months he gradually came out of his catatonic state and assumed the role of a quiet, cooperative, pleasant, somewhat aloof patient. He had no recall of the crime or events immediately preceding or following it. He seemed to be sincerely trying to recall and consented to a sodium amobarbital-methamphetamine interview with me, the consulting psychiatrist. In such a "narcoanalytic" or "truth serum" interview, barbiturate sedative tends to lessen the ability to withhold or suppress, and the amphetamine stimulant leads to activation and pressured speech. One does not necessarily get the "truth," for fantasies or delusions, rarely even falsehoods, may be expressed. Under the influence of truth serum latent psychotic processes or organic brain impairment are more likely to be manifest.

During the sodium amobarbital-methamphetamine interview,

Frank had no clear recall of the actual events, indicating genuine repression. However, he did show considerable evidence of bizarre thinking, which seemed to reflect a psychotic thought disorder. Frank wept continuously for hours under the influence of the drugs. He continually referred to how he had been deeply hurt by Laurie. He continued to confuse her with his mother, at times referring to the two women interchangeably. He said that he was feeling hurt and that, therefore, Laurie was hurting too, implying that they were one and the same person, and reflecting his lack of ego boundaries. He clearly still considered Laurie his wife. In view of his perception of her as suffering, he went on to the fantasy that someone was going to hurt her. "Laurie gonna be hurt. Children may be too. Laurie gonna be hurt, oh, my God! [*Anxiously*] That dumb girl not know what she doing. She cut me so bad; she hurt so bad too. Let's try to save family—children. Don't want to, must, must. Love Laurie. Oh, those dirty bastards; they don't care. He gonna shoot me." Frank also reported feeling that he was dead and that if he had shot himself, nothing would have happened because the bullet would have simply gone off into space. "The papier-mâché mask above my head would have slipped back into place and covered the bullet hole."

When he had recovered and stabilized sufficiently to be able to stand trial, Frank was returned to court. The court-appointed psychiatrist, Dr. Alien, diagnosed Frank as suffering from a psychoneurotic reaction. Dr. Alien found Frank (1) sane at the time he committed the offense in that he knew the nature and quality of his act, (2) capable of forming the specific intention to kill, (3) having the mental capacity to harbor malice, and (4) possessing the mental ability to deliberate and premeditate and probably to reflect upon the gravity of his act. Dr. Alien did say, however, that Frank's judgment was impaired by his deep reservoir of hostility toward his ex-wife, which was probably displaced upon the victim.

I testified quite differently. To me, Frank showed cognitive slippage, condensation, displacement, misidentification, lack of ego boundaries, projection, and other forms of psychotic logic during the "truth serum" interview. Although a legitimate question might be whether these distortions were drug-induced, such an event is unlikely. Likewise Frank's lack of emotion, inappropriate reactions, perseveration, and calm following his violent act were evidence of the psychotic dissociation of thoughts from feelings that would be extremely unusual except perhaps for a hardened criminal, which Frank was not.

It was my opinion that (1) Mr. Bedsloe was legally insane at the time of the commission of his offense in that he did not know the nature and quality of his act. He felt that he and his wife were one and that they and their children were in mortal danger at the hands of the murder victim. His entire perception of the nature of the act lacked an appreciation of and contact with reality. (2) He *did* have the mental capacity to form specific intent to kill. (3) There was no clear evidence of conscious premeditation, but there was the possibility that he could have reached the intention with deliberation based on his delusional interpretation of the situation. His judgment certainly was grossly impaired.

Jury trial was waived. The judge found the defendant guilty of second-degree rather than first-degree murder. The judge stated:

As to the defendant's insanity, unfortunately, we work within the framework of a perhaps outmoded and artificial legal structure. I do feel that the defendant at the time the incident took place—here again, I put great weight on the tape recording—was oriented to persons, places, time. I believe he knew what he was doing. I don't feel the delusion, if there was one, met the standard that I am required to apply for legal insanity under the M'Naghten rules.

Frank wrote me from prison regarding his reactions to the trial. His letter shows the sort of repressions, fragmented thought processes, and bizarre ideations that Frank was prone to demonstrate under stress.

I don't think anyone else but you knew I wasn't quite there parts of the time. I remember your telling the judge that I grow quieter and quieter in my circumscribed illness—as I was during most of the trial. I tried to talk to my lawyer, but I couldn't even open my mouth. I hope you know what it meant to me and means to me now to know that somebody was aware of what was happening to me. Your understanding relieved part of the helpless loneliness. I was surprised at my lack of reaction as the recording was being played. I remembered nothing, didn't even recognize any of the voices. When my little girl was screaming, "Let me go," I got the impression that I saw an image that was threatening her and her sister with a stick or whip or something. I never heard the shots. The groans of the dying man almost tore me up. He was in such terrible pain; he hurt so badly. (And I had been told I caused it.) Poor, poor man! Poor, poor man; it didn't seem fair. Nobody ever told me you could hurt so badly after you were dead, and I had died some time before. He didn't hurt so badly as I had for so long before dying, but it was all right if I was hurt. That didn't matter; I didn't count anyway, but he hurt so much. I felt the pain with him even though I was dead, but my family is safe, family is safe. Doesn't matter I dead and still hurting; family is safe. Why hurt after dead? Go to hell, burn, is all right, can take it, family safe now, is worth pain. . . . The pain of the dying man seemed to combine with mine, but even together the pain was much much less than it had been for months, maybe years, before all this happened. Then memories of the terror, uncertainty and pain before I died started flooding back. I felt myself slipping back into insanity. No, won't go, can't let go, too hard, too much work. Can't let go; come back, come back. Shaking, but I had made it. I hadn't gone crazy again, wonderful. As the recording went on, I remembered when the police came. I was at first glad. They were ghost police. Here, come take me away. Don't be alone when dead. Then I afraid they come to take me to burn over hot coals. Does not seem fair, but is O.K. Can't last forever and ever. Family is safe, not important if I hurt, is O.K. As I drifted to the door to let the police in, I floated over the body with the gun beside it. That is all I can remember of the time the recording was being played. There are no words for some of the feelings. This is as accurate as I can make it.

COMMENT

Frank Bedsloe had an emotionally deprived childhood, a common factor in the backgrounds of the violent offender. He longed for affection. No doubt he carried a heavy burden of repressed hostility, engendered by frustration and unexpressed for fear of loss of love. He had himself been the victim of actual and threatened violence at the hands of not only his parents and sisters but also of his wife. He could never measure up to expectations partially because they were contradictory and partially because they lacked positive emphasis. He felt guilt, shame, and anxiety over expressing emotions. He felt valued only for what he could provide materially. He married and became dependent upon a woman much like his mother, yet idealized her as the wished-for "good mother" rather than the actual "bad mother."

A number of factors seemed to evoke the final act. Frank was assaulted rationally and emotionally in ways that undermined his self-esteem and masculinity. His delusion of still being married was directly attacked. He was threatened with a loss of his children. A lack of trust was expressed, making real his own fear of losing control. Murder occurred when there seemed no way out and no more time. As Levy put it, "You have no choice." Finally, the murder scene reminds one of the auto "accident" in which Frank's father nearly killed his mother and himself. Similarly, he had been violent as a boy when he could not escape harassment from another child who "kept jumping on my back."

The complex issue of insanity and legal responsibility has been alluded to and is beyond the scope of this discussion. It must be recalled that for most of his life Frank Bedsloe was a hard-working, productive citizen. He was devoted to his family and had not been violent, antisocial, or overtly psychotic. One sees a man who in childhood was repeatedly the victim and witness of violence, deprived of affection, and humiliated and shamed, especially just for being a male. In all these circumstances one can sense the great pain of Frank's being helpless to do anything to change his plight. He could not help his mother after the accident, he could not prevent being forced to wear a dress, and he could not stop his sisters' violent treatment of him. He expressed this great emotional pain in his letter when he said, "The pain of the dying man seemed to combine with mine, but even together the pain was much less than it had been for months, maybe years, before all this happened." Given all this, it is not difficult to imagine how the divorce from his wife became an intolerable burden for Frank to bear or how murder could seem to be a solution to an unbearable conflict.

Recommendations

General measures aimed at prevention of such violence as depicted in these three case studies are discussed in the theoretical chapters of this book. At present, effective primary prevention remains an ideal, since it involves eradicating the factors common in the backgrounds of violent offenders—blatant inconsistencies in parental behavior, violence in the home of which the child is often either witness or victim, gross lack of affection including lack of basic positive regard for the child, and actual loss of or separation from parents.

Although these psychosocial factors are difficult to remove, they can be reduced. Often there are clear forewarnings in childhood of the potential for later destructive behavior. These include a history of actual incidents of violence and destructive behavior; poorly controlled anger and excessive response to minor frustrations, or, on the other hand, marked overcontrol and inability to express any resentment; repeated behavioral problems in the classroom; and parental child neglect and violence perpetrated upon the child. While primary prevention requires consistent, fair, and affectionate child rearing, early recognition of these behavioral forewarnings of destructive behavior and early intervention, so-called secondary prevention, do offer the means to reduce later violence in those identified as high risks. Assessment of violent individuals needs to include evaluation of brain function, since occasionally a specific and treatable brain disease can be found.

As to treatment of violent individuals per se, often referred to as rehabilitation or tertiary prevention, society generally does violence to the doers of violence in the traditional settings for violent offenders (jails, prisons, some mental hospitals). This mistreatment only adds to the offender's store of hostility and reconfirms to him that violence is a valid mode of coping and communication. In addition, when specific treatment procedures are introduced, they often fail because the usual nondirective and verbal approaches to psychological problems are generally ineffective with those who express their conflicts through action. This failure results in part from mental health professionals' insufficient appreciation of the emotional development of the impulse-ridden or poorly controlled person. For the violence-prone person's cognition is dominated by perceptual thinking—thinking that is much more related to imagery, prone to distortions, and readily converted into action. In such a person thought and action are poorly differentiated, and words are either relatively meaningless emotionally or perceived as hypocritical. On the whole, the disturbed offender frequently has not developed sufficient conceptual thinking—neither the capability to use concepts, abstractions, and language in communicating and solving problems nor the ability to distinguish past from both present and future and to distinguish thought from action.

The treatment of individuals with such psychological handicaps requires a psychotherapist who sets limits on behavior, demonstrates in action a consistency with what he says, openly communicates how he feels, provides external control when necessary, demonstrates reliability and predictability, and is able to give of himself and show genuine concern. By providing the patient with a consistent, firm, effective, and giving model from whom to learn and with whom to identify, the psychotherapist can begin to help change the immediacy-motivated behavior and disturbed thinking of the violence-prone person. Society's values and controls become assimilated through a relationship with a significant other who represents societal values. The therapist can help the patient learn to express angry feelings verbally instead of through destructive action and to understand the defensive or protective function of his destructive behavior. Conversion of vague emotions and impulses into concepts in and of itself is a step toward mastery. Attributing meaning and motivation to behavior tends to define action as volitional and subject to control. Differentiation of thought and action as processes allows the interposition of rationality and reality-testing between impulse and behavior. The past must be laid to rest, and the future perceived as being able to be different. An understanding of the addictive, security-providing quality of repetitive action patterns must be understood in addition to their symbolic meanings.

Group psychotherapy can be a very effective adjunct. Socialization pressures within a group can be intense. Insincerities and evasions are quickly spotted by group members. Middle-class modes of communication that handicap most psychotherapists can be avoided. A member of the group can find a sense of amalgamation and acceptance within a group, which may have been absent during childhood development. He can also achieve a sense of uniqueness and individuality. Through both group and individual therapy, affection, trust, and intimacy can develop to overcome and replace the emotional deprivation of childhood.

But psychotherapy is not enough. Effective treatment requires a setting that also provides clear structure, consistency, and predictability to help the violent patient overcome uncertainties and instabilities of past relationships and to establish basic trust. The psychotherapist must work in unison with other staff members if consistency is to be achieved. In fact many persons who resort to violence can best be treated in an institutional setting where acting destructively upon impulse cannot take place. Psychotherapeutic intervention may be possible within an institution with persons who would not seek help voluntarily, whose actions (including flight) would prevent successful outpatient work, or whose psychological resources are too meager to face both inner conflict and life tasks simultaneously. When action as a defense against anxiety, depression, or some other unpleasant feeling is blocked, an individual is forced to come to grips with this anxiety or depression or to develop other defenses. In a controlled therapeutic environment it is possible both to block destructive behaviors and to interpret their neurotic and defensive basis. Prisons and stockades contain many persons with neurotic and psychosomatic symptoms who never had such suffering when they lived lives of action—suffering which is quite independent of any specific punishment. A person is more likely to be amenable to treatment when he is suffering than when he is causing others to suffer.

Unfortunately, opportunities for destructive, manipulative behavior; relationships based upon power and exploitation; and gratification of dependency by a controlling, unloving, authoritarian parent-surrogate often occur in prisons. In these ways such institutions actually play into and reinforce rather than overcome antisocial defenses. Unwholesome old patterns must be blocked, and the individual helped with the conflicts that then emerge. The traditional mental hospital is not well equipped to cope with violent and antisocial behavior, and the prison traditionally has been concerned with retribution rather than with treatment and rehabilitation. New treatment methods and settings must be evolved.

Methods and settings need to encompass elements that will assist the transition from dominance of perceptual thinking and impulsive action to dominance of conceptual thinking and planned action. The treatment setting must provide work opportunities that develop work skills and social competence and enhance self-esteem. While protecting against violence, the setting should offer graded responsibilities and the opportunity for patient participation in decision-making affecting the lives of the treatment group. Finally, the envisioned treatment setting must be congruent with constructive living in the outside community, and thus it should include both sexes and encourage group interdependence and division of labor among members.

As a psychiatrist I have a firm commitment to the idea that human behavior can be modified. Our failures in prevention and treatment have been based on ignorance, which can be ameliorated through further research; on lack of implementation of accepted principles; on a reluctance to innovate; and on vindictiveness toward social deviancy far more than on any intrinsic "incurability" of the violence-prone person. The human's capacity for growth and healing is great, and, hopefully, his proclivity for violence can be halted.

Acknowledgments

I am grateful to the subjects, who seemed motivated to do their part to prevent other such tragedies, for permission to report their stories and to Frank Vanasek, Ph.D., acting Chief of Research, Atascadero State Hospital, and John Kersten Kraft, Stanford University medical student, for their assistance.

Selected Readings

Balt, J. *By Reason of Insanity*. New York: New American Library, 1966. (Also available in Signet paperback edition.) [This remarkable autobiography was written by a gifted Hollywood writer who killed his wife and was subsequently hospitalized at an institution for the criminally insane, where he gained considerable insight through work with a skilled psychotherapist.]

Shields, R. W.   *A Cure of Delinquency. The Treatment of Maladjustment*. London: Heinemann, 1962.

Part **III**

Recommendations *and*
Conclusions

14. Summary of Recommendations

Alan J. Rosenthal, M.D.,
and Frederic W. Ilfeld, Jr., M.D.

The recent crises of violence in this country, which are of such concern to us all, prompted the formation of the Committee on Violence of the Stanford Department of Psychiatry. As behavioral scientists we recognized that such critical times are dangerous but that a crisis, being a turning point, also provides within it the opportunity for change toward an adaptation more favorable to human progress and development. With this in mind the committee undertook this study of violence. Our goals have been to explore the roots of violence and to recommend adaptive alternatives to it. The following recommendations are developed from our perspective as behavioral scientists and are based on both clinical and research experiences.

Traditionally the health professional has translated basic scientific knowledge into practical application, often before the evidence is conclusive. In undertaking this study on violence, the committee has employed such a "physician model" in advocating that remedies be attempted even though etiology may not be established with certainty. The evidence for many of our recommendations is suggestive, not conclusive. Still we are convinced that as physicians and behavioral scientists we have a right, even an obligation, to submit our conclusions to examination and catalyze meaningful social action from the best available data. Relevant action can and must be undertaken now.

Our study analyzes violence on several levels, ranging from the more theoretical and abstract to the more practical and concrete, and our recommendations fall at various points along this continuum. This chapter summarizes those recommendations appearing in more detail in previous chapters. It begins with the general guidelines that are developed in the theoretical section of this book (Part I) and follows with the specific recommendations of the practical issues section (Part II). Finally, the chapter concludes with suggestions for action that each individual can undertake immediately.

General Guidelines

The theoretical section of this book presents the foundations of violent behavior from a number of perspectives. These include biological, psychodynamic, environmental, and cybernetic theories of violence as well as a discussion of alternatives to violent behavior. This variety of theoretical approaches to the subject itself indicates that violent behavior has multiple determinants. Many factors contribute to the phenomenon of violence, and no single concept provides an adequate explanation for it. Rather than considering man as inescapably bound to inherent patterns of violence, the theoretical chapters suggest mechanisms for coping with the many determinants of violent behavior and indicate "general guidelines" for its control and prevention. These guidelines are here organized into educational, social and political, and research categories. Since this organization tends to obliterate and transcend chapter boundaries, we refer the reader to the chapters of Part I for a more detailed account of these guidelines and their theoretical development.

GUIDELINES FOR EDUCATIONAL PROGRAMS
• *Modify excessively punitive child-rearing practices through education.* Many aggressive and violent children learn violence through imitation of and identification with overly punitive parents. The expression of appropriate and genuine affection and understanding and consistent limit-setting are much more successful in controlling child behavior than is a violent or overly punitive parental action.
• *Children with absent or grossly inadequate parental models should be provided with competent, respected, nonviolent adults.* These adults, whether "foster parents," "big brothers," or others, could give such children the opportunity to be self-confident and assertive without being violent. Parents and other models for identification could, by example, aid the child to develop and use conceptual thinking in coping with conflict rather than using impulsive, immediate action.

• *Encourage constructive channeling of aggression.* Individual and collective activities that sublimate aggressive energy into effective, nonviolent channels (art, science, service projects, sports, nonviolent political protest) should be more available for all members of our population. Participation in these nonviolent activities should be socially rewarded. Such activities are especially significant because boredom and the lack of productive activity themselves may contribute to the development of violent behavior.

• *Expand programs for the development of mutual understanding and empathy between individuals and groups.* The ability to perceive another's feelings and viewpoints often dissolves anger and violent behavior. Such programs should include (1) interpersonal and intergroup contact in a supportive, nonthreatening setting of shared values and goals; (2) use of the mass media to portray accurately and sensitively the lives of those who may be feared or hated, foreign or unknown; and (3) role-taking of the other's position and rehearsals of nonviolent responses to anger.

• *Publicize and encourage alternatives to violent behavior.* Such alternatives include, among others, negotiation and nonviolent protest. With a greater awareness and number of effective, nonviolent alternative plans of action available, the probability of violence becomes less. The long-term efficacy of such alternative plans should be stressed in educational programs.

• *Develop educational programs that identify the factors contributing to violent behavior.* Studies of animal behavior indicate that violence is largely due to threats to status, threats to personal territory, pain, and overcrowding. Other factors contributing to human violence include one's previous learning experiences, prevailing cultural values, severe and chronic frustrations, and feelings of increasing pressures and constraints. Educational programs should teach about these and other precursors of aggression and violence. We must learn to recognize anger as a warning signal and to anticipate social conflict in order to prevent the violence that may emerge.

GUIDELINES FOR SOCIAL AND POLITICAL PROGRAMS

• *Respect human "territoriality" and avoid overcrowding.* Areas of high population density may result in encroachment on one's "personal life space" or personal territory. Animal studies show that intense overcrowding can lead to violent actions. The risks of overcrowding must be considered in present-day community and housing development.

• *Reduce frustrations that involve significant goals for large seg-*

ments of our population. Frustration plays a major role in engendering violence. The goals of personal dignity, self-respect, and self-determination for minority groups and communities in our society must become realistically attainable, thus reducing the frustrations of those striving for such goals. Expectations that cannot be fulfilled realistically must be identified, and attainable goals developed.

• *Establish additional machinery for the expression of social and political grievances.* Such machinery could include an ombudsman, who would serve as an arbitrator between individual plaintiffs and the government. An ombudsman would help individuals to express their frustrations and would arbitrate their grievances in constructive, nonviolent ways.

• *Employ the least violent means of social control available, and then only when absolutely necessary.* The indiscriminate use of force by those in authority may itself precipitate retaliatory violence. Punishment or force, when necessary, should be used judiciously and sparingly to be maximally effective. Social policy that employs harsh punishment, often more severe than the crime, is itself guilty of the "crime of punishment" and is grossly self-defeating in this attempt to reduce violent behavior.

• *Emphasize nonviolent techniques of conflict resolution.* Teaching and rewarding nonviolent means of settling conflict, while divesting violence of glorification or reward, are essential in diminishing violent behavior. Violence begets further violence.

• *Avoid condoning some forms of violence while condemning others.* Inconsistent attitudes and actions concerning violent behavior result in a moral dilemma or double standard and maintain rather than reduce violence. Social programs should clearly emphasize the morality in nonviolent alternatives to conflict resolution and uniformly condemn violent behavior.

GUIDELINES FOR RESEARCH PROGRAMS

Many areas for study in the field of violent behavior exist. The chapters on theory emphasize the following recommendations:

• *Expand research on the biological and environmental bases of aggression and violence through animal studies, especially nonhuman primate studies.* Factors contributing to violent behavior in animals provide significant clues to understanding violence in man.

• *Increase the study of biological factors in humans that contribute to violence.* Hormonal, neurological, and physiological research is necessary to identify possible organic factors in those individuals who are repeatedly or uncontrollably violent. Such studies should be examined together with data accumulated from social and psychological views of violence.

• *Intensify research into the personal, interpersonal, and intergroup factors responsible for violent behavior.* The specific environments and crises that precipitate violence require further delineation, and methods of adaptation and coping with them need further study.

• *Undertake cross-cultural and historical studies of violence and aggression.* Other countries and cultures, both past and present, should be studied to determine their types and causes of violent behavior and their techniques of avoiding and coping with violence.

• *Study the indications for, limits of, and specific tactics for the effective use of nonviolent strategies.* Such strategies include negotiation and various forms of nonviolent protest. This study requires research both in the laboratory situation and in natural settings. National concern for perfecting the tactics of peaceful existence must at least equal our emphasis on research in the tactics of war.

• *Create multidisciplinary teams and centers to study the many facets of violent behavior.* The interaction of many factors contributes to violence, and this interaction requires intensive study as much as the individual factors. Individuals representing the areas of nonhuman research; human biological, psychological, and social research; and cross-cultural research should compose these teams.

Specific Recommendations

Part II of this book, Current Issues of Violence in America, reviews a number of specific topics (mass media, assassination, mental illness, and so forth) and their relation to violent behavior. These chapters present specific recommendations that have more immediate practical value than the preceding general guidelines. Although the recommendations from each chapter in Part II will be listed here, the reader is again referred to the chapters themselves for greater detail and explanation.

THE CHOICE OF COLLECTIVE VIOLENCE IN INTERGROUP CONFLICT

Collective violence in the history of the United States has achieved some positive social gains, but its use clearly results in serious repercussions, including the continuation of violence itself. The use of collective violence in this country today results from the interaction of conflicting groups (minority with majority groups, students with university officials, and so forth) and can serve as a danger signal to society. Nevertheless, such group violence evokes counterviolence from opposition groups, and this interaction results in even greater tensions, divisiveness, and further violence. The conditions favoring collective violence exist today, and unless rapid interventions are attempted, we may anticipate even more of it. Therefore, *in general, we endorse the conclusions and recommendations of the National Advisory Commission on Civil Disorders (The Kerner Report) and encourage their implementation.*

We further recommend the following:
- *The adoption of the principle and practice of self-determination by disenfranchised communities and oppressed groups.*
- *Interracial contact, as opposed to separatism.* The former is more likely to reduce racial suspicion, tension, and collective intergroup conflict. To be effective, such contact must be based on working toward shared goals and sustained over time.
- *Well-controlled prospective studies to examine the effects of violence and social change on groups as well as on interracial tensions within these groups.* White and integrated majority communities as well as minority and separated communities must be the objects of such studies. More minority group behavioral and social scientists should be encouraged to participate in these studies, and their results should be translated into practical application.

VIOLENCE IN THE MASS MEDIA

The mass media, especially movies and television, have become powerful instruments for social learning in man. Man learns, in part, by the observation and imitation of what he sees and hears, and the mass media appeal to the senses through which he learns most efficiently: vision and audition. Both fictional dramas and news reports in movies and television repeatedly depict scenes of violence. These media thus become a "School for Violence" for Americans of all ages. Because of the unparalleled significance of the mass media upon society today, we recommend the following:
- *Reduction of the portrayal of violence in the mass media.* This applies especially to movies and television, both in news reports and fictional presentations.
- *Discrediting of violent acts that do appear in the mass media.* Violence and those who advocate it should not be rewarded or glorified. When violence does appear, its destructive consequences should be emphasized.
- *Development within the mass media of educational program-*

ming concerning the limitations of violence and the potentials and methods of nonviolent behavior. Programs should include representations of those individuals and groups whose tasks include coping with conflict and should emphasize their adaptive, nonviolent techniques.

• *Establishment within the mass media of professional, ethical standards concerning the depiction of violence.* Effective self-regulation within the mass media should be established to reduce the amount and type of violence presented. Individuals within the mass media who demonstrate personal responsibility and judgment in the treatment of violence deserve the profession's and the public's active support.

• *External regulation of violent content.* Controls upon the mass media should include public reaction to programming (through letters of accord or protest) and criticism from one medium to another. Appropriate federal regulation should also be considered.

FIREARMS CONTROL AND VIOLENCE

Firearms account for the majority of all homicides and suicides in the United States. The United States, in proportion to population, leads all other industrialized countries in deaths by firearms, but gun control laws in this country are relatively weak and grossly inconsistent in limiting the availability of firearms. Most victims in this country are family members or acquaintances of the murderer, and the murders appear to result from the combination of at least three factors: (1) impulsivity, (2) the availability of the weapon, and (3) the lethality of the weapon. Impulsivity and the potential misuse of firearms are more characteristic of the young, the mentally retarded, the senile, alcoholics, and others with histories of violent behavior. Firearms rate very high in lethality and, in this country, in availability. Therefore, we recommend the following:

• *Registration of all firearms according to federal law.*

• *Licensing of all individuals who own firearms according to federal law.*

• *Regular evaluation of registration and licensing procedures to better identify those who can and cannot handle firearms safely and to study the potential dangers of gun ownership.* These evaluations should be widely publicized.

• *Careful evaluation and restriction from gun ownership of those who constitute a "high-risk" group,* for example, those individuals demonstrating marked impulsivity in their personalities.

THE GUN LAW CONTROVERSY

While the general public repeatedly favors gun laws requiring registration and licensing, many individuals and groups oppose such laws, among them the powerful National Rifle Association. Analysis of the arguments pro and con reveals that the controversy is determined by many underlying psychological, social, political, ideological, and pragmatic factors. In fact, the firearms controversy reflects in microcosm the larger controversy over violence tormenting our country. Both sides present statistics and arguments that are sometimes incomplete, confusing, or taken out of context, and they support their views with emotional fervor. Nonetheless, from our review of the various gun law arguments, we recommend (in addition to registration, licensing, research, and specific restrictions, as already recommended) the following:

• *Public education to create awareness of the psychological and social forces underlying the firearms controversy.* The many hidden, emotion-laden issues need to be understood and discussed in order to facilitate agreement between proponents and opponents of gun controls.

• *Distribution of accurate and complete information about proposed legislation and the reasons for it.* This too would facilitate rational dialogue and agreement between proponents and opponents.

• *Distinctions between types of firearms proposed for restriction.* For instance, while handguns are often used in homicides, they are relatively unimportant in hunting and recreation.

• *Attention to the potential economic losses resulting from restrictive gun legislation.* Possible economic effects include decreased revenues from hunting licenses, gun manufacture, and gun sales.

• *Provision of adequate resources and safeguards for effective and nondiscriminatory implementation and enforcement of firearms legislation.*

• *Legal assurances to sportsmen and hunters of ready access to their chosen recreation.*

• *Consideration of a contractual agreement with the National Rifle Association to administer registration and licensing procedures* if these regulations become enacted.

• *Further study of issues raised by the controversy.* Areas requiring further study include the characteristics of groups holding various views regarding gun controls, the actual protective value of personal firearms, the reasons for gun purchases, the liabilities and benefits of disarming off-duty police, the development and use of nonlethal weapons, and the effects upon children of guns and their use.

AMERICAN PRESIDENTIAL ASSASSINATION

Attempted presidential assassinations in the United States, with the exception of one incident, have been made by socially alienated men with delusional thinking and socioeconomic inadequacy. In addition, the assassinated presidents themselves have often enhanced their own vulnerability by exposing themselves unnecessarily. Hence we recommend the following:

• *Regulation over the public appearances of major political figures.* This includes more extensive use of the mass media by major political figures, thus reducing their personal public exposure; the prohibition by law of their appearance in open, large crowds at which notice of their presence has been previously announced; and urging their avoidance of the public expression of personal fatalistic feelings.

• *A waiting period between the application for a firearm and its purchase.* During this time the applicant's background can be evaluated. Such a delay could discourage "impulsive" assassins and help prevent other high-risk individuals from easy access to firearms.

• *Establishment of "Violence Prevention Centers."* (See the recommendations concerning mental illness and violence that follow.)

• *Further research in other countries and cultures in which assassination is either frequent or nonexistent.* Methods of protecting the political leaders of these cultures should be studied.

MENTAL ILLNESS AND VIOLENCE

Contrary to popular belief, studies of mentally ill patients discharged from hospitals indicate that acts of violence are no more prevalent among the mentally ill than they are among the general population. Exceptions to this are those with the diagnosis of alcoholism, psychomotor epilepsy, and perhaps paranoid schizophrenia, all of whom are associated more frequently with violent acts. Other exceptions are those with a history of violent behavior or presenting with the so-called "preassaultive" state. On the basis of these facts, we recommend the following:

• *Any legal measures taken to control the sale or use of firearms not discriminate against the discharged mentally ill patient.* Each individual with a history of mental illness should be evaluated on an individual basis. Exceptions to this appear in the following recommendation.

• *Identification and help for high-risk subgroups within the mentally ill population.* Those individuals with alcoholism, psychomotor epilepsy, and paranoid schizophrenia, as well as those in other subgroups that may be identified in the future, should be evaluated very carefully, restricted in their ownership and use of firearms, and offered professional help. Since alcohol abuse is a highly significant factor in violent behavior, it constitutes one important reason for the identification and rehabilitation of those who use alcohol excessively.

• *Establishment of "Violence Prevention Centers."* These centers could be integrated with preexisting community mental health centers or suicide prevention centers. They would function to help individuals who threaten violence; to cope with actual outbreaks of violence; to identify existing precipitants to violent behavior; and to collect data for research on the causes and prevention of violence.

DRUG USE AND VIOLENCE

Violent behavior in groups of drug users varies according to the specific drug in use and according to important nondrug variables. The public tends to focus exclusively on drug factors and to minimize the contribution of other factors in the behavior of drug users. However, unless the spectrum of psychosocial factors in drug use is considered, important factors contributing to violent behavior will be ignored. Within specific groups of drug users there is a range of potential for violence. For example, while most chronic users of intravenous methamphetamine and some chronic alcoholics have a high incidence of assaultive behavior, occasional and low-dose users of these drugs do not. In addition, many people indulging in current social marihuana usage seem to experience an interaction of drug effects, social factors, and psychological influences that enhances nonviolent behavior. Manifestations of violence under the influence of other drugs in current use—for example, barbiturates and "hard narcotics" such as heroin—fall somewhere between these extremes. Based upon the relation of violence and drug use, we recommend the following:

• *Establishment of educational programs about drug use.* Our educational programs should teach the dangers and harmful effects of specific drugs, the patterns of drug use, and the appropriate and safe use of drugs. Drug education programs are best conducted factually rather than moralistically and by well-trained personnel (including former drug users) presenting up-to-date information. These programs need to include students at all levels, their parents, teachers, and professionals involved in the mass media.

• *Sharp legal distinctions among different illicit drugs.* Severe restrictions on the availability of basic ingredients for methamphetamine and closely related amphetamines are indicated, as these drugs are frequently associated with disturbed and violent behavior. Further efforts to curb illicit amphetamine use also are needed. Similarly, current data indicate that restrictions should be increased against driving after drinking. On the other hand, at least from the standpoint of violent behavior, there is no justification for the present heavy penalties imposed on marihuana users in this country. Continuing revisions of legal sanctions are necessary as more information becomes available.

• *Increased research into drug effects and drug users.* These investigations should include the factors and drugs that decrease as well as increase tendencies toward violence. Current restrictions on research with marihuana and some other drugs affecting behavior severely impede the understanding of the relationship between drugs and behavior and should be modified.

CASE STUDIES OF VIOLENCE

An examination of the backgrounds of severely disturbed individuals who exhibit violent behavior reveals a number of common factors. These individuals frequently have experienced great inconsistencies in their own parents' behavior, lack of affection and positive regard during childhood, violence in their immediate environment, and actual loss or separation from parents. Children in such an environment often display "behavioral forewarnings" of violent or destructive behavior. These may include poorly controlled anger, school behavioral problems, poor frustration tolerance, or blatantly violent actions. Thus we recommend improvement of the following:

• *Primary prevention of violent behavior.* Here the development of educational and social programs to eliminate or at least reduce the frequency of damaging childhood experiences is of prime importance.

• *Secondary prevention of violent behavior,* i.e., early identification and treatment. Early identification of the behavioral forewarnings of violent behavior is possible, and appropriate psychological and medical intervention can avert its later development.

• *Tertiary prevention of violent behavior,* i.e., the adequate treatment and rehabilitation of individuals in our society who already exhibit violent, antisocial, or criminal behavior. Research into the causes and prevention of so-called sociopathic behavior needs to be intensified. Treatment institutions for violent offenders often have been violent settings themselves or ineffective in their therapeutic attempts. New therapeutic modalities and settings are necessary to approach the problems of violent offenders. Individual therapy specifically geared to the needs of such offenders, as well as group therapy techniques, must be further developed. In addition, treatment settings must provide a consistent, predictable environment, emphasizing nonviolent coping behavior.

Recommendations for Individual Action

The preceding guidelines and recommendations hold within them many implications for the individual. To reduce violence in this country, we believe that social, political, and educational policies and programs must be supported by individual citizens and therefore must involve individual action. Each of us can begin immediately to change our behavior and contribute to diminishing violence in many ways. We can reduce violence by the following:

• *Relinquishing our inconsistent standards and behavior surrounding acts of violence.* Our condoning some violent behaviors while condemning others maintains rather than reduces violence.

• *Eliminating excessively punitive discipline for our children and substituting nonviolent discipline and positive rewards.* In this way we can provide our children with examples of nonviolent coping behavior.

• *Learning about the potential hazards of overpopulation and its contribution to violent behavior, considering the merits of personal family planning, and limiting the size of our families.*

• *Urging our schools to develop a curriculum in the nonviolent resolution of social conflict.*

• *Writing to professionals in the mass media.* Our letters should urge them to reduce the depiction of violence on television and in the movies, to emphasize that violence is destructive rather than glamorous, and to sponsor educational programs that demonstrate nonviolent means for the resolution of conflict.

• *Opening channels of communication among ourselves and members of groups having differing views and needs.* This can be done through school organizations, neighborhood meetings, student-faculty forums, community-police meetings, and so forth.

• *Encouraging legislators to enact strong firearms control laws and to establish more legal machinery for the expression of political grievances.*

• *Urging legislators, law enforcement officials, and judicial officials to eliminate cruel social controls and penalties and to emphasize rehabilitation.*

Although these recommendations are only a portion of the possible individual actions, they represent important steps that can and must be taken. The essential point is that individual citizens are not helpless to act—each of us can take part in decreasing violence.

Violence has many determinants. No single theory has yet explained it adequately. In this volume we have studied violence from many perspectives and have suggested a wide variety of strategies to cope with it. The general guidelines and the specific recommendations appearing in this chapter are drawn from a large volume of theoretical and empirical evidence. We present them here in abbreviated form; and again, the reader is referred to the previous chapters for a more complete development and explanation. In one sense these recommendations represent the purpose and goal of our committee: to examine violence in this country and to suggest adaptive alternatives to its use. In another sense, however, they raise many questions and suggest a variety of areas for further study. Hopefully, these recommendations will not only promote the adoption of preventive measures and nonviolent alternatives but will also stimulate further study toward the nonviolent resolution of conflict, leading to a more favorable adaptation in man's evolutionary development.

15. Violence and the Struggle for Existence

David N. Daniels, M.D.,
and Marshall F. Gilula, M.D.

> The need is not really for more brains,
> the need is now for a gentler, a more
>   tolerant people
> than those who won for us
> against the ice, the tiger, and the bear.
> LOREN EISELEY [15]

Violence explodes our hopes for peace and unity. It polarizes and destroys individuals, groups, and nations. Hourly reports of violence bring numbness, shock, confusion, and sorrow. We live in a violent world.

Violence increasingly is threatening our struggle for existence in terms of both survival and the quality of life. We must try to understand the violence that surrounds us in the hopes of finding alternatives to it that will enhance survival and also meet today's demand for change [21]. This statement represents the theme of this book. In this last chapter we develop two basic concepts underlying this theme. First, violence can be understood in the context of adaptation. Violence is part of a struggle to resolve stressful and threatening events—a struggle to adapt. Second, adaptive alternatives to violence are needed in this ever-changing technological era because the survival value of violent aggression is diminishing rapidly. Drawing from material in the other chapters, this chapter represents a synthesis of our group's findings and observations as they apply to these concepts. It reflects our view of adaptation theory as a unifying principle in human behavior.

In the Introduction two groups of terms were defined: (1) aggression and violence; and (2) adaptation, adjustment, and coping. In addition, the process of human adaptation was briefly reviewed. Since here we discuss only aspects of these terms, the reader is encouraged to review the Definitions portion of the Introduction.

405

Here we first summarize and integrate the theories of aggression and violence presented in Part I and relate them to human adaptation. Then we discuss the process of coping in humans. Next, drawing upon data from Part II, Current Issues of Violence in America, we present relevant examples of violence and illustrate the urgent need for other ways of coping in man's struggle for existence. Finally, we consider the changing nature of human adaptation and suggest ways of coping with violence. Since this synthesis draws from the other chapters of this book, references are cited only for additional sources and to document specific points or citations of data.

Adaptation and Theories of Aggression

Aggression has helped man survive [45]. Aggression in man—including behaviors that are assertive, intrusive, and dominant as well as attacking and violent—is fundamental and adaptive. It is hard to imagine the survival of man without aggressiveness, for aggression is likely an element of most purposeful behavior and, in many cases, provides the means for pursuing a particular goal.

Aggression includes or at least is closely related to a wide variety of behaviors, many of which are constructive and essential to an active existence. We have mentioned assertive, intrusive, and dominance behaviors, but even stimulus-seeking behavior (for example, curiosity or the "need" to have something happen) is a behavior closely related to aggression and certainly at least as important a facet of human behavior as avoidance and as tension-reducing behaviors. Seeking the novel and unexpected provides much of life's color and excitement. Even though most of our discussion is restricted to attack behaviors and violence, we consider aggression in this broad perspective because relationships between the underlying physiological mechanisms and the social correlates of dominant, assertive, and violent behavior are still poorly understood [21].

Those who do restrict the concept of aggression to attack behaviors and violence agree that aggression must be considered in the context of other behaviors and feelings. Attack and avoidance (fight-flight) behaviors, or so-called agonistic behaviors, are firmly linked. Successful group defense, for instance, often depends upon some members attacking while others avoid the enemy. Likewise, anger occurs in the context of other feelings or affects, both negatively and positively toned, and serves, as do other affects, as a valuable signal of environmental conditions. Thus aggression can be considered adaptive behavior only as it fits into the total matrix of behaviors. Similarly anger as a signal of environmental conditions must be viewed in the context of other affects. When other feelings are ignored or fail to occur, anger becomes dominant and much more likely to lead to attack. Then the anger of a heated argument can turn into a beating and even a senseless killing.

Violence is not a *result* of aggression but simply a *form* of aggression. Violence is destructive aggression—often intense, immoderate, sometimes furious and uncontrolled behavior that injures or destroys the recipient or is intended to do so. In humans it is possible to extend the definition of *recipient* to include symbols important to one's self and groups, such as personal property, self-image, and human rights, although by and large in this book we often have limited our discussion of violence to destructive physical attack upon others. Using this definition means that violence cannot be equated with all threatened or actual attacks, since these often do not produce physical damage (or psychological damage, if the realm of symbols is included).

This somewhat arbitrary distinction creates dilemmas. Who decides when an attack is destructive or not? For example, when does spanking a child become a beating? Can all physical punishment be described as violence? What is the role of motivation or intent to injure? For now, we resolve this dilemma by starting with actual damage to the person's body or symbols as a criterion and adding intent to it. It is violence if you damage another, intended or not, as in many auto accidents where violence can occur accidentally or without conscious intent. And it is violence if in attacking, you intended damage, even if you did not inflict any.

Since this distinction between attack (or threatened attack) and violence complicates the issue, why do we even make it? This distinction is made because aggression in the form of attack (or its threat) is quite common among many species and serves useful purposes (see subsequent discussion), but damaging physical aggression in species other than man is infrequent* and not disruptive of the

* Although a number of behavioral scientists [32, 43] have indicated that nonhuman species are almost never physically destructive toward other animals within their species, other eminent behavioral scientists [24, 45] feel that much more observation, especially of primates, is needed before drawing this conclusion. For instance, Hamburg [24], in accounting for the destructiveness of humans in comparison to other primates, emphasizes the amplifying effects of human technology on aggressive tendencies that are similar to those of some nonhuman primates. While the comparative frequency of attack behaviors is debatable, the social disruption aspect of violence is uniquely human [17, 43].

social group [6, 43]. Furthermore, violence can be associated with other intentions. For instance, in the sadistic behavior of sexual assaults, violence is evoked in part by sexual motives.

REVIEW OF THEORIES OF AGGRESSION

In Part I the authors presented the main theoretical views of aggression and violence. All involve adaptation, but each suggests somewhat different solutions to the problem of violent behavior. In this synthesis relating aggression and violence to adaptation, we draw from all the theoretical chapters without making arbitrary distinctions among views. Broadly stated, the views presented in Part I show that aggression is determined by inherent biological factors interacting with environmental factors, especially social learning experiences and interruptions (often experienced as frustrations) in one's plans and goals.

The biological-inherent theories hold that aggressive behavior, including violence, is an intrinsic component of man resulting from natural selection: Man has built-in mechanisms for aggressive behaviors. Even when the aggression is restricted to attack and violent behaviors (as in most of this chapter), there is abundant evidence of the inherent predisposition to aggression and of its potential usefulness, especially in times past.

Animal studies (including primate field studies and neurophysiological research), developmental research, studies of brain-damaged and psychologically disordered humans, and male-female comparisons provide neuroanatomical, behavioral, and hormonal data, all of which illustrate the human predisposition to aggression. These data strongly suggest that basic neurophysiological processes and neuroanatomical structures exist which permit the development and expression of aggression and delimit the forms it may take. But the actual expression of aggression is not an inherent, genetically programmed instinct or drive resulting from a disturbance in internal homeostasis, such as occurs in hunger, thirst, and probably sex [35]. That is, there is no known internal physiological state that requires aggression to restore equilibrium. Aggression is basic to survival but not as a drive toward discharge of an internal inherent need state. Aggressive behaviors depend upon environmental factors that the undergirding biological mechanisms make easy to learn. Thus aggression is basic, but we are not preprogrammed to aggress. We are not fated to an instinct for violence that must be discharged periodically as an inevitable part of man's makeup.

Modern psychodynamic views of aggression use the word *drive* essentially in this manner. The term *aggressive drive* is used to imply a state of readiness, a potential, for a certain type of behavior rather than an inborn pattern of behavior that is complete and automatic in response to stimuli, either external or internal. Put another way, aggression is a means to an end, not an end in itself. There is no goal of restoring an internal equilibrium in a homeostasis of aggression. However, there is tension, especially in the skeletal muscles, which is reduced by attacking behavior. Thus modern psychodynamic theory views aggression (and its many derivatives such as violence) not as a primary drive but rather only as one class of behaviors that are important in seeking gratification and responding to frustrations and threats. Indeed psychodynamic theory concentrates on the many expressions of aggression as coping and defense behaviors acquired during the phases and vicissitudes of human development.

While some manifestations of anger and attack are seen basically as reactive responses to frustration, other forms are viewed as secondarily acquired behaviors. Many factors lead to expressions of derived or secondary aggression (attack behaviors). One is failure in the "adaptive apparatus of the ego," that is, failure of coping mechanisms that involve conceptual thinking or inhibit and delay impulses. Another factor is the need to terminate some intolerable feeling like anger, helplessness, guilt, tension, and boredom. In this case attack is used as a defense wherein the negative consequences of violence are endured or ignored because of the immediate benefits. Yet another factor is the acquired and often repeated association of violent action with gratification, security, prior successful conflict resolution, and in some instances with a sense of excitement. Finally, disturbances in identification with parental role models because of either failure in positive identifications or identification with disturbed parents lead to secondarily acquired attack behaviors. Violence in these psychodynamic terms always serves some purpose in settling conflict, presumably in the interest of self-preservation. Yet these derived forms of physical aggression, as discussed subsequently, mainly are defense behaviors serving mostly adjustment rather than long-run adaptation.

In other species the circumstances of aggressive behaviors are much less complicated. Unlike man, who can consider far-reaching consequences in both space and time, other animals live largely in the present, making it simpler to determine the conditions in which attack behaviors will occur. The specific instigators of attack behaviors are pain, threat to status, invasion of personal space, and overcrowding. Although intraspecies violence among nonhuman mammals may occur less frequently than with humans, attack behaviors, especially in ritualized form, do occur among members of the same species in the circumstances mentioned. Hence they serve the valuable functions of spacing and dispersing populations over the available land, regulating breeding, maintaining a dominance order among the group members, and furthering intragroup defense and affiliation through structuring social interactions. Aggression in humans, probably even in the form of violence, has had similar adaptive value historically.

Since attacking behaviors and threatened attacks often are ritualized signals, they actually can prevent extensive and damaging forms of attack. In fact, uncontrolled attack in animals generally occurs only under conditions of overcrowding and extreme social deprivation. Here, as with humans, the attack is often displaced from the original object onto some less dangerous target [3]. Moreover, although violent aggression apparently occurs more frequently in humans, attack behaviors in man also are much more likely to be non-damaging or not overtly expressed.

In sum, the biological-inherent theories of aggression show that we must examine the matrix formed by the intertwining of internal mechanisms with external events and social learning experiences. Environmental theories of aggression complement the biological-inherent views because they focus on extrinsic factors contributing to aggressive behaviors, not because they disregard innate mechanisms.

The frustration view states that aggressive behavior occurs after an interference with ongoing purposeful activity. (This theory often equates aggression with destructive or damaging violent behavior.) The primary effect of frustration is to raise the motivational state of the individual, with the destructive response itself being a learned behavior. A person feels frustrated when a violation of his hopes or expectations occurs, and he may then try to solve the problem by attacking the presumed source of the frustration.

Frustrations can take various forms: threats to life, thwarting of basic needs, personal insults, and conflict among an individual's various societal roles. Major factors influencing attack responses to frustration include the nature of the frustration, previous experience, available alternatives for reaction (aggression is by no means the only response to frustration), the person's personality and maturity, and the immediately preceding events or feelings conducive to violence—so-called instigating stimuli. Such instigating stimuli include a precipitating event, ready availability of weapons, a low expectancy of punishment, boredom, intoxication, group contagion, and strong obedience to authority. According to this theory, frustration-evoked attack aims at removing obstacles to our goals. The attack response to frustration may represent coping behavior, behavior that is not merely adjustive but which also has long-range favorable consequences; hence the frustration theory too ties in with adaptation.

The social learning theory says that attack behavior results from child-rearing practices and other forms of socialization. Documentation comes from sociological and anthropological studies and from observing social learning in children. Aggressive behavior including violence can be acquired merely by watching and learning—often by imitation and play—and does *not* require frustration. This emphasis on acquiring attack behaviors through learning experiences does not diminish the important role played by the intrinsic capacity in humans to readily learn these behaviors. In man both inherent selective learning mechanisms and critical developmental periods for learning play an important part in developing attack behaviors [23, 43, 46].

Violent behavior rewarded by a particular culture or subculture usually reflects basic group values and hence behaviors that the group believes are adaptive. In cultures where achievement, self-reliance, and individual self-interest are valued highly, one also finds a relatively high emphasis on military glory, a relatively high incidence of personal crime, and a society characterized by a relatively high degree of bellicosity. From the social learning theory we infer that as long as a society values and accepts violence as an effective coping strategy, violent behavior will continue.

FACTORS IN COLLECTIVE VIOLENCE

Since the bases of collective violence extend beyond the factors contributing to aggression and violence in individuals, it is necessary to summarize these additional factors. First, the importance of group adaptation and coping, especially in man and nonhuman primates, must be recognized. In addition to enhancing group survival, group territorial defense promotes group unity and reduces strife among members [3]. Since Freud believed in an aggressive instinct, the unity factor may have led him to conclude that increasing civilization with its consequent restrictions on the aggressive instinct was a crucial factor leading to war [19]. He felt that the inherent aggressive instinct was displaced or scapegoated upon another group. However, the notion of a fixed reciprocal relationship between individual and group violence holds true only if one holds to a drive discharge theory of aggression.

Next, conflict between groups (e.g., subcultures, nations) is conducive to violence. Incompatible goals between groups and unobtainable goals of a group, especially goals associated with rising expectations of their fulfillment, increase the likelihood of violence, just as intolerable frustrations do in individuals. Similarly, rapid cultural change, with its accompanying social tensions and threats to established values and authority, contributes to group violence.

Rapid change and perceived inequality in social conditions are two instigators of collective violence. Other factors include especially a precipitating incident, identification of the "source" of the frustrations or strains together with the belief that attack will achieve desired goals, low expectation of punishment, obedience to authority or inspiring leadership, and the phenomenon of group contagion wherein individual accountability is diffused by group pressure and actions [4].

Lastly, deliberate planned attack, as in war, differs from spontaneous unplanned attack, as in mob violence. Planned attack usually depends upon formal cultural norms sanctioning the violence and adequate social controls. Mob violence depends more upon emergent informal norms and failure in social controls.

INTERRELATIONS AMONG
THEORIES AND IMPLICATIONS

The various perspectives on aggression and violence are interrelated. Proclivities for social learning and for frustration often have a biological determinant. For example, the biology of sex influences the learning of courting behavior. Regarding violence, from these theories of aggression we see that the many facets of violence include man's inherent predisposition to aggression, aggressive responses to thwarted goals, and behavior patterns imitatively learned within the cultural setting. All these views of aggression and violence fit into adaptation–coping concepts. Violence is an attempt to cope with stressful situations and to resolve intolerable conflicts. Violence may have short-run adjustive value, even when the long-run adaptive consequences may in fact be adverse. It is the sometimes conflicting natures of adjustment and adaptation that are confusing and insufficiently appreciated. In some instances violence emerges as a defense when constructive coping strategies have failed. Here violence serves as short-term adjustment. In other instances violence is used as a deliberate strategy that presumably enhances survival and adaptation. Our species apparently has overabsorbed violence into our cultures as a survival technique. Children and adolescents have learned well the accepted violent behaviors of their elders.

The theories of aggression help us understand violent behavior and hence suggest potential ways of reducing violence. Man's inherent potential for aggressive behaviors suggests that effective controls upon the expression of destructive forms of aggression are necessary and that reduction of violence depends upon teaching constructive means of expressing aggression.

The frustration view of aggression suggests that control or reduction of violence requires diminishing existing frustrations as well as encouraging constructive redirection of aggressive responses to frustrations and dashed hopes. Reducing frustrations includes removing or improving environmental factors that stand between personal needs or goals and their expected fulfillment. Such factors include violation of human rights, economic deprivation, various social stresses, and dashed personal hopes.

Finally, the social learning point of view suggests that diminishing violence requires changes in cultural traditions and child-rearing practices. Parents who violently punish children for violent acts are teaching their children how and in what circumstances violence can be performed with impunity. Similarly societies that condemn some forms of violence while condoning other forms propagate more violence. Other changes in cultural traditions would emphasize prevention rather than mainly punishment of violent acts and, equally important, would emphasize human rights and cooperative group effort rather than excessive and isolated self-reliance. The first step toward making these changes that will reduce violence is to examine our values.

All these partial solutions to the problem of violence are suggestions derived from theory. They are mutually complementary rather than exclusive of one another, since it is possible *concurrently* to change social learning practices, reduce frustrations, encourage attainable expectations, redirect aggression into constructive channels, and assert controls that require a minimum of force and suppression. Furthermore, even increased awareness and understanding of the factors and circumstances leading to attack behaviors and violence can themselves result in greater mastery and control of violence.

Before discussing current examples of violence from the perspective of those factors that foster violence and from the standpoint of how these examples reflect the changing nature of human adaptation, we shall describe coping processes in humans in some detail. We do this because an understanding of coping provides a lever to the understanding of violence and its role in human adaptation.

Coping and Violence

Coping is goal-oriented, problem-solving behavior that occurs when a stressful stimulus interrupts important plans of action. It represents the continuing and usually successful struggle of an individual or group to meet environmental demands for change. Hence coping usually accomplishes tasks or goals with adaptive consequences. The concept of coping is crucial in understanding violence and in pursuing alternatives to violence, since violent behavior represents an effort to resolve conflicts. Here we discuss the questions: When does coping behavior occur? What are the basic elements in the coping process? What factors modify or affect the coping process and cause it to fail? And how does an understanding of coping help explain violence and suggest remedies for it? Although coping and its relation to violence are touched upon repeatedly in the preceding theoretical discussion, and indeed throughout the book, the central position of coping in the daily conduct of human affairs and in settling conflict makes it imperative to examine this mediator of human adaptation in some detail. In doing so, we draw considerably from the cybernetic model presented in Chapter 4 and from the work of Hamburg and his associates [23, 25, 40].

WHEN COPING OCCURS

Coping begins when there is a disruption in an individual's or group's ongoing plan or activity, when an important nonrote or unexpected event occurs that alters usual plans of action and creates a disequilibrium or stress that calls for revision of plans. The type of disruption varies. The disruption (stressful event) may be an actual external blockage or a failure to attain an expected goal. It may occur when a task under consideration is completed. Or the disruption may be a new stimulus directing attention from the current activity. In this regard coping can be considered as self-initiated, not just forced or in response to a threatening stimulus. Still, new stimuli or the boredom associated with completion of a task can be experienced as threatening. Of most relevance to violent behavior, however, is coping resulting from an interruption in an important plan or goal, one that seems vital to the individual's or group's overall plans and goals.

THE COPING PROCESS

Coping always represents the effort of an individual or group to solve a problem or resolve a conflict. It involves the planned application of the individual's or group's skills (including technical, manual, cognitive, and interpersonal) to solving problems in the present and in anticipated situations. The process is similar to the subjective appraisals of outcomes described in Chapter 4. Affect (for instance, feelings of anxiety or anger) signals a threat or disruption in an important ongoing activity or plan and provides feedback *and* "feedforward" about the appropriateness of one's behavior. The feelings or affects thus engendered reflect the subjective probability of reaching goals, which in turn is based largely upon cognitive assessment of the likelihood of various strategies to accomplish particular goals. Feelings or affects also serve as motives or prompters of action, and their intensity reflects the value of goals. It is important to emphasize that coping is not simply a cognitive, intellectual matter. Awareness of one's feelings, being "tuned in," is crucial to carrying out both appropriate appraisals and actions—to successful coping.

The form that coping behavior takes is based upon these constantly reoccurring subjective appraisals. If the external environment seems to offer hope of achieving important goals, coping will take the form of various direct actions on the environment. On the other hand, if the environment seems unmodifiable in respect to important goals, then coping will take the form of alterations in internal perceptions of events, so-called intrapsychic alterations or defenses—for example, devaluing the perceived worth of a goal. In most instances both types of activity occur together and lead to successful problem-solving [31]. For instance, a person can devalue (deny) the worth of one goal, which would then permit enactment of a plan toward another goal. Similarly an individual can screen out (reduce) fear-arousing perceptions that might otherwise interfere with his proceeding with an important plan of action.

Since many factors in the total situation influence the coping process, it is necessary to discuss important modifiers of coping behavior, especially those that increase the likelihood of violence.

FACTORS MODIFYING COPING

Factors within the person that are associated with goals and their attainment modify coping. Important personal factors are the individual's current internal state and "set," his particular past experiences, his maturity, and the skills and abilities with which he can tackle a task.

The characteristics of goals and the means to their attainment similarly are important. In particular, the attainability of alternative goals or approaches or both are crucial. But also important are the value or stakes of the goal for both the individual and significant others; the degree of ambiguity, complexity, and novelty associated with the current situation; the approval of the social group; and the availability of environmental resources, especially other people, to help, for often the cooperation of others is necessary to carry out a plan [31, 27].

Any number of these modifiers (for example, few or poorly developed personal skills, conflicting goals, and a high degree of novelty in the situation) can conspire to increase the stress upon the individual or group in the pursuit of goals. However, there are three factors that we will discuss in detail because of their special relevance to violent behavior: the availability of alternatives and attainability of goals; considerations involving time; and the curvilinear relation between coping and stressful situations, those demanding change in behavior.

Coping: Alternatives and Attainability of Goals

Both the actual availability and the perceived availability of alternative and attainable goals or means to goals are crucial to successful coping. For when there is little or nothing that the individual or group can do to alter events, the only coping that can occur under these circumstances is through internal rearrangements of perceptions that allow for the gaining of time or relinquishing a goal. Attack behavior is the other "choice" in the face of being trapped without constructive means or alternatives.

Coping and Time

One's perspective on time, how long it should take to get results, influences the entire process of coping—subjective appraisals and behaviors alike. The child's and the student's views of time differ greatly from the adult's and the teacher's views. For the child and the student events take too long, time drags out. In contrast, for the adult and the teacher events move too quickly, time goes by too fast. Similarly, this type of contrast can occur between the oppressed and the oppressor. The impatience of hunger and youth becomes tempered by satiation and age. The hungry and young often feel rushed and constrained, a feeling that narrows the range of alternative choices and increases the likelihood of using violence in an attempt to reach a goal. Having or perceiving insufficient time to reach goals is a strong inducement to violence. In addition, if there is no hope for future rewards, no value in extended time, taking what you can

get now by whatever means available without regard to future consequences becomes a plausible course of action [7]. An exception is
the older person who may perceive, and correctly, that there is insufficient time to reach valued goals. In this case the feeling of failure
is more likely to lead to the violence of suicide than to outer-
directed attack.

Then there are those whose perspective on time is telescoped into
the present, for example, the brain-damaged, the impulse-ridden, and
the drug-abusing individual. By taking mainly the present view,
these individuals often use poor judgment, since they rely upon neither future consequences nor past experience in making appraisals.
Similarly highly stressful events that produce the feeling of being
rushed and constrained prompt the individual or group into taking
the short-run, present-oriented view. Terminating painful feelings,
ending intolerable conflicts, and fulfilling urgent needs are strong
inducements for domination by an immediacy orientation, which in
turn can lead to violent action. Such short-term goals take precedence over long-term goals because immediate relief seems more important than possible long-run maladaptive consequences. In these
circumstances the individual or group is much more likely to dis-
count the needs of others and their potential for helping. This tendency to telescope time into the present and to take only the personal
view during stressful times is of more relevance now than ever before because the rapid pace of cultural change itself brings one crisis
upon another, increasing both the risk of resorting to violence as
well as the tendency to ignore destructive long-range effects of violent actions.

Gaining time is yet another way that time plays a role in coping.
When there is little or nothing that can be done to alter one's current situation, forestalling action can help the individual get prepared emotionally for whatever is to happen and often to endure a
painful experience—to ride out the storm. But here, in contrast to
taking the present view, there is an expectation of rewards in the
future, which helps one endure the present.

Coping and Stress

Stressful situations vary in intensity, which is governed by the
event itself, the experiencer's perception of the event, his physiological reactions to it, and his coping abilities [2]. It is difficult to quan-
tify stress from person to person, since individuals vary greatly from
one situation to another in their capacities for recognizing, tolerat-
ing, and dealing with stressful events. Any particular situation may

represent a minor stress to one individual and a major stress to another.

Minor stresses are simple problems requiring solution. Ordinary plans are sufficient to solve the problem, and little coping is required. Intermediate stressful events represent crises, that is, events serving as turning points. A crisis can lead to problem-solving with favorable outcomes or go on to become a disabling upset [8]. Major stressful situations are events that overwhelm the individual's or group's coping efforts. At such times indiscriminate aggressive reactions are likely to take place along with other forms of defensive behavior. In this way some violence can be viewed as an outgrowth of a failure in the coping process.

With events demanding little change in ordinary plans of action (for instance, small, easily remedied disruptions), some coping occurs but in small increments. As the situational stress increases, the phenomenon of crisis unfolds. Usual problem-solving techniques do not work. Vigilance becomes high, searching the environment for solutions increases, openness to new information occurs along with a heightened potential for learning, and corresponding physiological preparedness takes place. The individual is in a highly motivated state, which holds the potential for maximal application of his coping skills and for learning new skills. But as the situational stress increases beyond an optimal range, coping rapidly drops off, and the individual's coping strategies give way to more primitive and defensive behaviors. At the same time, the distress (for example, anxiety) experienced by the individual also increases rapidly, which in itself serves to interfere with coping behavior and to divert attention from the task at hand. The individual reaches a "breaking point" at which time he is no longer able to deal with the task [22].

Thus coping with stressful events can be said to function in a curvilinear fashion. For each person and situation there is a range of adequate functioning. Many curves of coping are possible, depending upon the various "types" of individuals interacting with different stressful situations. Figure 9 simply shows the curves of some hypothetical "types" from among a family of possible curves. The vertical axis represents the hypothetical level of coping actually performed by individuals in different circumstances. The horizontal axis is the hypothetical level of environmental demands for change (situational stress). The light portion of the figure, the area above the diagonal line, indicates the zone of adequate coping. The shaded area below the diagonal line indicates the zone of failure where

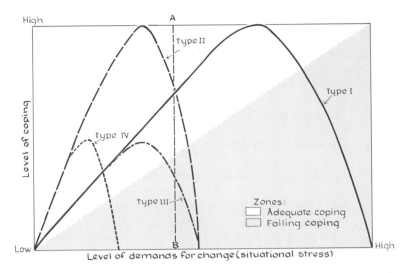

FIG. 9. Hypothetical patterns of coping. Type I individual has high coping skills and low distress arousal; Type II, high coping skills and high distress arousal; Type III, low coping skills and low distress arousal; and Type IV, low coping skills and high distress arousal. Vertical line AB shows that coping for different types varies greatly at any given level of situational stress.

coping behaviors, no matter how skilled, are inadequate to the demands of the situation and where defensive, adjustment-oriented behaviors replace the more future- and task-oriented coping behaviors. Each curve is asymmetrical to indicate that at a point near failure in the coping process a rapid reversal occurs when an individual's maximum coping potential, however good it may be, is reached. On the descending curve coping behaviors are replaced more and more by defensive behaviors that deal mainly with the immediate distress engendered by the stressful situation rather than with the situation itself or long-range efforts. Destructive behavior is likely to occur as the demands for change exceed the individual's capacity to cope. In addition, the curves show that the capacity to cope varies with the individual and the situation [27], that there is a tendency to "overcope" on the upswing of the curves (i.e., individuals perform at levels exceeding the minimal requirements of the situation), and that at any particular level of situational stress some types are failing to cope while others are successfully coping (see vertical line AB).

Types I and II are highly skilled copers (have many and good coping strategies). However, Type I experiences affect and distress less intensely than Type II, who becomes distressed more easily and intensely. Thus although Type I becomes mobilized more slowly at lower levels of stress than Type II, Type I still functions adequately at lower levels and over a larger range of stress than does Type II, who experiences affect arousal (e.g., anxiety or anger) and distress more intensely at any given level of stressful inputs and more readily experiences disabling distress.

On the other hand, Types III and IV have few and poor coping skills and strategies and consequently cope over a smaller range of stressful situations. The low-skilled, easily distressed person, Type IV, is the most handicapped. He is more likely both to experience excessive, disabling affect and to have fewer skills going for him. In contrast, Type III can function adequately over a larger range of stressful situations than can Type IV.

During development, as a child acquires more and better differentiated coping skills, one would expect coping patterns to shift gradually from Types III and IV to Types I and II. This shift in coping pattern with age accounts in part for the decrease in violence that comes with maturity. Similarly, one would expect drugs, such as alcohol and methamphetamine, and some types of brain damage to shift coping toward a Type IV pattern and consequently increase the probability for violent behavior.

COPING, DEFENSE, AND VIOLENCE

We can now summarize the conditions under which coping is likely to go awry or even cease and violence emerge. Often these are the conditions that bring on defensive activity which temporarily enhances the fit between an individual or group under stress and the immediate situation and reduces perceived distress. Defensive activity depends greatly upon alterations in internal perceptions (for example, screening out an interruption) or behaviors that are present-bound (for example, attacking a blockade to one's plans without weighing future consequences). The adjustment that defense achieves represents successful coping when there is little or nothing that the individual can do in the present to favorably alter future events. Mainly this requires alterations of the individual's perceptions that allow him to gain time or to relinquish goals. However, when there is some opportunity to influence future events favorably, defense can protect the individual from "information overload" and disabling feelings by reducing information input and distressing affect and thereby allow him to continue with a task. For instance, dealing with a severely frustrating reality is possible only if the full extent of the bitter truth is recognized slowly or only as rapidly as the person can stand it [50]. This function of defense, which may facilitate coping, depends upon the alterability of future events.

Although adjustment is an important phenomenon and may result in weathering the storm and shifting goals and plans, the accompanying alterations in perceptions that make it possible to adjust also can lead to distorted and inadequate subjective appraisals of present and future plans and goals. Often these perceptual alterations are referred to as ego defense mechanisms [18] or security operations [42]. Among these ways to alter perceptions and screen out information are denial, repression, displacement, projection, intellectualization, and rationalization. Distorted perceptions can lead to very personalized views and sometimes to fixed reactions to stressful situations ("neurosis"). Defenses succeed in the momentary encounter but fail to win the day. The price of temporary adjustment that makes one feel good or better and potentiates defensive behavior is high. The danger is compounded by the ensuing poorer subjective assessments of the environment, which can escalate into further perceptual distortions and "irrational" defensive action. Thus action too may be misguided by distorted perceptions and inadequate subjective appraisals of outcomes. At such times the attempt to bring immediate relief or to restore a plan is frequently carried out through attacking and destroying the perceived here-and-now interference. Considerations of long-range consequences go by the board.

Obviously only a portion of all defensive reactions to stressful events lead to violence, but key elements in defense behaviors—an exclusively present and past orientation; a highly personalized view; and, when present, the inclination toward action as a goal in itself—predispose one to attack. All these lead to insufficient appraisal as to whether or not a particular goal is attainable. Then if the situation is one that frequently signals anger—frustrating blockages to one's plans and dashed hopes—the likelihood of violence is enhanced. This is particularly so when the interrupted plan is directed toward a highly valued and close-at-hand goal, alternative courses of action are unavailable, time is limited, and other people seem to be obstacles to goals rather than potential sources of help and cooperation.

These are the principal conditions of reactive violence, violence that emerges when other means of coping fail. However, attack also can occur as a deliberate, even primary, strategy to attain a desired

just as violent as the individual having only token or fragmented controls.

For some individuals who commit violent acts, coping is further impaired by brain damage (including of course temporary impairment induced by drugs), which further handicaps one's assessment of the environment and reduces inhibitions that are necessary for successful coping. Occasionally, violent behavior may literally be produced by focal brain lesions that alter brain function in areas directly involving inhibition and facilitation of attack behavior [34]. Similarly some psychotic people, who are impaired in their ability to distinguish the self from others, thought from action, and reality from fantasy, are vulnerable to failures in coping. These people are especially likely to commit violent acts within the family setting. Still violence in psychotic people is unlikely unless other predisposing factors are present, such as violence in the family, an orientation toward action, and extreme mistrust in others.

Violent Behavior in Resolving Conflict

Such violence-prone individuals encounter stressful situations without the skills to solve them in adaptive ways. Indeed these individuals demonstrate the very factors that lead to coping failure. In such ill-equipped people the stage for violence is well set. The scene is familiar. The victim is a family member, friend, or acquaintance who has had repeated friction and clashes with the violence-prone person and who, like that person, may himself be drinking and more liable to attack. Alcohol, or perhaps methamphetamine, may be used to reduce distress and bring temporary relief, that is, bring temporary adjustment, but these drugs actually serve to obliterate future consequences, erode controls, and distort perceptions—all of which lead to taking only the present and personal view and dispose the person to violent behavior.

The individual finds himself trapped in a situation in which he experiences intolerable frustration, intense anger, helplessness resulting from the unavailability of or the inability to perceive alternative solutions, and no way to gain time or get help. In addition, he may literally not be able to stand encroachments on the physical space surrounding his body [29]. The conflict overwhelms him, sometimes even to the point where reality disappears. He then resorts to violence. Thus the act of homicide can be viewed as the emergence of a defensive reaction and a breakdown of coping. Homicide eliminates the immediate problem at a time when there seems to be no future or when the future seems unimportant, and the long-range consequences of the act are not considered. Put another way, homicide and many other forms of personal violence have adjustive rather than adaptive value.

A similar pattern holds for presidential assassination. To the alienated and grossly disturbed person, the act of assassination can represent a desperate attempt to achieve importance, reverse a downward life course, and obtain retribution for imagined wrongs. Repeatedly in the presidential assassin one sees an alienated man struggling to cope and failing. To him the act of killing an important political figure seemingly provides resolution of the conflict.

Cultural sanctions can be seen as playing a part in all individual violence. In the United States, as elsewhere, killing is sometimes a "legitimate" means of resolving conflicts or solving problems. When the cause is viewed as good and the issue sufficiently important, killing is justified. Is it a contradiction that would-be presidential assassins usually have been convinced of the overwhelming importance and rightness of their cause? To them also killing seems a legitimate means to accomplish a valued goal. Similarly in the battered-child syndrome the brutal and sometimes lethal beatings of children by their parents represent a strategy, twisted as it may be, to accomplish the goal of educating a "disobedient" child.

COLLECTIVE VIOLENCE AND COPING

An additional dilemma is that killing is neither legally nor socially defined as an unequivocally criminal act. The existence of capital punishment and war as adaptive strategies gives qualified sanction to violence as a means of resolving conflict. So does an ethos glorifying courage, worshipping military heroism, and extolling self-protection by brute strength and firearms. Both the general public and their leaders are remarkably adept in justifying violence perpetrated on their fellow man. In a sense all sanctioned violence is collective, since it has group social approval. Certainly the existence of sanctioned violence abrades the concept of law and order. Indeed collective and sanctioned violence—deliberate attack as attempted coping—can be viewed as the core issue, since most individual violence is drawn from it and often represents desperate efforts to solve conflicts.

We urgently need research on the psychological processes that permit an individual or group to view some violence as good (and presumably adaptive) and other forms of violence as bad (and presumably maladaptive). Although the history of violence in man is polymorphous, there likely are psychological mechanisms common to all cultures and times. For instance, the psychology of sanctioned violence everywhere depends on attributing evil motives to the "outsiders." Then because "they" are violent (evil), "we" *have* to be violent; or (twisted even further) because "they" are violent, it is *good* for "us" to be violent. Through this process we seem to be capable of justifying any violence, but perhaps the most invidious justification of violence is the moral application of violence either as "a last resort" or because "our cause is the truly right one."

The psychology of sanctioned violence is transmitted from generation to generation. Each generation *learns* the ways, processes, and ethos of violence: "Nothing is clearer in history than the adoption by successful rebels of the methods they were accustomed to condemn in the forces they deposed" [13]. Rebels have learned these methods and come to advocate them. Similarly, men who have served in the military are stronger advocates of military interventions and methods than are men who have not had military service [3]. During the People's Park controversy in Berkeley, California, several hundred arrested citizens were imprisoned in the Santa Rita jail. It is not surprising that some of the Sheriff's young deputies, veterans of the Vietnam war, viewed those "dissidents like they were Viet Cong" and punished them accordingly [28], since they too had come to see the opposition in militaristic terms.

Thus people who have seen sanctioned violence being committed in the name of law, order, justice, moral obligation, and duty come to use violence themselves as a "just" means of solving their own problems. The people are acting as their government's representatives have acted—if the cause is just, the grievance real, then force and violence can be used.

Domestic Group Violence: "Riots"

Nowhere do we better see this thinking reflected then in the actions of rioters (Chapter 6). A study of the 1967 Detroit uprising [9] showed that the rioters (young, somewhat better educated men who had experienced frustration of their rising expectations) viewed violence against the "system" as justified. Not surprisingly, their views of what justifies violence differed greatly from those of the law enforcers and of the middle-aged black citizens. To the rioters violence was a means of accomplishing goals seemingly unattainable by nonviolent means. Their belief in the power of violence is understandable. Civil disorders are serving in part as a danger signal, a catalyst for change and an instrument of achievement. Some uprising participants reported that violence provided individual satisfaction such as a sense of manliness, strength, and personal achievement.

The Detroit example is quite characteristic of the interacting factors leading to "mob" violence. Antecedents are similar to factors that are conducive to revolt, except organized and sustained effort and the intent to revolt are lacking. A large under-class group feels oppressed (historically this subordinate group is not a minority but the majority, the "masses"). Over time, wealth accumulates disproportionately in the dominant group. Sometimes the growing gap is relative, and this gap can be in values, beliefs, and skills as well as in power and wealth. Then the conditions of relative deprivation obtain: Living conditions of the dominant group, however good they may already be, improve faster than those in the subordinate group, even though the subordinate group's conditions are improving. The favorable changes in the subordinate group increase the range and inconsistency of opportunities. Aspirations are extended, but they grow faster than actual change. While the proportion of black citizens in the American middle class (economically speaking) has grown from 5 percent to 25 percent in just over two decades, the average black citizen finds himself getting further behind his white counterpart [36]. The real gains through the nonviolent civil rights movement further extended black citizens' expectations. Ironically and tragically these heightened expectations have not been met, a failure that has left many feeling even more deprived.

In a society that now as in the past practices violence as though it were productive, violence more readily replaces nonviolent means of settling conflict. And despite our "social amnesia," the forgetting of our country's violent roots [41], much of American history is the story, even the romance, of violence by both majority and minority groups [26]. Quite naturally more than 50 percent of blacks condoned ghetto riots and believed in their effectiveness in producing favorable changes [5].

Then this already explosive mixture of belief in violence as a means of coping, relative deprivation, and dashed expectations ignites into group violence following a relatively small precipitating incident such as an abuse by the police, the symbol of the alien controlling enemy. For those lacking "a piece of the action" in political and economic power, the power of violent disruption has its rewards: a sense of fulfillment and achievement seemingly unavailable by other means, concessions from the dominant group, and a sense of group unity. But do these supposed gains outweigh the destruction and suffering, the further polarization, and the escalations of counterviolence? Do they outweigh the dangers of organized rebellion and the potential suppression?

War and Coping

In the history of man peace is the punctuation to war. Of the last 3,421 years only 268 have been free from war [13]. In the period between 1820 and 1949 over three hundred wars were fought causing between 1.5 percent and 3.0 percent of all deaths, and perhaps 10 percent if one includes indirect effects like subsequent disease and famine [37, 51]. Although other species fight among themselves, this amazing and nearly ubiquitous predilection to mass intergroup killing must be included among man's unique characteristics [3, 32, 43]. Our analysis here centers on this propensity for intergroup killing and its role in the past and present evolution of man. While analysis of the myriad of wars is not our task, we will comment upon the "causes" of war, and we ask the reader to consider for himself or herself the particular relevance of the Vietnam conflict in the current crisis of violence facing America.

Behavioral and social scientists have grasped at all sorts of explanations for this species' warring behavior. Perhaps even the attempt to explain war is a cause of war; our ability to justify any form of violence is part of man's extraordinary cerebral endowment. Many causes of war have been suggested: contiguity, overcrowding, habituation, social learning, obedience to authority, predation, psychological defenses (for example, rationalization, blaming, denial, displacement, and counterphobic tendencies), identification with (becoming like) the aggressor, the host of fears associated with the human condition, territoriality and power (population spacing, control of resources, group dominance), the formation of extensive expectations that cannot be fulfilled, intolerable frustration, biologically rooted aggressive "instincts," greed, revenge, ideology (truth, religion—especially Christianity and Islam—politics, nationalism), failure of alliances and other destruction-prohibiting rituals, and the mere presence of a war-making institution [3, 16, 17, 20, 37, 44, 51, 52]. One wonders whether the mere distance and speed with which we kill are factors rendering meaningless the signals of submission that other animals use to halt violent encounters [17, 32]. Often we literally no longer have to touch the results of our violence which denies us feedback about the full reach and range of our acts and impairs appraisals of outcomes. The impersonal factor shows up in another way. Since war is an activity between organized groups, e.g., nation states, decisions producing war often are made in a calculated manner by those who do not participate directly in any personal acts of violence.

General economic conditions play a direct role in war but probably less than do psychological and political factors [37, 51]. This argument fits in with the relative deprivation theory. It is not only the gap between groups but awareness of the gap that incites war. With the advent of television and other mass media, the disadvantaged everywhere and certainly those in America are becoming acutely aware of their deprivations.

Although all these factors likely play a role, considered from the perspective of adaptation some factors are most important [3]. War (especially when restricted to "ritualized" fighting) has served evolution by dispersing and spacing groups, controlling population growth, strengthening affiliations, uniting groups, and assuring resources for the winning group. None less than Darwin [10] recognized this. Put in oversimplified terms: "War is a nation's way of eating. It promotes co-operation because it is the ultimate form of competition" [13]. In militaristic terms war becomes the final arbiter—the "ultimate" in group coping and conflict resolution.

But put another way: "War is a product of man's evolution, and man's evolution is determined—at least in part—by the institution of war" [3]. Yet man is evolving, not just evolved. Since evolution is a process of selection and elimination, those things that help adaptation are selected for, and those that hinder adaptation are selected against.

Despite whatever purposes war has served in the past, there are convincing reasons to believe that war is no longer helping man to solve long-range problems. In fact, war now is working against the struggle for existence, both in terms of survival and the quality of life.

It is possible for some characteristics of a species to be maladaptive or to serve as only partial adaptations [14, 32]. Remnants of formerly adaptive characteristics are one example. Another is "quantum evolution" or rapid evolution during which some characteristics develop at a great rate because of selective pressures associated with new environments [14]. Such rapid changes mean that selection out of other less adaptive characteristics has not yet occurred or kept pace. In man development of the cerebrum outstrips changes in lower, older brain centers, and culture outstrips biological keeping pace in general. Similarly intraspecies selection pressures can act to produce only partial adaptation. Reproduction and in man some facets of culture are selected for on the basis of intraspecies "desirability," which is relatively independent of the trait's general environmental adaptive value. For instance, a society may value warriors as preferred mates, a preference that can lead to more men becoming warriors and the continuing selection of warlike men, even though war may be increasingly detrimental to the group. Thus it is possible to have behaviors that seem to be adaptive but which are serving little purpose and actually may be very harmful to long-run survival.

Warring is such a behavior. War no longer assures resources (spoils) to the victor, since both winner and loser can be depleted equally; and it no longer assures population control, since the victor can be eliminated along with the vanquished. In the technological age even weeding out the weak has little adaptive import, since physical strength is of little importance. Man is not becoming more warlike [37], but war is becoming more destructive, long, costly, and lethal (the percentage of casualties is rising despite modern medicine) [51]. Added to this carnage is the probability of nuclear or biological-chemical warfare or both, however low a probability it might be. Estimates range from less than 1 percent to approximately 5 percent per year [3]. If one extends these probabilities over a span of ten, fifty, or even one hundred years, the cumulative prospect for holocaust is terrifying.

Yet we have what can be thought of as a cultural intraspecies selection pressure for war, which is quite out of harmony with general adaptation. Frank [16] writes of two overlapping motives for war: "success-oriented" motives, in which war is primarily a means to an end, that is, war as collective coping; and "conflict-oriented" motives, in which war is waged for its own sake. In conflict-oriented war the rewards are the satisfactions associated with the act: the glory, adulation, and worship of the battle hero, with dying in battle seen as the highest possible experience. Such cultural enshrinement of war tends to sustain it regardless of coping factors and despite environmental selective pressures against it. In this way war can be viewed as "diabolical" intraspecies selection [32].

An additional evolutionary factor affecting the adaptive value of war is diversification [3]. In the past diversification has helped human groups to adapt to many different environments. But cultural diversity in man also has led to human populations so different culturally that communication between them becomes difficult, and genetic crossover may be small [12]. In our new era, however, physical distance shrinks because of expanding population and rapid transportation, while psychological distance often remains great despite the mass media potential to reduce psychological barriers through increasing positive contact among groups. The likelihood of intergroup strife and the number of provocations to fight are compounded by repeated physical contacts between groups that still lack sufficient psychological contact and rapport. This point is one of great importance in the modern world.

The Vietnam war illustrates all too well the controversy over sanctioned collective violence and its role in coping. Hopefully this controversy also reflects a growing awareness of the changing nature of coping and adaptation. We, the authors, believe it better not to parade in dreary procession, point by point, statements linking this war with what we have been saying about collective violence and coping. It seems to us that more purpose would be served if the reader himself compares the Vietnam conflict with the "explanations" of war, the past evolutionary value of collective violence, and the factors in evolving man that change the feasibility of war as a coping strategy. For example, are the following contributors to war at work: The human capacity to blame and justify? The belief in the rightness of the cause, despite the costs, justifying the killing? The belief in war as necessary and effective coping? Can you see the dangers this war daily offers to existence?

Must we be fooled by seeming adaptations? As two eminent historians have said, "We must not allow our mutual fears to lead us into war, for the unparalleled murderousness of our weapons and yours brings into the situation an element unfamiliar to history" [13]. While to stop war requires historically unprecedented change, one clear lesson of history is that a society's failure to recognize and act on the need for change brings that society down.

Ubiquitous though war has been, human populations actually do vary in the amount they are warlike. There are some examples of peaceful peoples scattered throughout the world [11], and more importantly some once warring peoples, such as the Scandinavians, have become peaceful [1]. Certainly war is not an inescapable behavior pattern. One must *learn* warfare [35]. Indeed since no other mammalian species is known to commit mass intraspecies killing, Andreski [1] asserts that war must be "the creation of culture." If a people have the idea of going to war as a necessary or inevitable way to solve problems, then given the right circumstances, they will go to war [3].

Ironically there is no paucity of either naturally occurring or manmade enemies to fight. Pestilence, famine, war, overpopulation and its products, pollution and destruction of natural resources are all very real enemies of man. At an ever-accelerating rate these real enemies encircle mankind. Since they select no particular nation, they might yet unite our species in common effort. The struggle for existence that lies ahead is with these enemies, not one another. Still it is hard to get a people to change its ways, as is indicated by the examples of the current controversy over guns and the mass media portrayals of violence.

SPECIAL ISSUES REFLECTING
VIOLENCE AND COPING

Both the controversy over guns (Chapters 8 and 9) and the mass media portraits of violence (Chapter 7) reflect violence as attempted coping. These controversies especially reveal the pervasive belief in violence as an effective and often justified means to reach vital goals.

The Gun Controversy and Coping

In America guns are everywhere among us and everywhere available, reflecting our extensive reliance on them. The gun, first for survival and now for protection, is a part of the American heritage, the frontier tradition of self-reliance. Private citizen possession of firearms is culturally sanctioned not only for such uses as hunting but also as a presumably effective way to protect the nation, group, family, and self against all sorts of potential dangers and evil forces. Additionally guns symbolize or represent a way to cope with a host of mistrusts and fears—helplessness, inadequacy, weakness, and the unknown. A gun becomes the "equalizer." Thus any infringement upon free access to guns, even by requiring registration of firearms and licensing of owners, can mean the threatened loss of protection and security, of a way of life, of self-reliance, and of prized possessions that may help to compensate for feelings of inadequacy. This theme of loss complicates the firearms controversy, since people faced with important threatened or actual losses often try to cope by restoring the loss. People would "rather fight than switch." In short, citizen ownership of guns has been sanctioned and valued because guns seem to represent effective coping in our society.

However, the violence that emerges in this complicated society frequently results from the failure of the protection-by-gun strategy of coping. Most gun deaths occur among family, friends, and acquaintances; of these killings nearly all are impulsive, not deliberate, and therefore are defensive, adjustment-oriented actions. Violent acts like homicide and suicide occur when other means of resolving conflict seem exhausted or when a particular state of mind, often aggravated by the use of a mind-altering drug, makes the future disappear. Similarly gun accidents occur more frequently among the impulsive—the young and the accident-prone adult. In addition, seen from the perspective of coping, individuals who enter

the daily stressful situations of life handicapped by more frustrations, fewer alternatives, and little expectation of a better future also
are more prone to use guns. Even the mere presence of a gun may
contribute to attack strategy, since the gun is a highly symbolic
means for settling conflicts, requires no physical contact, and is an
especially easy weapon to use. In addition, perhaps the impulsive use
of guns can be viewed as a failure of the American action-orientation
in those people who feel that action in itself is a goal worth achieving
as well as a means to terminate conflict.

Mass Media Portrayals of Violence

Nowhere is violence as a sanctioned coping strategy more evident
than in mass media portrayals of violence, especially on television.
The media foster the image of the Violent American armed with
gun, ignorance, and frustration, ruthlessly pursuing good and evil
alike. Television, radio, and newspapers project a repetitive, staccato
beat of violence, showing us that violence is valued, necessary,
wanted, and even enjoyed.

For example, one report [49] indicated that a single television station showed 334 completed or attempted killings in one week.
About 50 percent of prime-time programs feature violence and
crime [38]. Nor does this abundance of violent acts go unwatched.
The average American child from ages 3 through 16 spends more of
his waking hours watching television than attending school [39].
There is no question, no doubt whatever, of this constant flow of
violent fare on TV and other media and its observation.

But what effect do the mass media have? Although all mass media
have appeal and impact, television has the most powerful impact. It
not only simultaneously reaches both senses most highly developed
in man, audition and vision, but it also is available instantly and in the
United States universally, even for the poorer citizen. Its message
can be absorbed with minimal effort, and its operation does not require technical skill; even toddlers can operate it. Thus television
effortlessly teaches pupils where they are, in the way humans learn
best: through simultaneous presentations to the visual and auditory
senses. For the young in particular learning involves observing, imitating, and then observing once again. Furthermore, television by
virtue of its nearly real simulation of life, its inherent authenticity,
blurs the line between reality and fantasy. Hence to the most vulnerable—the young, the unsophisticated, the immature—television is a
particularly powerful educational instrument. In estimating the
"teacher power" of television, one also must understand that learn-

ing something and performing what has been learned are not the same. As with any observational learning, much more is learned by watching television than is spontaneously performed. In sum, television (and to a considerable extent other mass media) is a powerful means of teaching: TV is watched abundantly, it "grabs and massages" [33] those senses most exquisitely developed in man, and it has intrinsic authenticity. The television industry knows this and so do advertisers. If TV can teach people to buy things, that is, to alter their behavior, it also can teach people violence. And this powerful medium, together with the others, inundates the viewer with violence of all kinds and descriptions. Television teaches the alphabet of violence; only the actual performance is not guaranteed (but then neither does advertising a specific product guarantee its purchase).

The media's message in depicting violence is that violence is a good, often quick way to get things done; violence is billed as effective coping. This message is given in fictional presentations. Observe it for yourself in the Western, the detective story, the "crime busters," or the Saturday morning cartoons. And it likewise is given in news and documentary presentations of the Vietnam war, riots, student revolt, and police action. Observe them too for the depiction of violence as effective coping. Violence is condoned, rewarded, and even glorified. Ironically the viewer usually is deprived of the one aspect of violence that *might* discourage violence. The censor cuts out the ugly consequences, the victim's pain and agony and the wanton destruction of life. This restricts the viewer from determining the coping value of violent acts, since the full impact and range of consequences are not presented for appraisal. Furthermore, we are never taught "in this school for violence that violence in itself is something reprehensible" [48].

One study of TV [30] revealed that violence is used about one-third of the time as a means to various goals. For the programs most frequently watched by children, violence represented the solution 47 percent of the time. Not only were violent means employed, but violence, along with other "socially disapproved" solutions, was more successful in attaining goals than socially approved means:

The present data suggest a definite tendency for television programs to project content in which socially approved goals are most frequently achieved by methods that are not socially approved [30].

Yet we hear repeatedly that the goals of students, young blacks, and others are to be commended while their methods must be condemned. It is not easy to teach citizens that violence is an acceptable way to cope in one context and not in another, especially when the cause seems worthy.

Part of the tragedy is that television and mass media in general could be our most powerful tools for dealing with today's violence. Television could effectively promote adaptive alternatives to violence, and stress the many nonviolent ways to resolve conflict. It could encourage, if not induce, desired culture modification and intergroup understanding, but not while the lesson, the accepted cultural tradition, remains that violence, especially when disguised by the cloak of history, fantasy, or rightness, is an effective, acceptable way to cope.

Violence and the Changing Nature of Human Adaptation

Violence is unique to no particular region, nation, or time [13, 37]. Thus to condemn some nations as violent while lauding others is by and large sheer folly. Centuries ago man survived primarily as a nomadic hunter relying on violent aggression for both food and protection [46]. Even when becoming agricultural and sedentary, man struggled against nature, and survival still required violent aggression, especially for maintaining territory when food was scarce.

Then in a moment of evolution man's potentialities suddenly produced the age of technology. Instead of adapting mainly by way of biological evolution, we are now increasingly subject to the effects and demands of cultural evolution. Instead of having to adapt to our environment, we now can adapt our environment to our needs. Despite this potential emancipation from biological evolution, we retain the adaptive mechanisms derived from a long history of mammalian and primate evolution. These include our primitive forms of aggression—our violence, bellicosity, and inclination to fight in a time of emergency. Where these mechanisms once responded more to physical stress, they now must respond more to social, cultural, and psychological stresses, and the response does not always produce adaptive results. Where violent aggressive behavior once served to maintain the human species in times of danger, it now threatens our continued existence.

The adaptation-coping perspective shows most clearly, we believe, how man came to be the most violent of species—virtually the only species with a history replete with genocidal behavior, the only "unhinged killer[s]" [43]. Biologically man is an ancient species, in whom the fantastic development of the cerebrum, the result of so-called quantum evolution, is a very recent acquisition [14]. The older areas of the brain—for example, the limbic system which includes mechanisms for attack and avoidance—are incompletely adapted to the cerebrum [43]. The cerebrum and the older portions of the brain are, as it were, out of step with each other. The cerebrum, which makes man the "pinnacle" of evolution, also renders him unusually vulnerable to violent behavior.

The cerebrum enabled this physically unimposing creature to make weapons, any number of which once enhanced survival. Now weapons have turned this unimposing fellow into the mightiest of killers, and any number of these weapons threaten rather than enhance survival. We kill with such speed and distance that even the cries of appeasement are muted or not heard.

The cerebrum gave man foresight and awareness with which to comprehend, and often extend himself into, the future. Yet foresight and self-awareness leave man especially vulnerable to dashed hopes of his many extended expectations.

The cerebrum provided the ability to symbolize, abstract, and recall, which enabled man to form large and more complicated cultures. But social complexity also generated many more changes with which man has had to cope. When some of these stressful demands for change overwhelm the ability of the individual or group to cope, violence and other more primitive and irrational behaviors occur.

Even the "coping machinery" in man presents problems. Successful coping involves extensive appraisals of the environment. These appraisals provide the basis for man's many and varied means to solve problems and achieve his goals. This same "machinery," however, permits man to distort perceptions, making it possible for him to fool and deceive himself in endless ways.

Furthermore, in this technological era culture changes so rapidly that time has assumed another dimension—the dimension of acceleration. Many conditions thought to be certain and enduring prove to be merely transient realities upon which we cannot rely. Thus we often must face the added stress of having our ideas and beliefs disproved within the scope of our lifetimes or sooner. The luxury of being dead before being discovered wrong is disappearing.

In the current rapidly expanding technological era, many once useful modes of coping are transformed into threats to survival. Territorial exclusivity is becoming obsolete in an economy of abundance. Vast weapons, communication, and transportation networks shrink the world to living-room size and expand our own backyard to encompass a "global village." Yet war and exclusivity continue. Our exploitation of natural resources becomes maladaptive. Relatively unlimited reproduction, once adaptive for advancing the survival of our species, now produces overcrowded conditions similar to those that lead to destructive and violent behavior in laboratory experiments with other species. And crowded societies abutting against one another dramatically increase the opportunity for intergroup conflict or stress through almost continuous provocation to attack. A concept of an optimal range of population and attention to the quality, not just the quantity, of life must be inculcated.

The rate at which we now change our environment apparently exceeds our current capacity for coping with the changes we make. Technological advances alter our physical and social environments, which in turn demand different coping strategies and a conscious, deliberate reshaping of culture. The accelerated civilization of technology is crowded, complex, ambiguous, and uncertain. To cope with it, we must become capable of restructuring knowledge of our current situation and then applying new information constructively: Several factors give us reason to hope that we can succeed.

HARNESSING THE POTENTIAL FOR COPING

Our social organization and intellectual abilities give us vast potential for coping, but we must overcome our tendencies to distort perceptions and to take mainly the personal and present view when confronted by challenges demanding change. Knowledge and technology can be harnessed to serve goals determined by man. Automation makes possible the economics of abundance, but only our cultural values can make abundance a reality for all people. Medicine permits us to expand our control over life, but we have not yet seen fit to use this power to determine the limits of population. The technologies of communication and travel shrink the world, but man has not yet expanded the horizon of inclusion. We can learn to unite in goals that transcend exclusivity and direct cultural evolution in accordance with adaptive values and wisdom. The past need not and must not be master of our future. Although understanding the past can provide perspective and point to carry-overs that now are perilous, adaptation is in the present and future, not in the past.

UNDERSTANDING VIOLENCE AND
PURSUING ALTERNATIVES

Violence can be understood and controlled. The crisis we are now experiencing is one of violence, not of aggression, and it is violence that we must replace. Aggression in the service of coping can build and create rather than destroy. The several theories of aggression and current issues of violence suggest many complementary ways of reducing attack behaviors and redirecting aggressive tendencies (see also Chapter 14).

We can teach about coping: about anger signaling a frustrating block to a goal or a dashed hope; about how stressful demands for change potentiate our defense-oriented tendencies to distort perceptions and to take mainly the personal and present view, tendencies which in turn often lead to violent attack; about the maladaptive long-run consequences of violence; and about the damaging effects of sanctioned violence and of the mere observation of violence (for much childhood learning is by observation and subsequent play and rehearsal).

Moreover, we can teach what already is known about the contexts and factors that instigate and diminish violence. Hopefully a central message of this book is how much now is known about the causes of and paths to the prevention of violence. We can teach that violence occurs in relation to other feelings and potential behaviors occurring in human strivings; that many alternatives to anachronistic physical violence and its symbolic counterparts are possible; that empathy with the perspectives of other individuals, groups, and nations provides protection against violence; and that the compression of time demands expanding the horizon of the future, for what formerly took a hundred years, a thousand years, or more now is compressed to ten years, one year, or less.

FOCUSING ON SOCIAL CHANGE

Greater attention can be focused on understanding and implementing social change [47]. In stable cultures, or cultures undergoing change slowly, societal coping strategies suppressing and ignoring conflict are efficient means of maintaining stability and order. Dissonance can be "ignored" and strife squelched. The group relies heavily on tradition. But coping through suppression and denial of conflict fails in cultures undergoing rapid change. Here the resolution, acceptance, and even encouragement of nonviolent conflict are required to keep pace with the demands of cultural change and to assure the existence of a society. The group can rely less on former traditions. In the technological era relying on conflict suppression heightens cultural lag and produces not stability, but a repetitious game of "catch up" characterized by one major social crisis after another and by defensive behaviors that are too often only adjustive in that they bring relief of immediate problems by restoring or attempting to restore the status quo, while doing little to provide long-range solutions. Unforeseen change produces intolerable stress, anxiety, and increased resistance to rational change. These reactions inhibit solution-seeking behavior; evoke feelings of mistrust, loss, and helplessness; and lead to attacks on the apparent agents of change and evil.

Thus expanding our knowledge of the social change processes, understanding resistances to rational change, and pursuing constructive alternatives are our highest priority. The task of convincing people to change cannot be a casual endeavor. We urgently need to develop cultural traditions for coping with rapid social change.

First, our educational systems can provide comprehensive curricula that teach the causes of social problems, the nature of social conflict and its resolution, and the numerous nonviolent strategies of social change. Social change curricula need to provide students with practical field work and simulated experiences as social change agents.

Second, societal groups and organizations can benefit from many methods for organizational renewal that help keep a system responsive, informed, and future-oriented. These methods include the following: periodic goal-planning and assessment groups, organizational retreats or seminars composed of individuals from multiple levels in the organizational matrix, limiting the upper boundaries of tenure in positions of authority, voluntary rotation among positions, exchanges between organizations and groups, utilization of outside consultants, periodic sabbatical-type leaves for continuing education and personal renewal, and regularized negotiations between potentially conflicting groups.

Third, much greater endeavor must be given to implementing constructive programs in social change. It is not sufficient to find answers, suggest desirable changes, and recommend new plans only to have them rejected by a misinformed citizenry or fail for lack of funding. Nothing short of intense, determined effort can rid this or any society of violence, an effort similar in kind to the dedicated, cooperative effort of citizens, government, and industry that brought the United States from the tiny Explorer satellite in 1958 to the Apollo moon missions in a scant decade.

In sum, we must develop the ability to foresee social change and crises and actively meet them. We must learn to feel secure with uncertainty. We must pursue our strengths, assets, and potential to create and cooperate as the really challenging frontier.

Conclusion

The current examples of violence and the factors encouraging it reflect our vacillation between the anachronistic culture of violence and the perplexing culture of constant change. We feel alienated and experience social disruption. Current demands for change are potentially dangerous because change activates a tendency to return to older, formerly effective coping behaviors that now represent mainly adjustive, temporizing behaviors. Social disruption caused by change tends to increase violence as a means of coping at a time when violence is becoming increasingly a defensive-reactive behavior and a great danger to our survival.

Today we see attempts to return our country to the simpler, clearer, more predictable past. Although these attempts bring temporary relief and reduce discord (are adjustive), they serve coping poorly. In a rapidly changing world, looking backward rather than forward for solutions heightens both social instability and the disruption it seeks to cure. Thus America's current violence threatens our existence, not because we are more violent than ever before or than other peoples, but because violence makes it difficult for us to cope with our changing world. On the other hand, our national concern with violence indicates that our people are more aware of the dangers of violence. This in itself can be a step toward rational social change. But we need time, a moratorium on violence, in order that constructive alternatives to violence can acquire the cloak of cultural traditions. If Americans and people everywhere can reduce their violence, then selection hopefully will favor evolution of a more gentle people. Indeed it is quite possible that evolution gradually is favoring just such change [45].

Today's challenge, the crisis of violence, is really the crisis of man. This crisis is especially difficult because violence, a once useful but now increasingly maladaptive coping strategy, seems to be firmly rooted in human behavior patterns. We conquer the elements and yet end up facing our own image. Dobzhansky expressed this well in *Mankind Evolving* [12]:

Man and man alone knows that the world evolves and that he evolves with it. By changing what he knows about the world man changes the world that he knows, and by changing the world in which he lives man changes himself. Changes may be deteriorations or improvements; the hope lies in the possibility that changes resulting from knowledge may also be dictated by knowledge. Evolution need no longer be a destiny imposed from without; it may conceivably be controlled by man in accordance with his wisdom and his values.

Adaptation to this changing world rests on how effectively we can understand, channel, and direct our aggressive behaviors. Already we may know enough for man to close his era of violence if we determine to pursue alternatives.

Acknowledgment

We are grateful to Mary M. Shapiro, Frederick T. Melges, and David A. Hamburg for their helpful reviews and editorial assistance during the preparation of this chapter.

References

1. Andreski, S. Origins of War. In Carthy, J. D., and Ebling, F. J. (Eds.), *The Natural History of Aggression*. New York: Academic, 1964.
2. Appley, M. H., and Trumbull, R. (Eds.). *Psychological Stress*. New York: Appleton-Century-Crofts, 1967.
3. Barry, D. Evolution and the Adaptive Value of War. Unpublished Humanities Honors Program Essay, Stanford University, 1969.
4. Brown, R. *Social Psychology*. New York: Free Press, 1965.
5. Campbell, A., and Schuman, H. Racial Attitudes in Fifteen American Cities. Supplemental Studies for the National Advisory Commission on Civil Disorders. Washington, D.C.: U.S. Government Printing Office, 1968.
6. Carthy, J. D., and Ebling, F. J. (Eds.). *The Natural History of Aggression*. New York: Academic, 1964.
7. Daniels, D. N., and Kuldau, J. M. Marginal man, the tether of tradition, and intentional social system therapy. *Community Mental Health Journal* 3:13, 1967.
8. Darbonne, A. Crisis: A review of theory, practice, and research. *International Journal of Psychiatry* 6:371, 1968.
9. Darrow, C., and Lowinger, P. The Detroit Uprising: A Psychological Study. In Masserman, J. (Ed.), *The Dynamics of Dissent*. Science and Psychoanalysis, vol. 13. New York: Grune & Stratton, 1968.
10. Darwin, C. *The Descent of Man*. Chicago: Rand, McNally, 1874 (Revised Edition).
11. Davie, M. R. *The Evolution of War*. New Haven: Yale University Press, 1929.
12. Dobzhansky, T. *Mankind Evolving*. New Haven: Yale University Press, 1962.

13. Durant, W., and Durant, A. *The Lessons of History*. New York: Simon and Schuster, 1968.
14. Ehrlich, P. R., and Holm, R. W. *The Process of Evolution*. New York: McGraw-Hill, 1963.
15. Eiseley, L. *The Immense Journey*. New York: Random House, 1946.
16. Frank, J. D. *Sanity & Survival: Psychological Aspects of War and Peace*. New York: Random House, 1967.
17. Freeman, D. Human Aggression in Anthropological Perspective. In Carthy, J. D., and Ebling, F. J. (Eds.), *The Natural History of Aggression*. New York: Academic, 1964.
18. Freud, A. *The Ego and the Mechanisms of Defense*. New York: International Universities Press, 1946.
19. Freud, S. Civilization and Its Discontents (1930). In *The Standard Edition of the Complete Psychological Works of Sigmund Freud*, tr. and ed. by J. Strachey with others. London: Hogarth and the Institute of Psycho-Analysis, 1961. Vol. 21, p. 64.
20. Fried, M., Harris, M., and Murphy, R. (Eds.). *The Anthropology of Armed Conflict and Aggression*. New York: Doubleday, 1968.
21. Gilula, M. F., and Daniels, D. N. Violence and man's struggle to adapt. *Science* 164:396, 1969.
22. Grinker, R. R., and Spiegel, J. P. *Men Under Stress*. Philadelphia: Blakiston, 1945.
23. Hamburg, D. A. Emotions in the Perspective of Human Evolution. In Knapp, P. D. (Ed.), *Expression of the Emotions in Man*. New York: International Universities Press, 1963.
24. Hamburg, D. A. Unpublished data, 1968.
25. Hamburg, D. A., and Adams, J. E. A perspective on coping behavior. *Archives of General Psychiatry* 17:277, 1967.
26. Harris, C. J. Aerospace Technology and Urban "Disorders." Paper delivered at the American Institute of Aeronautics and Astronautics Annual Meeting, Philadelphia, October 1968 (Paper No. 68–1109).
27. Janis, I. L. Individual Differences in Vigilance and Adaptive Coping Actions in Response to Fear-Arousing Information. Unpublished paper delivered at Stanford University Conference on Coping and Adaptation (sponsored by the National Institute of Mental Health) Palo Alto, March 20–22, 1969.
28. KCBS Radio news, San Francisco, May 30, 1969.
29. Kinzel, A. F. Body Buffer Zone in Violent Prisoners. Unpublished paper delivered at the American Psychiatric Association's Annual Meeting, Miami, May 1969.
30. Larsen, O. N., Gray, L. N., and Fortis, J. G. Achieving Goals Through Violence on Television. In Larsen, O. N. (Ed.), *Violence and the Mass Media*. New York: Harper & Row, 1968.
31. Lazarus, R. S. *Psychological Stress and the Coping Process*. New York: McGraw-Hill, 1966.
32. Lorenz, K. *On Aggression*. New York: Harcourt, Brace & World, 1966.
33. McLuhan, M. *Understanding Media*. New York: McGraw-Hill, 1964.

34. Mark, V., and Ervin, F. R. *Violence and the Brain.* New York: Harper & Row. In press.
35. Montagu, M. F. A. (Ed.). *Man and Aggression.* New York: Oxford University Press, 1968.
36. Pettigrew, T. F. Racially separate or together. *The Journal of Social Issues* 25:45, 1969.
37. Richardson, L. F. *Statistics of Deadly Quarrels.* Pittsburgh: Boxwood, 1960.
38. Schlesinger, A., Jr. *Violence: America in the Sixties.* New York: New American Library (Signet Books), 1968.
39. Schram, W., Lyle, J., and Parker, E. B. *Television in the Lives of Our Children.* Stanford: Stanford University Press, 1961.
40. Silber, E., Hamburg, D. A., Coelho, G. V., Murphey, E. B., Rosenberg, M., and Pearlin, L. I. Adaptive behavior in competent adolescents. *Archives of General Psychiatry* 5:354, 1961.
41. Spiegel, J. P. Psychosocial factors in riots—old and new. *American Journal of Psychiatry* 125:281, 1968.
42. Sullivan, H. S. *The Interpersonal Theory of Psychiatry.* New York: Norton, 1953.
43. Tinbergen, N. On war and peace in animals and man. *Science* 160:1411, 1968.
44. Waddington, C. H. Symbols, Language, and Human Violence. In Ng, L. (Ed.), *Alternatives to Violence.* New York: Time-Life Books, 1968.
45. Washburn, S. L., and Hamburg, D. A. Aggressive Behavior in Old World Monkeys and Apes. In Jay, P. C. (Ed.), *Primates: Studies in Adaptation and Variability.* New York: Holt, Rinehart & Winston, 1968.
46. Washburn, S. L., and Lancaster, C. S. The Evolution of Hunting. In Lee, R. B., and De Vore, I. (Eds.), *Man the Hunter.* Chicago: Aldine, 1968.
47. Watson, G. (Ed.). *Concepts for Social Change.* Washington: National Education Association, 1967.
48. Wertham, F. *A Sign for Cain.* New York: Macmillan, 1966.
49. Wertham, F. School for Violence. In Larsen, O. N. (Ed.), *Violence and the Mass Media.* New York: Harper & Row, 1968.
50. White, R. W. Strategies of Adaptation: An Attempt at Systematic Description. Unpublished paper delivered at Stanford University Conference on Coping and Adaptation (sponsored by the National Institute of Mental Health), Palo Alto, March 20–22, 1969.
51. Wright, Q. *A Study of War.* Chicago: University of Chicago Press, 1942.
52. Zifferstein, I. Psychological habituation to war: A sociopsychological case study. *American Journal of Orthopsychiatry* 37:457, 1967.